Introduction

You may think this book is simply a cynical way to cash in on the popularity of the strip without doing much of anything in the way of extra work. And you'd be largely correct about that. But look at it this way: After you enjoy it, you can give it to somebody else as a gift. That's something you can't do with, say, a bottle of wine (at least not gracefully). A Dilbert book is a rare opportunity to satisfy your greed and your nagging gift-giving guilt at the same time. It's a win-win scenario.

The only problem is that the book doesn't quite lay flat after you've pawed your way through it. You'll need an alibi.

I recommend that you get a felt-tipped pen and write "Best Wishes—Scott Adams" on the inside cover and try to pass it off as an autographed copy. You could even sketch a little Dogbert in there. If he looks a little deformed, just say my arm was in a sling.*

If the recipient hunts me down to verify your clam, I'll lie for you. You have my word on that.

On a related topic, many of you have written to ask how you can join a Dilbert/Dogbert fan club, mailing list, cult, or paramilitary force. So far, all we have is a mailing list. There are two benefits to being on the mailing list: 1.) You get a free Dilbert newsletter if we feel like it, and 2.) When Dogbert conquers the world, you will form a new ruling class.

To get on the mailing list, write:

E-mail: scottadams@aol.com

Snail Mail: Dilbert Mailing List
                United Media
                200 Park Avenue
                New York, NY 10166

Scott Adams

*If it looks better than I draw it, I hate you.

DOGBERT, SEE WHO'S AT THE DOOR.
DING DONG
HI. I'M FROM THE "BIG BALL WRECKING COMPANY." I HAVE A WORK ORDER TO DESTROY THIS HOUSE.
LOOKS LIKE YOU HAVE THE WRONG ADDRESS. THIS IS WALNUT AVENUE. WALNUT STREET IS CLEAR ACROSS TOWN.
OH PHLEGM! I DON'T HAVE TIME TO DRIVE WAY OVER THERE.
WOULD IT BE A BOTHER IF I JUST LEVELED THIS HOUSE INSTEAD.
THAT WOULD BE A TAD INCONVENIENT. TRY THE JOHNSONS, NEXT DOOR.
WHAT WAS THAT LOUD NOISE?
APPARENTLY THE JOHNSONS AREN'T HOME.

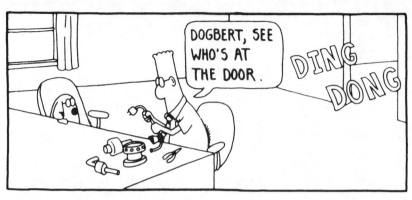

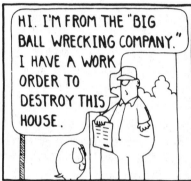

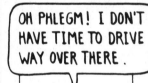

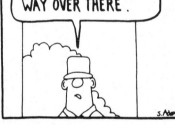

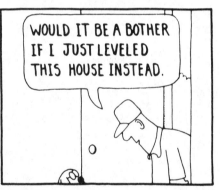

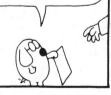

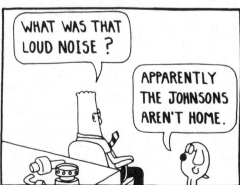

Shave the Whales

A Dilbert Book
by Scott Adams

BOXTREE

First published in the UK 1995 by Boxtree Limited, Broadwall House, 21 Broadwall, London SE1 9PL

First published in the USA in 1992 by Andrews and McMeel, 4900 Main Street, Kansas City, Missouri 64112, USA

Copyright © 1992 by United Feature Syndicate, Inc.
Cartoons copyright © 1989, 1990 United Feature Syndicate, Inc.

10 9 8 7 6 5 4

ISBN: 0 7522 0849 7

Printed and bound in Great Britain by Mackays of Chatham PLC, Kent

A CIP catalogue record for this book is available from the British Library

For Pam, my role model

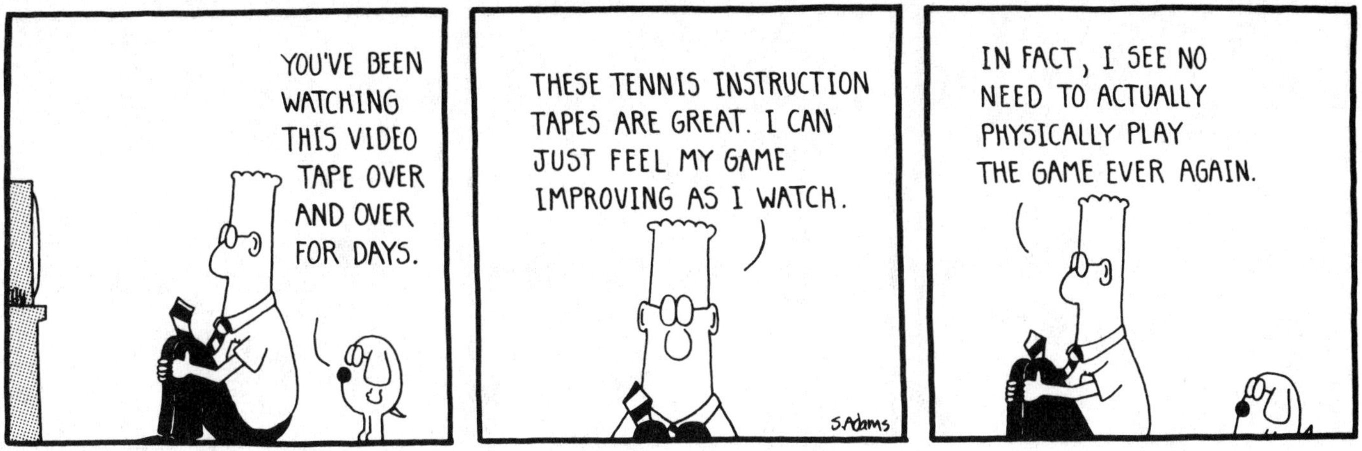
YOU'VE BEEN WATCHING THIS VIDEO TAPE OVER AND OVER FOR DAYS.
THESE TENNIS INSTRUCTION TAPES ARE GREAT. I CAN JUST FEEL MY GAME IMPROVING AS I WATCH.
S.Adams
IN FACT, I SEE NO NEED TO ACTUALLY PHYSICALLY PLAY THE GAME EVER AGAIN.

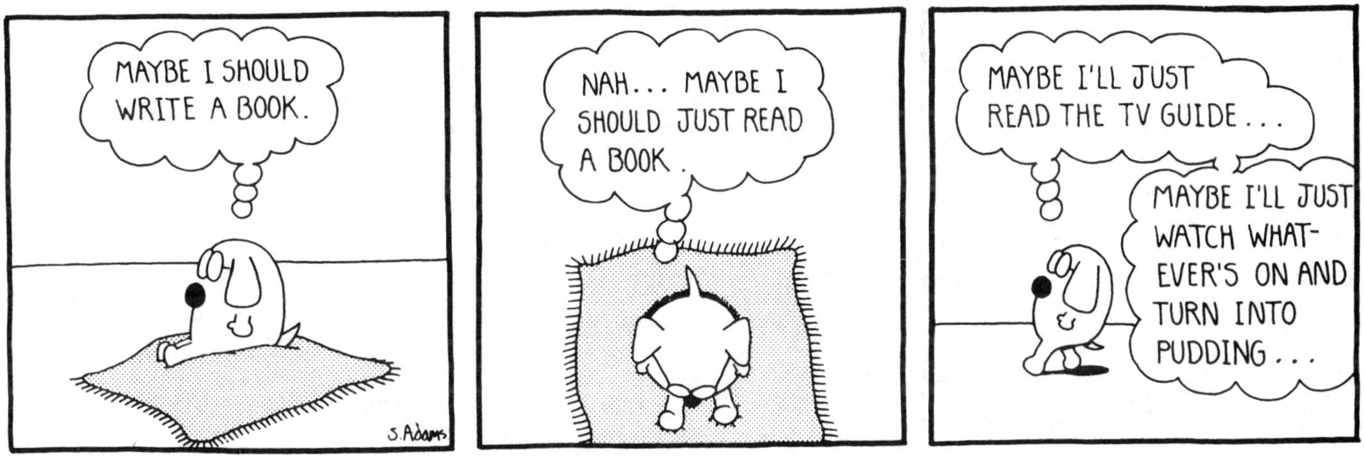
MAYBE I SHOULD WRITE A BOOK.
S.Adams
NAH... MAYBE I SHOULD JUST READ A BOOK.
MAYBE I'LL JUST READ THE TV GUIDE...
MAYBE I'LL JUST WATCH WHAT-EVER'S ON AND TURN INTO PUDDING...

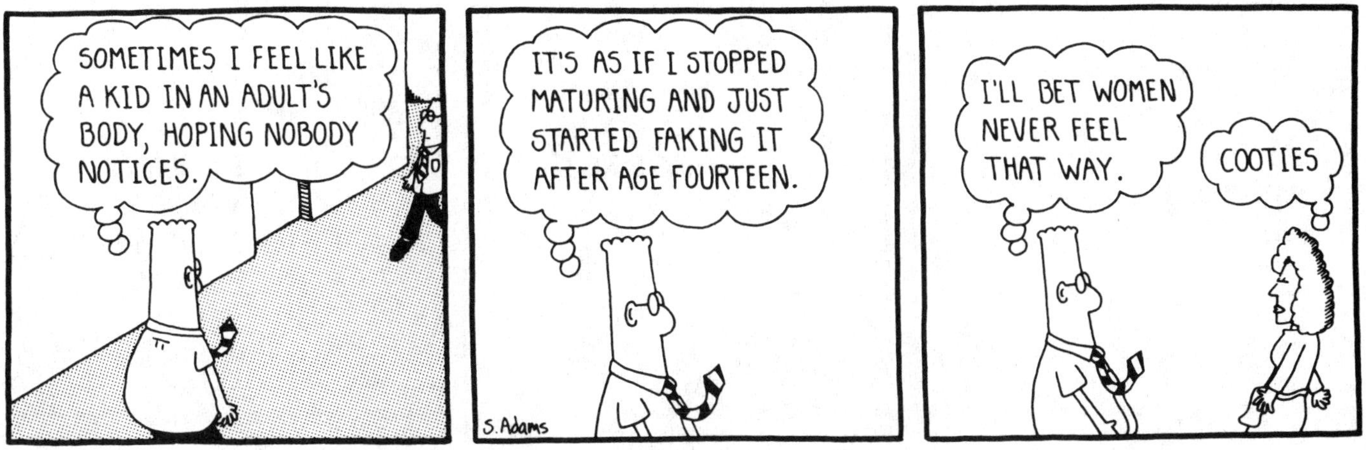
SOMETIMES I FEEL LIKE A KID IN AN ADULT'S BODY, HOPING NOBODY NOTICES.
IT'S AS IF I STOPPED MATURING AND JUST STARTED FAKING IT AFTER AGE FOURTEEN.
S.Adams
I'LL BET WOMEN NEVER FEEL THAT WAY.
COOTIES

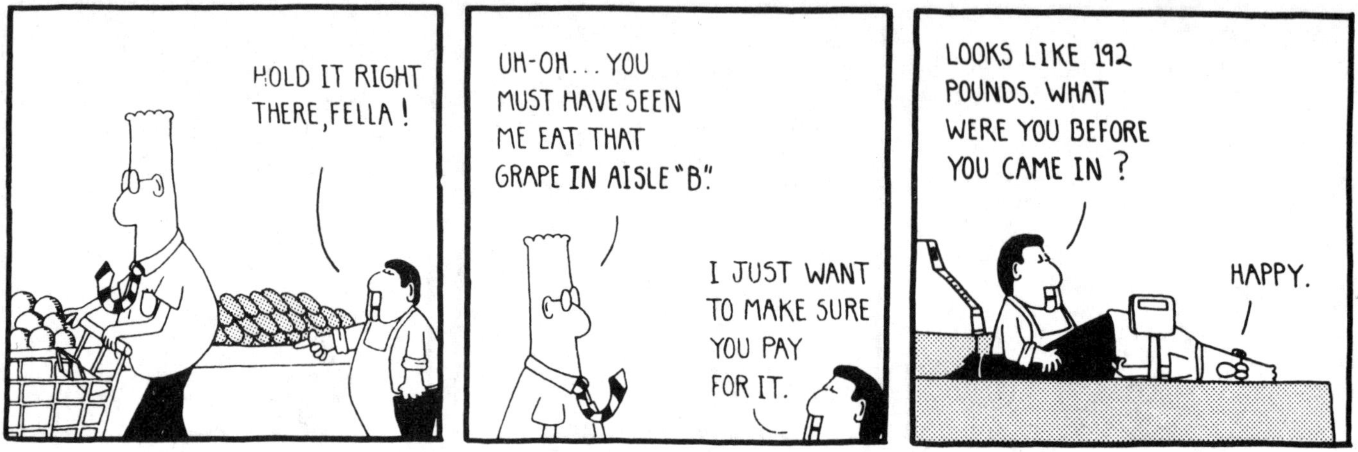
HOLD IT RIGHT THERE, FELLA!
UH-OH... YOU MUST HAVE SEEN ME EAT THAT GRAPE IN AISLE "B".
I JUST WANT TO MAKE SURE YOU PAY FOR IT.
LOOKS LIKE 192 POUNDS. WHAT WERE YOU BEFORE YOU CAME IN?
HAPPY.

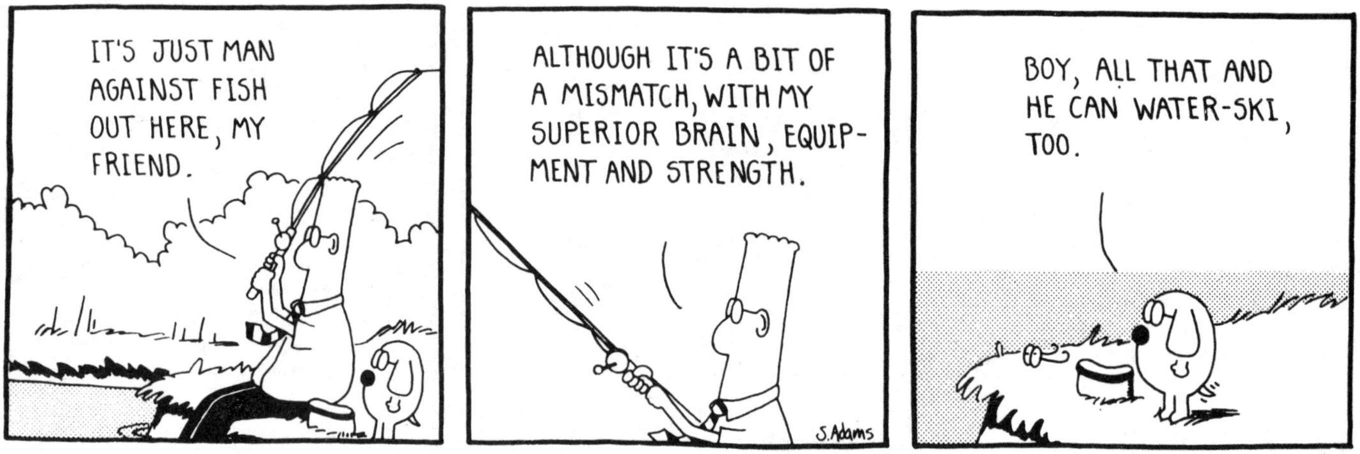
IT'S JUST MAN AGAINST FISH OUT HERE, MY FRIEND.
ALTHOUGH IT'S A BIT OF A MISMATCH, WITH MY SUPERIOR BRAIN, EQUIPMENT AND STRENGTH.
S. Adams
BOY, ALL THAT AND HE CAN WATER-SKI, TOO.

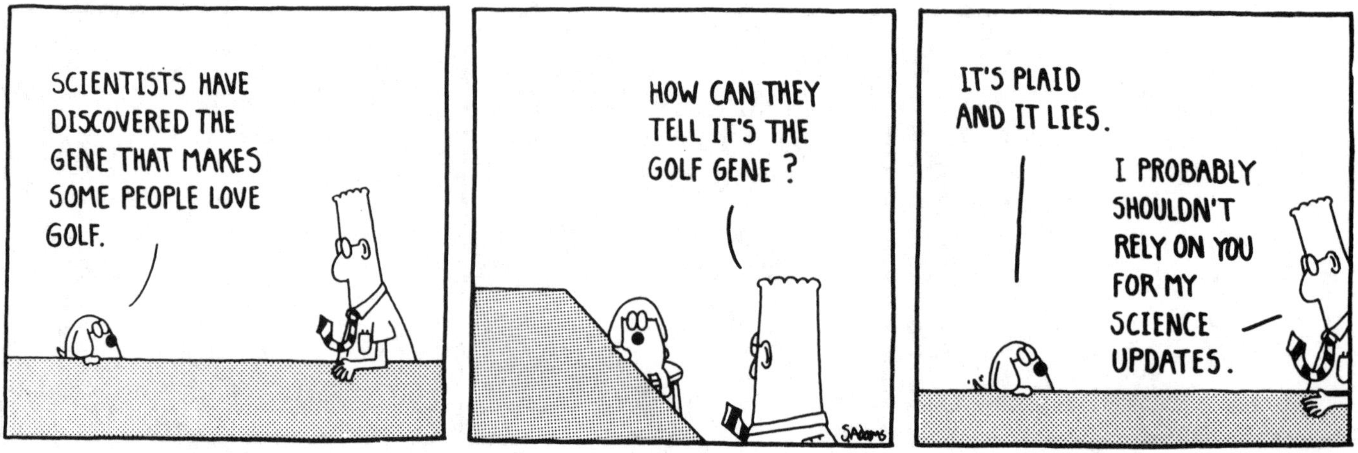
SCIENTISTS HAVE DISCOVERED THE GENE THAT MAKES SOME PEOPLE LOVE GOLF.
HOW CAN THEY TELL IT'S THE GOLF GENE?
S.Adams
IT'S PLAID AND IT LIES.
I PROBABLY SHOULDN'T RELY ON YOU FOR MY SCIENCE UPDATES.

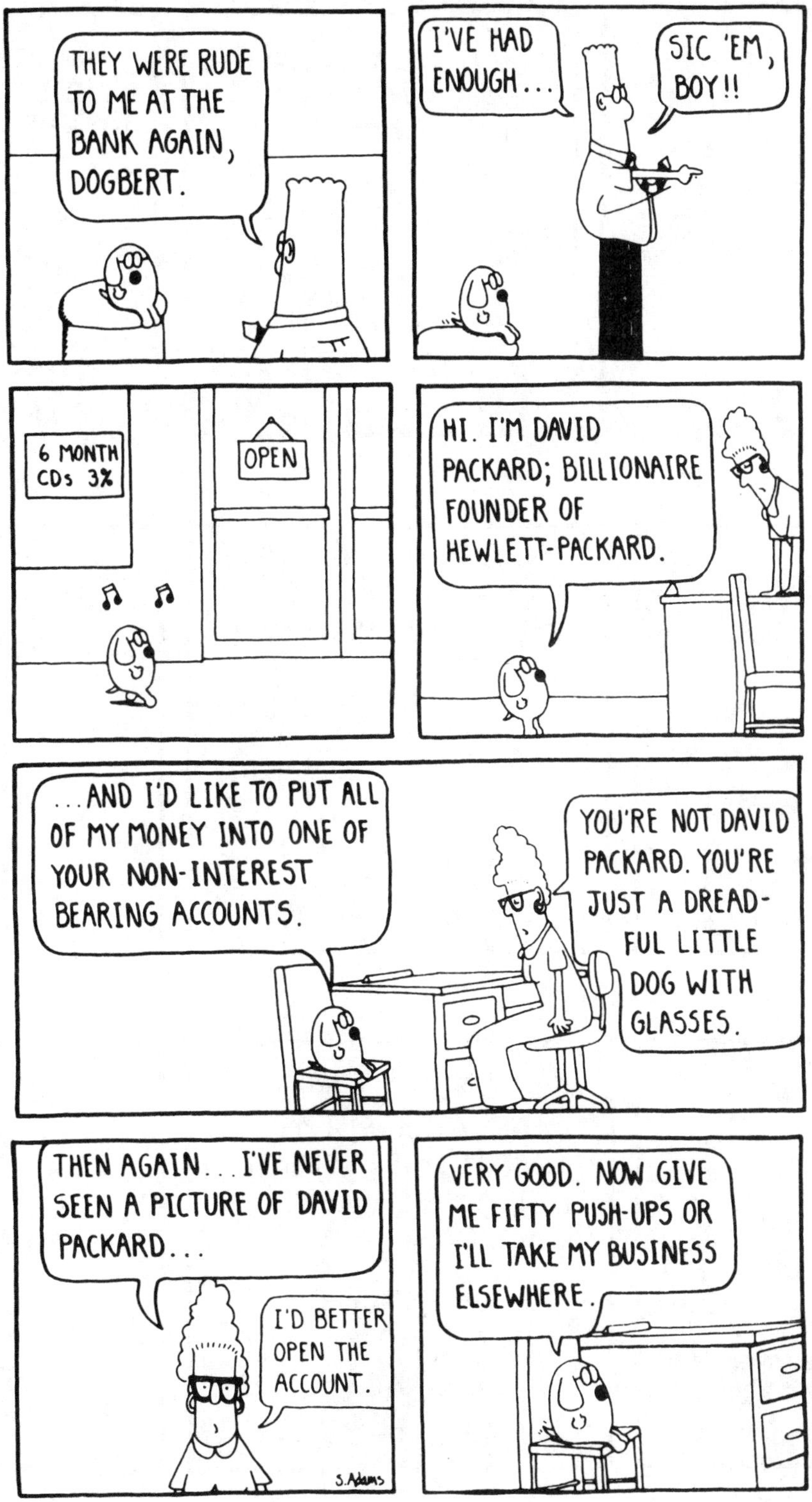
THEY WERE RUDE TO ME AT THE BANK AGAIN, DOGBERT.
I'VE HAD ENOUGH...
SIC 'EM, BOY!!
6 MONTH CDs 3%
OPEN
HI. I'M DAVID PACKARD; BILLIONAIRE FOUNDER OF HEWLETT-PACKARD.
...AND I'D LIKE TO PUT ALL OF MY MONEY INTO ONE OF YOUR NON-INTEREST BEARING ACCOUNTS.
YOU'RE NOT DAVID PACKARD. YOU'RE JUST A DREAD-FUL LITTLE DOG WITH GLASSES.
THEN AGAIN... I'VE NEVER SEEN A PICTURE OF DAVID PACKARD...
I'D BETTER OPEN THE ACCOUNT.
S. Adams
VERY GOOD. NOW GIVE ME FIFTY PUSH-UPS OR I'LL TAKE MY BUSINESS ELSEWHERE.

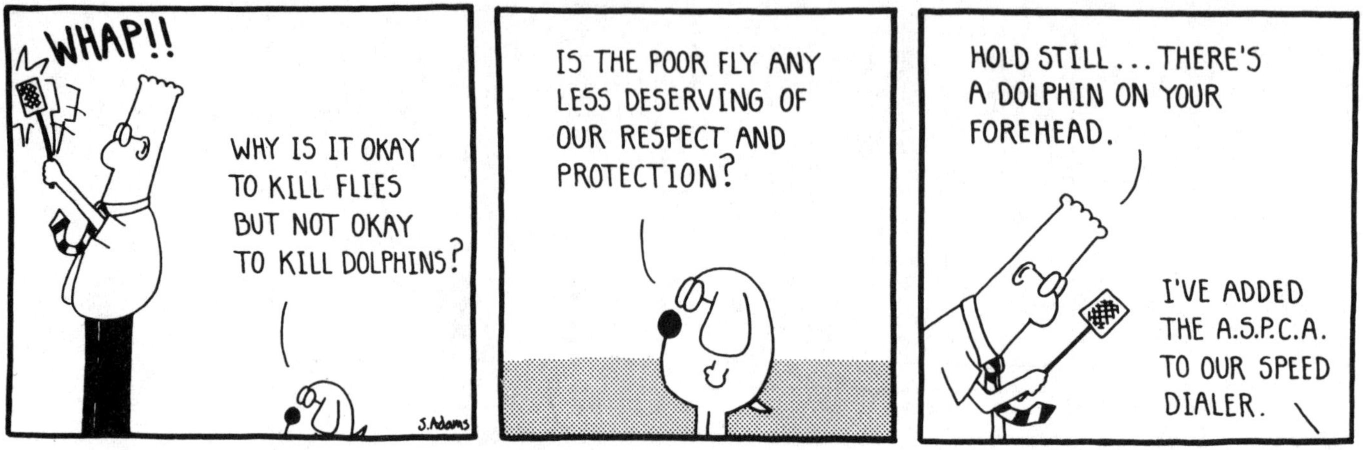
WHAP!!
WHY IS IT OKAY TO KILL FLIES BUT NOT OKAY TO KILL DOLPHINS?
IS THE POOR FLY ANY LESS DESERVING OF OUR RESPECT AND PROTECTION?
HOLD STILL... THERE'S A DOLPHIN ON YOUR FOREHEAD.
I'VE ADDED THE A.S.P.C.A. TO OUR SPEED DIALER.
S. Adams

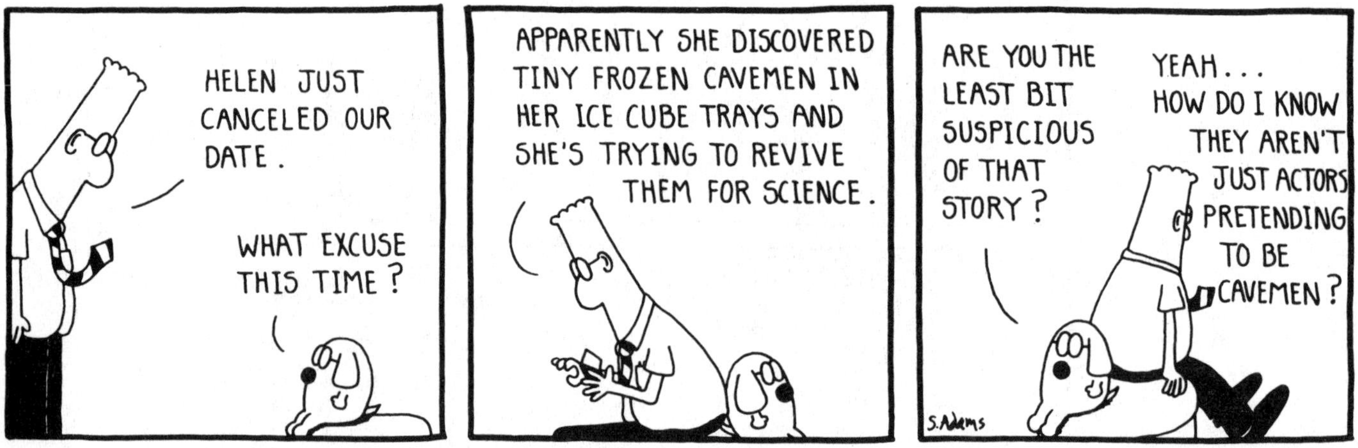
HELEN JUST CANCELED OUR DATE.
WHAT EXCUSE THIS TIME?
APPARENTLY SHE DISCOVERED TINY FROZEN CAVEMEN IN HER ICE CUBE TRAYS AND SHE'S TRYING TO REVIVE THEM FOR SCIENCE.
ARE YOU THE LEAST BIT SUSPICIOUS OF THAT STORY?
YEAH... HOW DO I KNOW THEY AREN'T JUST ACTORS PRETENDING TO BE CAVEMEN?
S. Adams

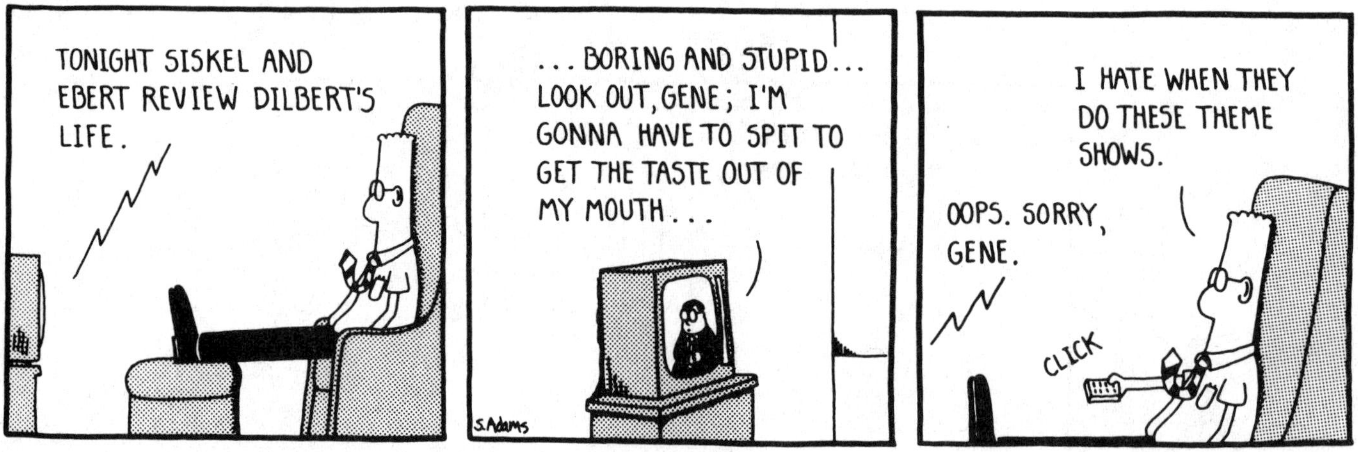
TONIGHT SISKEL AND EBERT REVIEW DILBERT'S LIFE.
... BORING AND STUPID... LOOK OUT, GENE; I'M GONNA HAVE TO SPIT TO GET THE TASTE OUT OF MY MOUTH...
S. Adams
I HATE WHEN THEY DO THESE THEME SHOWS.
OOPS. SORRY, GENE.
CLICK

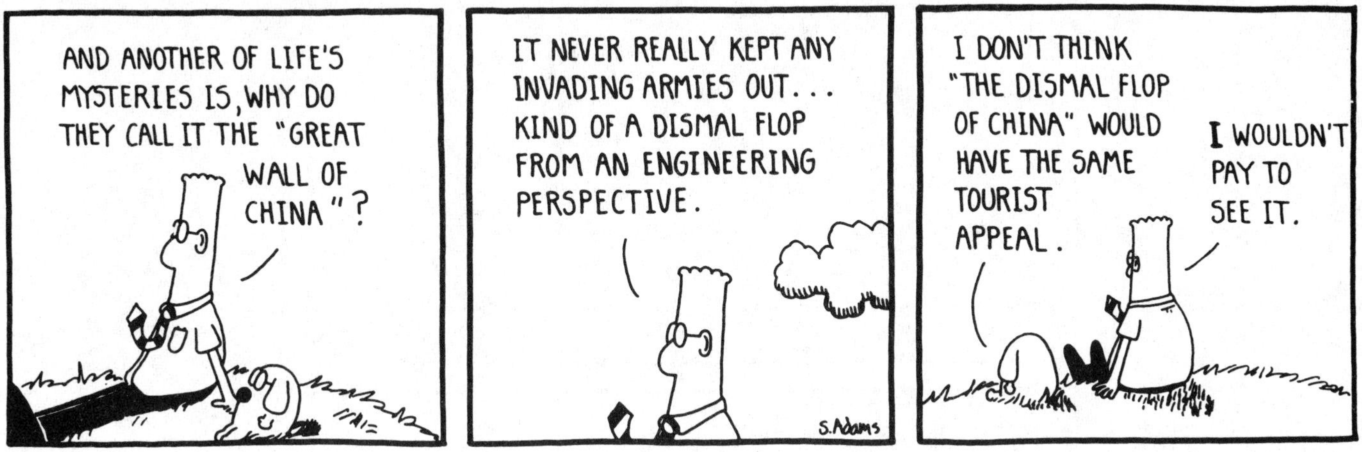
AND ANOTHER OF LIFE'S MYSTERIES IS, WHY DO THEY CALL IT THE "GREAT WALL OF CHINA"?
IT NEVER REALLY KEPT ANY INVADING ARMIES OUT... KIND OF A DISMAL FLOP FROM AN ENGINEERING PERSPECTIVE.
S.Adams
I DON'T THINK "THE DISMAL FLOP OF CHINA" WOULD HAVE THE SAME TOURIST APPEAL.
I WOULDN'T PAY TO SEE IT.

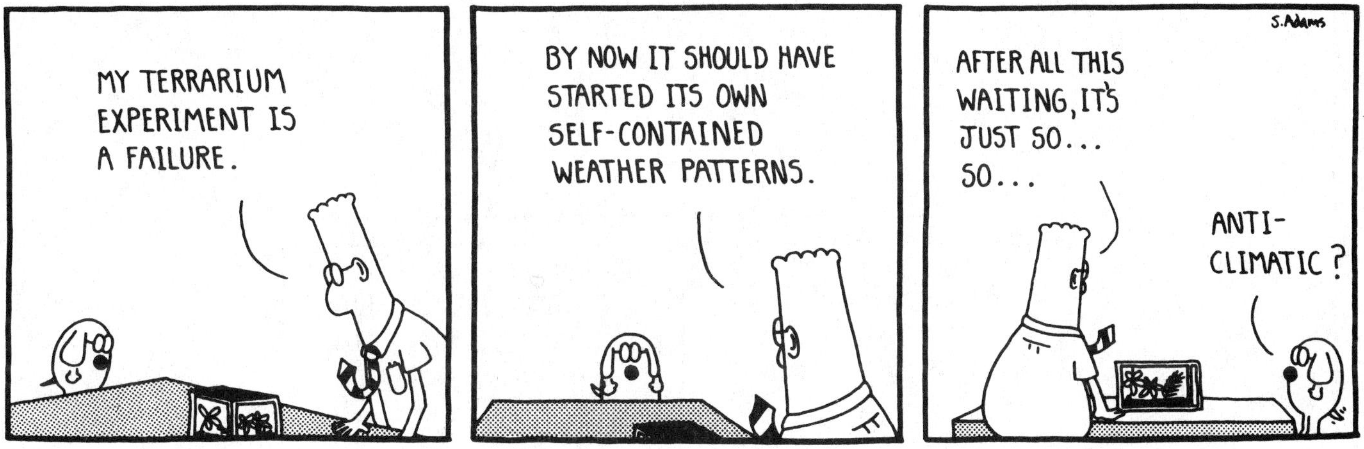
MY TERRARIUM EXPERIMENT IS A FAILURE.
BY NOW IT SHOULD HAVE STARTED ITS OWN SELF-CONTAINED WEATHER PATTERNS.
S.Adams
AFTER ALL THIS WAITING, IT'S JUST SO... SO...
ANTI-CLIMATIC?

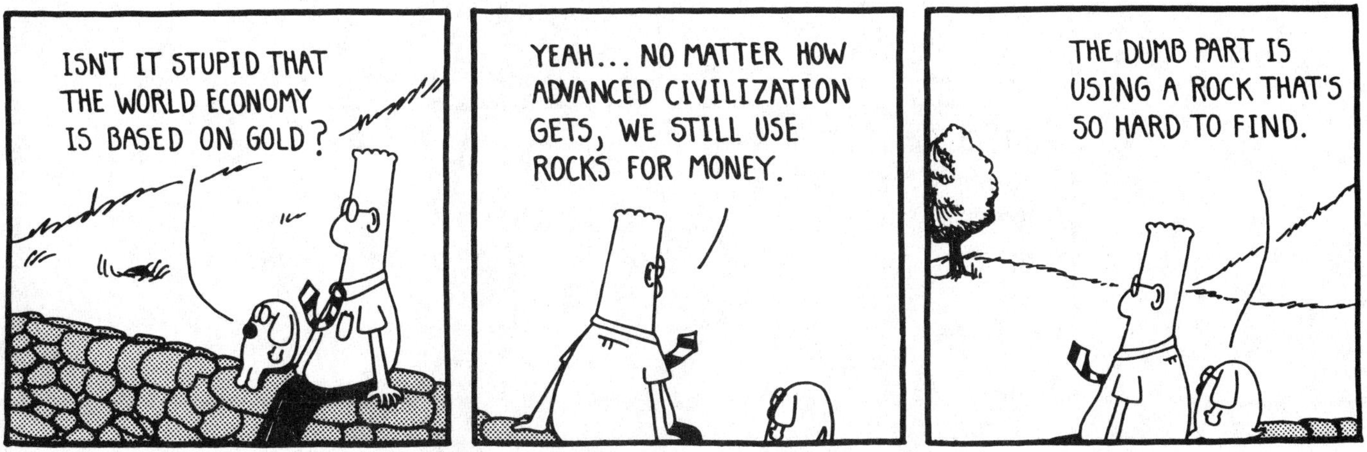
ISN'T IT STUPID THAT THE WORLD ECONOMY IS BASED ON GOLD?
YEAH... NO MATTER HOW ADVANCED CIVILIZATION GETS, WE STILL USE ROCKS FOR MONEY.
THE DUMB PART IS USING A ROCK THAT'S SO HARD TO FIND.

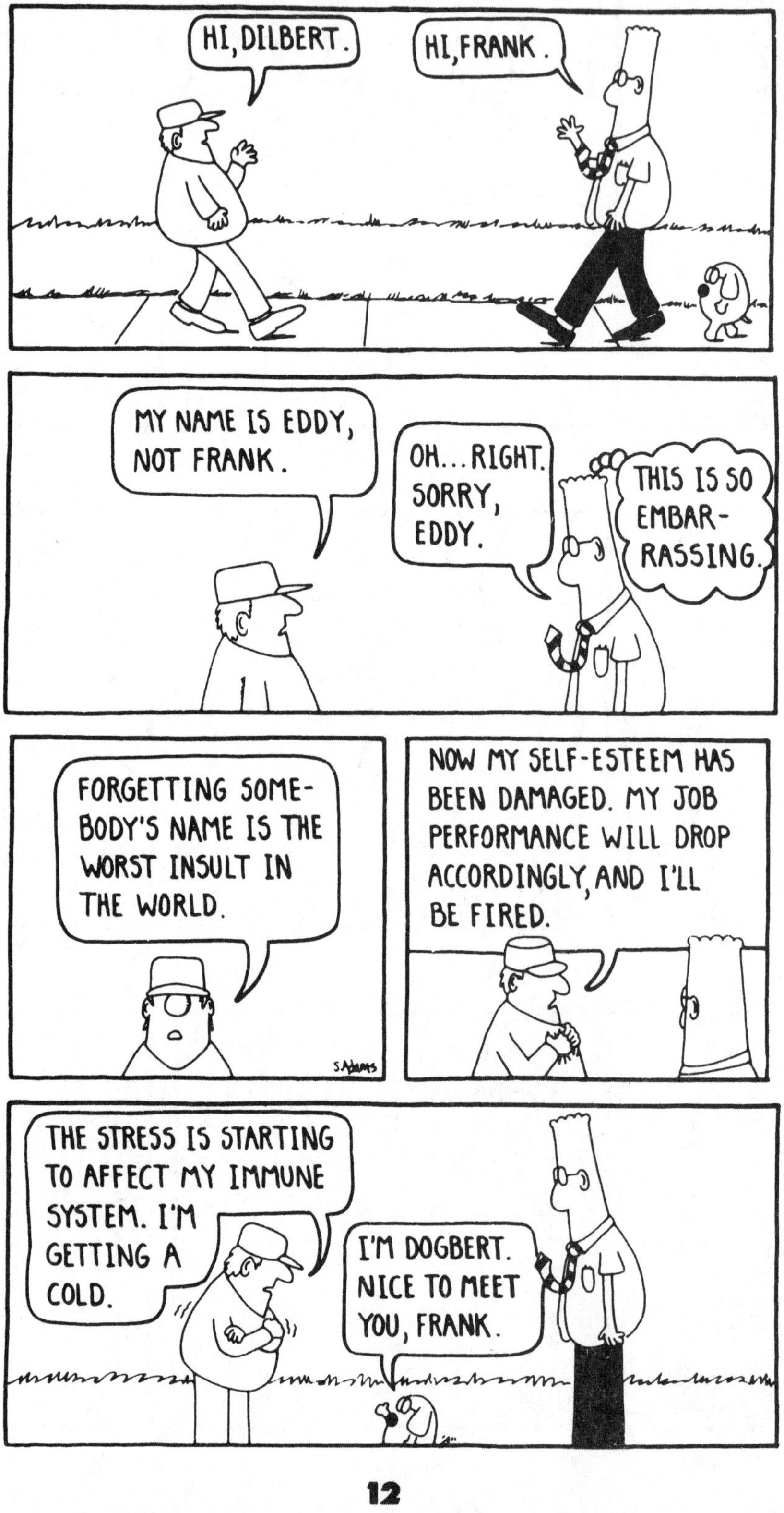
HI, DILBERT.
HI, FRANK.
MY NAME IS EDDY, NOT FRANK.
OH... RIGHT. SORRY, EDDY.
THIS IS SO EMBARRASSING.
FORGETTING SOMEBODY'S NAME IS THE WORST INSULT IN THE WORLD.
S.Adams
NOW MY SELF-ESTEEM HAS BEEN DAMAGED. MY JOB PERFORMANCE WILL DROP ACCORDINGLY, AND I'LL BE FIRED.
THE STRESS IS STARTING TO AFFECT MY IMMUNE SYSTEM. I'M GETTING A COLD.
I'M DOGBERT. NICE TO MEET YOU, FRANK.

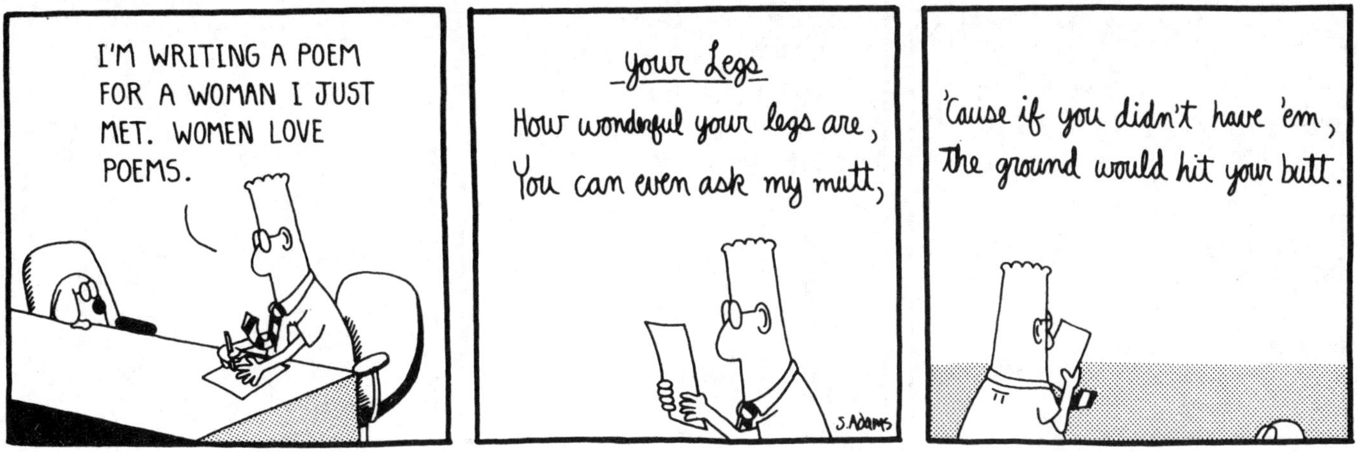
I'M WRITING A POEM FOR A WOMAN I JUST MET. WOMEN LOVE POEMS.
Your Legs
How wonderful your legs are,
You can even ask my mutt,
'Cause if you didn't have 'em,
The ground would hit your butt.
S. Adams

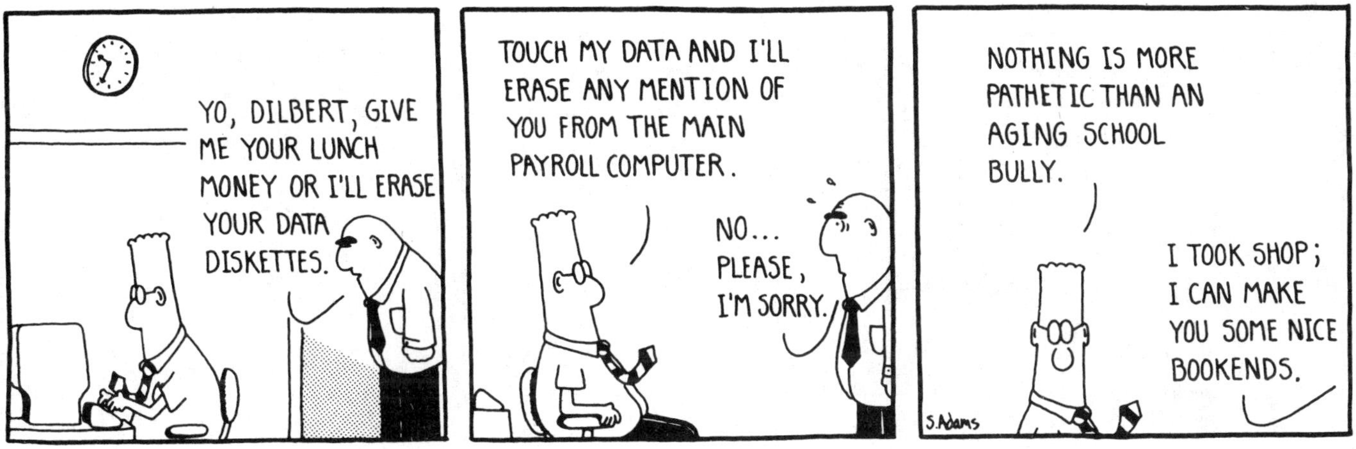
YO, DILBERT, GIVE ME YOUR LUNCH MONEY OR I'LL ERASE YOUR DATA DISKETTES.
TOUCH MY DATA AND I'LL ERASE ANY MENTION OF YOU FROM THE MAIN PAYROLL COMPUTER.
NO... PLEASE, I'M SORRY.
NOTHING IS MORE PATHETIC THAN AN AGING SCHOOL BULLY.
I TOOK SHOP; I CAN MAKE YOU SOME NICE BOOKENDS.
S. Adams

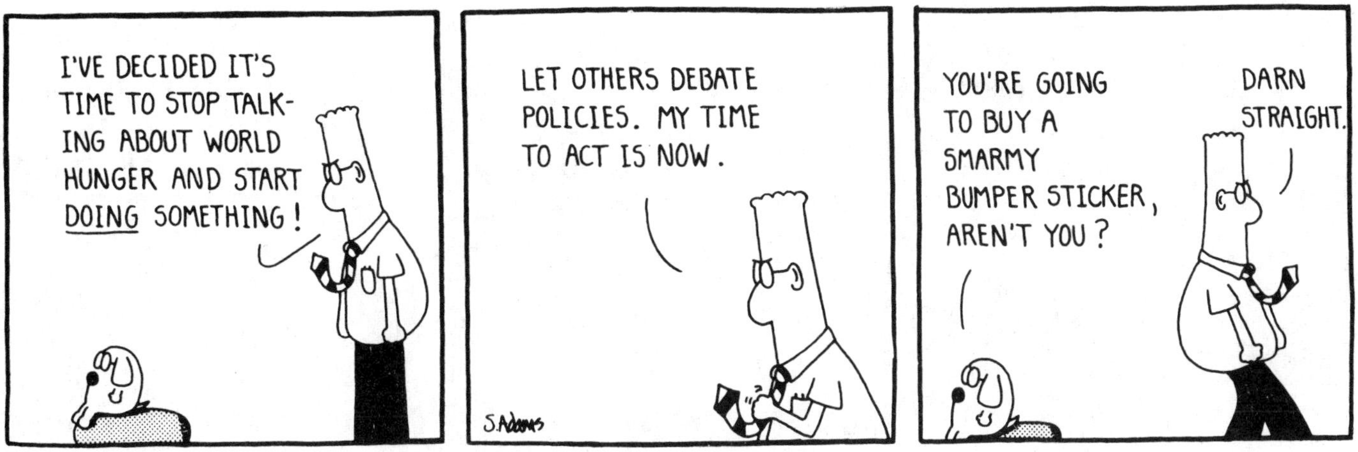
I'VE DECIDED IT'S TIME TO STOP TALKING ABOUT WORLD HUNGER AND START DOING SOMETHING!
LET OTHERS DEBATE POLICIES. MY TIME TO ACT IS NOW.
S. Adams
YOU'RE GOING TO BUY A SMARMY BUMPER STICKER, AREN'T YOU?
DARN STRAIGHT.

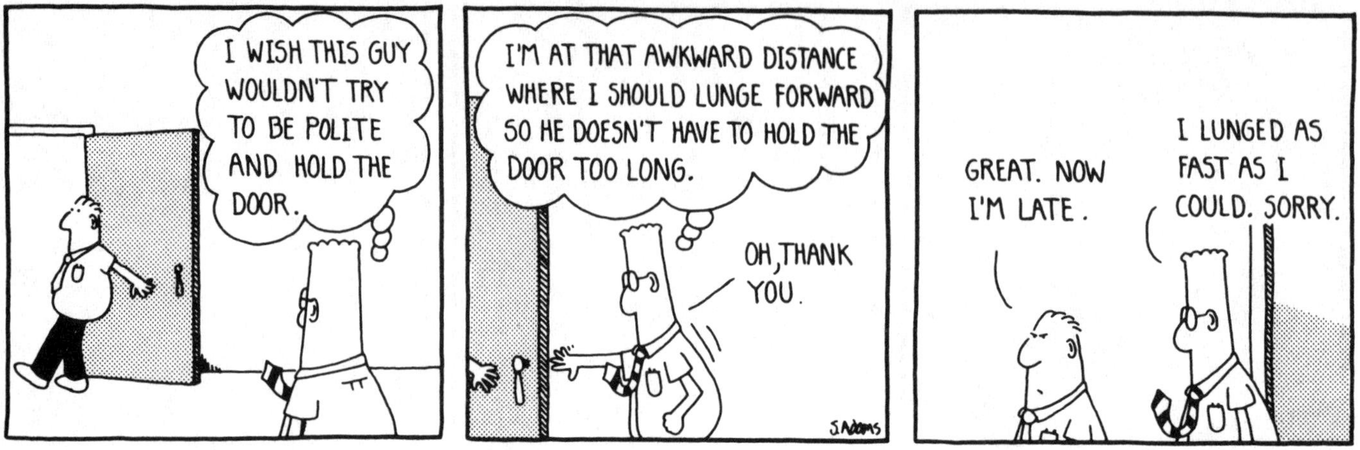
I WISH THIS GUY WOULDN'T TRY TO BE POLITE AND HOLD THE DOOR.
I'M AT THAT AWKWARD DISTANCE WHERE I SHOULD LUNGE FORWARD SO HE DOESN'T HAVE TO HOLD THE DOOR TOO LONG.
OH, THANK YOU.
S. Adams
GREAT. NOW I'M LATE.
I LUNGED AS FAST AS I COULD. SORRY.

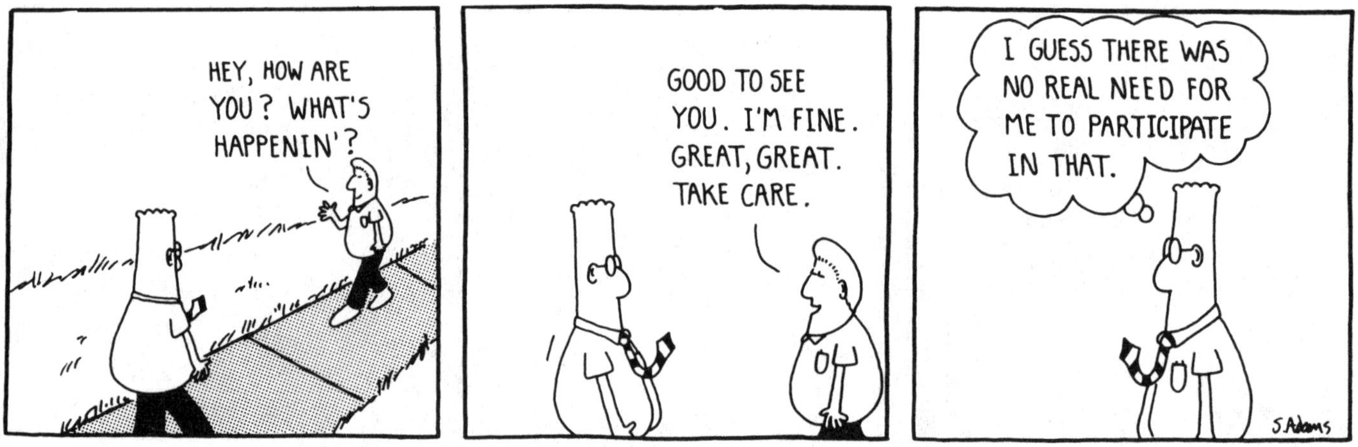
HEY, HOW ARE YOU? WHAT'S HAPPENIN'?
GOOD TO SEE YOU. I'M FINE. GREAT, GREAT. TAKE CARE.
I GUESS THERE WAS NO REAL NEED FOR ME TO PARTICIPATE IN THAT.
S. Adams

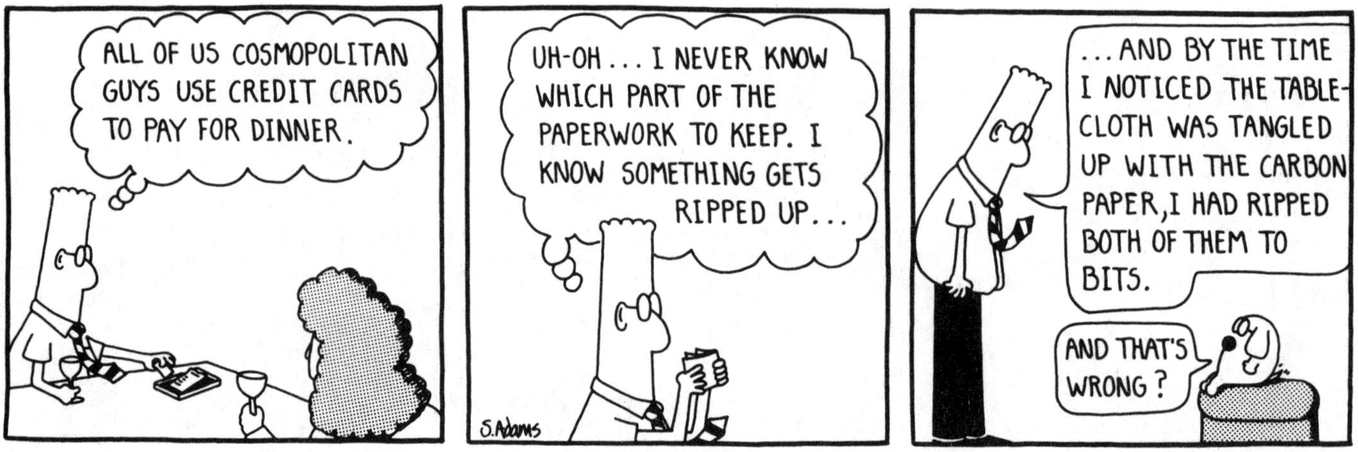
ALL OF US COSMOPOLITAN GUYS USE CREDIT CARDS TO PAY FOR DINNER.
UH-OH... I NEVER KNOW WHICH PART OF THE PAPERWORK TO KEEP. I KNOW SOMETHING GETS RIPPED UP...
S. Adams
...AND BY THE TIME I NOTICED THE TABLE-CLOTH WAS TANGLED UP WITH THE CARBON PAPER, I HAD RIPPED BOTH OF THEM TO BITS.
AND THAT'S WRONG?

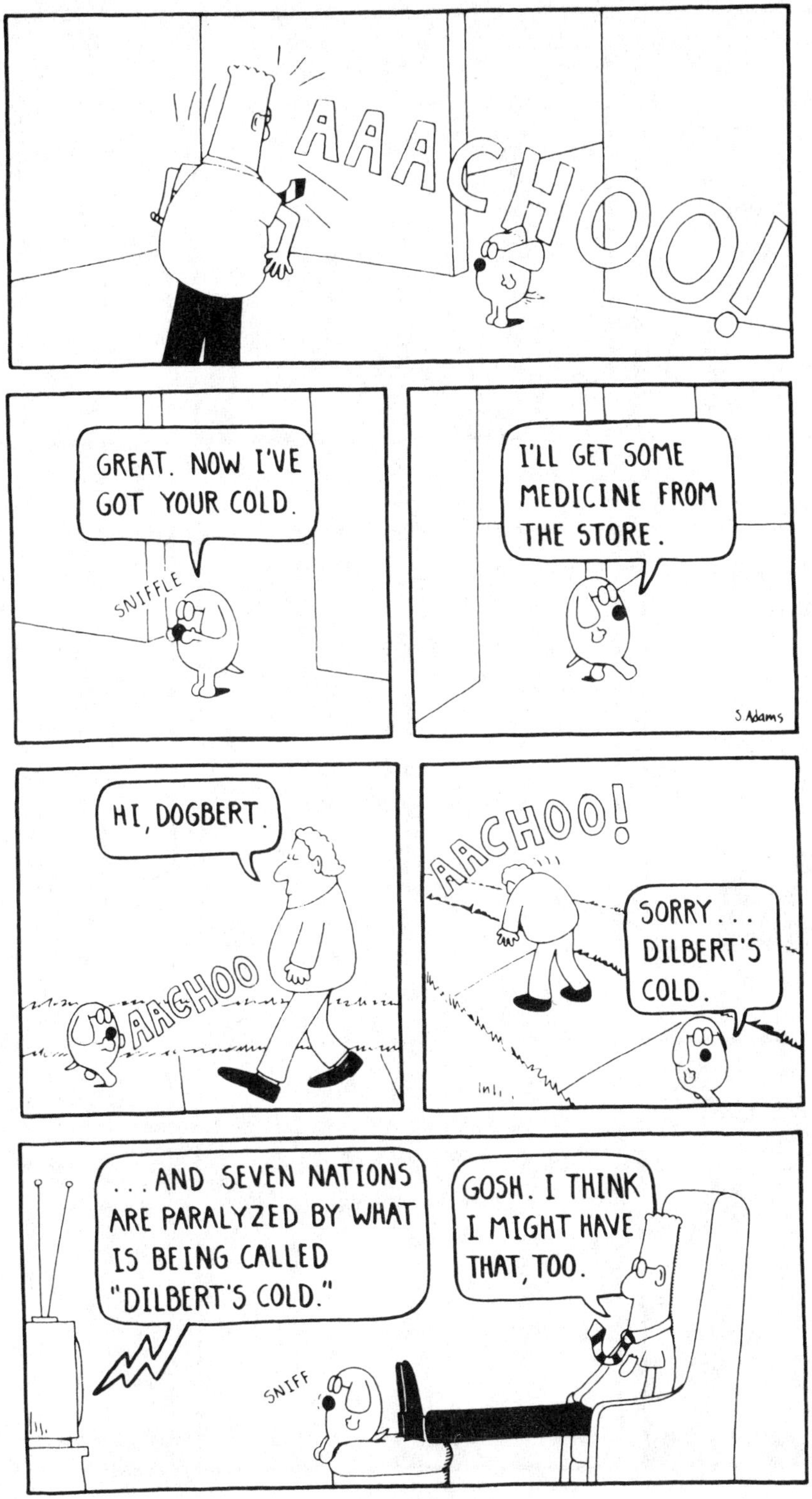
AAACHOO!
SNIFFLE
GREAT. NOW I'VE GOT YOUR COLD.
I'LL GET SOME MEDICINE FROM THE STORE.
S. Adams
HI, DOGBERT.
AACHOO
AACHOO!
SORRY... DILBERT'S COLD.
...AND SEVEN NATIONS ARE PARALYZED BY WHAT IS BEING CALLED "DILBERT'S COLD."
GOSH. I THINK I MIGHT HAVE THAT, TOO.
SNIFF

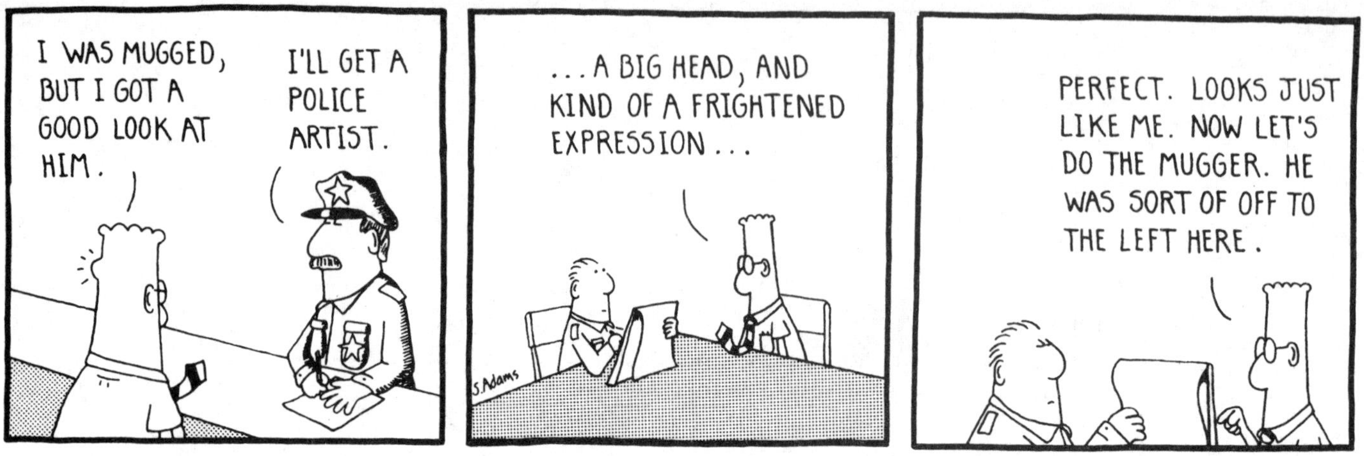
I WAS MUGGED, BUT I GOT A GOOD LOOK AT HIM.
I'LL GET A POLICE ARTIST.
...A BIG HEAD, AND KIND OF A FRIGHTENED EXPRESSION...
S.Adams
PERFECT. LOOKS JUST LIKE ME. NOW LET'S DO THE MUGGER. HE WAS SORT OF OFF TO THE LEFT HERE.

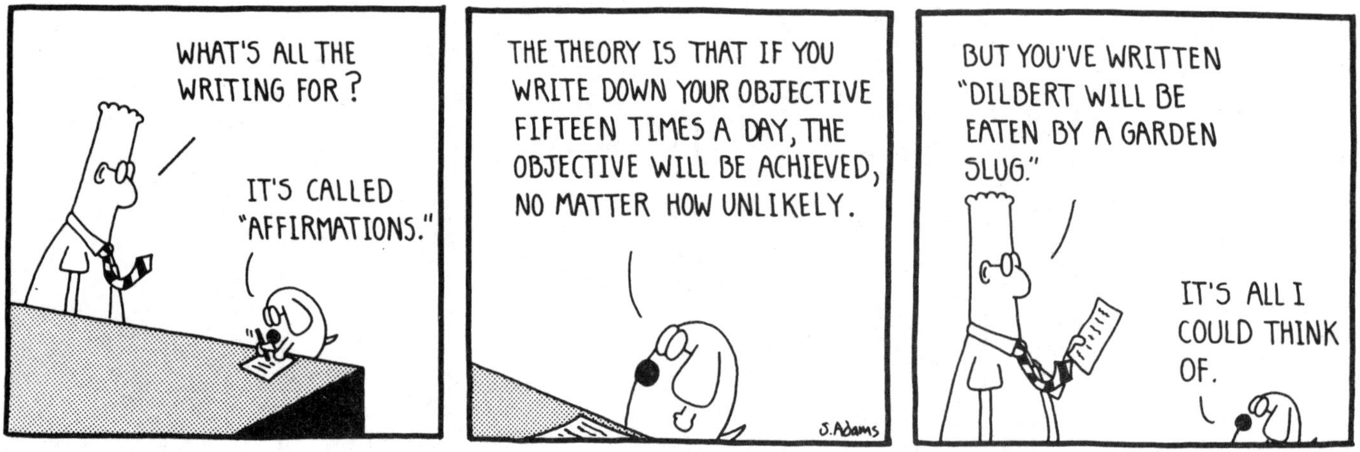
WHAT'S ALL THE WRITING FOR?
IT'S CALLED "AFFIRMATIONS."
THE THEORY IS THAT IF YOU WRITE DOWN YOUR OBJECTIVE FIFTEEN TIMES A DAY, THE OBJECTIVE WILL BE ACHIEVED, NO MATTER HOW UNLIKELY.
S.Adams
BUT YOU'VE WRITTEN "DILBERT WILL BE EATEN BY A GARDEN SLUG."
IT'S ALL I COULD THINK OF.

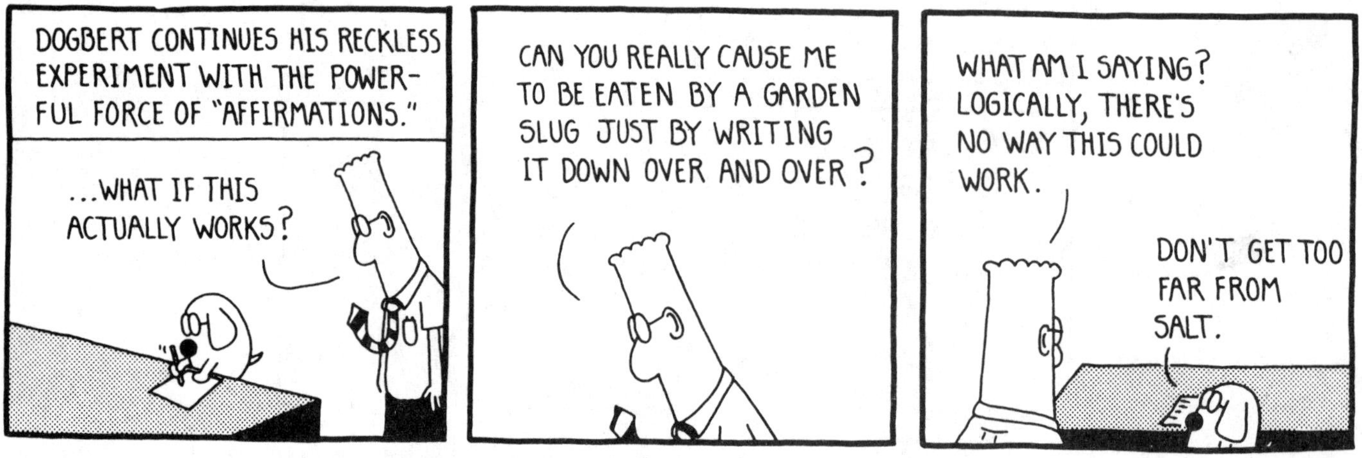
DOGBERT CONTINUES HIS RECKLESS EXPERIMENT WITH THE POWERFUL FORCE OF "AFFIRMATIONS."
...WHAT IF THIS ACTUALLY WORKS?
CAN YOU REALLY CAUSE ME TO BE EATEN BY A GARDEN SLUG JUST BY WRITING IT DOWN OVER AND OVER?
WHAT AM I SAYING? LOGICALLY, THERE'S NO WAY THIS COULD WORK.
DON'T GET TOO FAR FROM SALT.

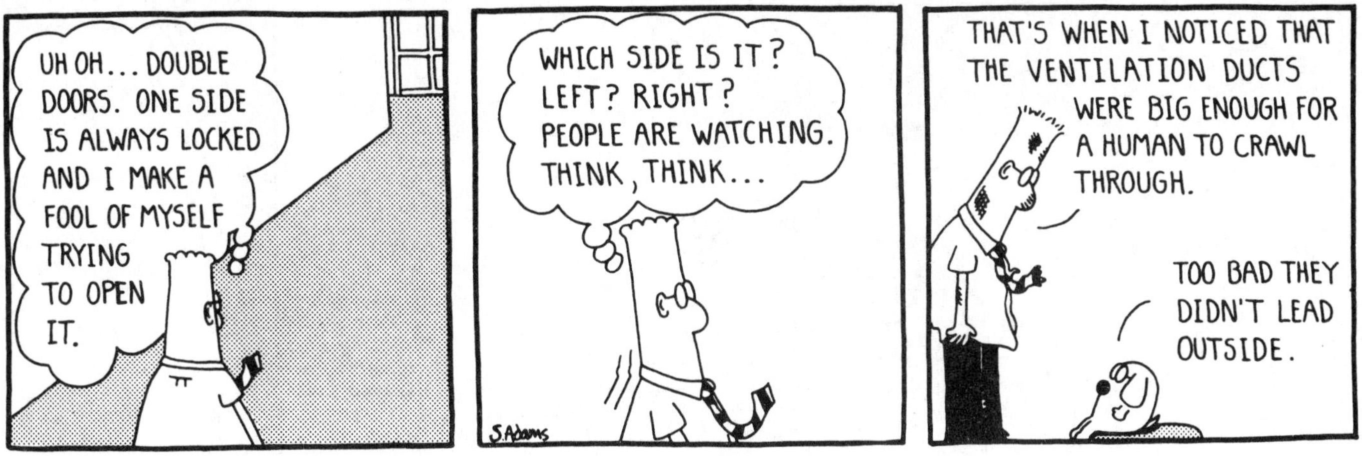
UH OH... DOUBLE DOORS. ONE SIDE IS ALWAYS LOCKED AND I MAKE A FOOL OF MYSELF TRYING TO OPEN IT.
WHICH SIDE IS IT? LEFT? RIGHT? PEOPLE ARE WATCHING. THINK, THINK...
S. Adams
THAT'S WHEN I NOTICED THAT THE VENTILATION DUCTS WERE BIG ENOUGH FOR A HUMAN TO CRAWL THROUGH.
TOO BAD THEY DIDN'T LEAD OUTSIDE.

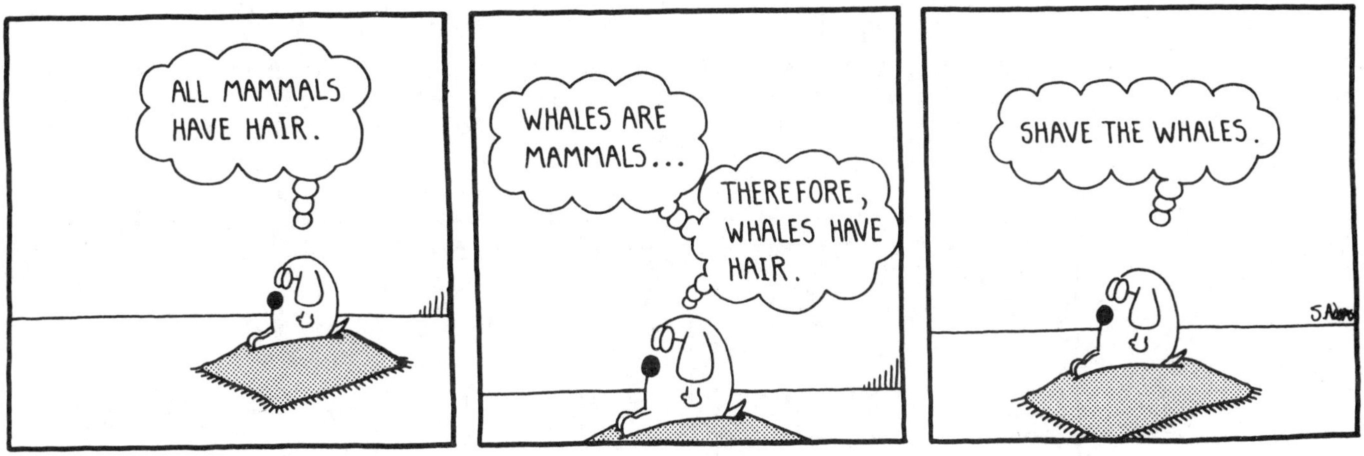
ALL MAMMALS HAVE HAIR.
WHALES ARE MAMMALS...
THEREFORE, WHALES HAVE HAIR.
SHAVE THE WHALES.
S. Adams

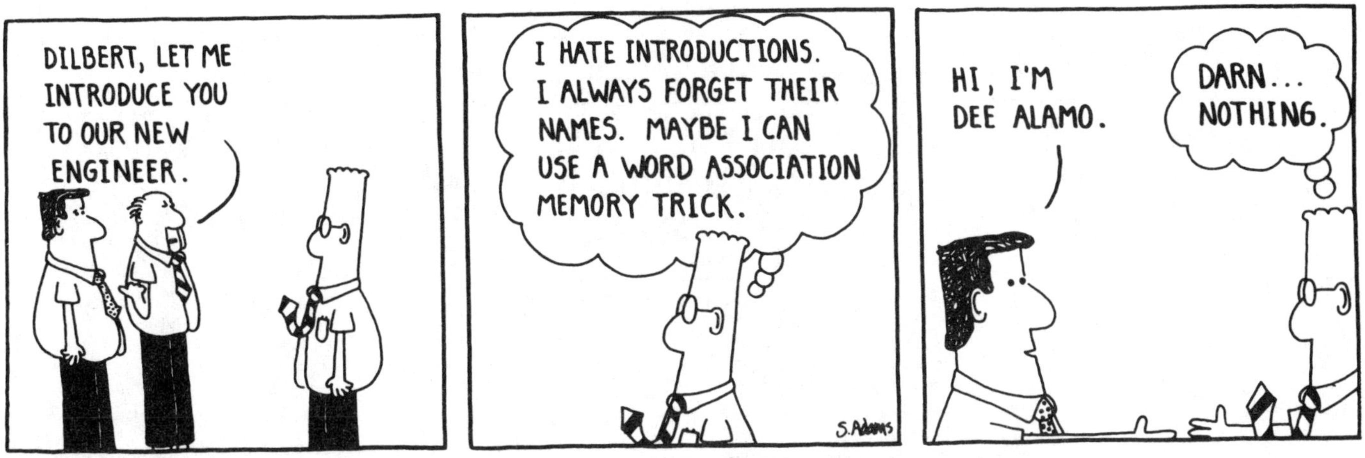
DILBERT, LET ME INTRODUCE YOU TO OUR NEW ENGINEER.
I HATE INTRODUCTIONS. I ALWAYS FORGET THEIR NAMES. MAYBE I CAN USE A WORD ASSOCIATION MEMORY TRICK.
S. Adams
HI, I'M DEE ALAMO.
DARN... NOTHING.

PUFF
PUFF PUFF
HOW WAS YOUR RUN?
GREAT... I FEEL AWFUL.
PARDON A SIMPLE DOG FOR ASKING, BUT WHY DO YOU RUN IF IT FEELS AWFUL?
WELL, IF I DO IT EVERY DAY, I'LL LIVE A LONGER LIFE.
SO, LIFE WILL FEEL AWFUL, BUT AT LEAST IT WILL LAST A LONG TIME.
UNLESS I GET HIT BY A TRUCK...
S Adams

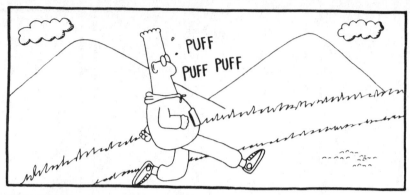

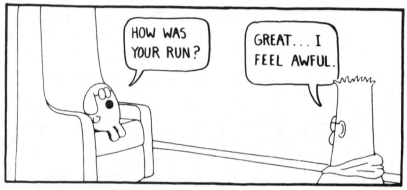

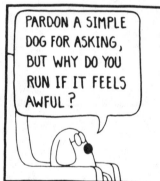

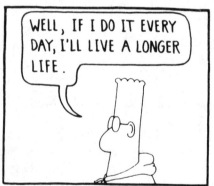

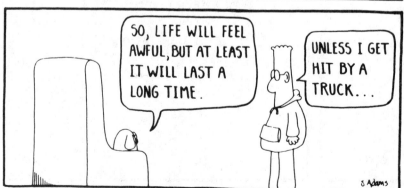

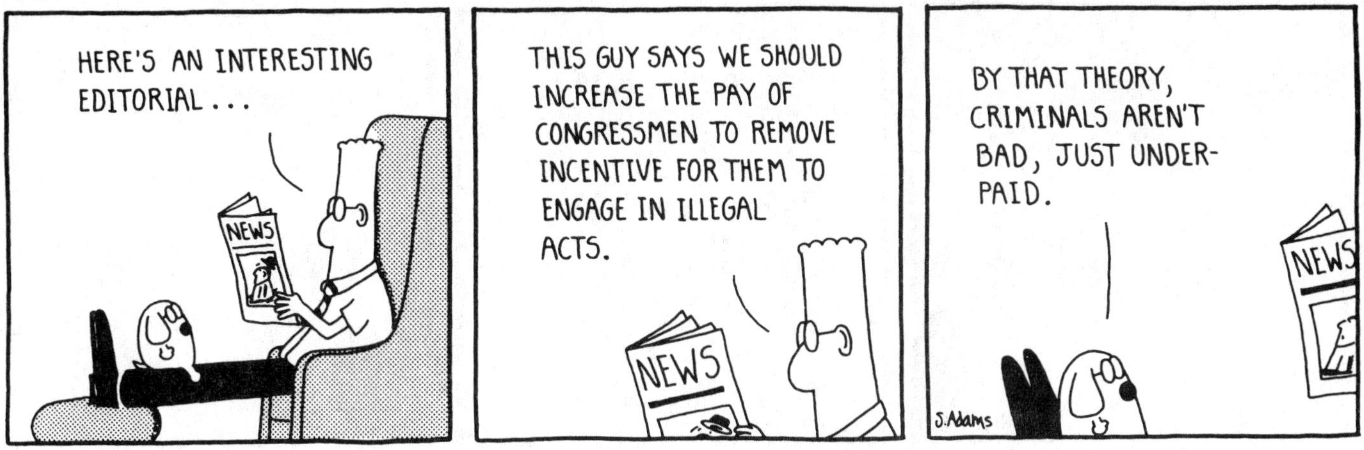
HERE'S AN INTERESTING EDITORIAL . . .
NEWS
THIS GUY SAYS WE SHOULD INCREASE THE PAY OF CONGRESSMEN TO REMOVE INCENTIVE FOR THEM TO ENGAGE IN ILLEGAL ACTS.
NEWS
BY THAT THEORY, CRIMINALS AREN'T BAD, JUST UNDER-PAID.
NEWS
S.Adams

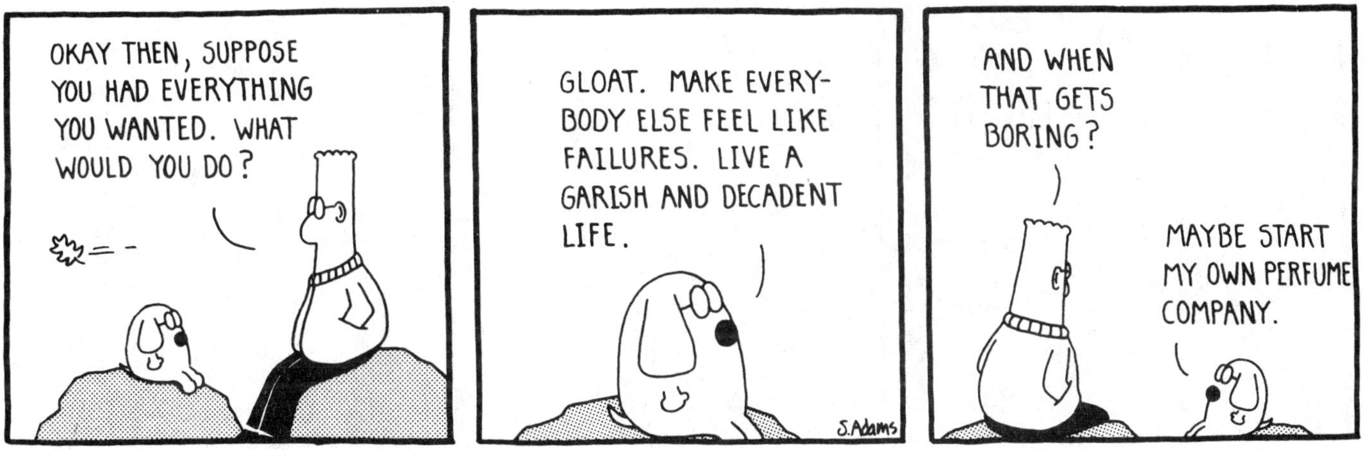
OKAY THEN, SUPPOSE YOU HAD EVERYTHING YOU WANTED. WHAT WOULD YOU DO?
GLOAT. MAKE EVERY-BODY ELSE FEEL LIKE FAILURES. LIVE A GARISH AND DECADENT LIFE.
S.Adams
AND WHEN THAT GETS BORING?
MAYBE START MY OWN PERFUME COMPANY.

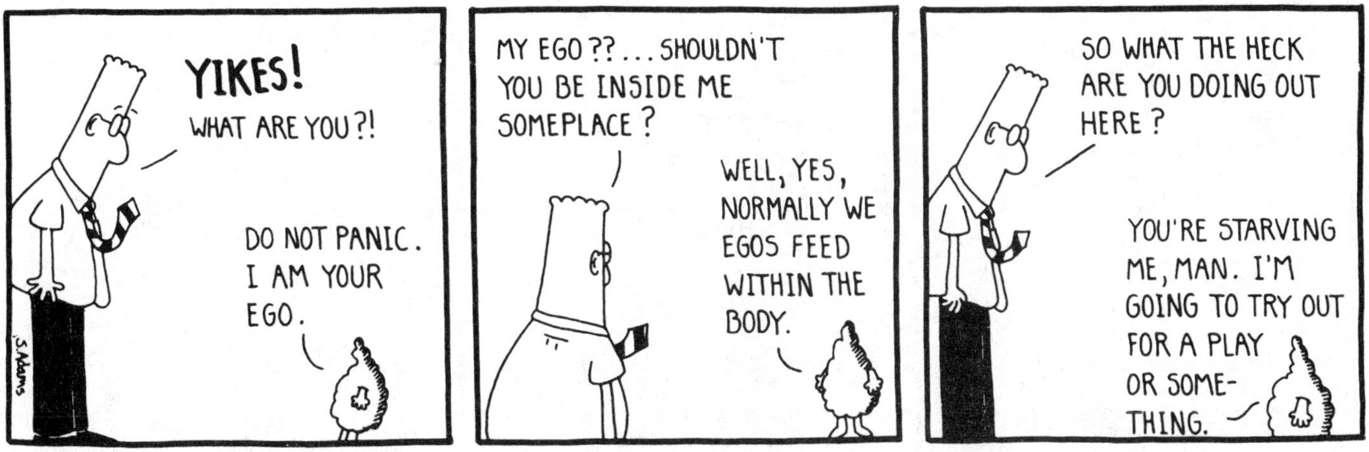
YIKES!
WHAT ARE YOU?!
DO NOT PANIC. I AM YOUR EGO.
S.Adams
MY EGO??... SHOULDN'T YOU BE INSIDE ME SOMEPLACE?
WELL, YES, NORMALLY WE EGOS FEED WITHIN THE BODY.
SO WHAT THE HECK ARE YOU DOING OUT HERE?
YOU'RE STARVING ME, MAN. I'M GOING TO TRY OUT FOR A PLAY OR SOME-THING.

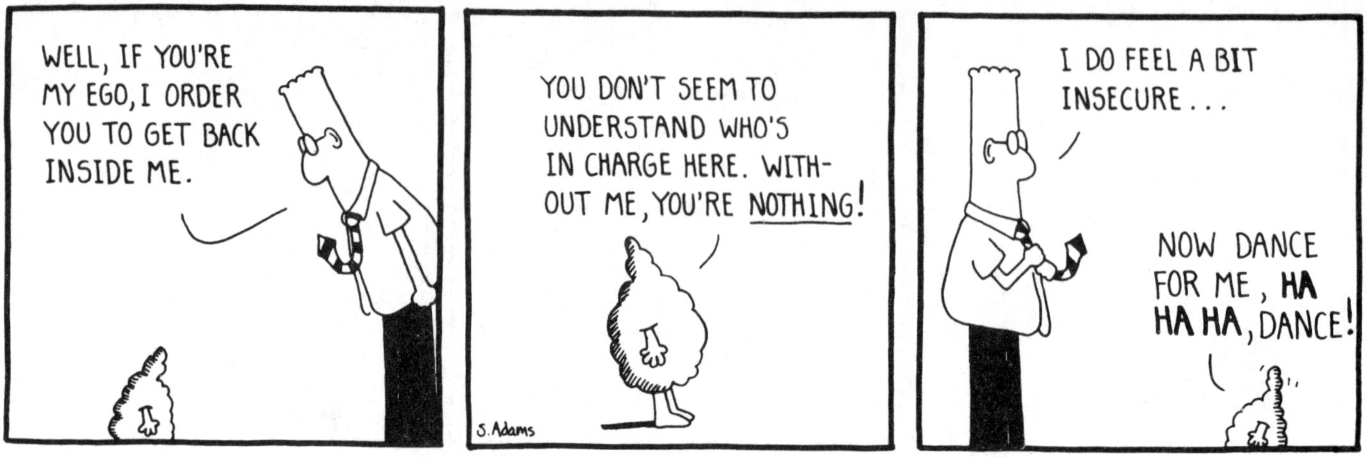
WELL, IF YOU'RE MY EGO, I ORDER YOU TO GET BACK INSIDE ME.
YOU DON'T SEEM TO UNDERSTAND WHO'S IN CHARGE HERE. WITH-OUT ME, YOU'RE NOTHING!
S. Adams
I DO FEEL A BIT INSECURE . . .
NOW DANCE FOR ME, HA HA HA, DANCE!

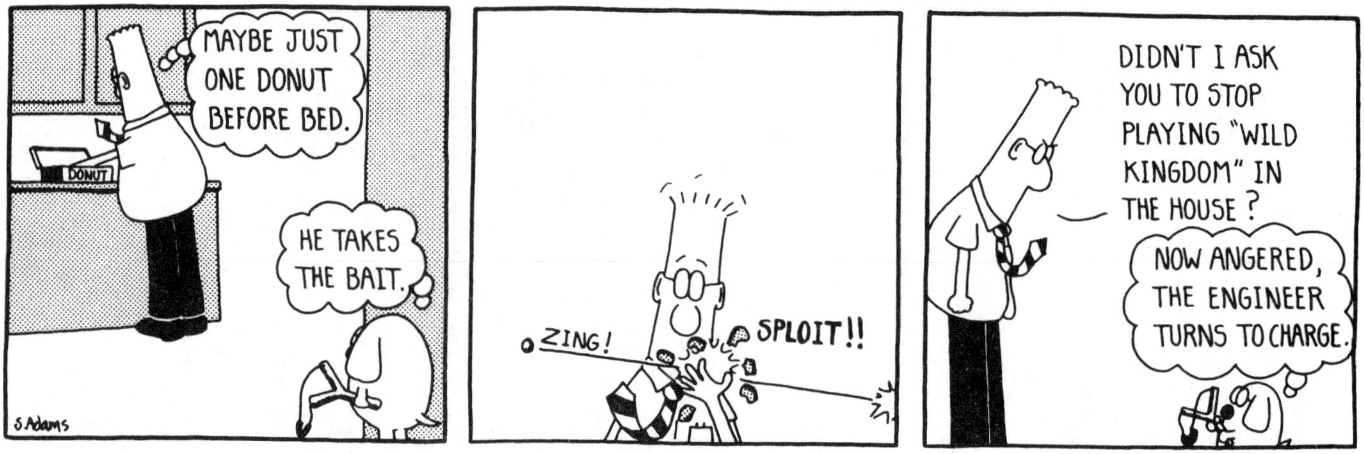
MAYBE JUST ONE DONUT BEFORE BED.
DONUT
HE TAKES THE BAIT.
S. Adams
ZING!
SPLOIT!!
DIDN'T I ASK YOU TO STOP PLAYING "WILD KINGDOM" IN THE HOUSE?
NOW ANGERED, THE ENGINEER TURNS TO CHARGE.

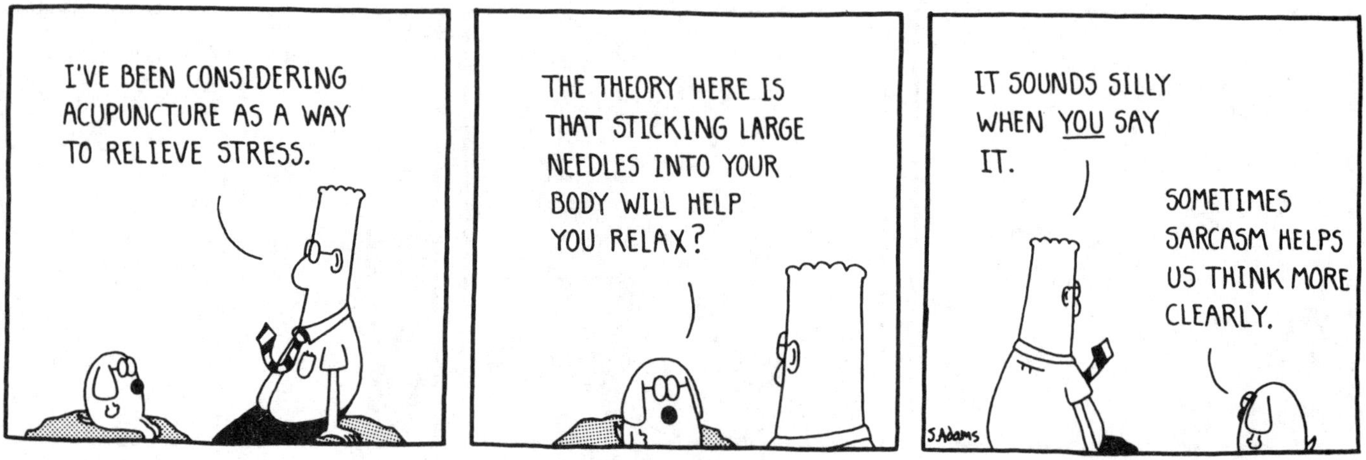
I'VE BEEN CONSIDERING ACUPUNCTURE AS A WAY TO RELIEVE STRESS.
THE THEORY HERE IS THAT STICKING LARGE NEEDLES INTO YOUR BODY WILL HELP YOU RELAX?
IT SOUNDS SILLY WHEN YOU SAY IT.
SOMETIMES SARCASM HELPS US THINK MORE CLEARLY.
S. Adams

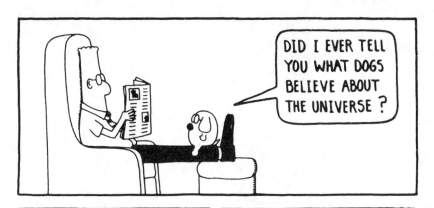

DID I EVER TELL YOU WHAT DOGS BELIEVE ABOUT THE UNIVERSE ?
WE BELIEVE IN INFINITE PARALLEL UNIVERSES, ALL SLIGHTLY DIFFERENT.
FOR EXAMPLE, IN OUR UNIVERSE, VINCENT VAN GOGH CUT HIS EAR OFF TO DEMONSTRATE HIS LOVE FOR A WOMAN.
BUT, IN A PARALLEL UNIVERSE, VAN GOGH LOSES THE EAR IN A TRAGIC TOE-NAIL CLIPPING ACCIDENT...
...VINNIE CLIPS THE NAIL, AND IT JUST GOES FLYIN' UP AND RIPS HIS EAR CLEAN OFF.
IN YET ANOTHER UNIVERSE, MAYBE HE HAD A DOG WHO TALKED HIS EAR OFF.
THIS IS WHY DOGS RARELY DISCUSS THEIR BELIEFS.
S Adams

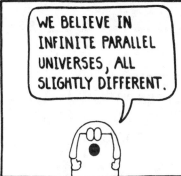

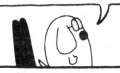

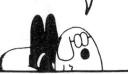

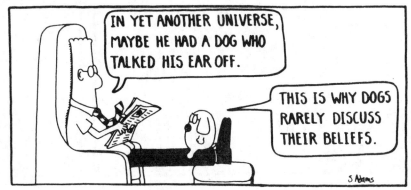

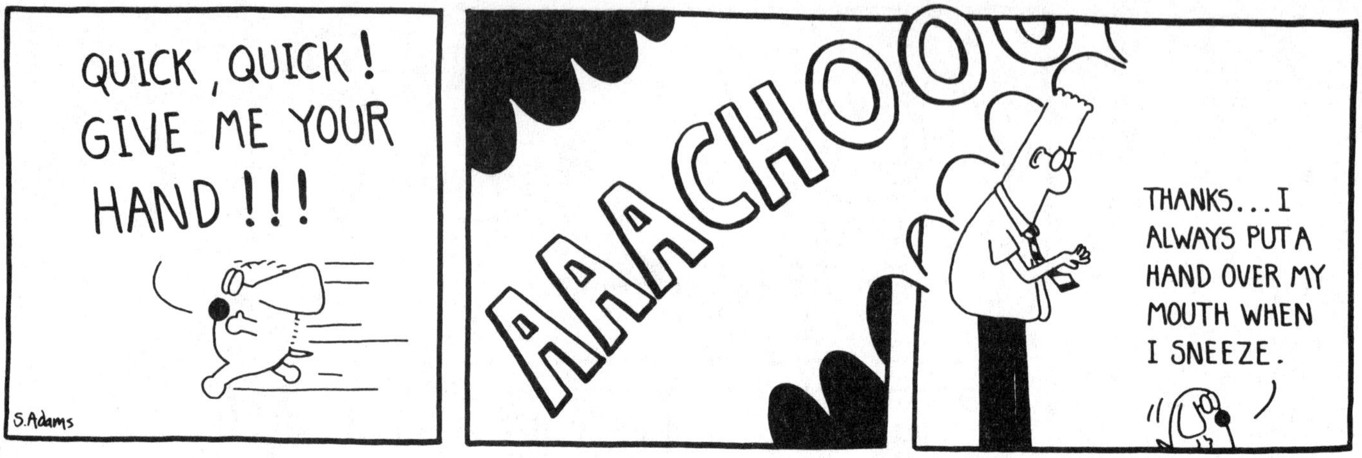
QUICK, QUICK! GIVE ME YOUR HAND!!!
S.Adams
AAACHOOO
THANKS... I ALWAYS PUT A HAND OVER MY MOUTH WHEN I SNEEZE.

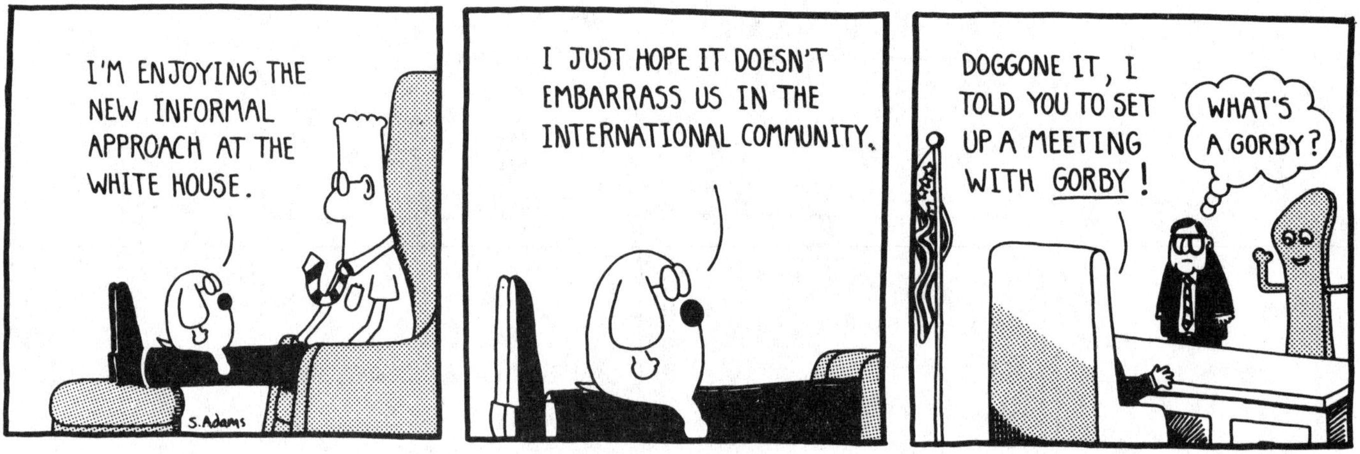
I'M ENJOYING THE NEW INFORMAL APPROACH AT THE WHITE HOUSE.
S.Adams
I JUST HOPE IT DOESN'T EMBARRASS US IN THE INTERNATIONAL COMMUNITY.
DOGGONE IT, I TOLD YOU TO SET UP A MEETING WITH GORBY!
WHAT'S A GORBY?

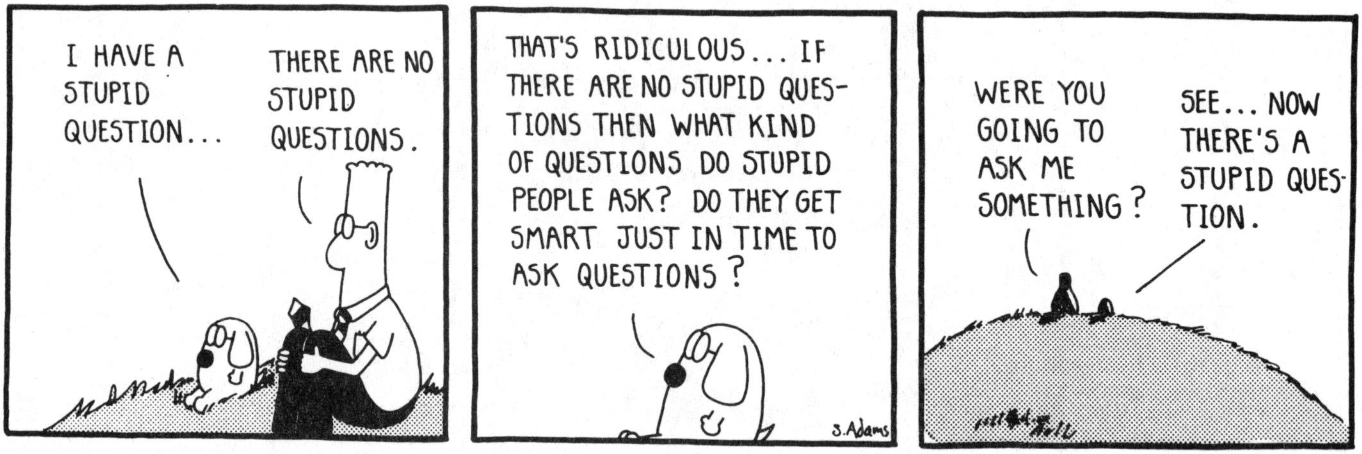
I HAVE A STUPID QUESTION...
THERE ARE NO STUPID QUESTIONS.
THAT'S RIDICULOUS... IF THERE ARE NO STUPID QUESTIONS THEN WHAT KIND OF QUESTIONS DO STUPID PEOPLE ASK? DO THEY GET SMART JUST IN TIME TO ASK QUESTIONS?
S.Adams
WERE YOU GOING TO ASK ME SOMETHING?
SEE... NOW THERE'S A STUPID QUESTION.

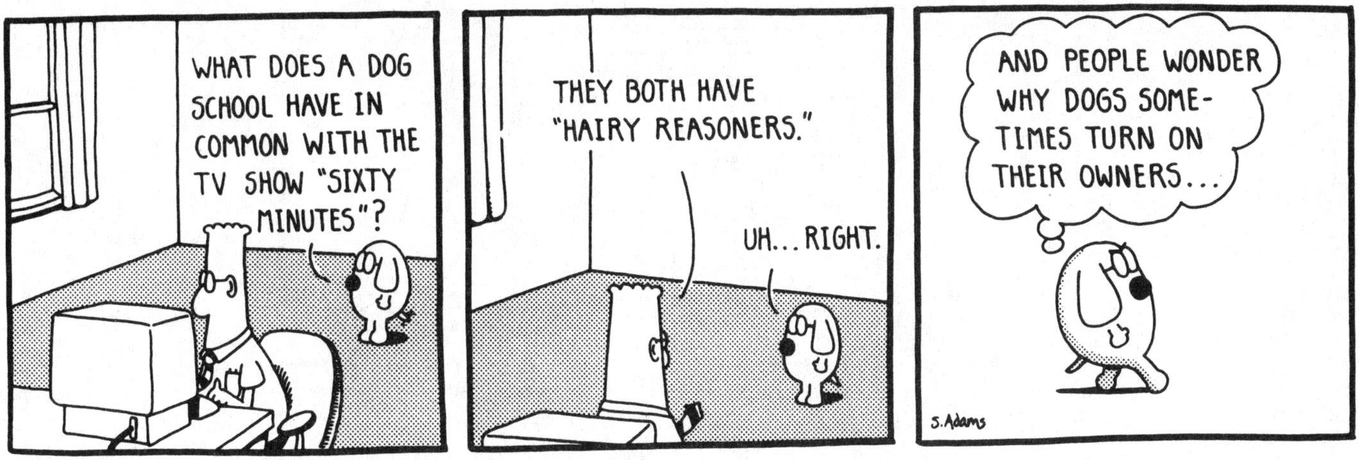
WHAT DOES A DOG SCHOOL HAVE IN COMMON WITH THE TV SHOW "SIXTY MINUTES"?
THEY BOTH HAVE "HAIRY REASONERS."
UH... RIGHT.
AND PEOPLE WONDER WHY DOGS SOMETIMES TURN ON THEIR OWNERS...
S. Adams

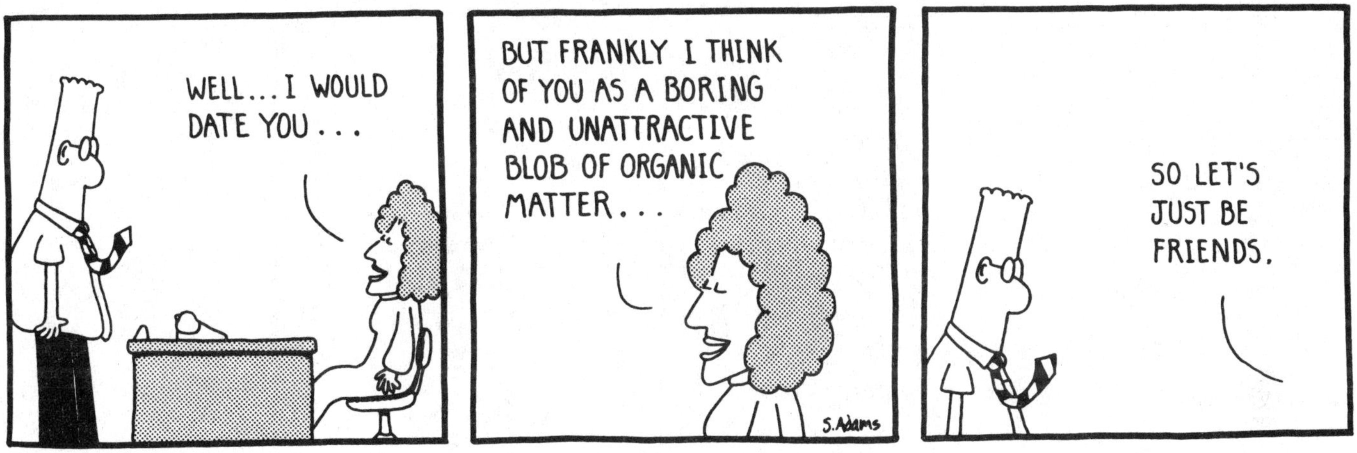
WELL... I WOULD DATE YOU...
BUT FRANKLY I THINK OF YOU AS A BORING AND UNATTRACTIVE BLOB OF ORGANIC MATTER...
S. Adams
SO LET'S JUST BE FRIENDS.

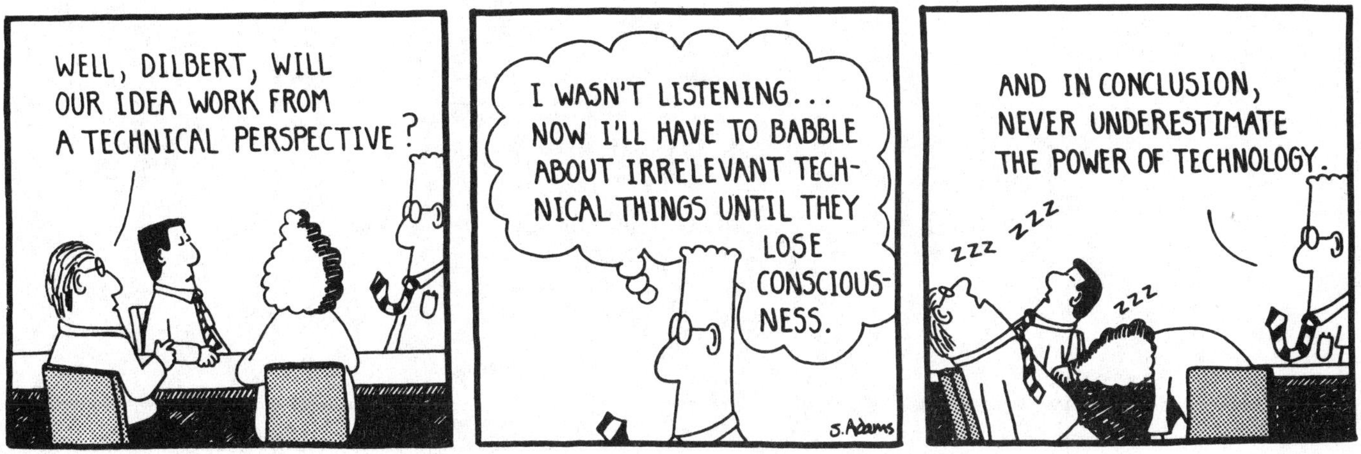
WELL, DILBERT, WILL OUR IDEA WORK FROM A TECHNICAL PERSPECTIVE?
I WASN'T LISTENING... NOW I'LL HAVE TO BABBLE ABOUT IRRELEVANT TECHNICAL THINGS UNTIL THEY LOSE CONSCIOUSNESS.
S. Adams
AND IN CONCLUSION, NEVER UNDERESTIMATE THE POWER OF TECHNOLOGY.
ZZZ ZZZ
ZZZ

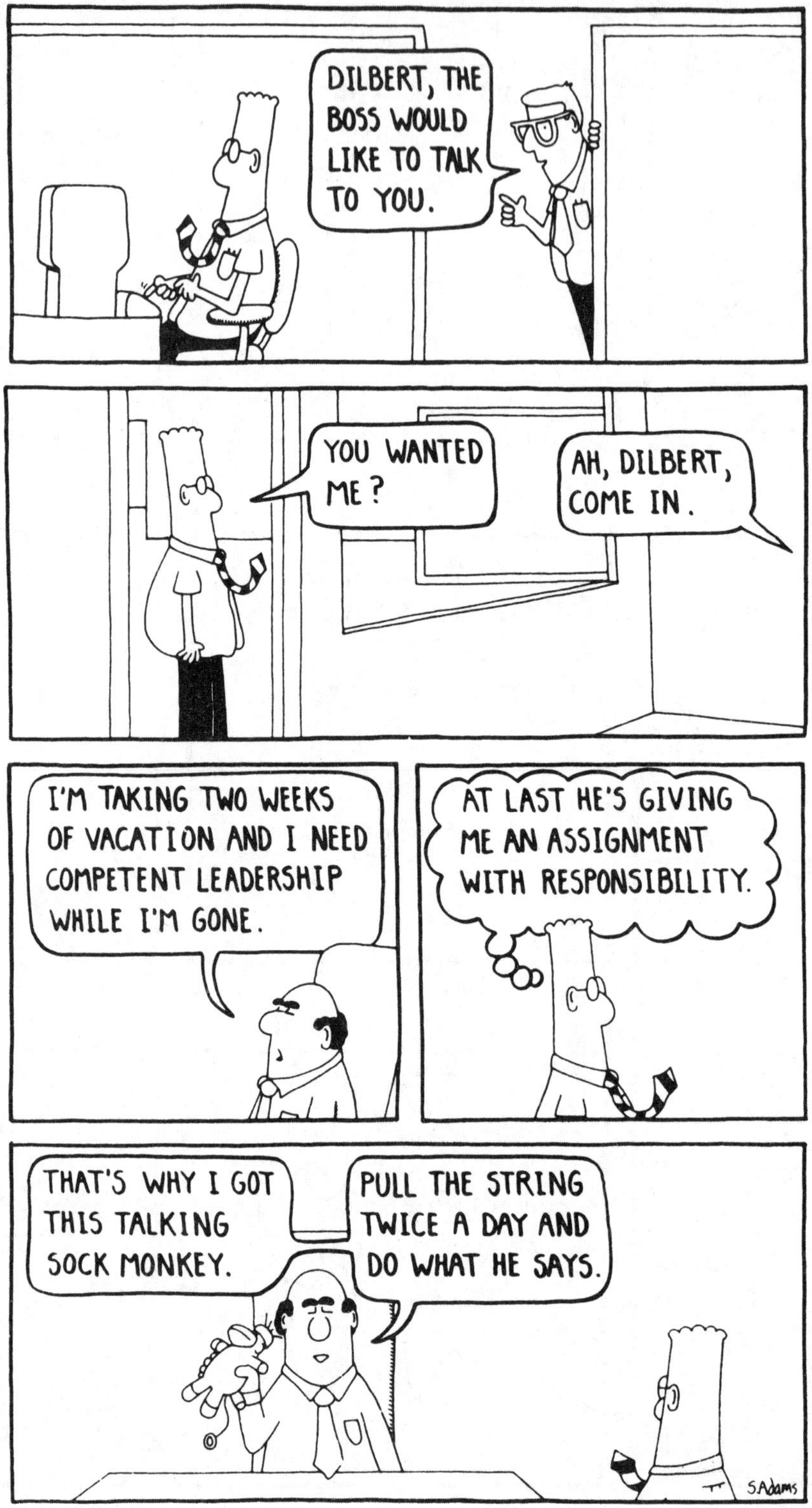
DILBERT, THE BOSS WOULD LIKE TO TALK TO YOU.
YOU WANTED ME?
AH, DILBERT, COME IN.
I'M TAKING TWO WEEKS OF VACATION AND I NEED COMPETENT LEADERSHIP WHILE I'M GONE.
AT LAST HE'S GIVING ME AN ASSIGNMENT WITH RESPONSIBILITY.
THAT'S WHY I GOT THIS TALKING SOCK MONKEY.
PULL THE STRING TWICE A DAY AND DO WHAT HE SAYS.
S.Adams

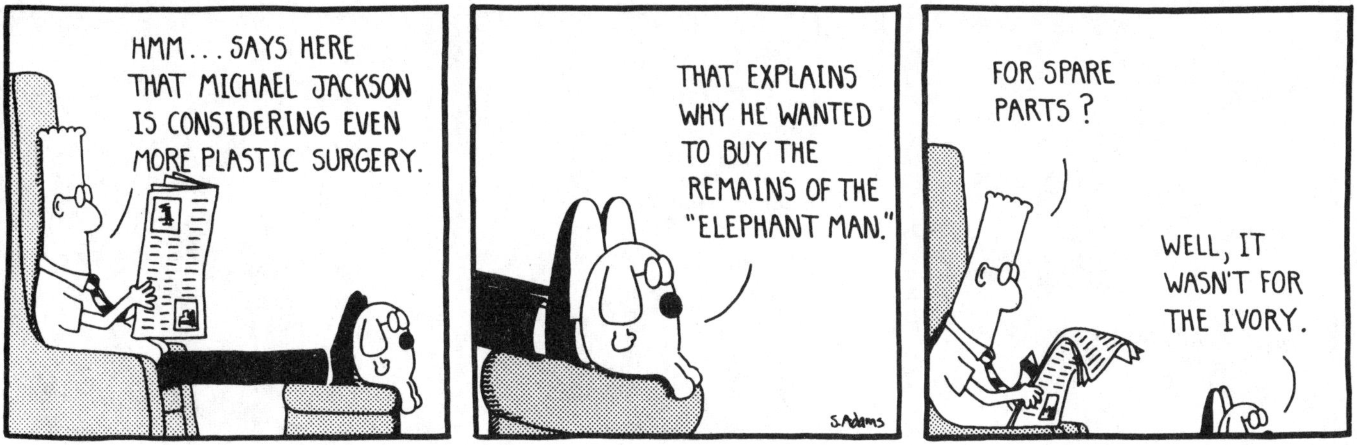
HMM... SAYS HERE THAT MICHAEL JACKSON IS CONSIDERING EVEN MORE PLASTIC SURGERY.
THAT EXPLAINS WHY HE WANTED TO BUY THE REMAINS OF THE "ELEPHANT MAN."
S.Adams
FOR SPARE PARTS?
WELL, IT WASN'T FOR THE IVORY.

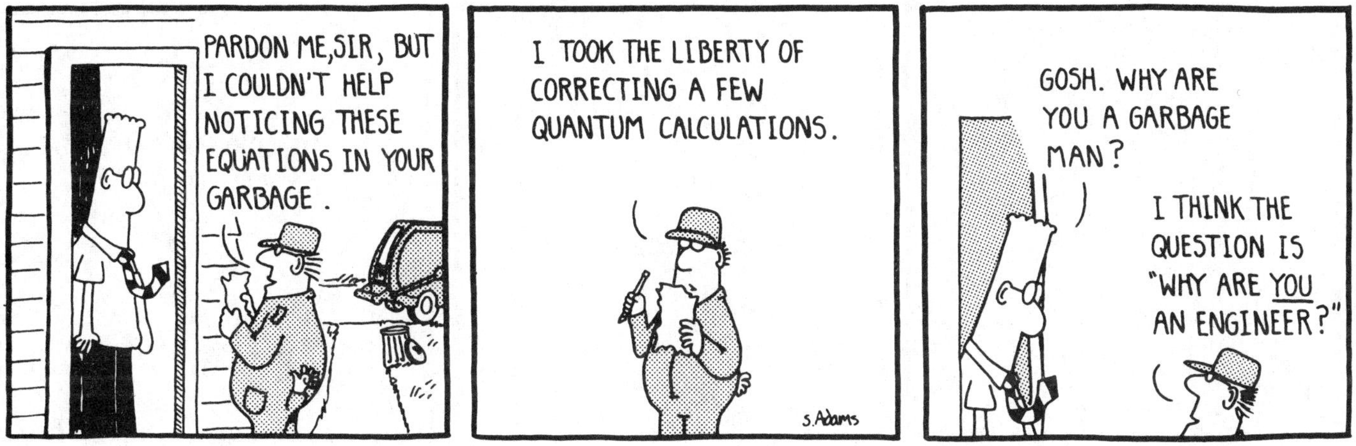
PARDON ME, SIR, BUT I COULDN'T HELP NOTICING THESE EQUATIONS IN YOUR GARBAGE.
I TOOK THE LIBERTY OF CORRECTING A FEW QUANTUM CALCULATIONS.
S.Adams
GOSH. WHY ARE YOU A GARBAGE MAN?
I THINK THE QUESTION IS "WHY ARE YOU AN ENGINEER?"

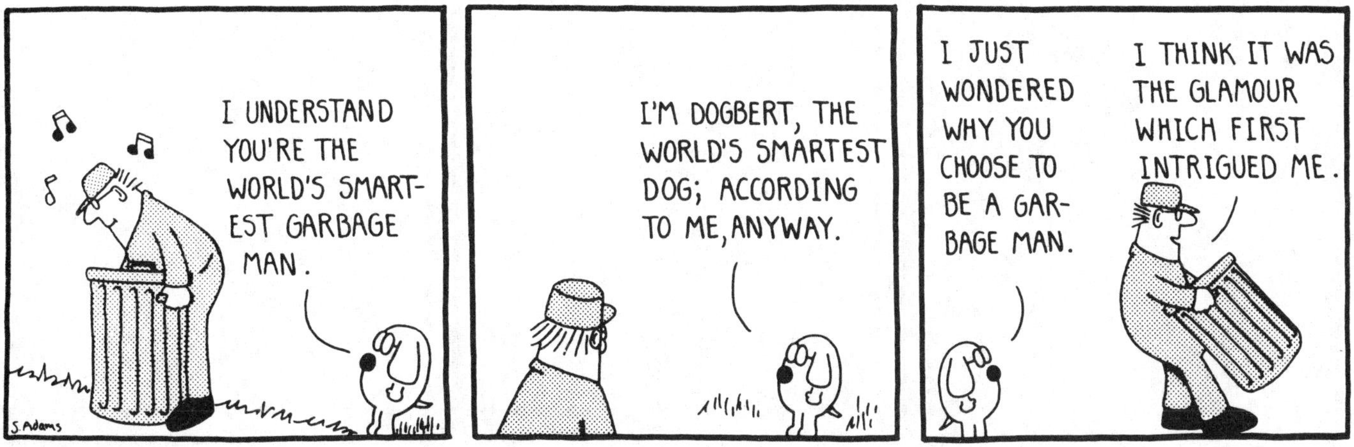
I UNDERSTAND YOU'RE THE WORLD'S SMART-EST GARBAGE MAN.
S.Adams
I'M DOGBERT, THE WORLD'S SMARTEST DOG; ACCORDING TO ME, ANYWAY.
I JUST WONDERED WHY YOU CHOOSE TO BE A GAR-BAGE MAN.
I THINK IT WAS THE GLAMOUR WHICH FIRST INTRIGUED ME.

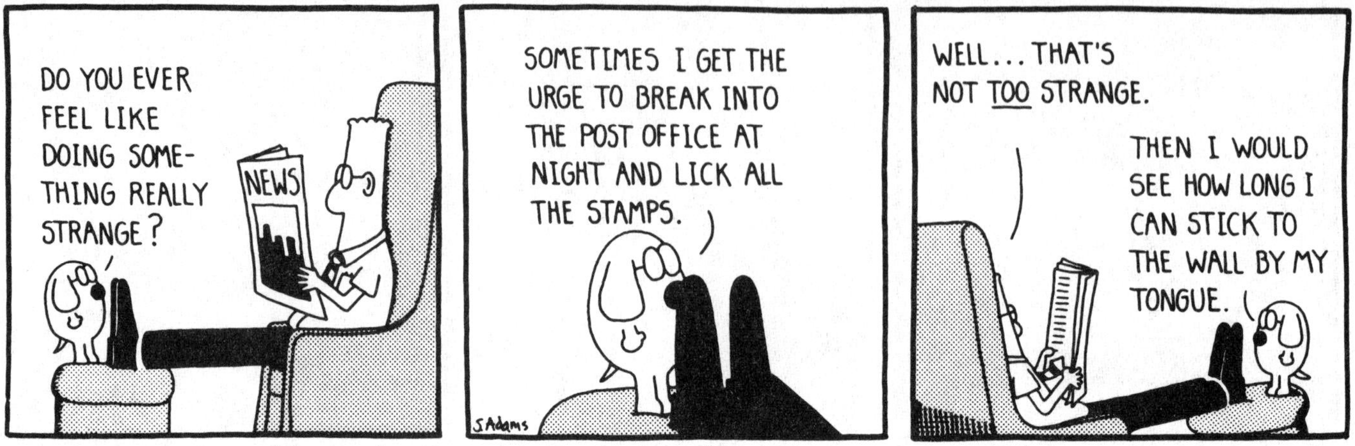
DO YOU EVER FEEL LIKE DOING SOME- THING REALLY STRANGE?
NEWS
SOMETIMES I GET THE URGE TO BREAK INTO THE POST OFFICE AT NIGHT AND LICK ALL THE STAMPS.
S.Adams
WELL... THAT'S NOT TOO STRANGE.
THEN I WOULD SEE HOW LONG I CAN STICK TO THE WALL BY MY TONGUE.

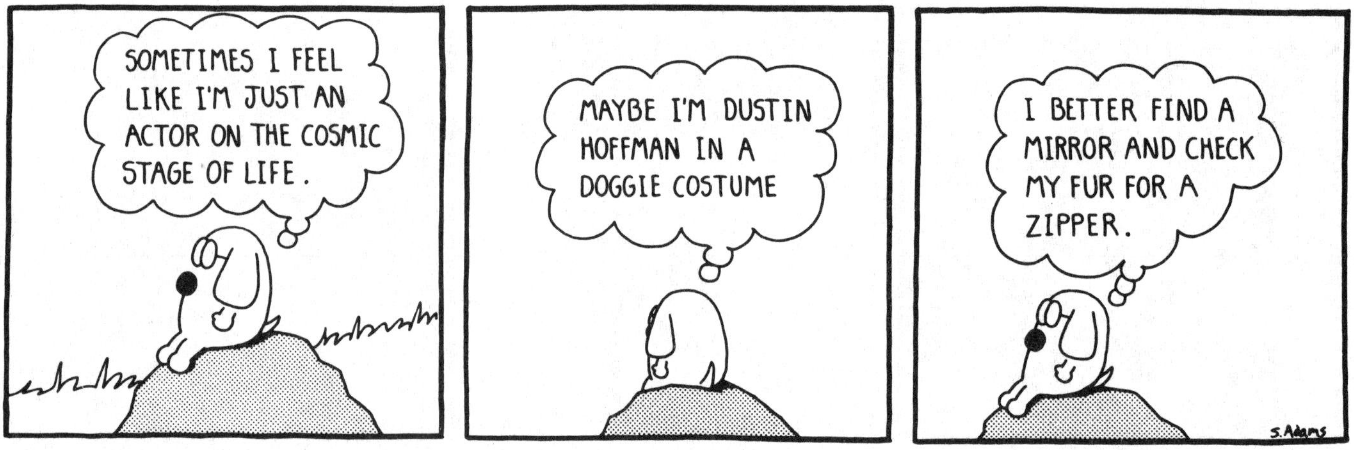
SOMETIMES I FEEL LIKE I'M JUST AN ACTOR ON THE COSMIC STAGE OF LIFE.
MAYBE I'M DUSTIN HOFFMAN IN A DOGGIE COSTUME
I BETTER FIND A MIRROR AND CHECK MY FUR FOR A ZIPPER.
S.Adams

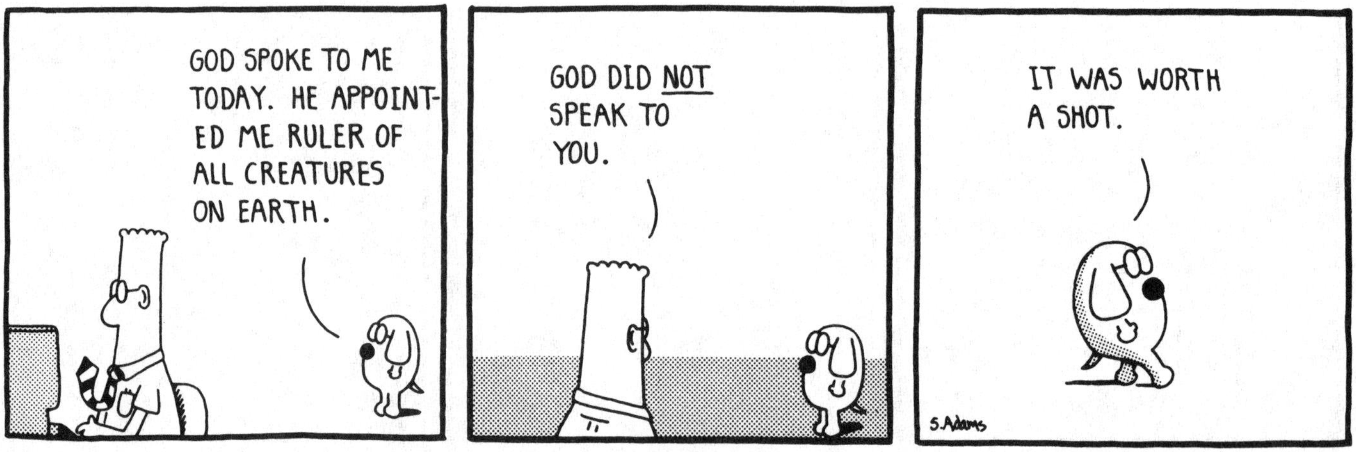
GOD SPOKE TO ME TODAY. HE APPOINT- ED ME RULER OF ALL CREATURES ON EARTH.
GOD DID NOT SPEAK TO YOU.
IT WAS WORTH A SHOT.
S.Adams

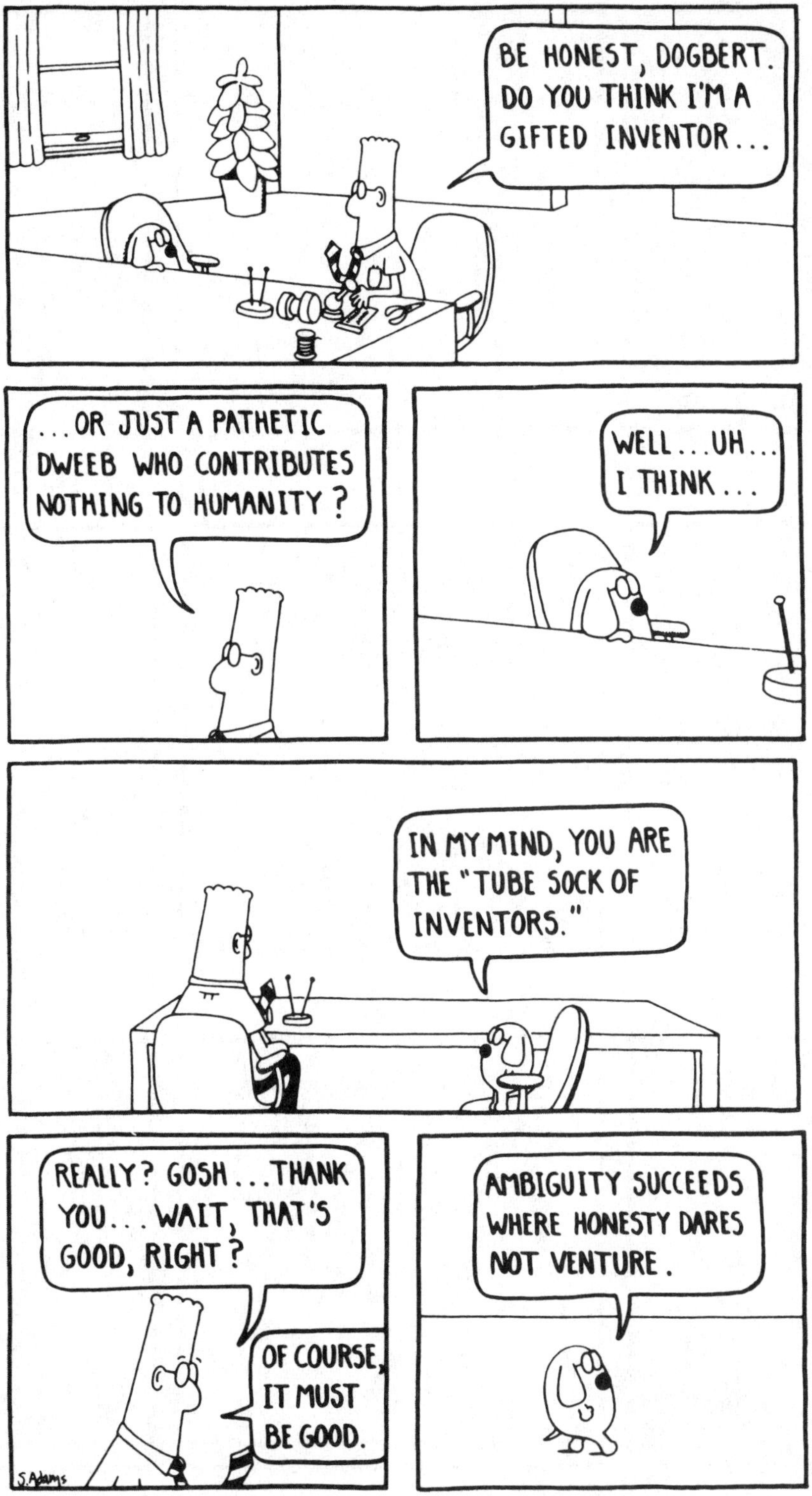
BE HONEST, DOGBERT. DO YOU THINK I'M A GIFTED INVENTOR...
...OR JUST A PATHETIC DWEEB WHO CONTRIBUTES NOTHING TO HUMANITY?
WELL...UH... I THINK...
IN MY MIND, YOU ARE THE "TUBE SOCK OF INVENTORS."
REALLY? GOSH...THANK YOU... WAIT, THAT'S GOOD, RIGHT?
OF COURSE, IT MUST BE GOOD.
AMBIGUITY SUCCEEDS WHERE HONESTY DARES NOT VENTURE.
S. Adams

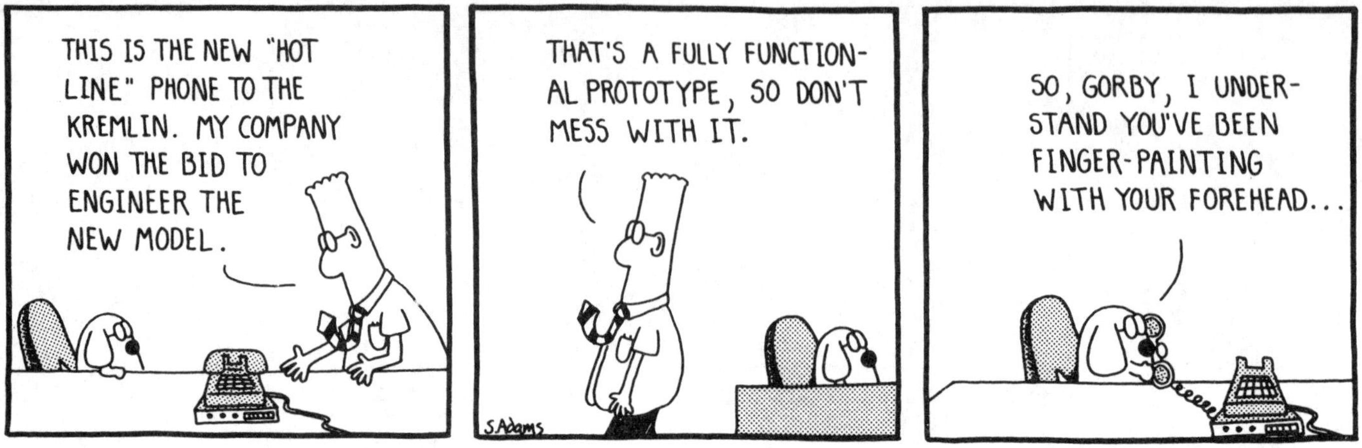
THIS IS THE NEW "HOT LINE" PHONE TO THE KREMLIN. MY COMPANY WON THE BID TO ENGINEER THE NEW MODEL.
THAT'S A FULLY FUNCTIONAL PROTOTYPE, SO DON'T MESS WITH IT.
S.Adams
SO, GORBY, I UNDERSTAND YOU'VE BEEN FINGER-PAINTING WITH YOUR FOREHEAD...

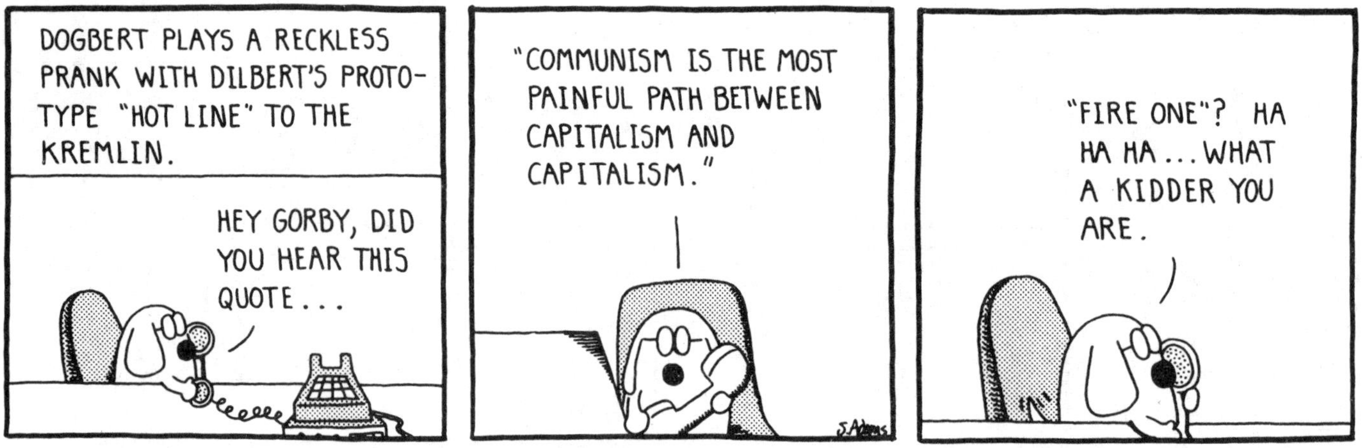
DOGBERT PLAYS A RECKLESS PRANK WITH DILBERT'S PROTOTYPE "HOT LINE" TO THE KREMLIN.
HEY GORBY, DID YOU HEAR THIS QUOTE...
"COMMUNISM IS THE MOST PAINFUL PATH BETWEEN CAPITALISM AND CAPITALISM."
S.Adams
"FIRE ONE"? HA HA HA... WHAT A KIDDER YOU ARE.

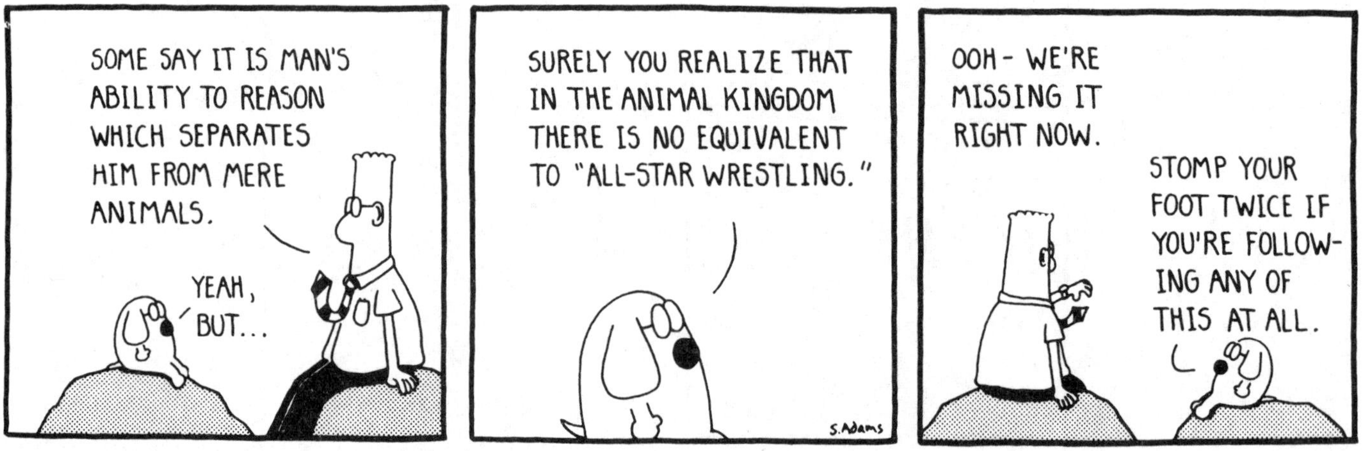
SOME SAY IT IS MAN'S ABILITY TO REASON WHICH SEPARATES HIM FROM MERE ANIMALS.
YEAH, BUT...
SURELY YOU REALIZE THAT IN THE ANIMAL KINGDOM THERE IS NO EQUIVALENT TO "ALL-STAR WRESTLING."
S.Adams
OOH - WE'RE MISSING IT RIGHT NOW.
STOMP YOUR FOOT TWICE IF YOU'RE FOLLOWING ANY OF THIS AT ALL.

YIKES!!! A SKUNK IN THE HOUSE!!!

HI.

OH, DON'T WORRY; WE SKUNKS ONLY SPRAY WHEN WE'RE SCARED... I CERTAINLY WOULDN'T USE MY THREATENING POWER TO FORCE YOU TO DO MY BIDDING.

S.Adams

THEN WHY IS YOUR TAIL TWITCHING?!

I'M SCARED YOU MIGHT NOT OFFER ME A BIG BOWL OF STRAWBERRY ICE CREAM.

DILBERT IS THREATENED BY AN ABUSIVE SKUNK.

THAT'S RIGHT: A BIG BOWL OF ICE CREAM COULD KEEP ME FROM BEING AFRAID AND REFLEXIVELY SPRAYING YOUR LIVING ROOM.

S.Adams

THIS IS BLACKMAIL!

MY GOODNESS, NO. IT'S JUST THAT I CAN'T CONTROL MY FEAR RESPONSE.

NOW I'M AFRAID THAT YOU WON'T SING THE SONGS FROM "CATS" WHILE I EAT.

DUST. WHERE DOES IT COME FROM? HOW DOES IT GET UNDER YOUR BED?

IS IT A NATURAL PHENOMENON OR A MESSAGE TO ANCIENT ASTRONAUTS?

S.Adams

TOMORROW ON "GERALDO," "DUST: WHAT'S IT ALL MEAN?"

IT MEANS YOU'RE PRETTY MUCH OUT OF TOPICS.

I BOUGHT A PHONE ANSWERING MACHINE.
WAS THE PHONE ASKING YOU QUESTIONS YOU COULDN'T ANSWER ON YOUR OWN?
THE HARD PART IS THINKING OF A GREETING MESSAGE.
"HI. THIS IS DILBERT. I'M NOT HERE RIGHT NOW."
"WELL, TECHNICALLY I AM HERE 'NOW'..."
"BUT 'NOW' IS A RELATIVE TERM, SO USE YOUR BEST JUDGMENT IN DECIDING WHETHER I'M HERE."
HMM...THAT WAS ACTUALLY A CREATIVE LITTLE MESSAGE.
DEMONSTRATING, ONCE AGAIN, THAT SUBTLE DIFFERENCE BETWEEN CREATIVITY AND COMPLEX STUPIDITY.
S Adams

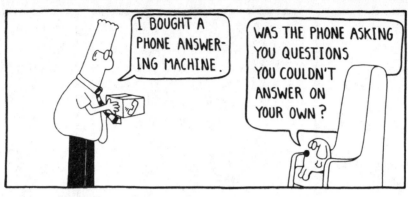

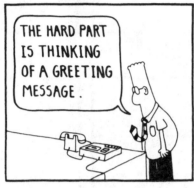

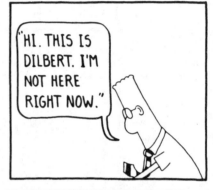

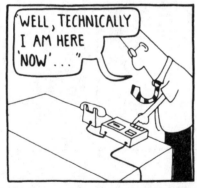

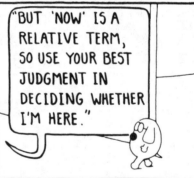

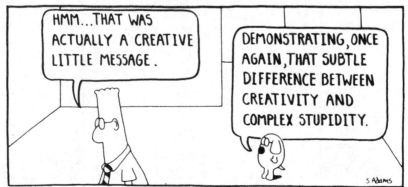

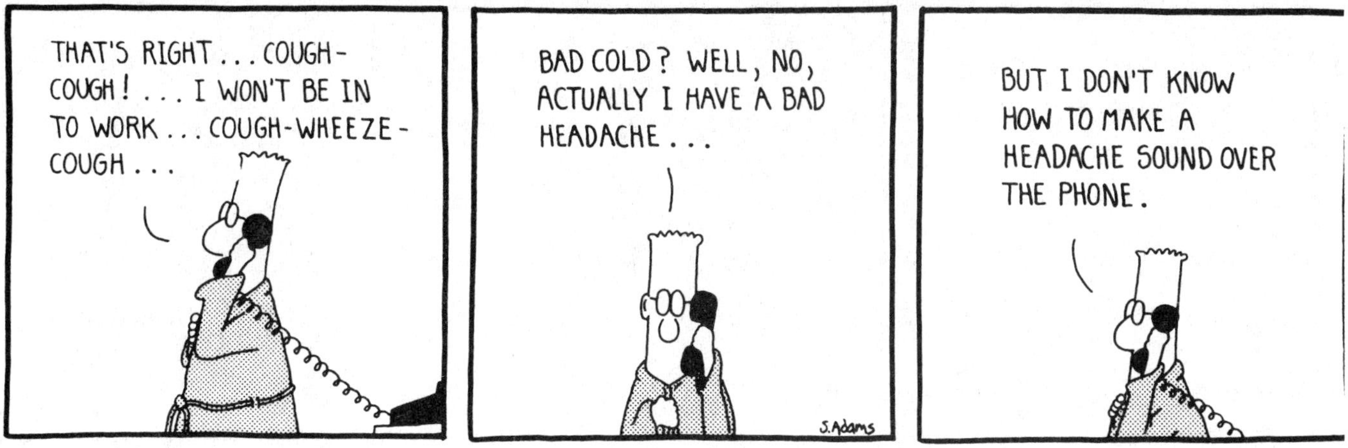
THAT'S RIGHT... COUGH-COUGH! ... I WON'T BE IN TO WORK... COUGH-WHEEZE-COUGH...
BAD COLD? WELL, NO, ACTUALLY I HAVE A BAD HEADACHE...
S.Adams
BUT I DON'T KNOW HOW TO MAKE A HEADACHE SOUND OVER THE PHONE.

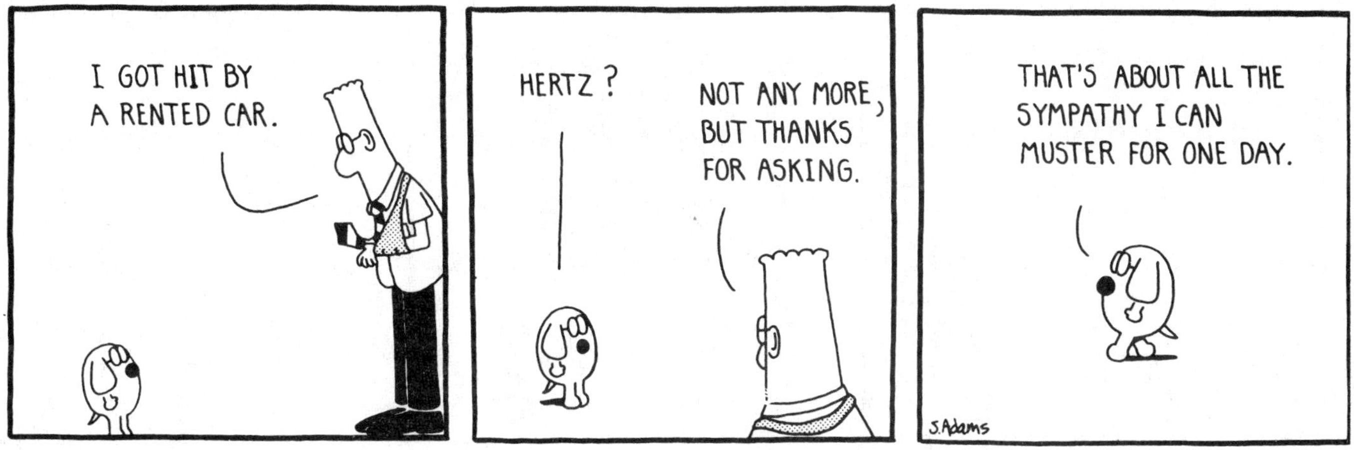
I GOT HIT BY A RENTED CAR.
HERTZ?
NOT ANY MORE, BUT THANKS FOR ASKING.
THAT'S ABOUT ALL THE SYMPATHY I CAN MUSTER FOR ONE DAY.
S.Adams

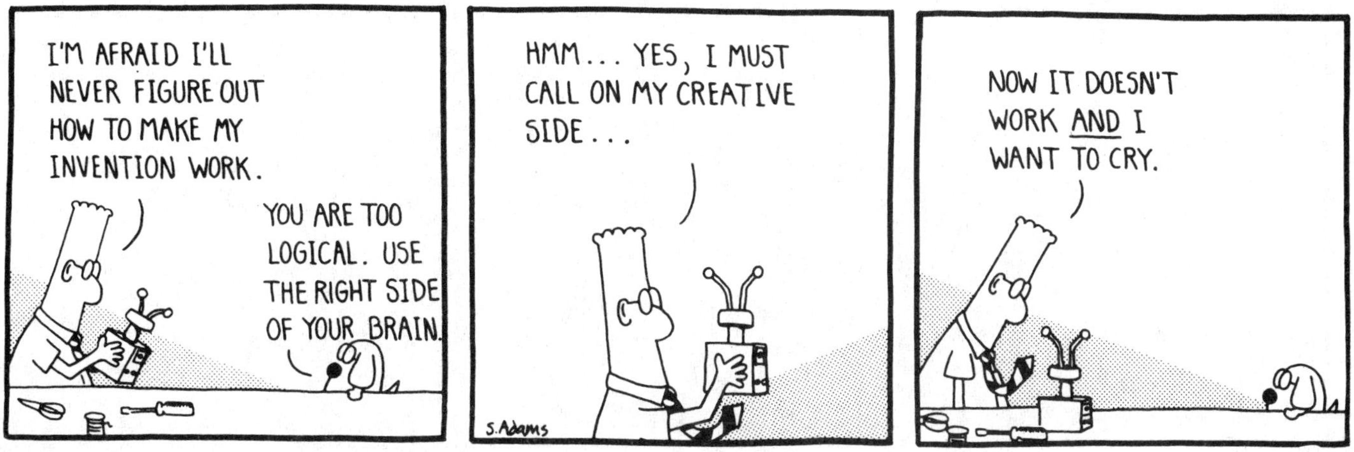
I'M AFRAID I'LL NEVER FIGURE OUT HOW TO MAKE MY INVENTION WORK.
YOU ARE TOO LOGICAL. USE THE RIGHT SIDE OF YOUR BRAIN.
HMM... YES, I MUST CALL ON MY CREATIVE SIDE...
S.Adams
NOW IT DOESN'T WORK AND I WANT TO CRY.

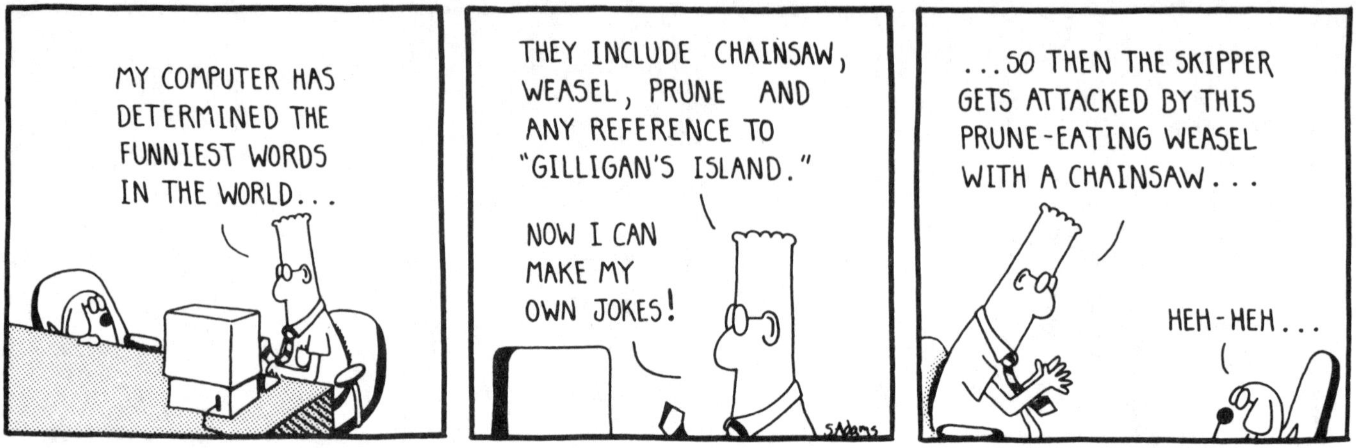
MY COMPUTER HAS DETERMINED THE FUNNIEST WORDS IN THE WORLD...
THEY INCLUDE CHAINSAW, WEASEL, PRUNE AND ANY REFERENCE TO "GILLIGAN'S ISLAND."
NOW I CAN MAKE MY OWN JOKES!
S.Adams
...SO THEN THE SKIPPER GETS ATTACKED BY THIS PRUNE-EATING WEASEL WITH A CHAINSAW...
HEH-HEH...

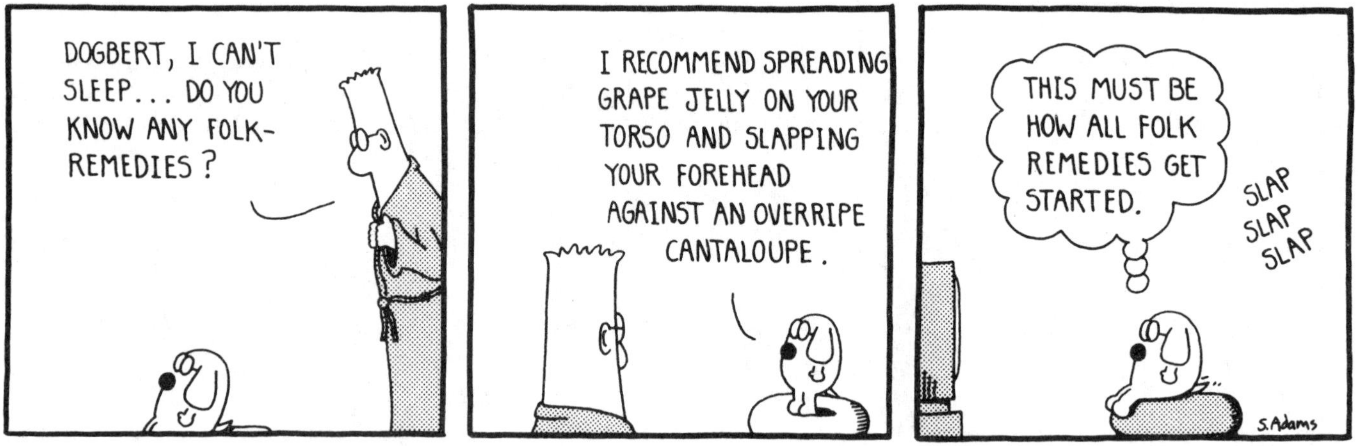
DOGBERT, I CAN'T SLEEP... DO YOU KNOW ANY FOLK-REMEDIES?
I RECOMMEND SPREADING GRAPE JELLY ON YOUR TORSO AND SLAPPING YOUR FOREHEAD AGAINST AN OVERRIPE CANTALOUPE.
THIS MUST BE HOW ALL FOLK REMEDIES GET STARTED.
SLAP SLAP SLAP
S.Adams

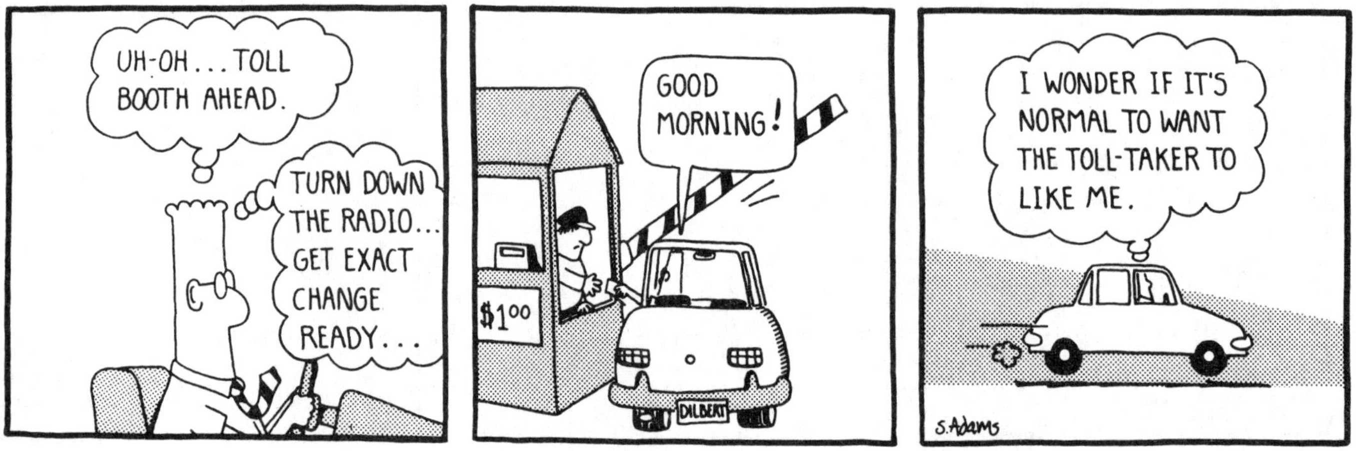
UH-OH... TOLL BOOTH AHEAD.
TURN DOWN THE RADIO... GET EXACT CHANGE READY...
GOOD MORNING!
$1.00
DILBERT
I WONDER IF IT'S NORMAL TO WANT THE TOLL-TAKER TO LIKE ME.
S.Adams

SANTA!
MERRY CHRISTMAS, DOGBERT!
DILBERT
DOGBERT
I'M GLAD YOU'RE UP... I'M HAVING A LITTLE TROUBLE WITH YOUR CHRISTMAS LIST.
IN YOUR LETTER YOU SAY YOU WANT TO BE NAMED SUPREME RULER OF EARTH.
IS THAT A PROBLEM?
FRANKLY, MY WORKSHOP IS MORE ORIENTED TOWARD SMALL CONSUMER GOODS...
CAN I HAVE AN ELF?
S.Adams
HAS G.I. JOE TAKEN UP BALLET, OR IS THIS SOME-THING I DON'T WANT TO KNOW ABOUT?

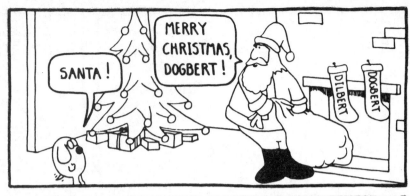

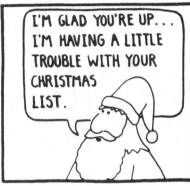

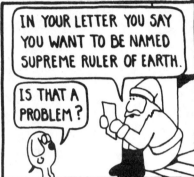

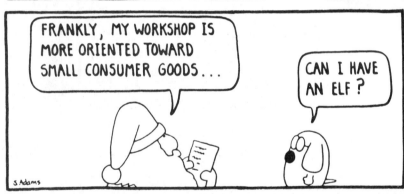

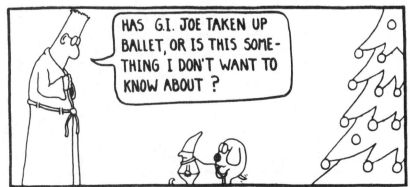

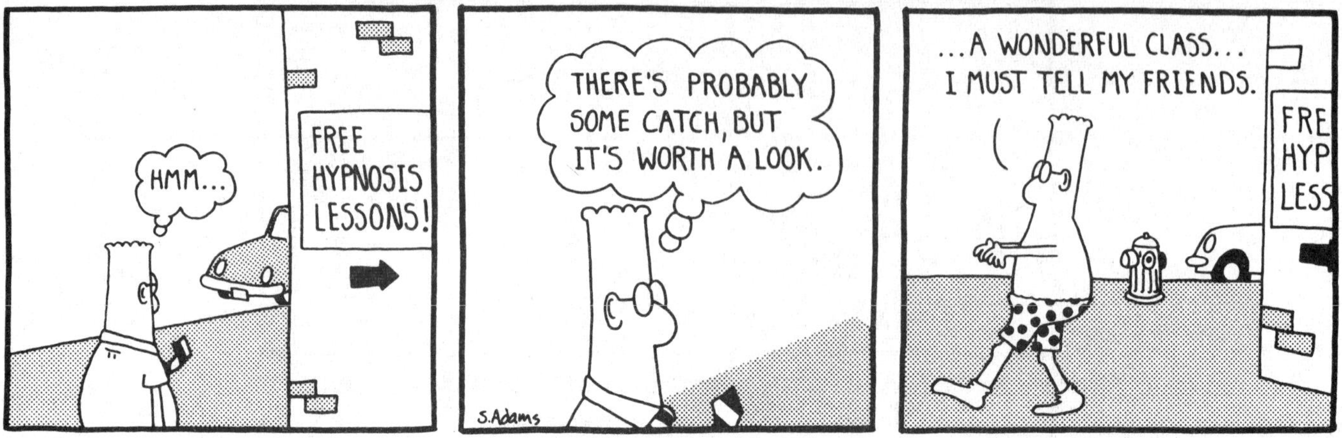
HMM...
FREE HYPNOSIS LESSONS!
THERE'S PROBABLY SOME CATCH, BUT IT'S WORTH A LOOK.
S.Adams
...A WONDERFUL CLASS... I MUST TELL MY FRIENDS.

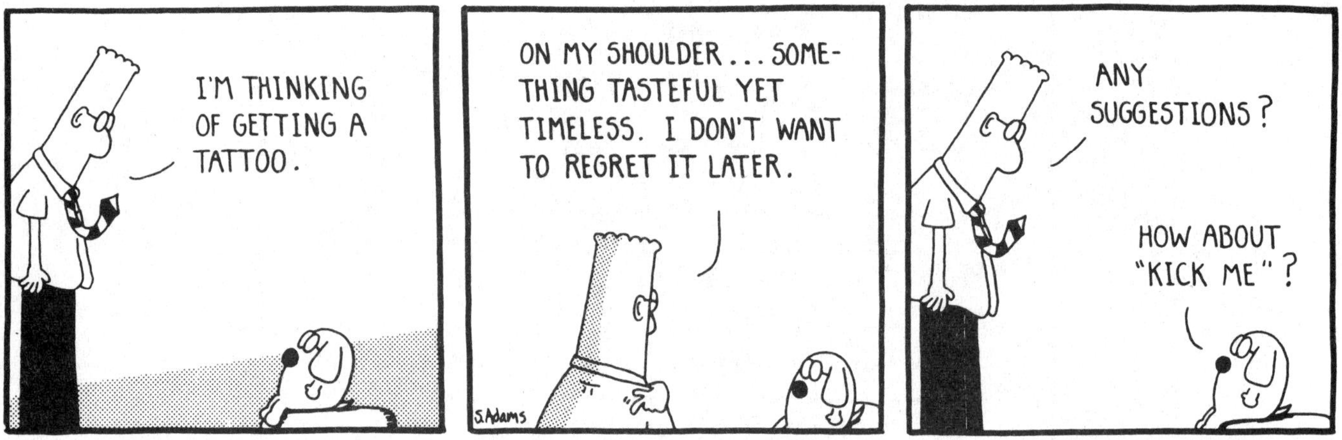
I'M THINKING OF GETTING A TATTOO.
ON MY SHOULDER... SOMETHING TASTEFUL YET TIMELESS. I DON'T WANT TO REGRET IT LATER.
S.Adams
ANY SUGGESTIONS?
HOW ABOUT "KICK ME"?

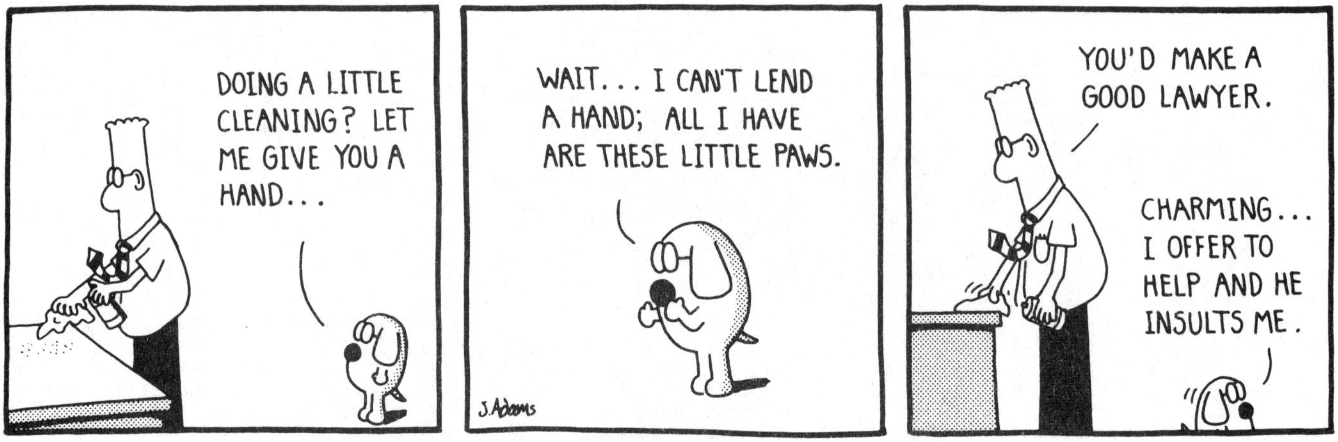
DOING A LITTLE CLEANING? LET ME GIVE YOU A HAND...
WAIT... I CAN'T LEND A HAND; ALL I HAVE ARE THESE LITTLE PAWS.
S.Adams
YOU'D MAKE A GOOD LAWYER.
CHARMING... I OFFER TO HELP AND HE INSULTS ME.

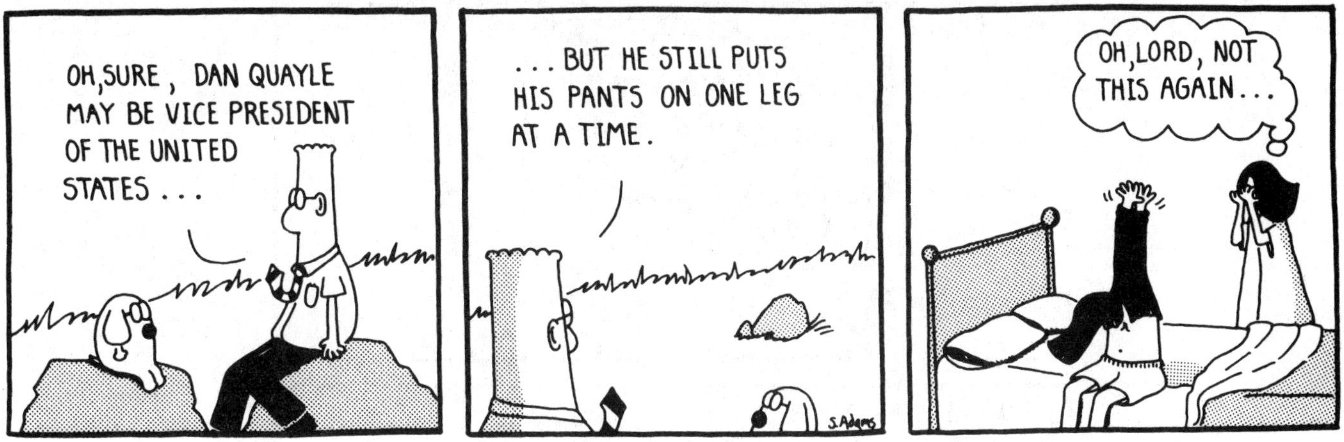
OH, SURE, DAN QUAYLE MAY BE VICE PRESIDENT OF THE UNITED STATES . . .
. . . BUT HE STILL PUTS HIS PANTS ON ONE LEG AT A TIME.
OH, LORD, NOT THIS AGAIN . . .
S. Adams

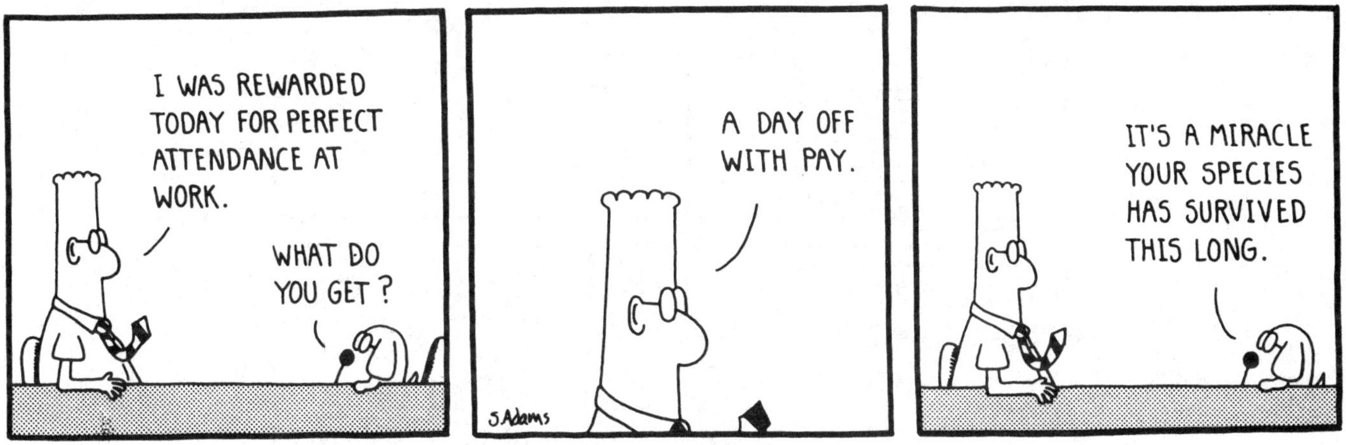
I WAS REWARDED TODAY FOR PERFECT ATTENDANCE AT WORK.
WHAT DO YOU GET?
A DAY OFF WITH PAY.
IT'S A MIRACLE YOUR SPECIES HAS SURVIVED THIS LONG.
S. Adams

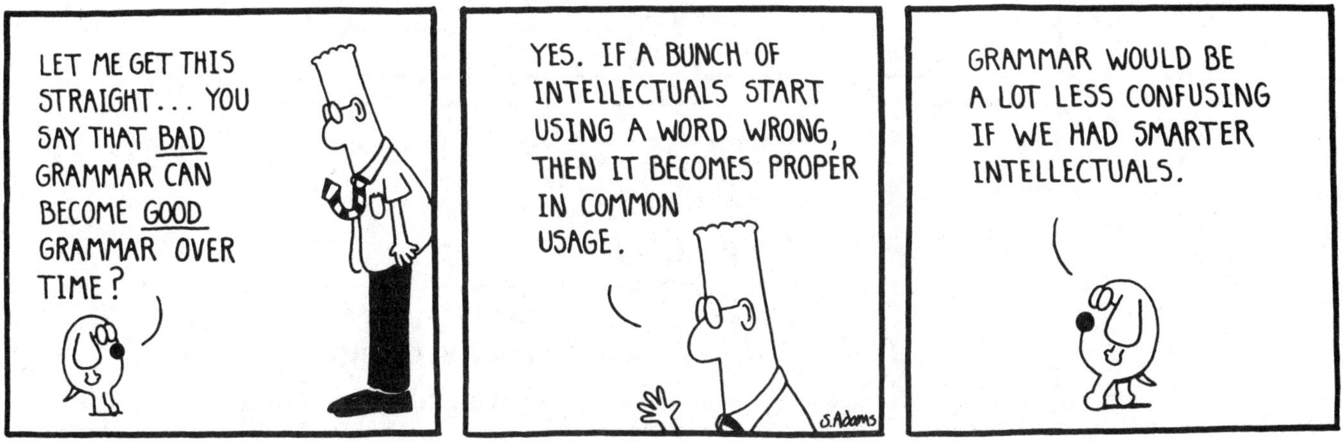
LET ME GET THIS STRAIGHT . . . YOU SAY THAT BAD GRAMMAR CAN BECOME GOOD GRAMMAR OVER TIME?
YES. IF A BUNCH OF INTELLECTUALS START USING A WORD WRONG, THEN IT BECOMES PROPER IN COMMON USAGE.
GRAMMAR WOULD BE A LOT LESS CONFUSING IF WE HAD SMARTER INTELLECTUALS.
S. Adams

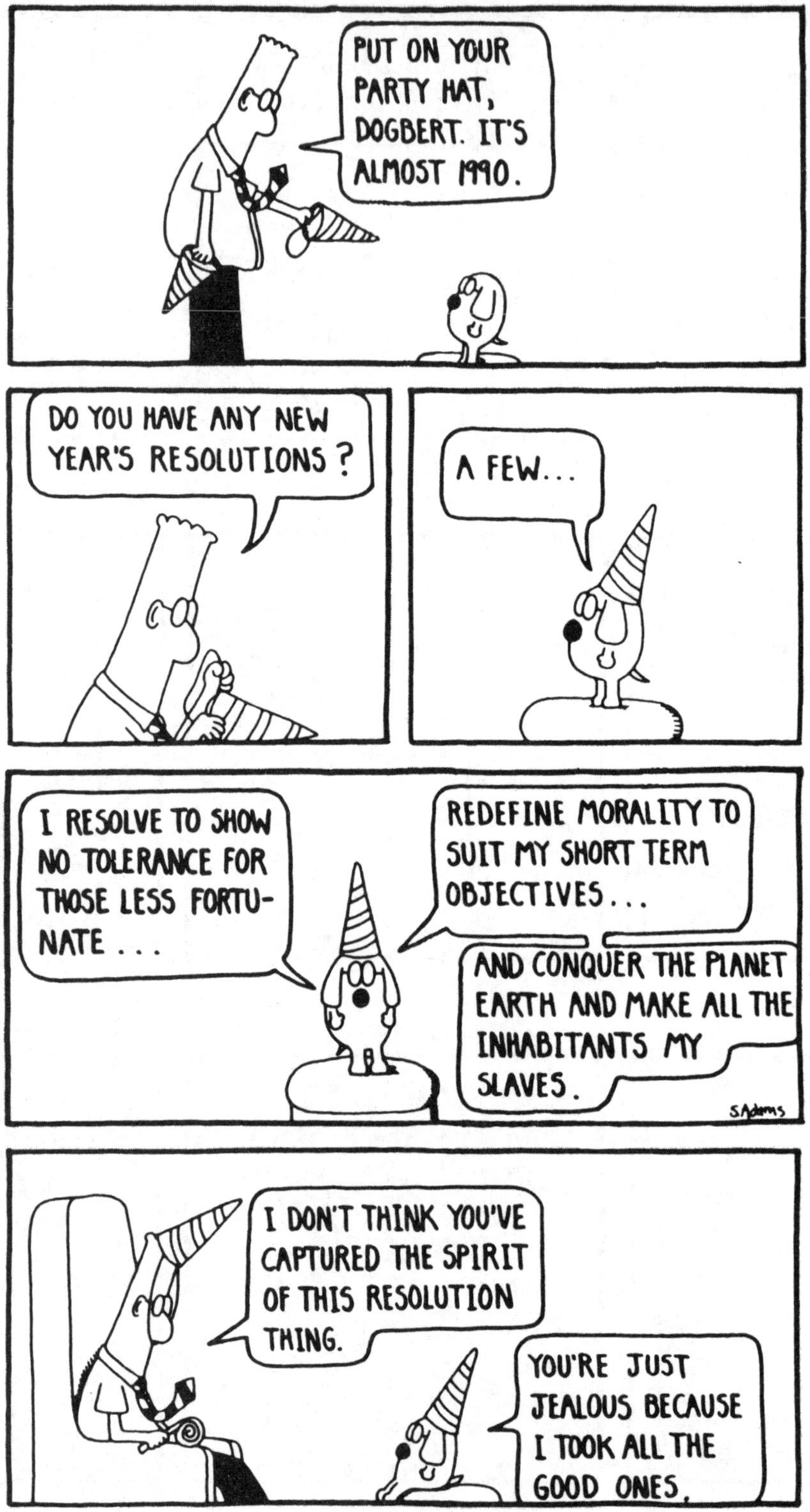
PUT ON YOUR PARTY HAT, DOGBERT. IT'S ALMOST 1990.
DO YOU HAVE ANY NEW YEAR'S RESOLUTIONS?
A FEW...
I RESOLVE TO SHOW NO TOLERANCE FOR THOSE LESS FORTU-NATE ...
REDEFINE MORALITY TO SUIT MY SHORT TERM OBJECTIVES...
AND CONQUER THE PLANET EARTH AND MAKE ALL THE INHABITANTS MY SLAVES.
S.Adams
I DON'T THINK YOU'VE CAPTURED THE SPIRIT OF THIS RESOLUTION THING.
YOU'RE JUST JEALOUS BECAUSE I TOOK ALL THE GOOD ONES.

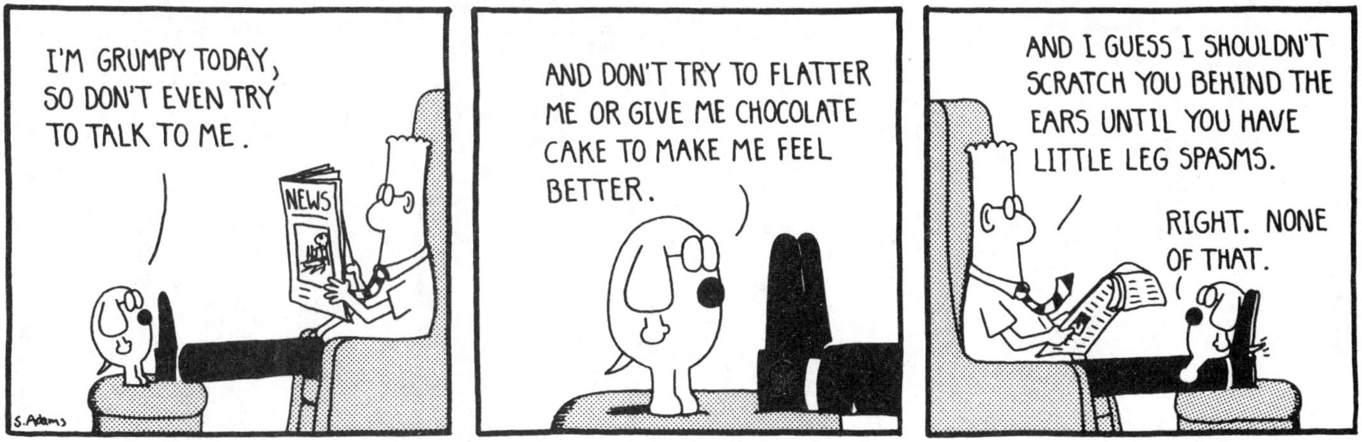
I'M GRUMPY TODAY, SO DON'T EVEN TRY TO TALK TO ME.
NEWS
S.Adams
AND DON'T TRY TO FLATTER ME OR GIVE ME CHOCOLATE CAKE TO MAKE ME FEEL BETTER.
AND I GUESS I SHOULDN'T SCRATCH YOU BEHIND THE EARS UNTIL YOU HAVE LITTLE LEG SPASMS.
RIGHT. NONE OF THAT.

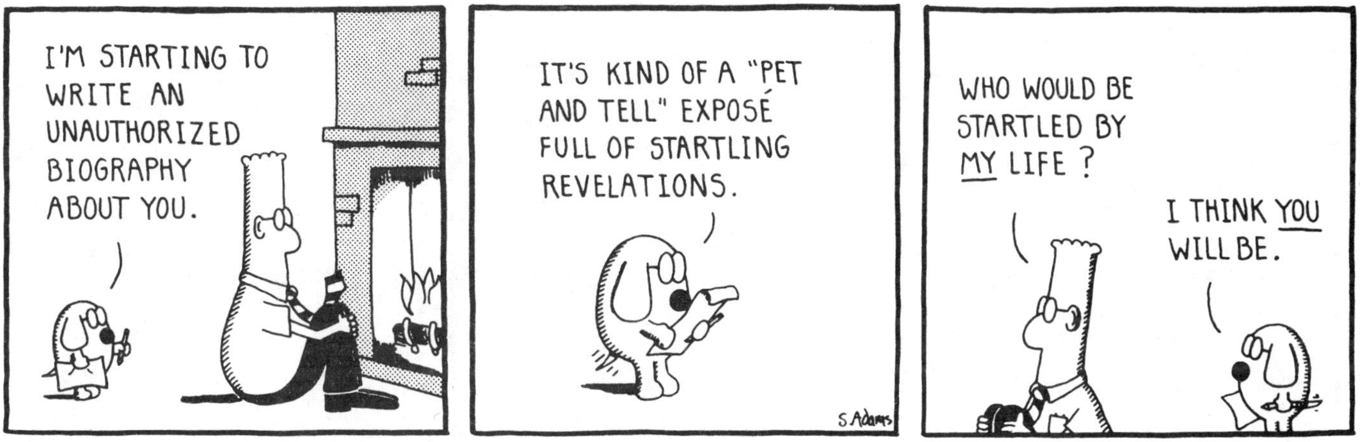
I'M STARTING TO WRITE AN UNAUTHORIZED BIOGRAPHY ABOUT YOU.
IT'S KIND OF A "PET AND TELL" EXPOSÉ FULL OF STARTLING REVELATIONS.
S.Adams
WHO WOULD BE STARTLED BY MY LIFE?
I THINK YOU WILL BE.

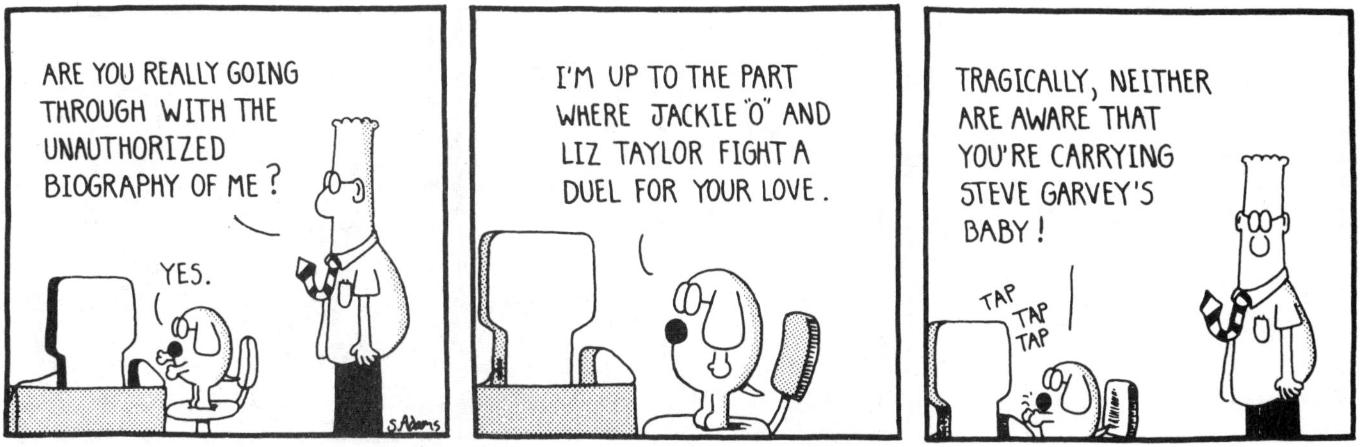
ARE YOU REALLY GOING THROUGH WITH THE UNAUTHORIZED BIOGRAPHY OF ME?
YES.
S.Adams
I'M UP TO THE PART WHERE JACKIE "O" AND LIZ TAYLOR FIGHT A DUEL FOR YOUR LOVE.
TRAGICALLY, NEITHER ARE AWARE THAT YOU'RE CARRYING STEVE GARVEY'S BABY!
TAP TAP TAP

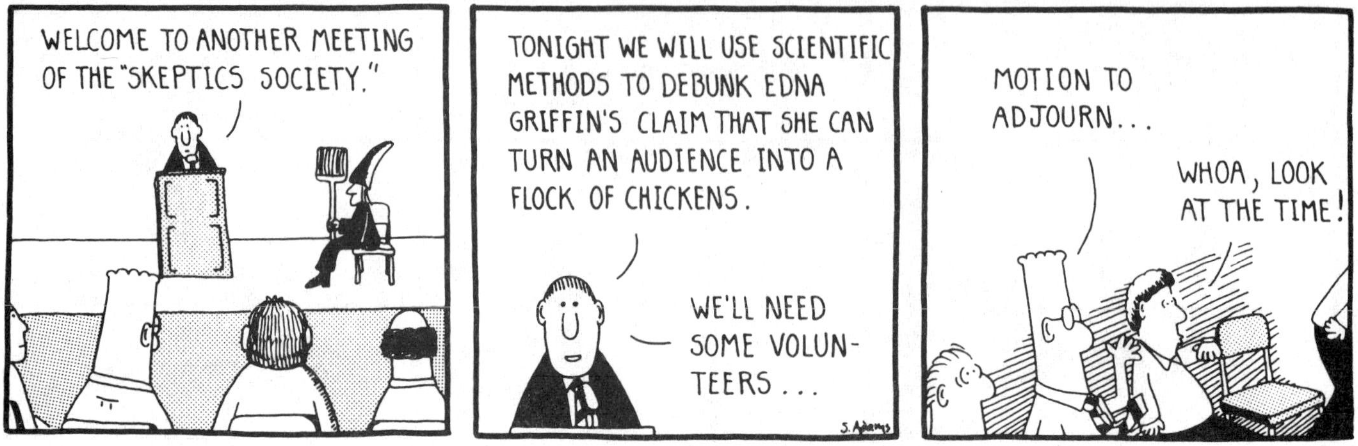
WELCOME TO ANOTHER MEETING OF THE "SKEPTICS SOCIETY."
TONIGHT WE WILL USE SCIENTIFIC METHODS TO DEBUNK EDNA GRIFFIN'S CLAIM THAT SHE CAN TURN AN AUDIENCE INTO A FLOCK OF CHICKENS.
WE'LL NEED SOME VOLUNTEERS...
S. Adams
MOTION TO ADJOURN...
WHOA, LOOK AT THE TIME!

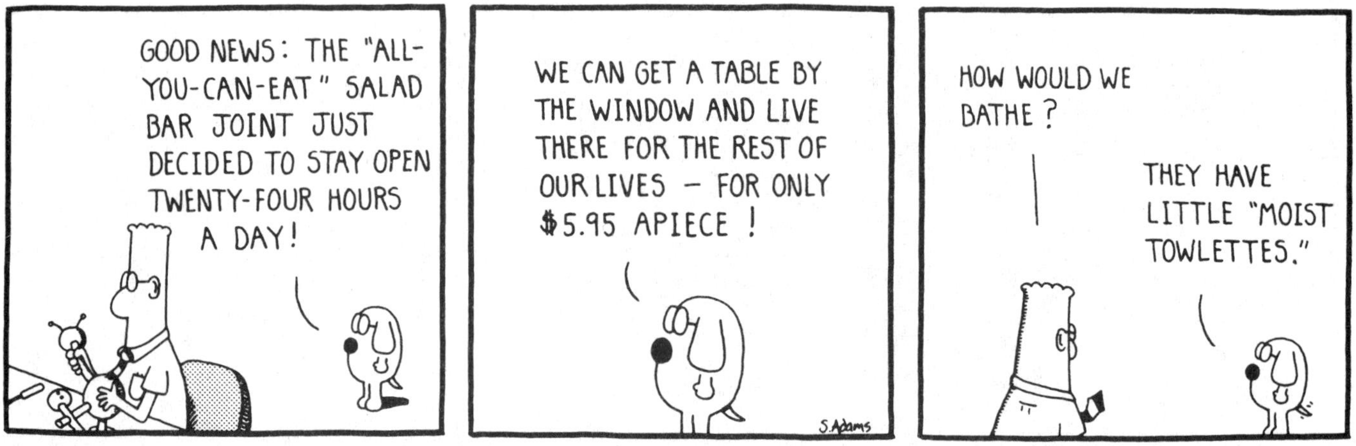
GOOD NEWS: THE "ALL-YOU-CAN-EAT" SALAD BAR JOINT JUST DECIDED TO STAY OPEN TWENTY-FOUR HOURS A DAY!
WE CAN GET A TABLE BY THE WINDOW AND LIVE THERE FOR THE REST OF OUR LIVES — FOR ONLY $5.95 APIECE!
S. Adams
HOW WOULD WE BATHE?
THEY HAVE LITTLE "MOIST TOWLETTES."

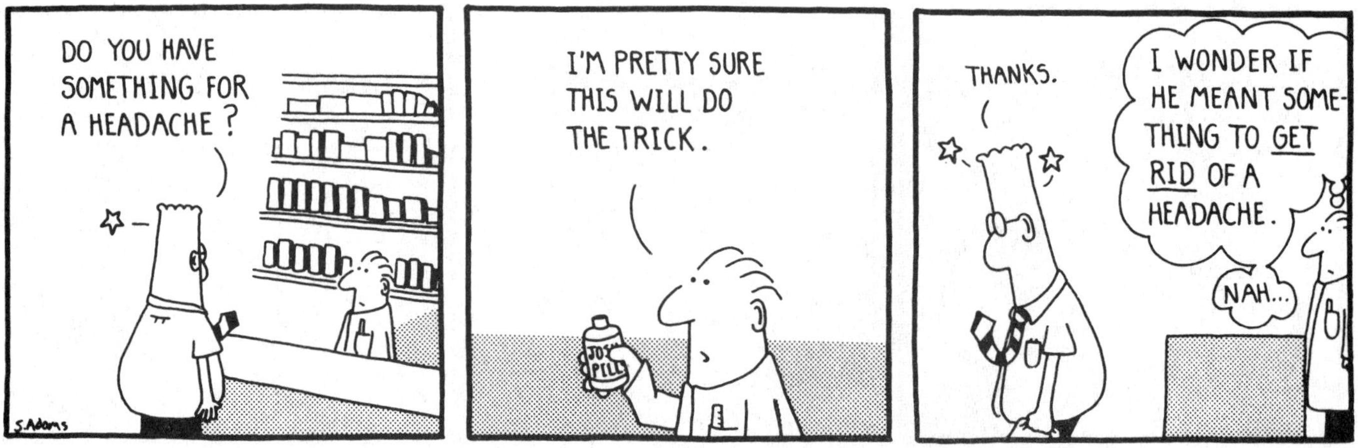
DO YOU HAVE SOMETHING FOR A HEADACHE?
S. Adams
I'M PRETTY SURE THIS WILL DO THE TRICK.
THANKS.
I WONDER IF HE MEANT SOMETHING TO GET RID OF A HEADACHE.
NAH...

OPEN
Bob's Classy Clothes
...AND YOU'RE QUITE CERTAIN THESE WILL SHRINK TO FIT?
YOU HAVE MY WORD AS A RETAIL SALES-MAN.
BOB'S CLASSY CLOT
S. Adams
YOU WERE TAKEN.
NO, THEY SHRINK IN THE WASH.
LIKE A GLOVE...
WILL THEY FIT NOW?
LIKE A GLOVE WITH TWO FINGERS.

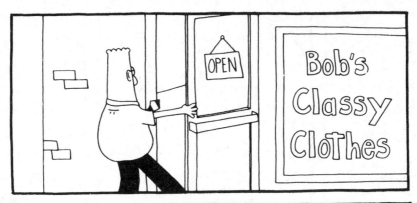

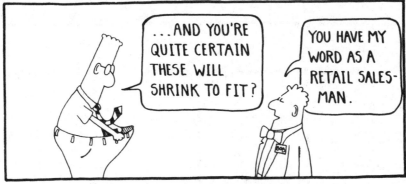

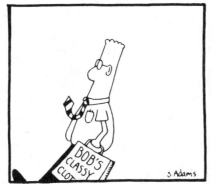

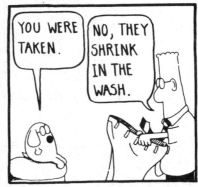

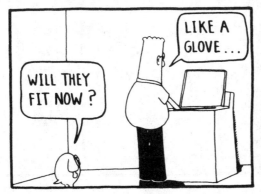

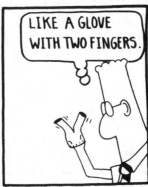

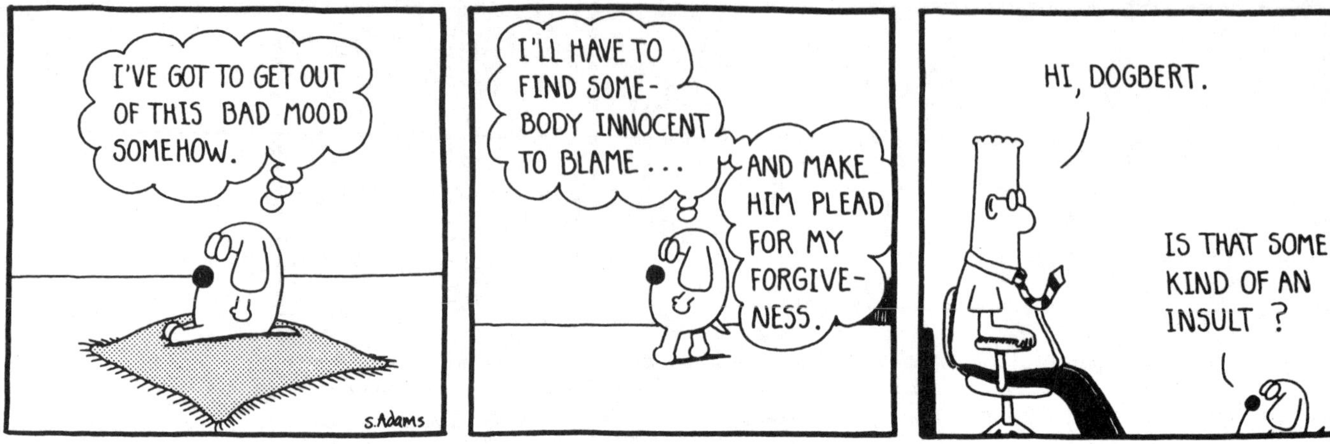
I'VE GOT TO GET OUT OF THIS BAD MOOD SOMEHOW.
S.Adams
I'LL HAVE TO FIND SOME-BODY INNOCENT TO BLAME . . .
AND MAKE HIM PLEAD FOR MY FORGIVE-NESS.
HI, DOGBERT.
IS THAT SOME KIND OF AN INSULT ?

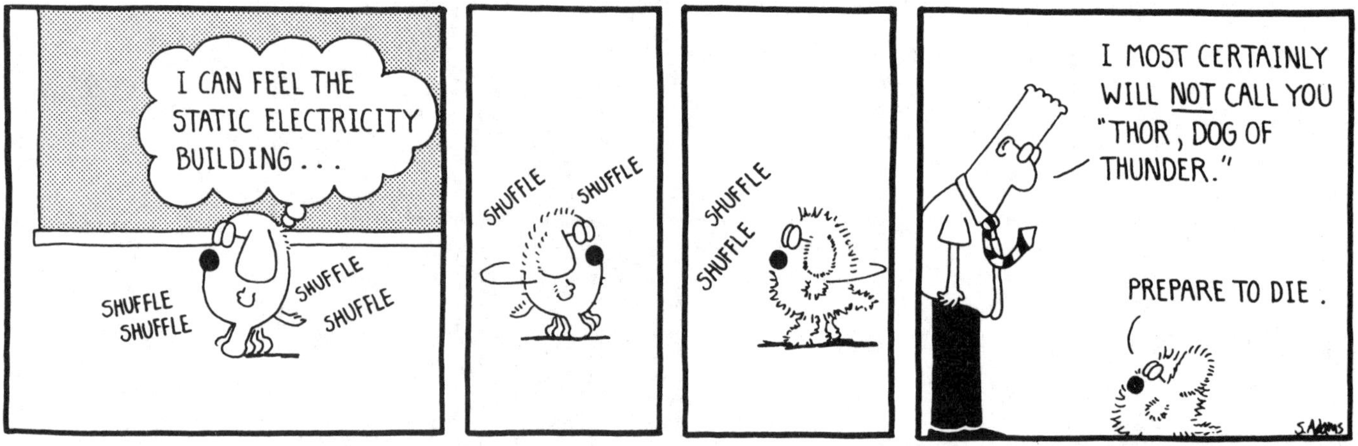
I CAN FEEL THE STATIC ELECTRICITY BUILDING . . .
SHUFFLE SHUFFLE
SHUFFLE SHUFFLE
SHUFFLE SHUFFLE
SHUFFLE SHUFFLE
I MOST CERTAINLY WILL NOT CALL YOU "THOR, DOG OF THUNDER."
PREPARE TO DIE .
S.Adams

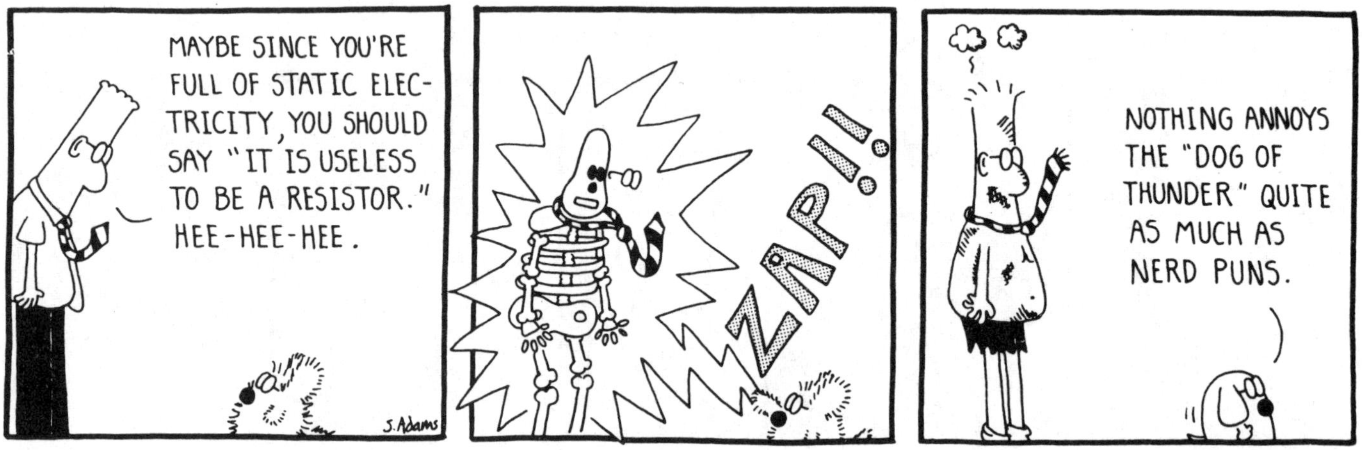
MAYBE SINCE YOU'RE FULL OF STATIC ELEC-TRICITY, YOU SHOULD SAY "IT IS USELESS TO BE A RESISTOR." HEE-HEE-HEE.
S.Adams
ZAP!!!
NOTHING ANNOYS THE "DOG OF THUNDER" QUITE AS MUCH AS NERD PUNS.

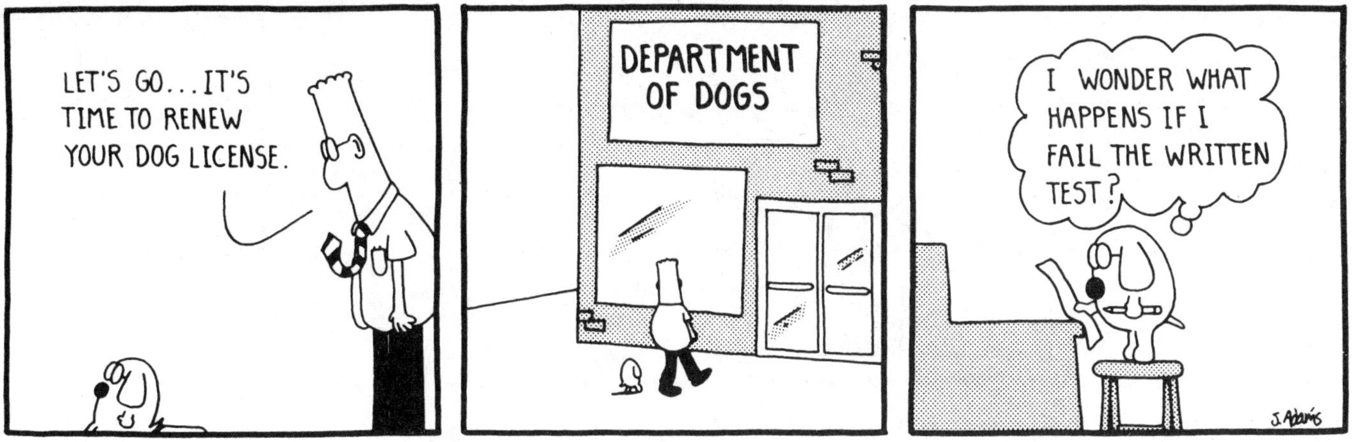
LET'S GO... IT'S TIME TO RENEW YOUR DOG LICENSE.
DEPARTMENT OF DOGS
I WONDER WHAT HAPPENS IF I FAIL THE WRITTEN TEST?
S. Adams

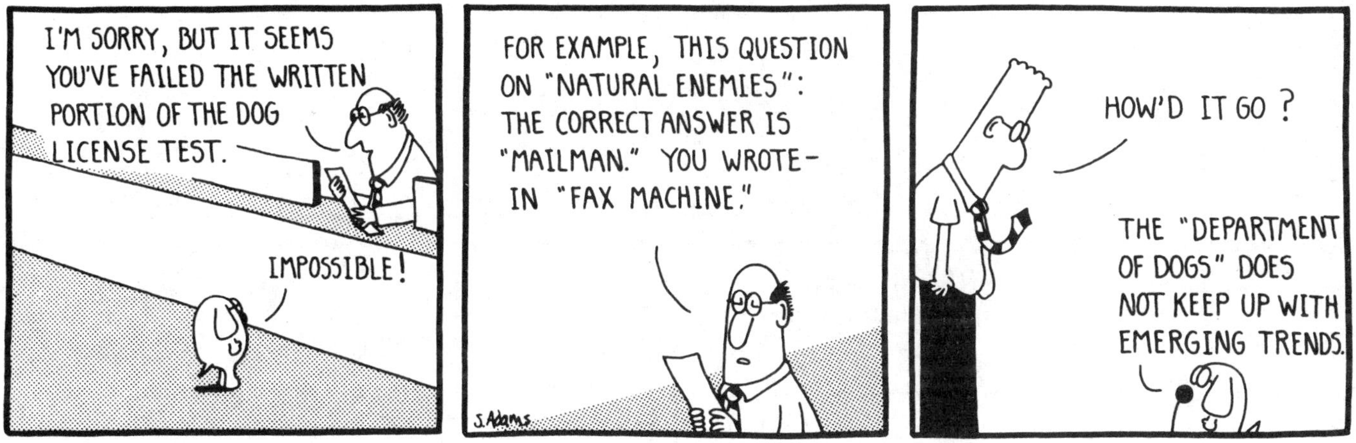
I'M SORRY, BUT IT SEEMS YOU'VE FAILED THE WRITTEN PORTION OF THE DOG LICENSE TEST.
IMPOSSIBLE!
FOR EXAMPLE, THIS QUESTION ON "NATURAL ENEMIES": THE CORRECT ANSWER IS "MAILMAN." YOU WROTE-IN "FAX MACHINE."
S. Adams
HOW'D IT GO?
THE "DEPARTMENT OF DOGS" DOES NOT KEEP UP WITH EMERGING TRENDS.

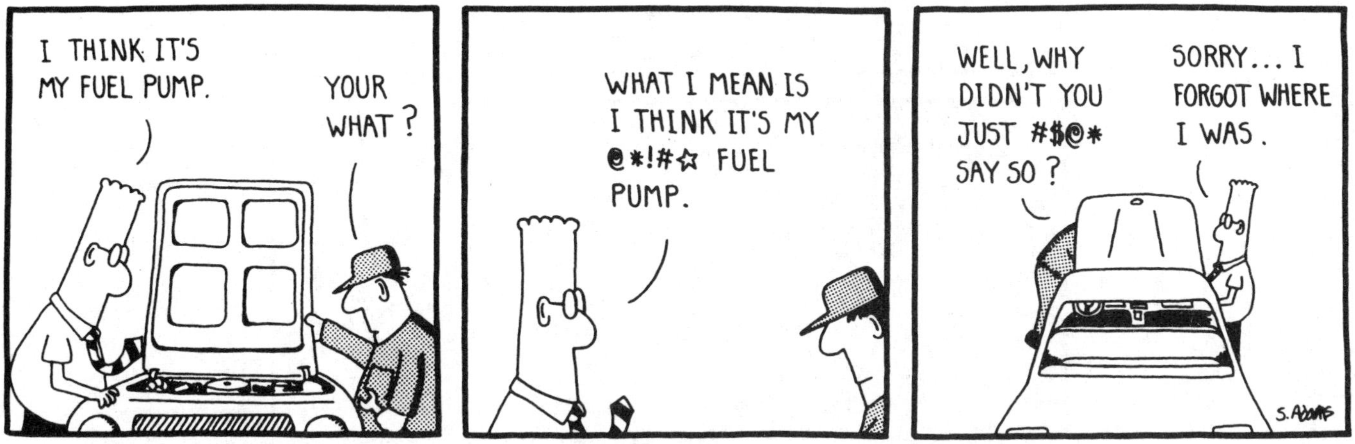
I THINK IT'S MY FUEL PUMP.
YOUR WHAT?
WHAT I MEAN IS I THINK IT'S MY @*!#☆ FUEL PUMP.
WELL, WHY DIDN'T YOU JUST #$@* SAY SO?
SORRY... I FORGOT WHERE I WAS.
S. Adams

YOU KNOW, MANY GREAT MEN KEPT DIARIES.
NOT TO MENTION THE ENTIRE KIRK CAMERON FAN CLUB.
Monday: Woke up. Went to work. Came home. Ate. Watched T.V. and went to bed
WELL, THIS WAS BOTH THERAPEUTIC AND SATISFYING.
DIARY
SOMETIMES IT'S GOOD TO BARE YOUR SOUL LIKE THAT.
S.Adams
WHO THE HECK IS KIRK CAMERON?
Tuesday: See "Monday."

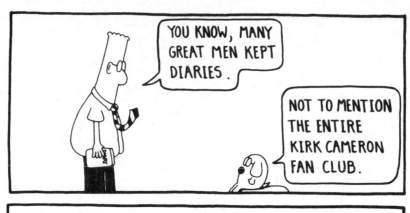

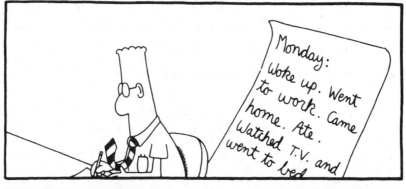

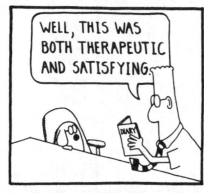

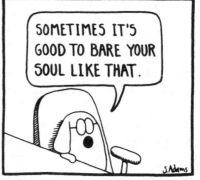

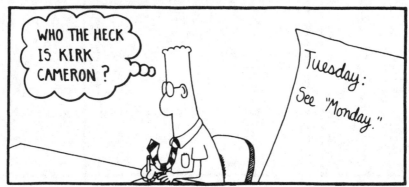

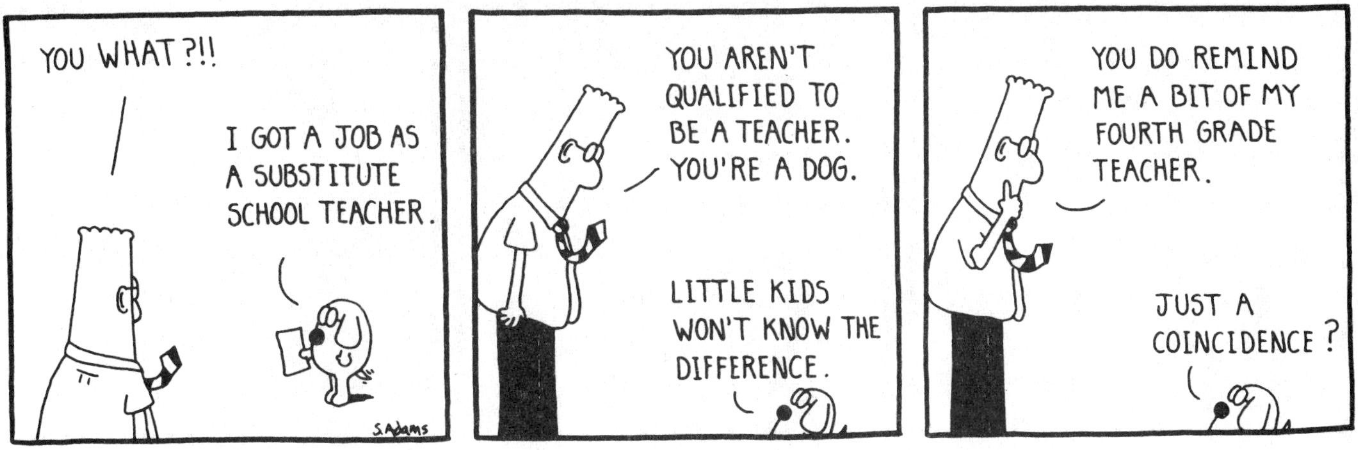
YOU WHAT?!!
I GOT A JOB AS A SUBSTITUTE SCHOOL TEACHER.
S.Adams
YOU AREN'T QUALIFIED TO BE A TEACHER. YOU'RE A DOG.
LITTLE KIDS WON'T KNOW THE DIFFERENCE.
YOU DO REMIND ME A BIT OF MY FOURTH GRADE TEACHER.
JUST A COINCIDENCE?

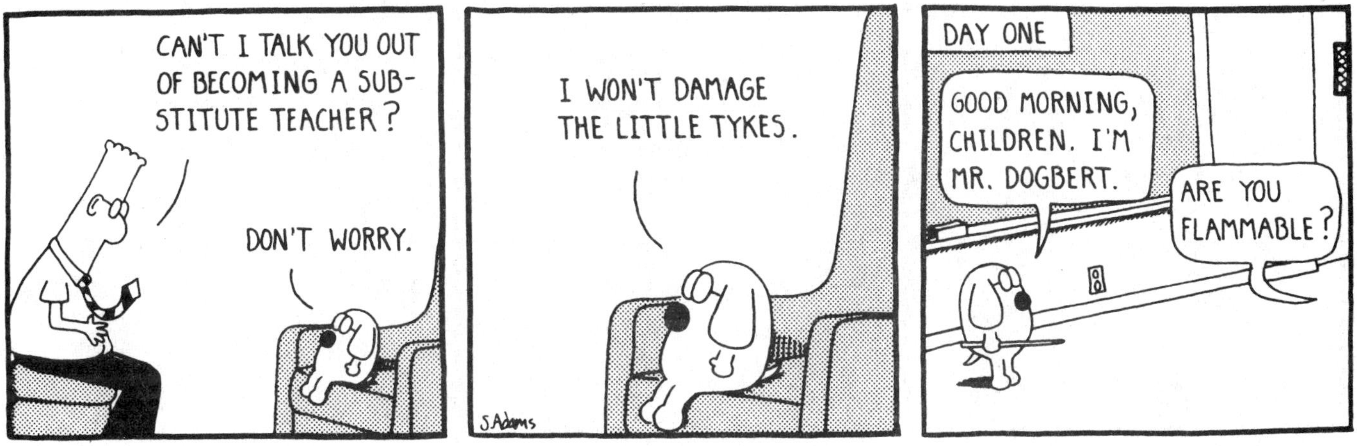
CAN'T I TALK YOU OUT OF BECOMING A SUB-STITUTE TEACHER?
DON'T WORRY.
I WON'T DAMAGE THE LITTLE TYKES.
S.Adams
DAY ONE
GOOD MORNING, CHILDREN. I'M MR. DOGBERT.
ARE YOU FLAMMABLE?

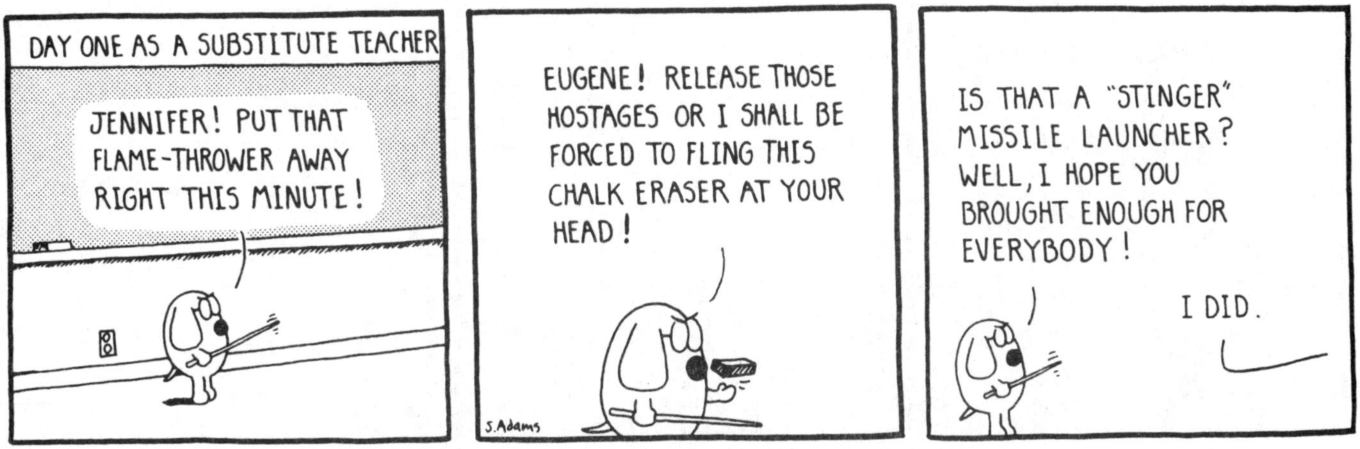
DAY ONE AS A SUBSTITUTE TEACHER
JENNIFER! PUT THAT FLAME-THROWER AWAY RIGHT THIS MINUTE!
EUGENE! RELEASE THOSE HOSTAGES OR I SHALL BE FORCED TO FLING THIS CHALK ERASER AT YOUR HEAD!
S.Adams
IS THAT A "STINGER" MISSILE LAUNCHER? WELL, I HOPE YOU BROUGHT ENOUGH FOR EVERYBODY!
I DID.

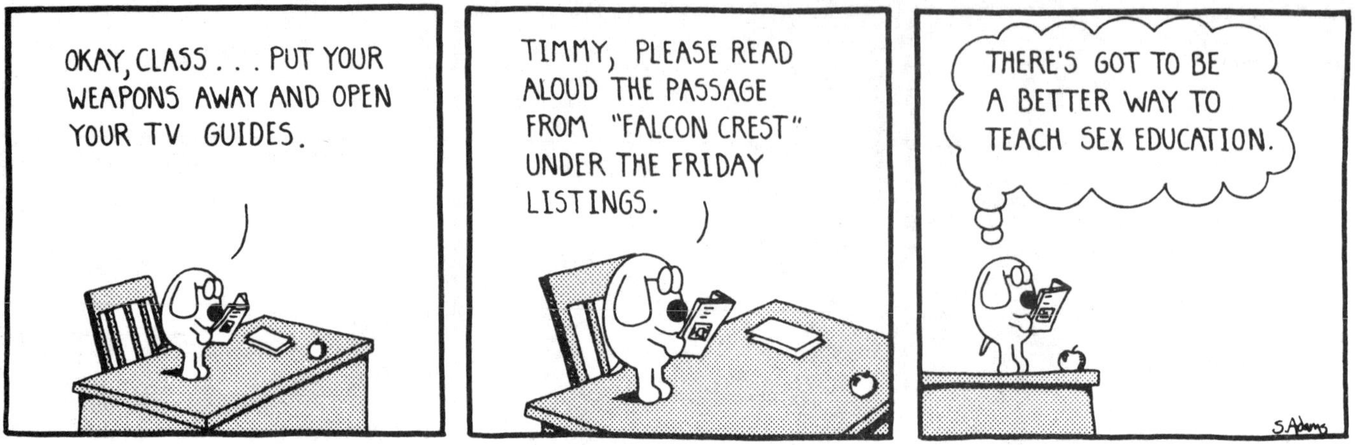
OKAY, CLASS . . . PUT YOUR WEAPONS AWAY AND OPEN YOUR TV GUIDES.
TIMMY, PLEASE READ ALOUD THE PASSAGE FROM "FALCON CREST" UNDER THE FRIDAY LISTINGS.
THERE'S GOT TO BE A BETTER WAY TO TEACH SEX EDUCATION.
S. Adams

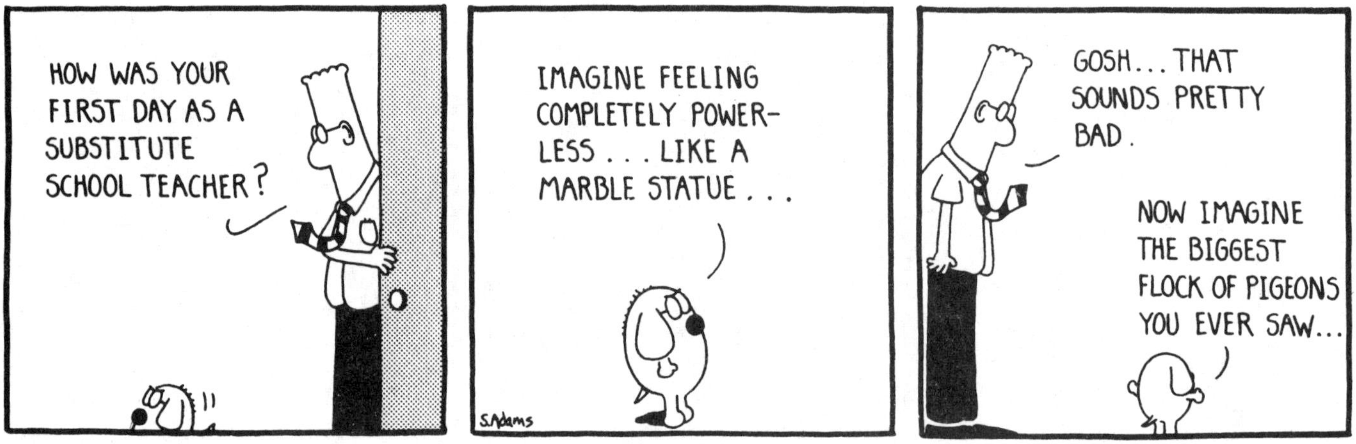
HOW WAS YOUR FIRST DAY AS A SUBSTITUTE SCHOOL TEACHER?
IMAGINE FEELING COMPLETELY POWER-LESS . . . LIKE A MARBLE STATUE . . .
S. Adams
GOSH . . . THAT SOUNDS PRETTY BAD.
NOW IMAGINE THE BIGGEST FLOCK OF PIGEONS YOU EVER SAW . . .

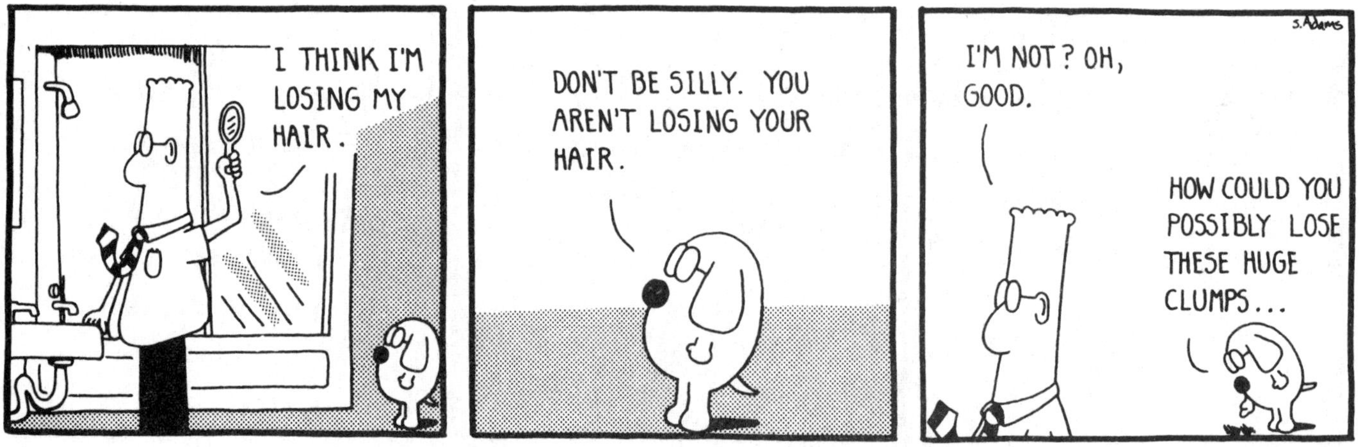
I THINK I'M LOSING MY HAIR.
DON'T BE SILLY. YOU AREN'T LOSING YOUR HAIR.
S. Adams
I'M NOT? OH, GOOD.
HOW COULD YOU POSSIBLY LOSE THESE HUGE CLUMPS . . .

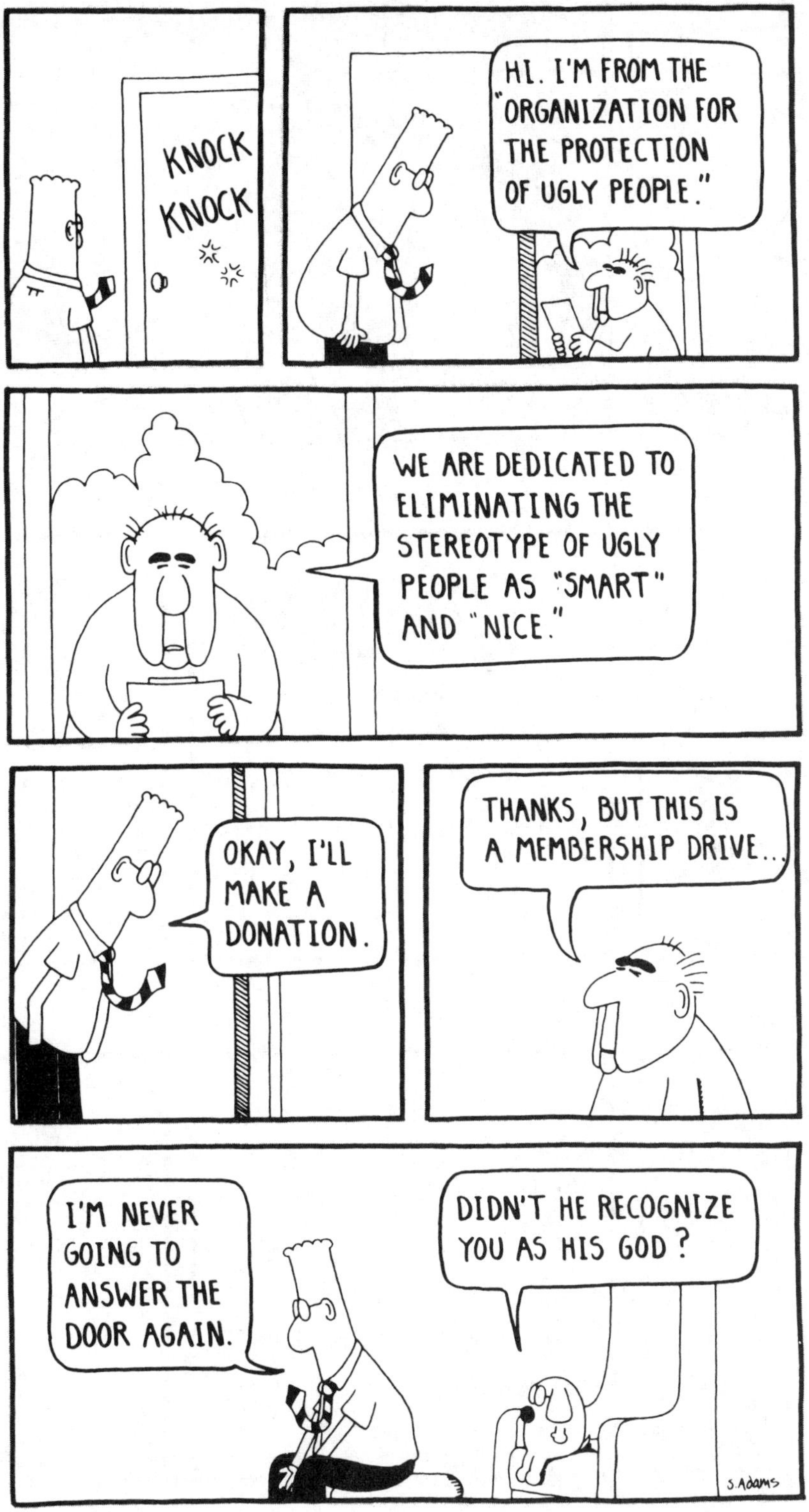
KNOCK
KNOCK
HI. I'M FROM THE "ORGANIZATION FOR THE PROTECTION OF UGLY PEOPLE."
WE ARE DEDICATED TO ELIMINATING THE STEREOTYPE OF UGLY PEOPLE AS "SMART" AND "NICE."
OKAY, I'LL MAKE A DONATION.
THANKS, BUT THIS IS A MEMBERSHIP DRIVE...
I'M NEVER GOING TO ANSWER THE DOOR AGAIN.
DIDN'T HE RECOGNIZE YOU AS HIS GOD?
S. Adams

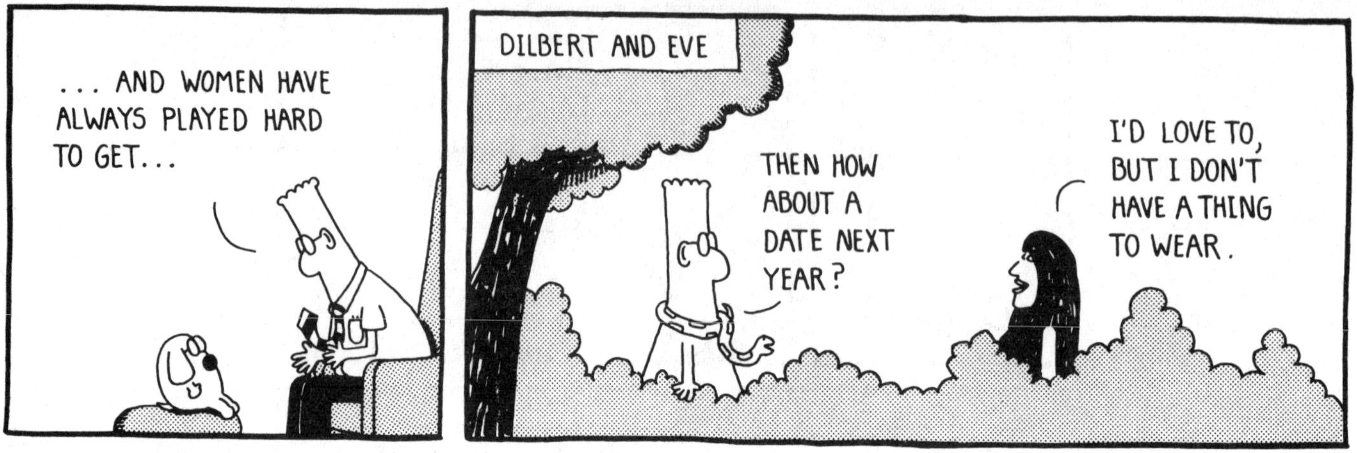
... AND WOMEN HAVE ALWAYS PLAYED HARD TO GET...
DILBERT AND EVE
THEN HOW ABOUT A DATE NEXT YEAR?
I'D LOVE TO, BUT I DON'T HAVE A THING TO WEAR.

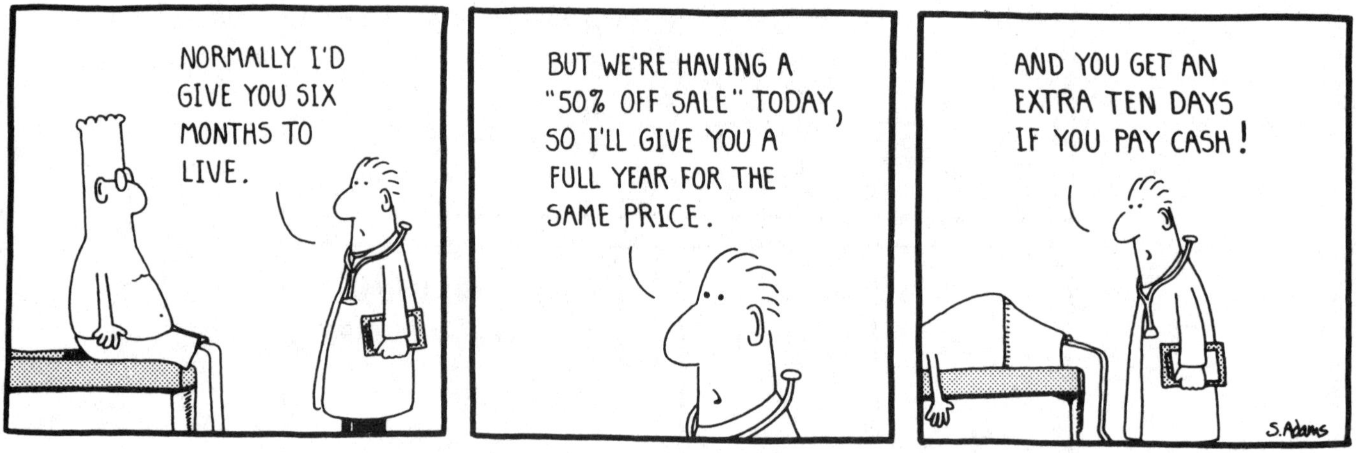
NORMALLY I'D GIVE YOU SIX MONTHS TO LIVE.
BUT WE'RE HAVING A "50% OFF SALE" TODAY, SO I'LL GIVE YOU A FULL YEAR FOR THE SAME PRICE.
AND YOU GET AN EXTRA TEN DAYS IF YOU PAY CASH!
S.Adams

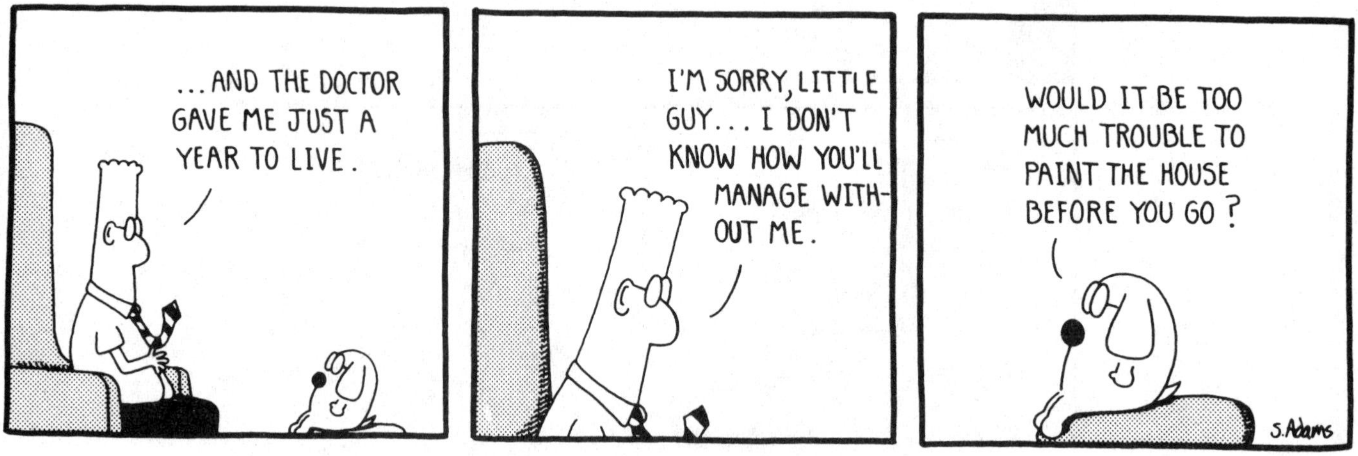
...AND THE DOCTOR GAVE ME JUST A YEAR TO LIVE.
I'M SORRY, LITTLE GUY... I DON'T KNOW HOW YOU'LL MANAGE WITH-OUT ME.
WOULD IT BE TOO MUCH TROUBLE TO PAINT THE HOUSE BEFORE YOU GO?
S.Adams

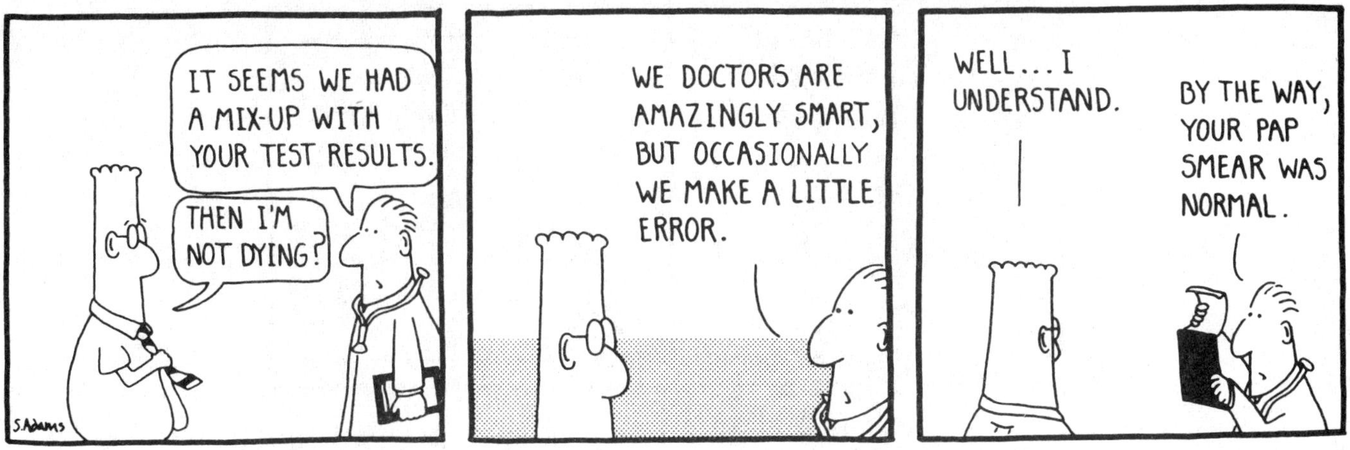
IT SEEMS WE HAD A MIX-UP WITH YOUR TEST RESULTS.
THEN I'M NOT DYING?
WE DOCTORS ARE AMAZINGLY SMART, BUT OCCASIONALLY WE MAKE A LITTLE ERROR.
WELL... I UNDERSTAND.
BY THE WAY, YOUR PAP SMEAR WAS NORMAL.
S.Adams

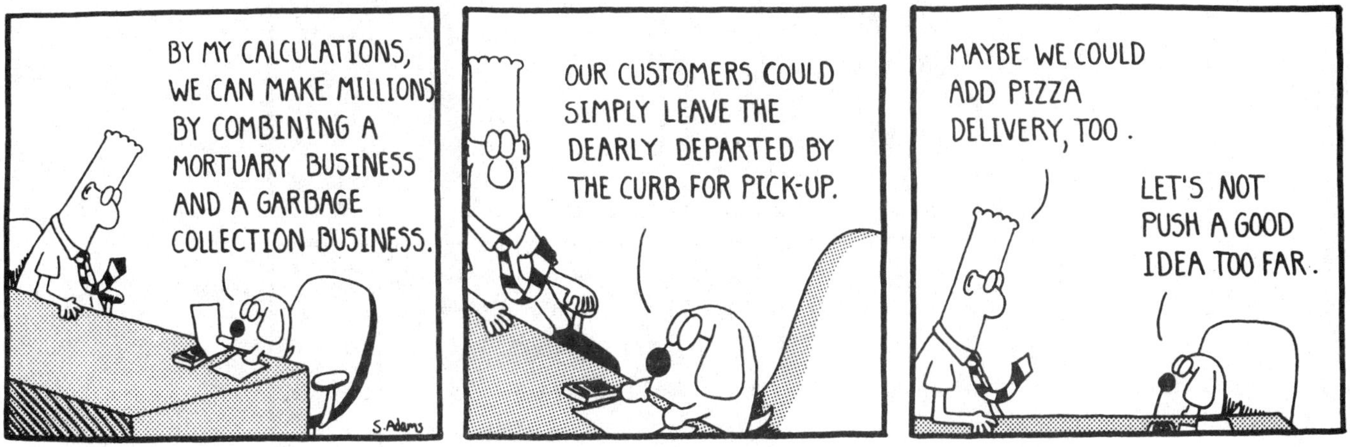
BY MY CALCULATIONS, WE CAN MAKE MILLIONS BY COMBINING A MORTUARY BUSINESS AND A GARBAGE COLLECTION BUSINESS.
S.Adams
OUR CUSTOMERS COULD SIMPLY LEAVE THE DEARLY DEPARTED BY THE CURB FOR PICK-UP.
MAYBE WE COULD ADD PIZZA DELIVERY, TOO.
LET'S NOT PUSH A GOOD IDEA TOO FAR.

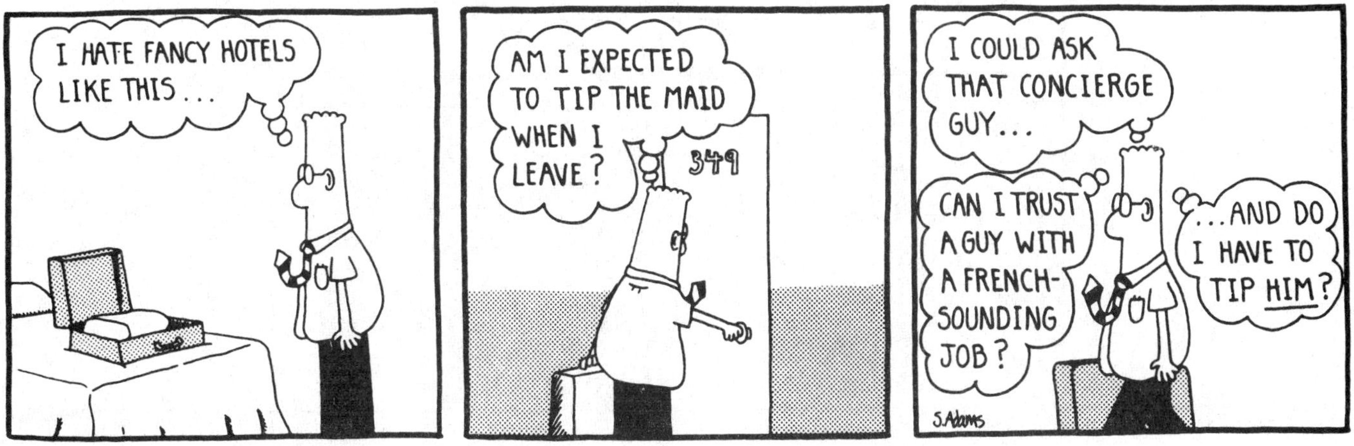
I HATE FANCY HOTELS LIKE THIS...
AM I EXPECTED TO TIP THE MAID WHEN I LEAVE?
349
I COULD ASK THAT CONCIERGE GUY...
CAN I TRUST A GUY WITH A FRENCH-SOUNDING JOB?
...AND DO I HAVE TO TIP HIM?
S.Adams

HA HA HA! MY SCHEME TO CONQUER EARTH IS RIGHT ON TRACK!
I'VE BEEN APPROVED FOR A MACYS CREDIT CARD!
I'LL USE THIS CREDIT HISTORY TO APPLY FOR VISA AND MASTERCARD.
SOON I'LL HAVE CREDIT CARDS FROM EVERY BANK IN THE WORLD.
THEN I'LL DO A CASH ADVANCE ON EVERY CARD, NETTING BILLIONS TO FORM A WORLD-WIDE LOTTERY PRIZE.
AND EVERYBODY WHO SUPPORTS ME AS SUPREME RULER OF EARTH GETS ONE FREE LOTTERY TICKET.
YOU KNOW, MOST DOGS WOULD BE DELIGHTED JUST TO GET A NICE CHEW-TOY.
S.Adams

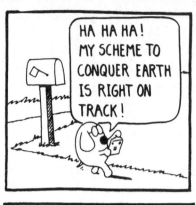

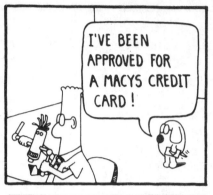

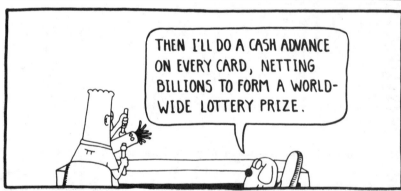

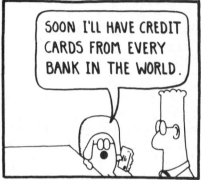

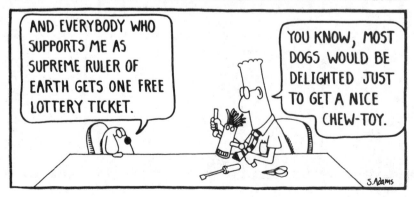

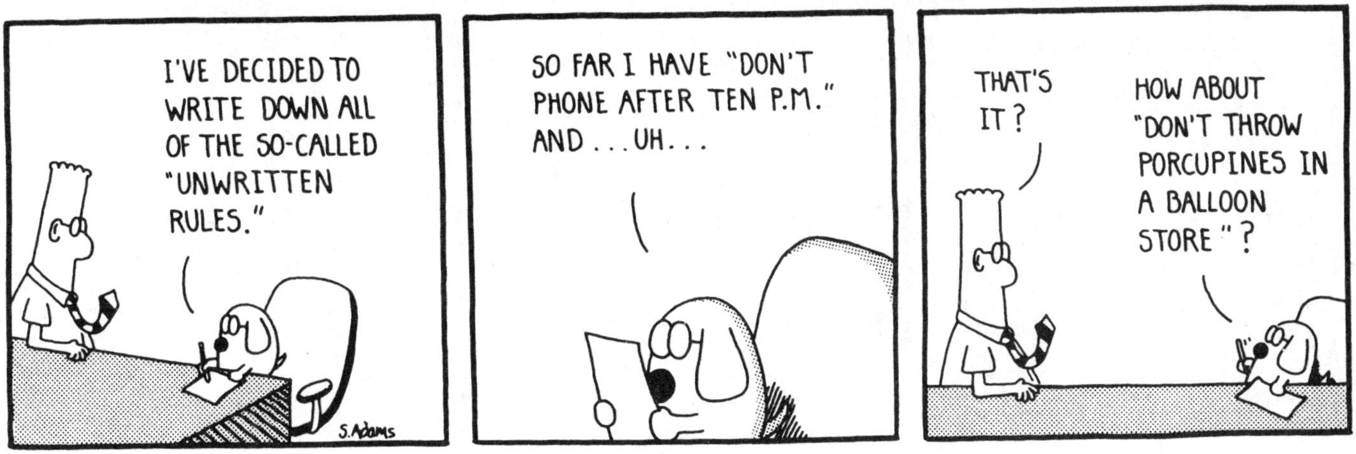
I'VE DECIDED TO WRITE DOWN ALL OF THE SO-CALLED "UNWRITTEN RULES."
SO FAR I HAVE "DON'T PHONE AFTER TEN P.M." AND . . . UH . . .
THAT'S IT?
HOW ABOUT "DON'T THROW PORCUPINES IN A BALLOON STORE"?
S. Adams

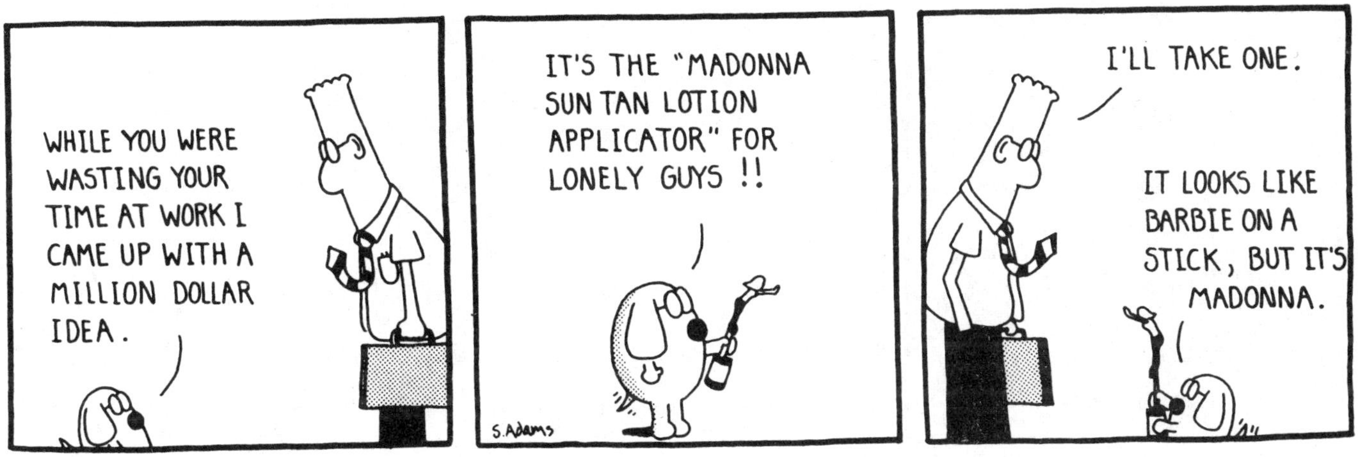
WHILE YOU WERE WASTING YOUR TIME AT WORK I CAME UP WITH A MILLION DOLLAR IDEA.
IT'S THE "MADONNA SUN TAN LOTION APPLICATOR" FOR LONELY GUYS!!
I'LL TAKE ONE.
IT LOOKS LIKE BARBIE ON A STICK, BUT IT'S MADONNA.
S. Adams

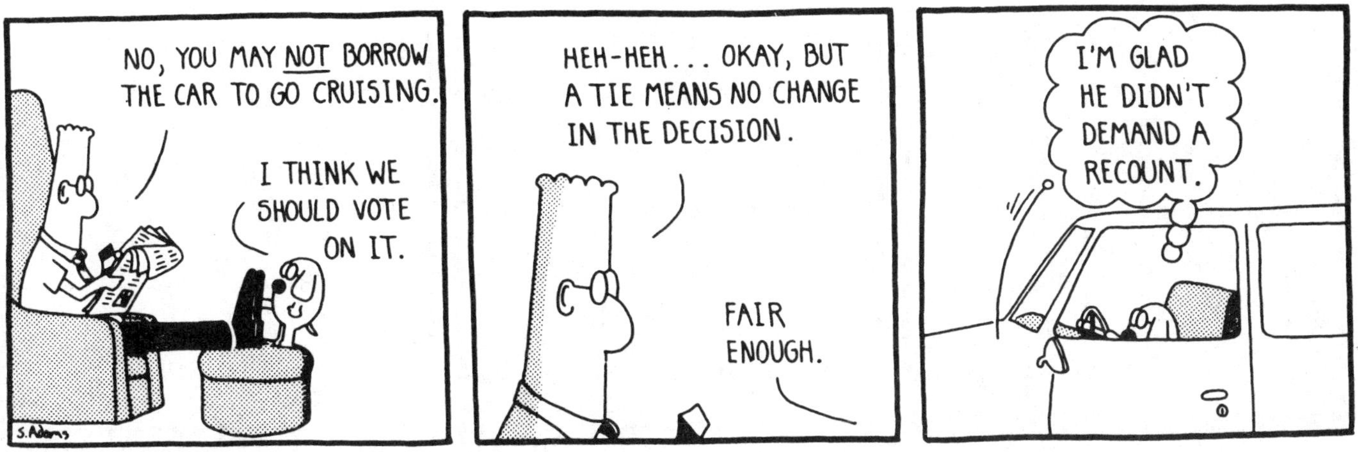
NO, YOU MAY NOT BORROW THE CAR TO GO CRUISING.
I THINK WE SHOULD VOTE ON IT.
HEH-HEH . . . OKAY, BUT A TIE MEANS NO CHANGE IN THE DECISION.
FAIR ENOUGH.
I'M GLAD HE DIDN'T DEMAND A RECOUNT.
S. Adams

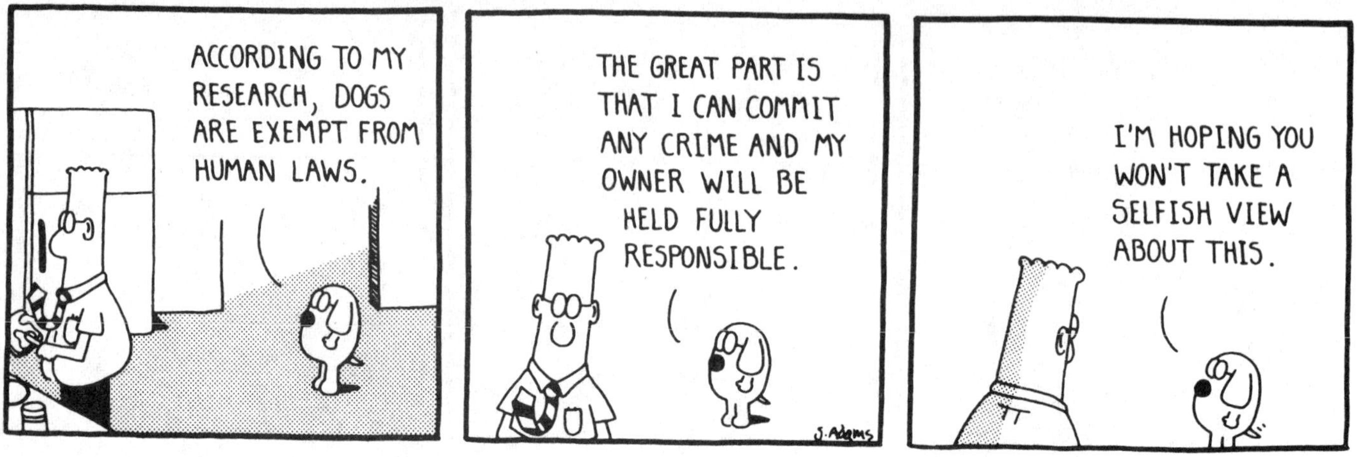
ACCORDING TO MY RESEARCH, DOGS ARE EXEMPT FROM HUMAN LAWS.
THE GREAT PART IS THAT I CAN COMMIT ANY CRIME AND MY OWNER WILL BE HELD FULLY RESPONSIBLE.
I'M HOPING YOU WON'T TAKE A SELFISH VIEW ABOUT THIS.

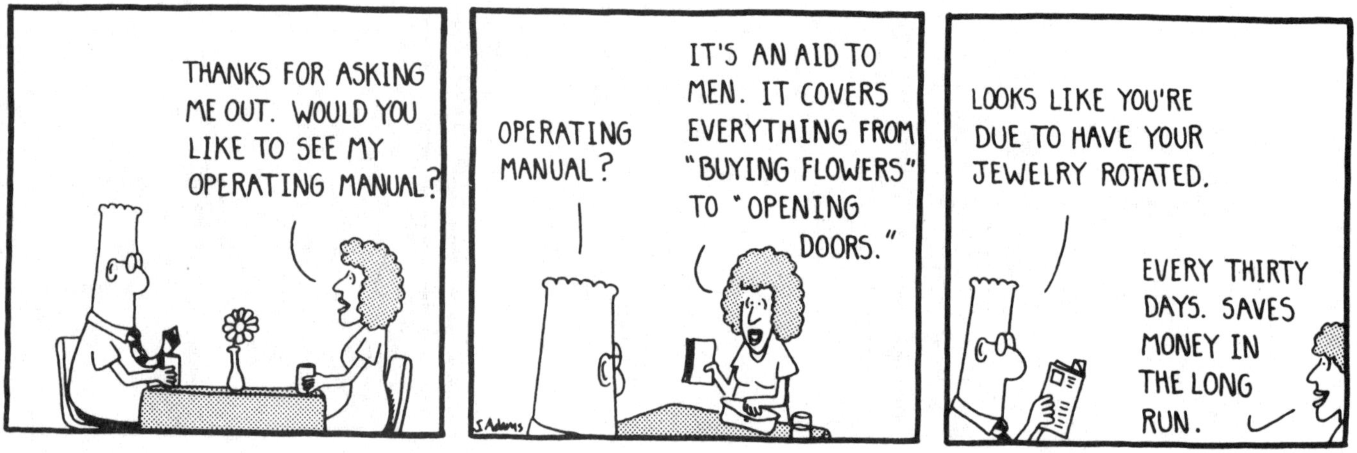
THANKS FOR ASKING ME OUT. WOULD YOU LIKE TO SEE MY OPERATING MANUAL?
OPERATING MANUAL?
IT'S AN AID TO MEN. IT COVERS EVERYTHING FROM "BUYING FLOWERS" TO "OPENING DOORS."
LOOKS LIKE YOU'RE DUE TO HAVE YOUR JEWELRY ROTATED.
EVERY THIRTY DAYS. SAVES MONEY IN THE LONG RUN.

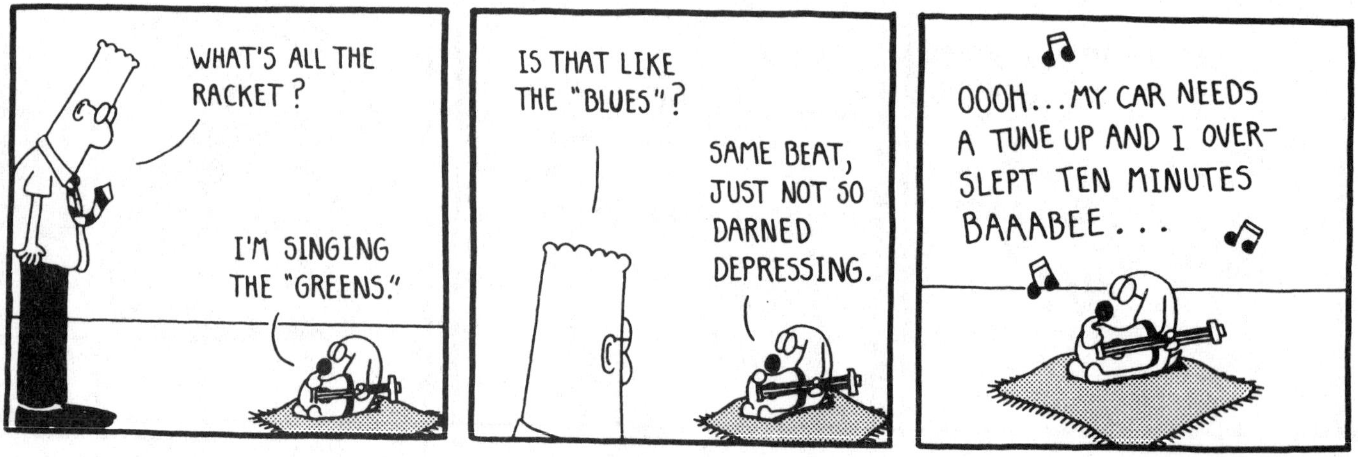
WHAT'S ALL THE RACKET?
I'M SINGING THE "GREENS."
IS THAT LIKE THE "BLUES"?
SAME BEAT, JUST NOT SO DARNED DEPRESSING.
OOOH... MY CAR NEEDS A TUNE UP AND I OVER-SLEPT TEN MINUTES BAAABEE...

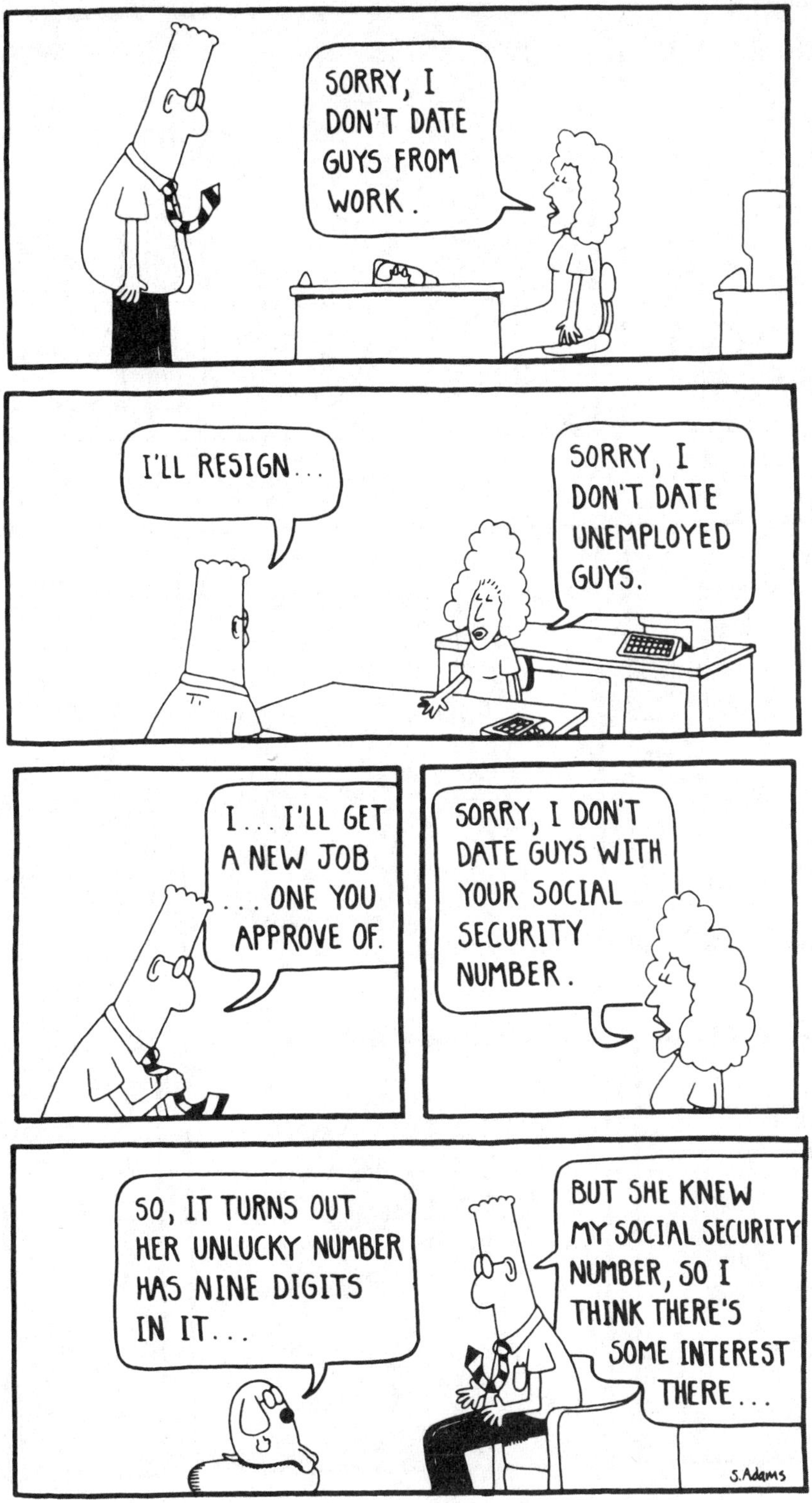
SORRY, I DON'T DATE GUYS FROM WORK.
I'LL RESIGN...
SORRY, I DON'T DATE UNEMPLOYED GUYS.
I... I'LL GET A NEW JOB ... ONE YOU APPROVE OF.
SORRY, I DON'T DATE GUYS WITH YOUR SOCIAL SECURITY NUMBER.
SO, IT TURNS OUT HER UNLUCKY NUMBER HAS NINE DIGITS IN IT...
BUT SHE KNEW MY SOCIAL SECURITY NUMBER, SO I THINK THERE'S SOME INTEREST THERE...
S.Adams

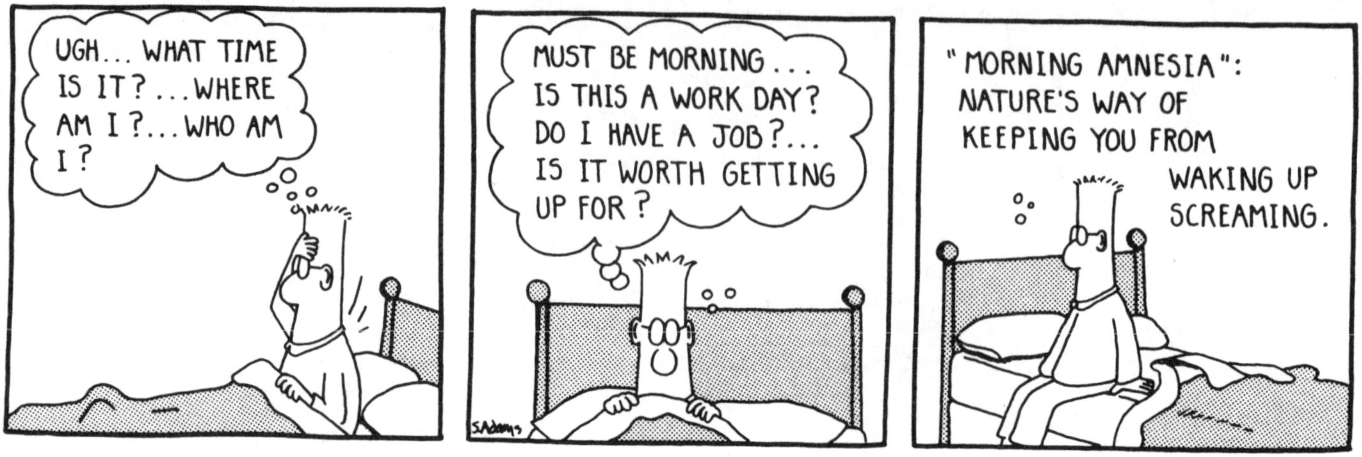
UGH... WHAT TIME IS IT?...WHERE AM I?...WHO AM I?
MUST BE MORNING... IS THIS A WORK DAY? DO I HAVE A JOB?... IS IT WORTH GETTING UP FOR?
"MORNING AMNESIA": NATURE'S WAY OF KEEPING YOU FROM WAKING UP SCREAMING.

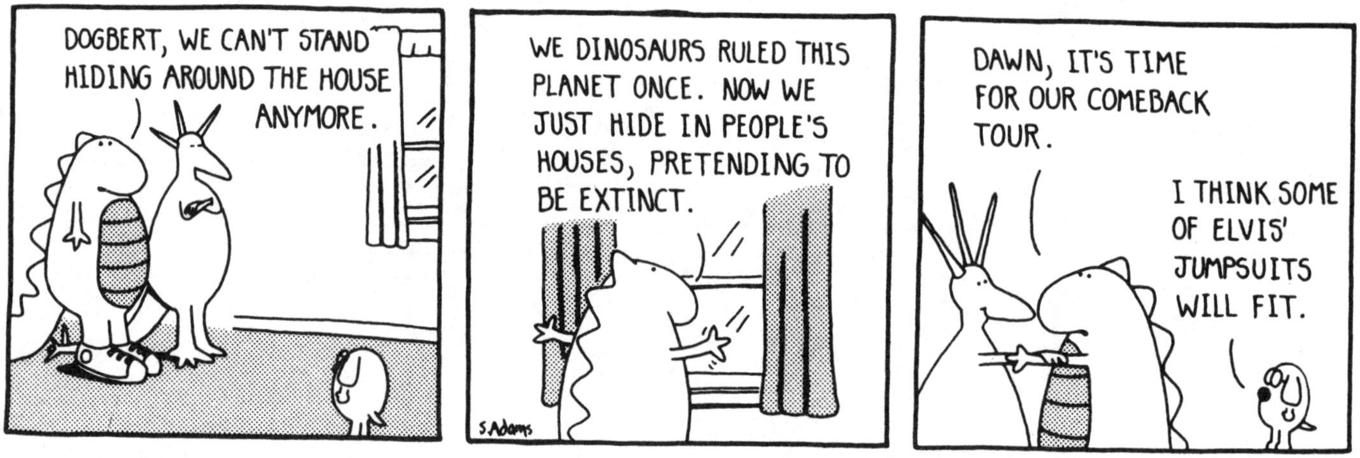
DOGBERT, WE CAN'T STAND HIDING AROUND THE HOUSE ANYMORE.
WE DINOSAURS RULED THIS PLANET ONCE. NOW WE JUST HIDE IN PEOPLE'S HOUSES, PRETENDING TO BE EXTINCT.
DAWN, IT'S TIME FOR OUR COMEBACK TOUR.
I THINK SOME OF ELVIS' JUMPSUITS WILL FIT.

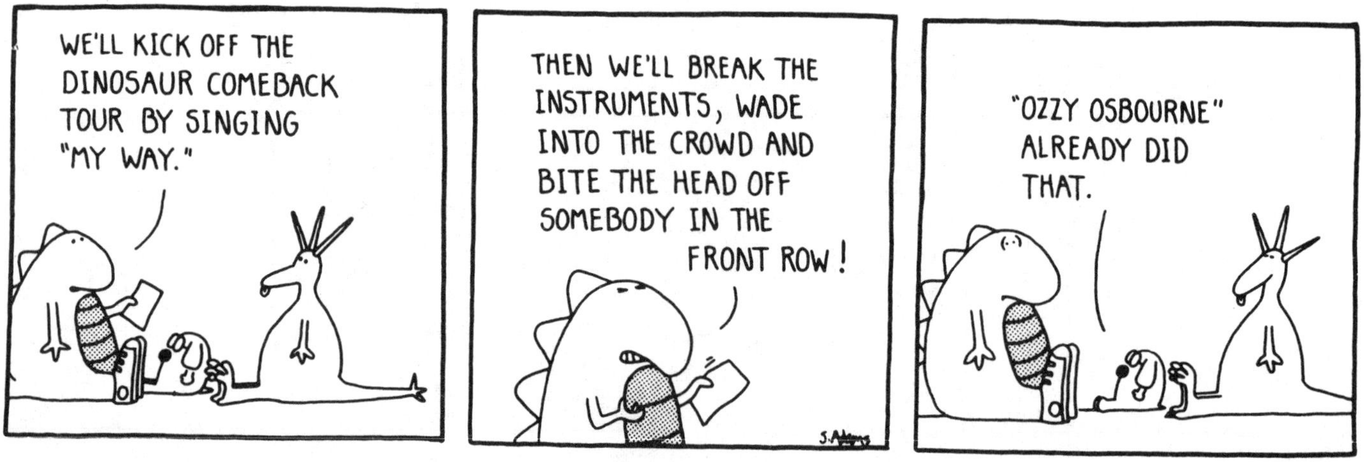
WE'LL KICK OFF THE DINOSAUR COMEBACK TOUR BY SINGING "MY WAY."
THEN WE'LL BREAK THE INSTRUMENTS, WADE INTO THE CROWD AND BITE THE HEAD OFF SOMEBODY IN THE FRONT ROW!
"OZZY OSBOURNE" ALREADY DID THAT.

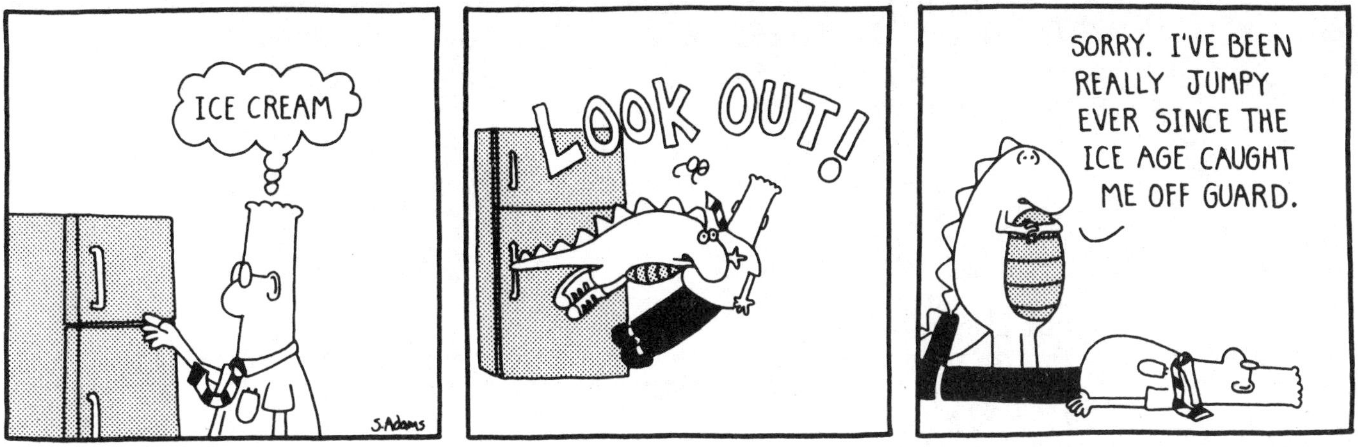
ICE CREAM
LOOK OUT!
SORRY. I'VE BEEN REALLY JUMPY EVER SINCE THE ICE AGE CAUGHT ME OFF GUARD.
S.Adams

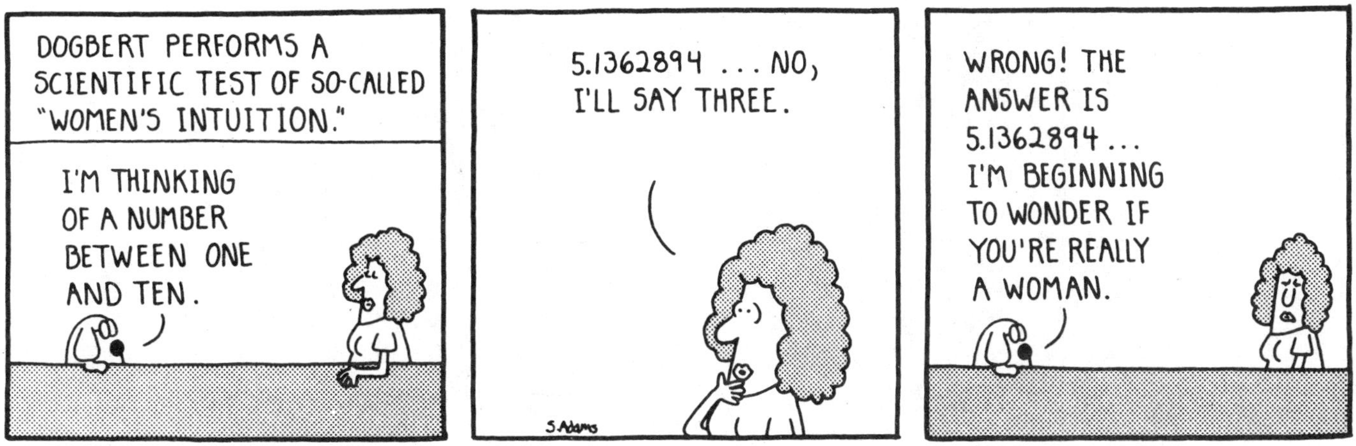
DOGBERT PERFORMS A SCIENTIFIC TEST OF SO-CALLED "WOMEN'S INTUITION."
I'M THINKING OF A NUMBER BETWEEN ONE AND TEN.
5.1362894 . . . NO, I'LL SAY THREE.
WRONG! THE ANSWER IS 5.1362894 . . . I'M BEGINNING TO WONDER IF YOU'RE REALLY A WOMAN.
S.Adams

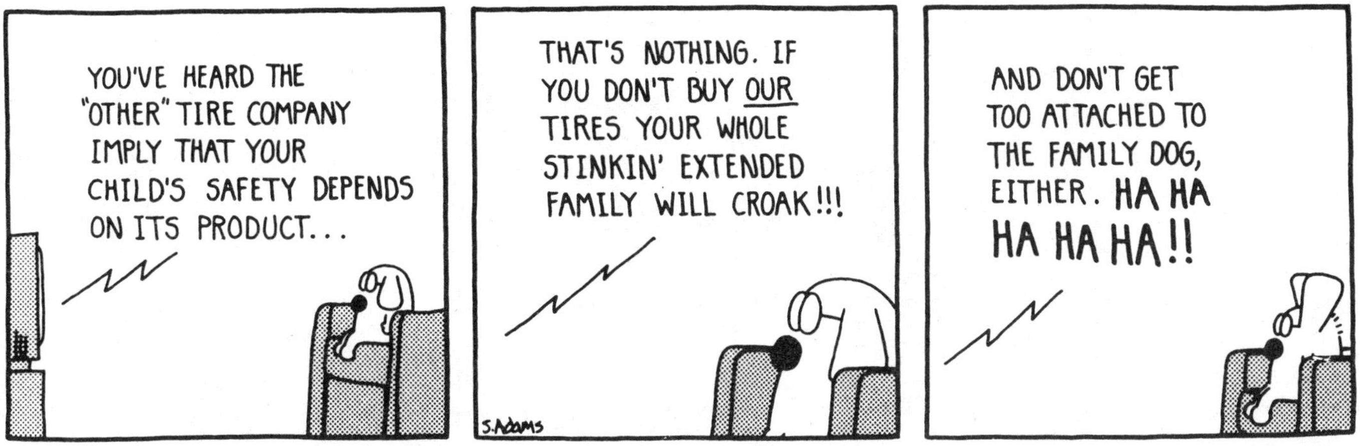
YOU'VE HEARD THE "OTHER" TIRE COMPANY IMPLY THAT YOUR CHILD'S SAFETY DEPENDS ON ITS PRODUCT . . .
THAT'S NOTHING. IF YOU DON'T BUY OUR TIRES YOUR WHOLE STINKIN' EXTENDED FAMILY WILL CROAK!!!
AND DON'T GET TOO ATTACHED TO THE FAMILY DOG, EITHER. HA HA HA HA HA!!
S.Adams

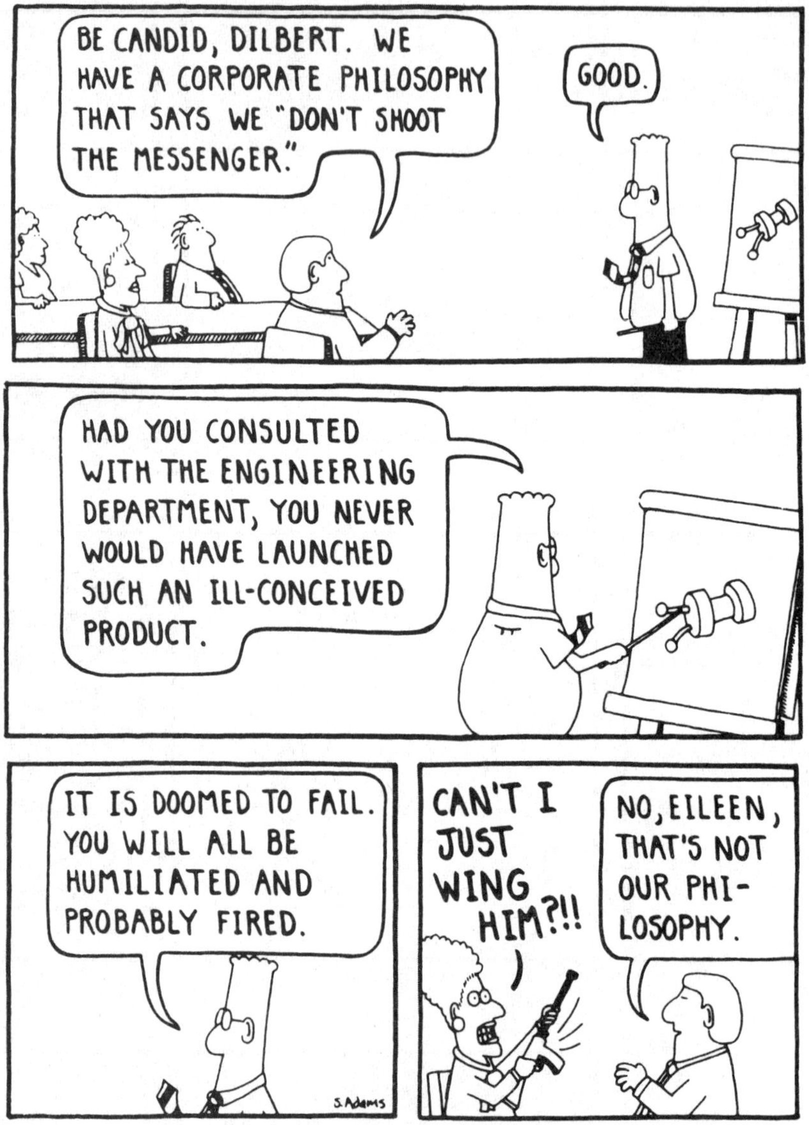
BE CANDID, DILBERT. WE HAVE A CORPORATE PHILOSOPHY THAT SAYS WE "DON'T SHOOT THE MESSENGER."
GOOD.
HAD YOU CONSULTED WITH THE ENGINEERING DEPARTMENT, YOU NEVER WOULD HAVE LAUNCHED SUCH AN ILL-CONCEIVED PRODUCT.
IT IS DOOMED TO FAIL. YOU WILL ALL BE HUMILIATED AND PROBABLY FIRED.
S.Adams
CAN'T I JUST WING HIM?!!
NO, EILEEN, THAT'S NOT OUR PHI-LOSOPHY.

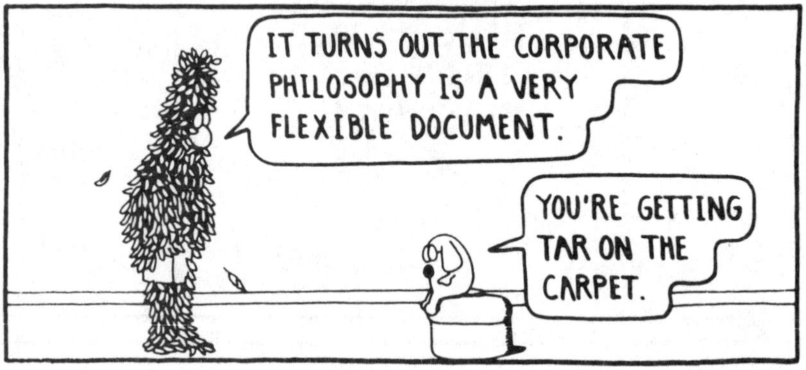
IT TURNS OUT THE CORPORATE PHILOSOPHY IS A VERY FLEXIBLE DOCUMENT.
YOU'RE GETTING TAR ON THE CARPET.

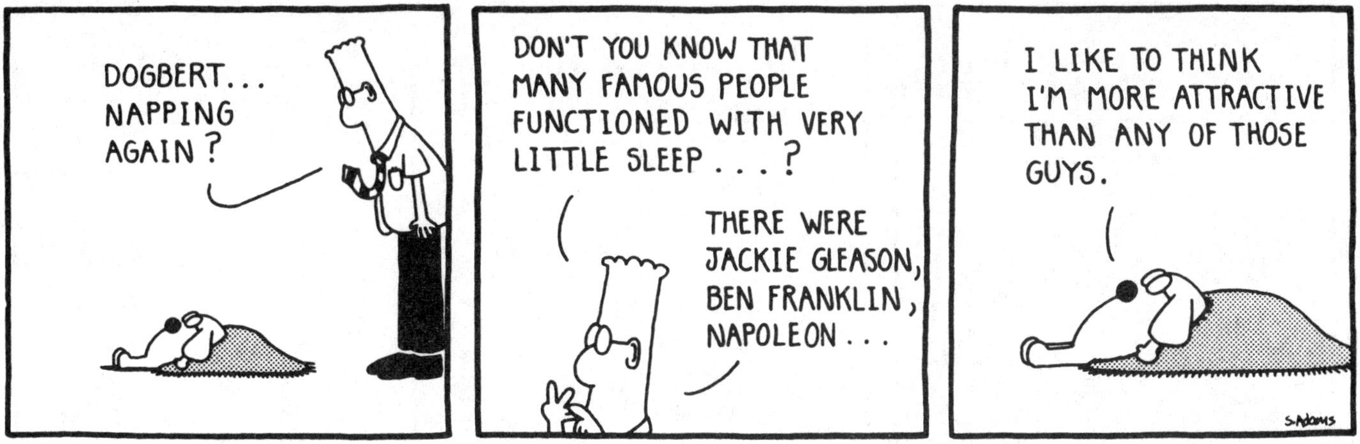
DOGBERT... NAPPING AGAIN?
DON'T YOU KNOW THAT MANY FAMOUS PEOPLE FUNCTIONED WITH VERY LITTLE SLEEP...?
THERE WERE JACKIE GLEASON, BEN FRANKLIN, NAPOLEON...
I LIKE TO THINK I'M MORE ATTRACTIVE THAN ANY OF THOSE GUYS.

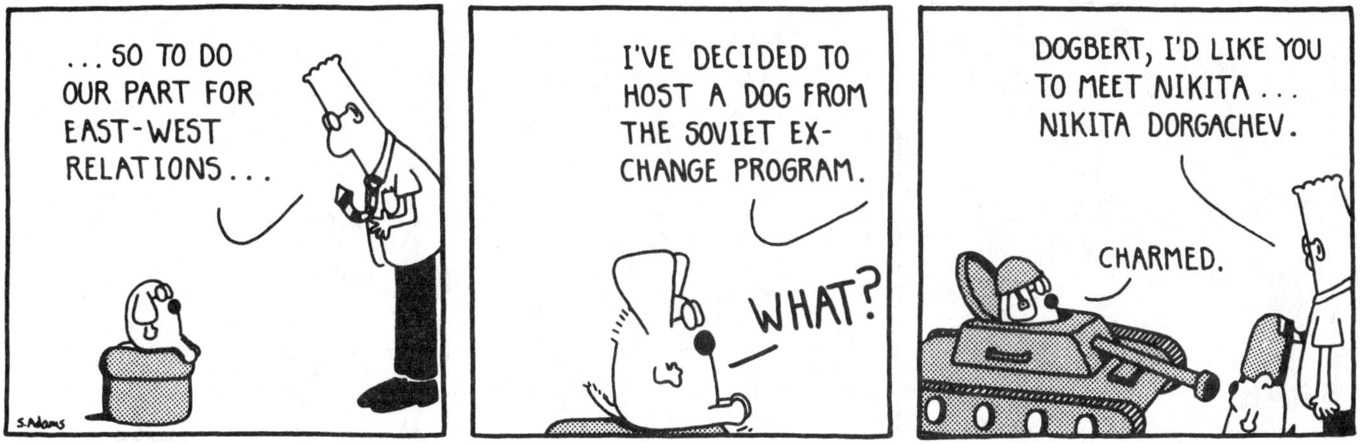
...SO TO DO OUR PART FOR EAST-WEST RELATIONS...
I'VE DECIDED TO HOST A DOG FROM THE SOVIET EX-CHANGE PROGRAM.
WHAT?
DOGBERT, I'D LIKE YOU TO MEET NIKITA... NIKITA DORGACHEV.
CHARMED.

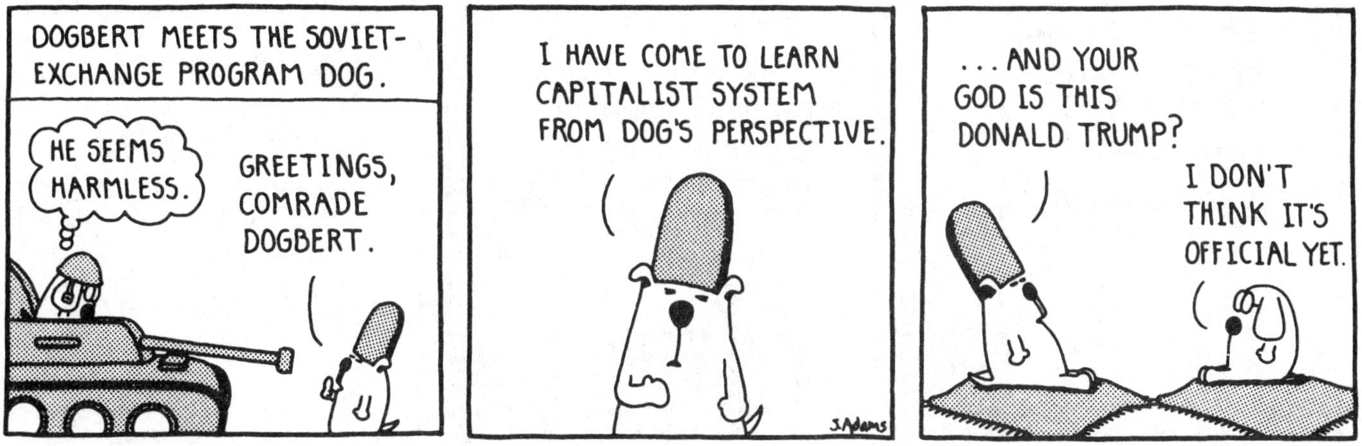
DOGBERT MEETS THE SOVIET-EXCHANGE PROGRAM DOG.
HE SEEMS HARMLESS.
GREETINGS, COMRADE DOGBERT.
I HAVE COME TO LEARN CAPITALIST SYSTEM FROM DOG'S PERSPECTIVE.
...AND YOUR GOD IS THIS DONALD TRUMP?
I DON'T THINK IT'S OFFICIAL YET.

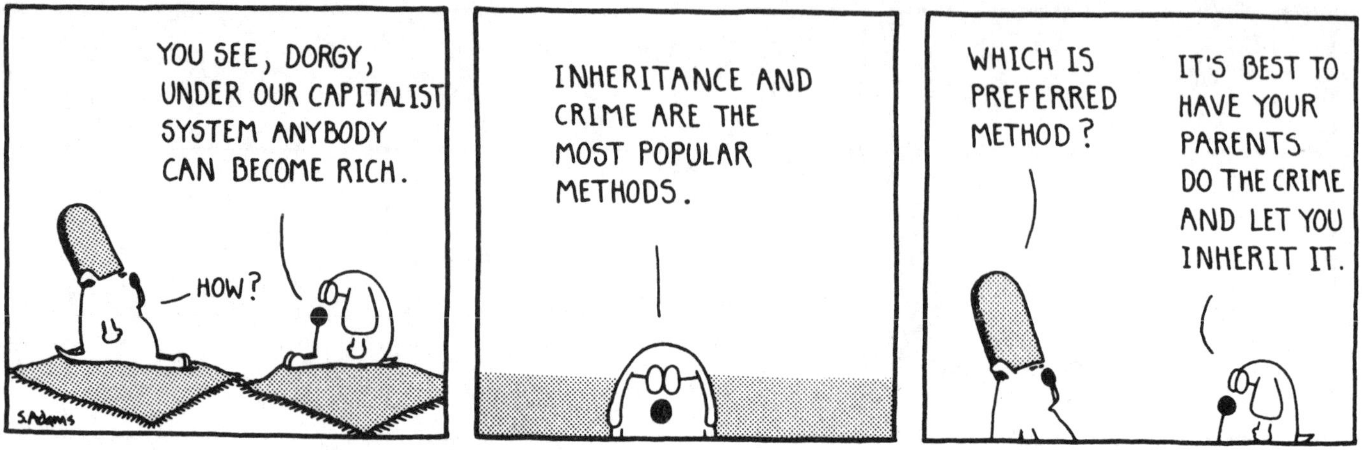
YOU SEE, DORGY, UNDER OUR CAPITALIST SYSTEM ANYBODY CAN BECOME RICH.
HOW?
INHERITANCE AND CRIME ARE THE MOST POPULAR METHODS.
WHICH IS PREFERRED METHOD?
IT'S BEST TO HAVE YOUR PARENTS DO THE CRIME AND LET YOU INHERIT IT.
S. Adams

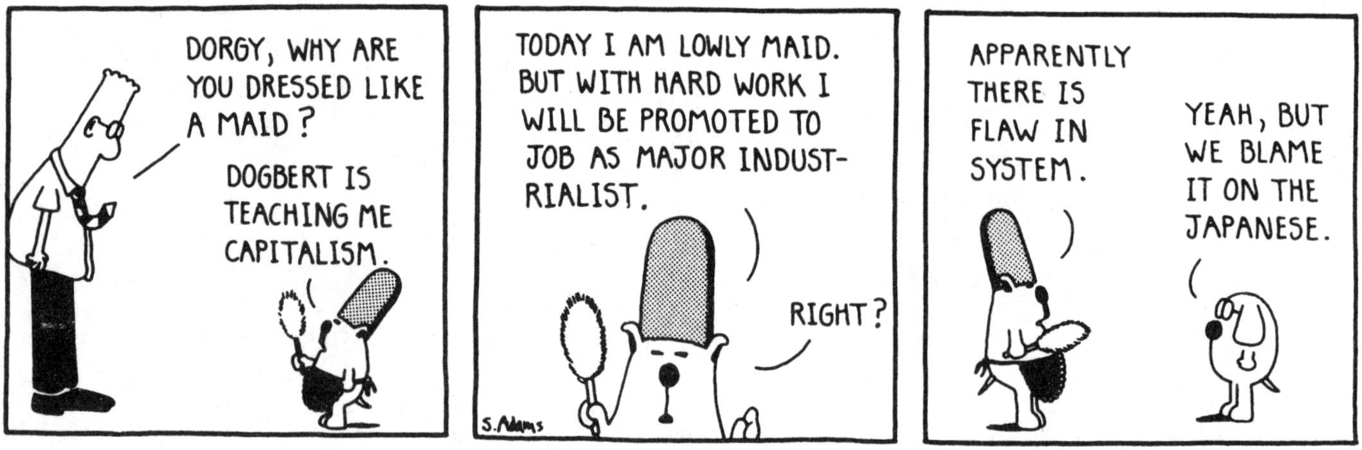
DORGY, WHY ARE YOU DRESSED LIKE A MAID?
DOGBERT IS TEACHING ME CAPITALISM.
TODAY I AM LOWLY MAID. BUT WITH HARD WORK I WILL BE PROMOTED TO JOB AS MAJOR INDUST-RIALIST.
RIGHT?
APPARENTLY THERE IS FLAW IN SYSTEM.
YEAH, BUT WE BLAME IT ON THE JAPANESE.
S. Adams

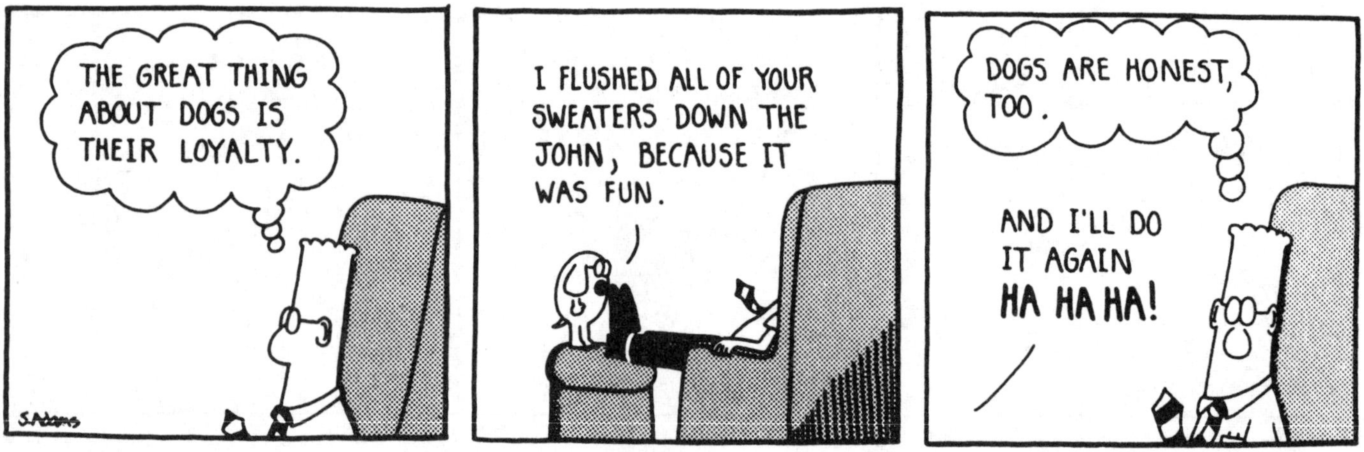
THE GREAT THING ABOUT DOGS IS THEIR LOYALTY.
I FLUSHED ALL OF YOUR SWEATERS DOWN THE JOHN, BECAUSE IT WAS FUN.
DOGS ARE HONEST, TOO.
AND I'LL DO IT AGAIN HA HA HA!
S. Adams

I READ THAT DINOSAURS EVOLVED INTO THE BIRD FAMILY.
THAT'S EXACTLY CORRECT, DOGBERT.
BUT MOST PEOPLE DON'T REALIZE THAT THERE WAS A VERY DIFFICULT PERIOD WHEN SOME DINOSAURS STARTED EVOLVING INTO BIRDS.
S. Adams
"LEARNING TO FLY WAS THE HARDEST PART."
"AND LIVING IN TREES WAS A REAL NUISANCE."
BOY, THAT SOUNDS TOUGH.
THE TRAGIC PART IS THAT WE DID IT JUST FOR THE "BONUS MILES."

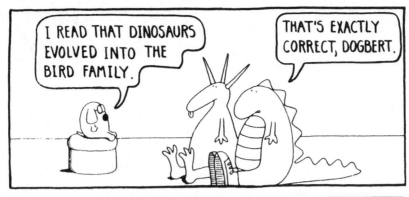

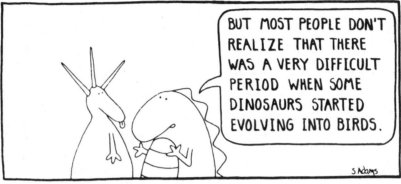

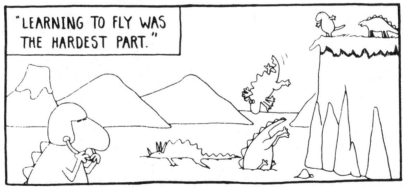

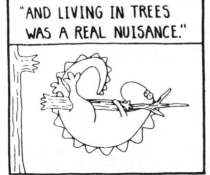

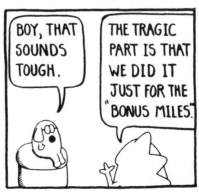

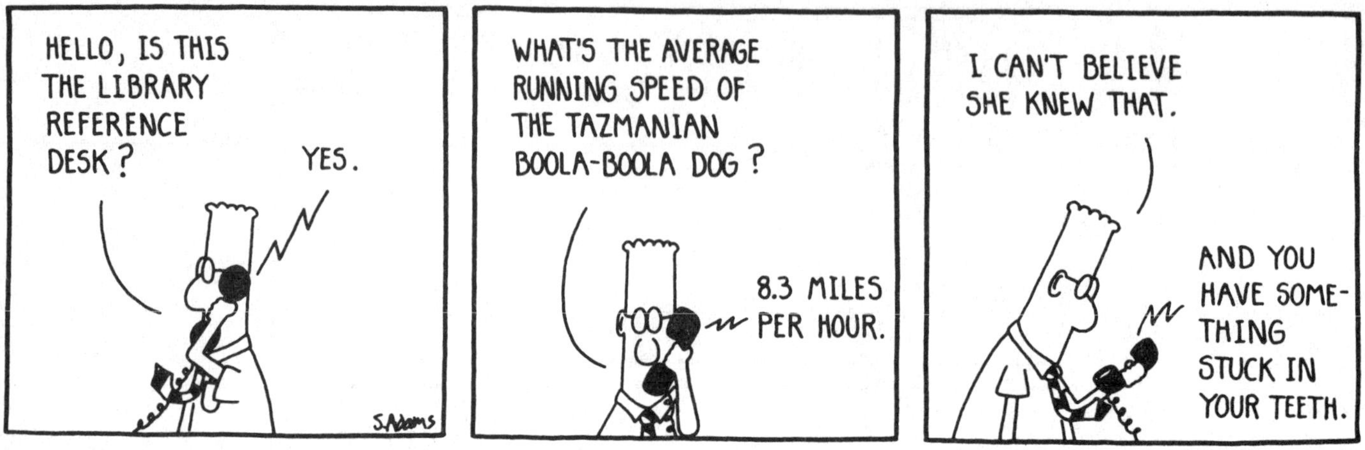
HELLO, IS THIS THE LIBRARY REFERENCE DESK?
YES.
WHAT'S THE AVERAGE RUNNING SPEED OF THE TAZMANIAN BOOLA-BOOLA DOG?
8.3 MILES PER HOUR.
I CAN'T BELIEVE SHE KNEW THAT.
AND YOU HAVE SOME-THING STUCK IN YOUR TEETH.
S.Adams

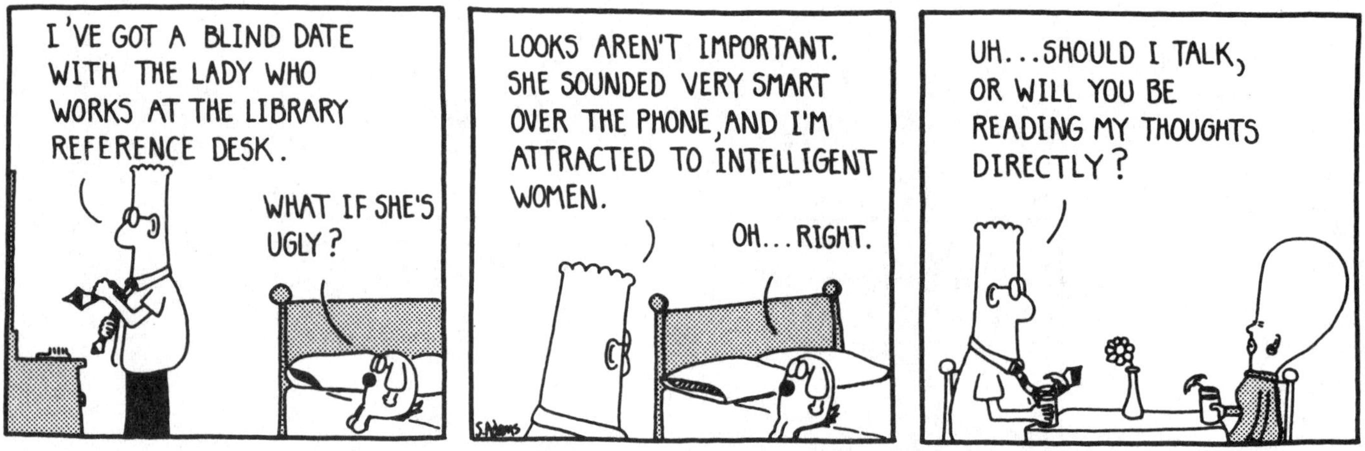
I'VE GOT A BLIND DATE WITH THE LADY WHO WORKS AT THE LIBRARY REFERENCE DESK.
WHAT IF SHE'S UGLY?
LOOKS AREN'T IMPORTANT. SHE SOUNDED VERY SMART OVER THE PHONE, AND I'M ATTRACTED TO INTELLIGENT WOMEN.
OH... RIGHT.
UH...SHOULD I TALK, OR WILL YOU BE READING MY THOUGHTS DIRECTLY?
S.Adams

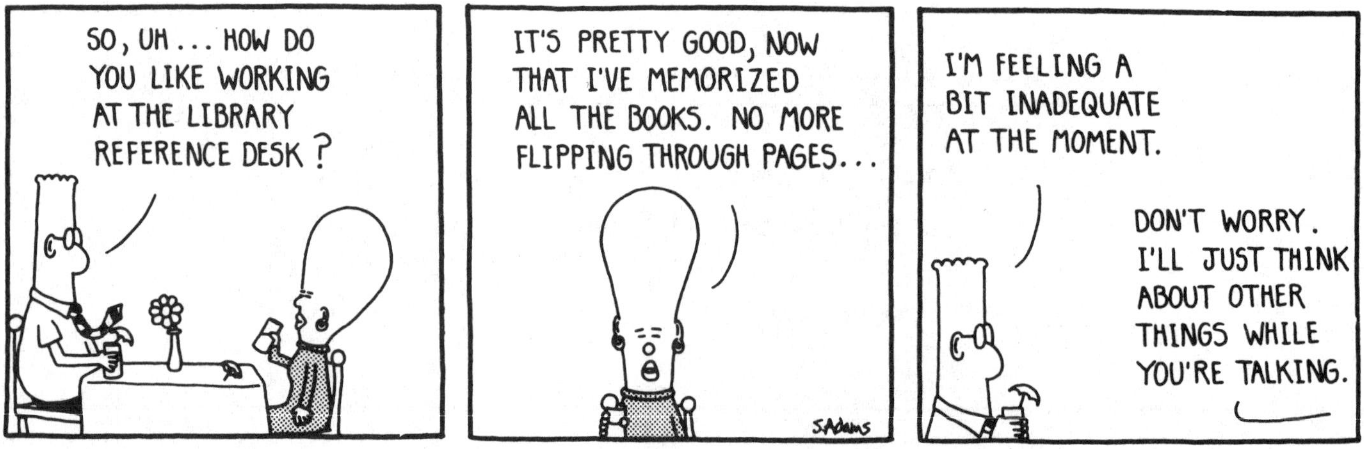
SO, UH... HOW DO YOU LIKE WORKING AT THE LIBRARY REFERENCE DESK?
IT'S PRETTY GOOD, NOW THAT I'VE MEMORIZED ALL THE BOOKS. NO MORE FLIPPING THROUGH PAGES...
I'M FEELING A BIT INADEQUATE AT THE MOMENT.
DON'T WORRY. I'LL JUST THINK ABOUT OTHER THINGS WHILE YOU'RE TALKING.
S.Adams

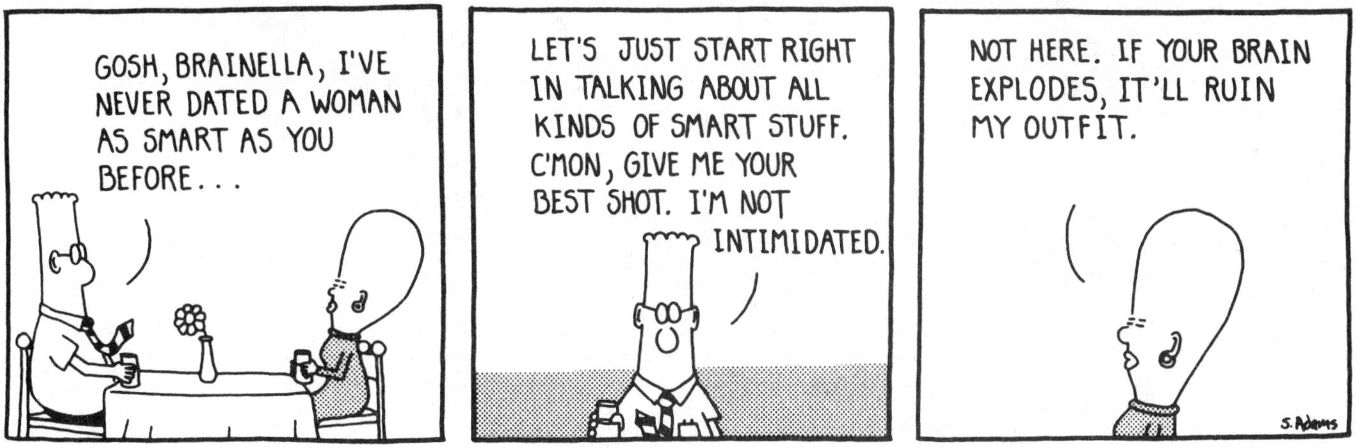
GOSH, BRAINELLA, I'VE NEVER DATED A WOMAN AS SMART AS YOU BEFORE...
LET'S JUST START RIGHT IN TALKING ABOUT ALL KINDS OF SMART STUFF. C'MON, GIVE ME YOUR BEST SHOT. I'M NOT INTIMIDATED.
NOT HERE. IF YOUR BRAIN EXPLODES, IT'LL RUIN MY OUTFIT.
S. Adams

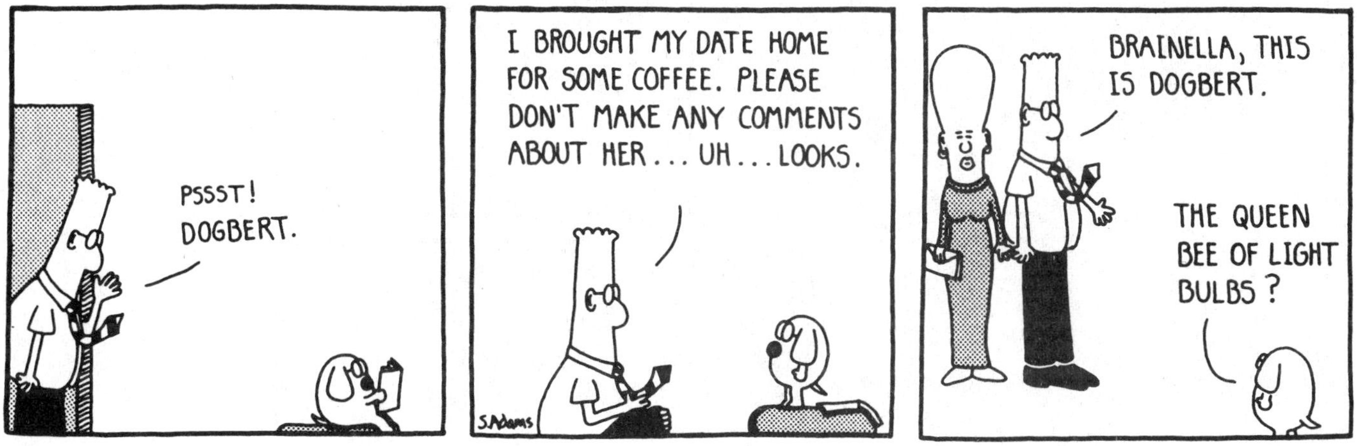
PSSST! DOGBERT.
I BROUGHT MY DATE HOME FOR SOME COFFEE. PLEASE DON'T MAKE ANY COMMENTS ABOUT HER... UH... LOOKS.
S. Adams
BRAINELLA, THIS IS DOGBERT.
THE QUEEN BEE OF LIGHT BULBS?

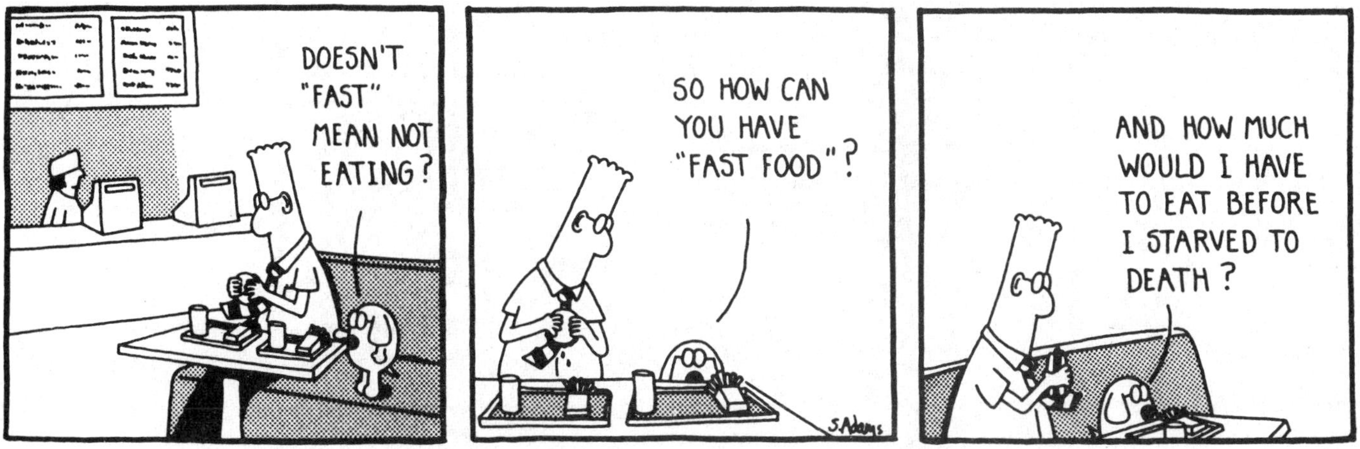
DOESN'T "FAST" MEAN NOT EATING?
SO HOW CAN YOU HAVE "FAST FOOD"?
S. Adams
AND HOW MUCH WOULD I HAVE TO EAT BEFORE I STARVED TO DEATH?

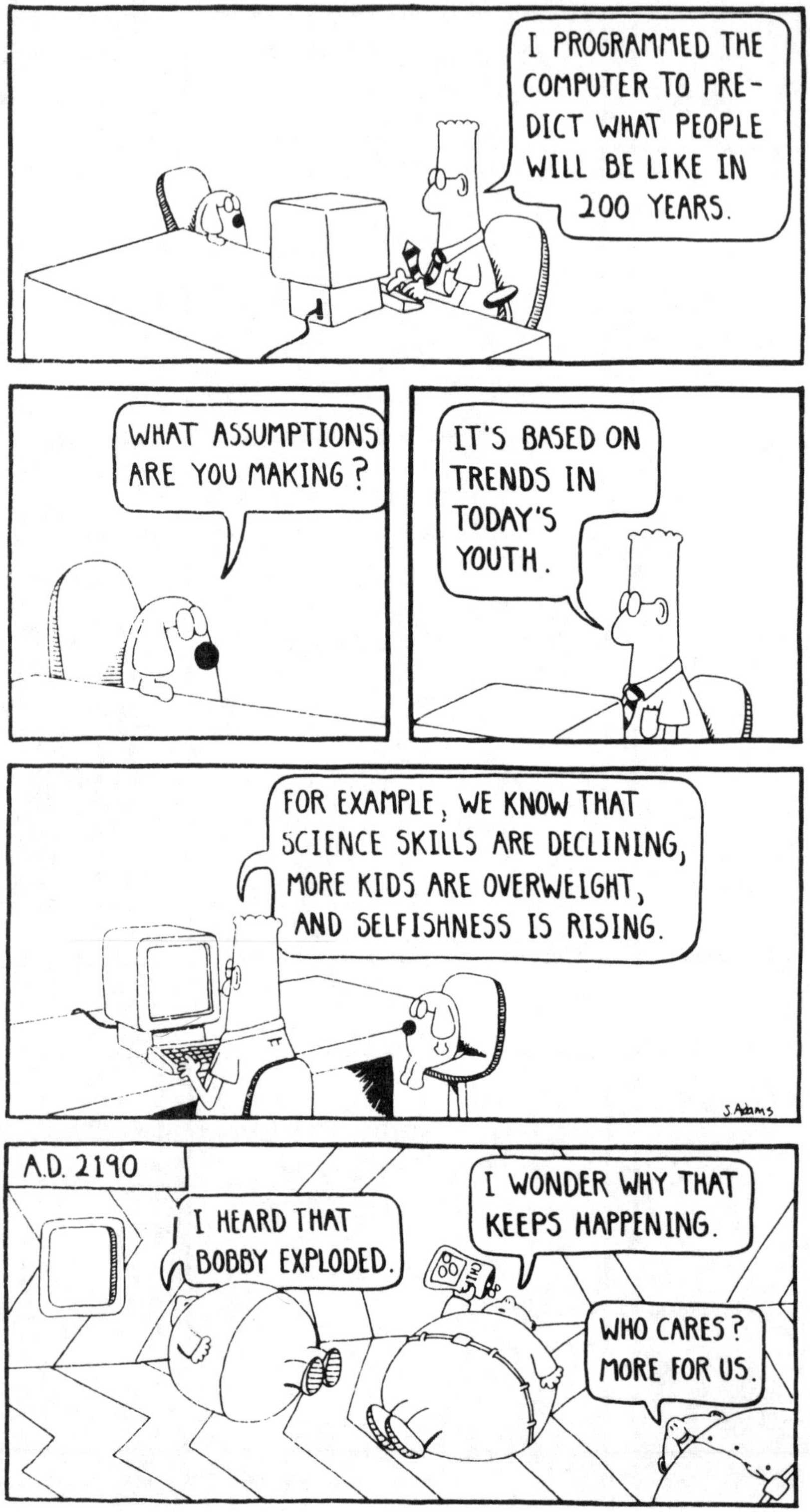
I PROGRAMMED THE COMPUTER TO PRE-DICT WHAT PEOPLE WILL BE LIKE IN 200 YEARS.
WHAT ASSUMPTIONS ARE YOU MAKING?
IT'S BASED ON TRENDS IN TODAY'S YOUTH.
FOR EXAMPLE, WE KNOW THAT SCIENCE SKILLS ARE DECLINING, MORE KIDS ARE OVERWEIGHT, AND SELFISHNESS IS RISING.
S. Adams
A.D. 2190
I HEARD THAT BOBBY EXPLODED.
I WONDER WHY THAT KEEPS HAPPENING.
WHO CARES? MORE FOR US.

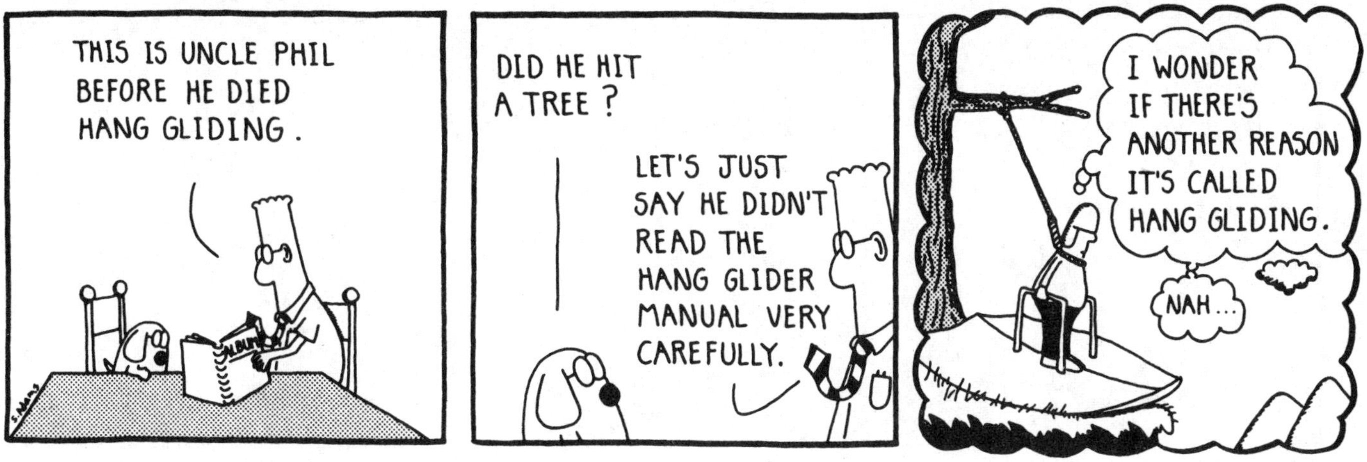
THIS IS UNCLE PHIL BEFORE HE DIED HANG GLIDING.
DID HE HIT A TREE?
LET'S JUST SAY HE DIDN'T READ THE HANG GLIDER MANUAL VERY CAREFULLY.
I WONDER IF THERE'S ANOTHER REASON IT'S CALLED HANG GLIDING.
NAH...

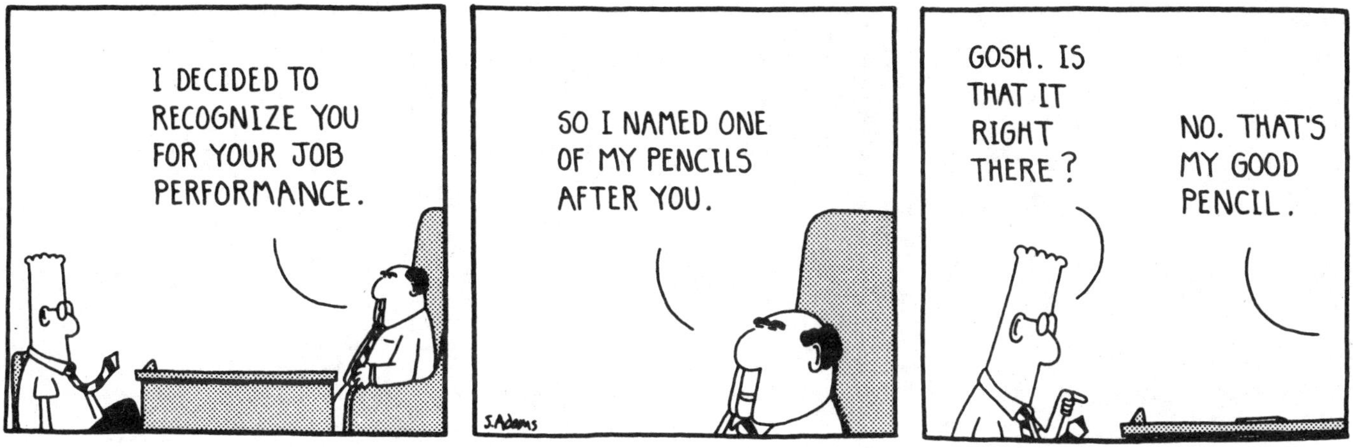
I DECIDED TO RECOGNIZE YOU FOR YOUR JOB PERFORMANCE.
SO I NAMED ONE OF MY PENCILS AFTER YOU.
GOSH. IS THAT IT RIGHT THERE?
NO. THAT'S MY GOOD PENCIL.

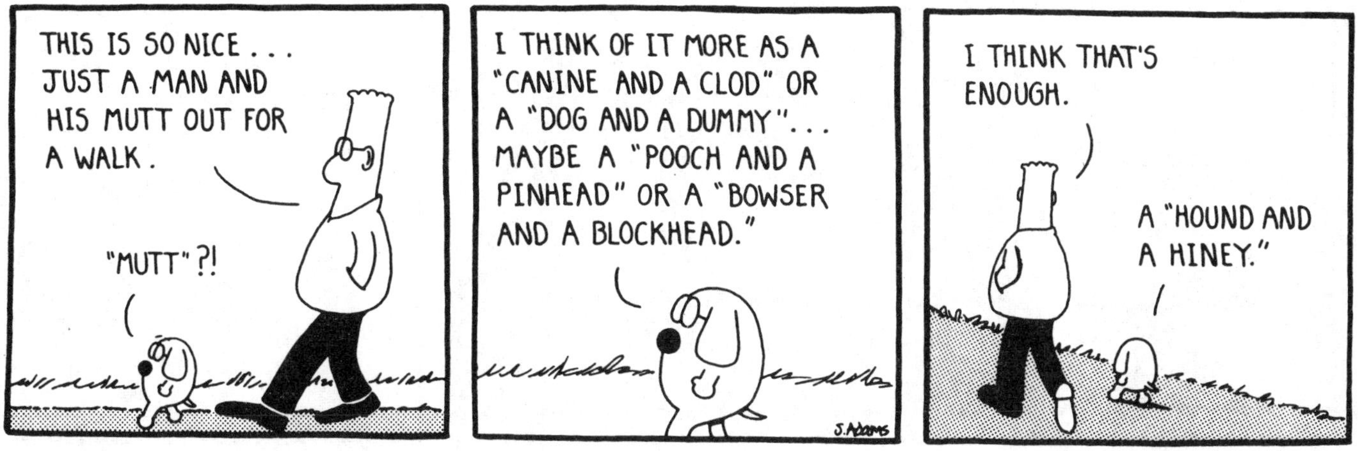
THIS IS SO NICE... JUST A MAN AND HIS MUTT OUT FOR A WALK.
"MUTT"?!
I THINK OF IT MORE AS A "CANINE AND A CLOD" OR A "DOG AND A DUMMY"... MAYBE A "POOCH AND A PINHEAD" OR A "BOWSER AND A BLOCKHEAD."
I THINK THAT'S ENOUGH.
A "HOUND AND A HINEY."

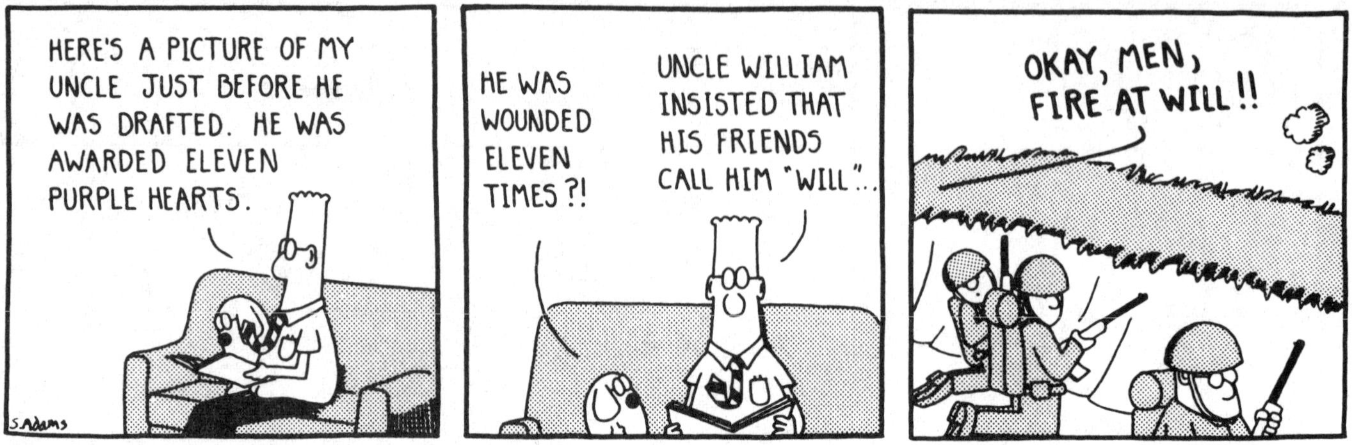
HERE'S A PICTURE OF MY UNCLE JUST BEFORE HE WAS DRAFTED. HE WAS AWARDED ELEVEN PURPLE HEARTS.
S.Adams
HE WAS WOUNDED ELEVEN TIMES ?!
UNCLE WILLIAM INSISTED THAT HIS FRIENDS CALL HIM "WILL"...
OKAY, MEN, FIRE AT WILL !!

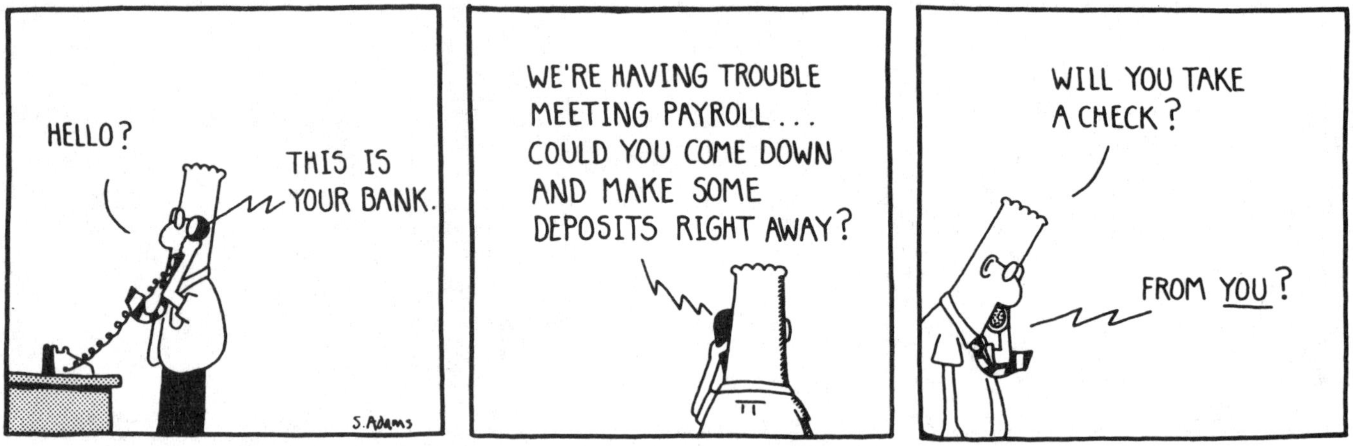
HELLO?
THIS IS YOUR BANK.
S.Adams
WE'RE HAVING TROUBLE MEETING PAYROLL... COULD YOU COME DOWN AND MAKE SOME DEPOSITS RIGHT AWAY?
WILL YOU TAKE A CHECK?
FROM YOU?

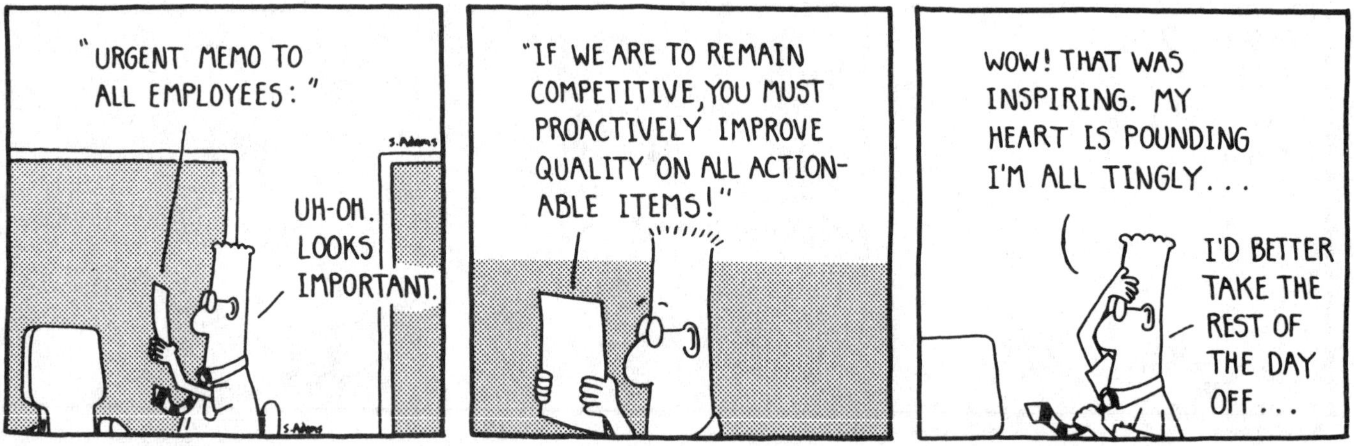
"URGENT MEMO TO ALL EMPLOYEES:"
UH-OH. LOOKS IMPORTANT.
S.Adams
"IF WE ARE TO REMAIN COMPETITIVE, YOU MUST PROACTIVELY IMPROVE QUALITY ON ALL ACTIONABLE ITEMS!"
WOW! THAT WAS INSPIRING. MY HEART IS POUNDING I'M ALL TINGLY...
I'D BETTER TAKE THE REST OF THE DAY OFF...

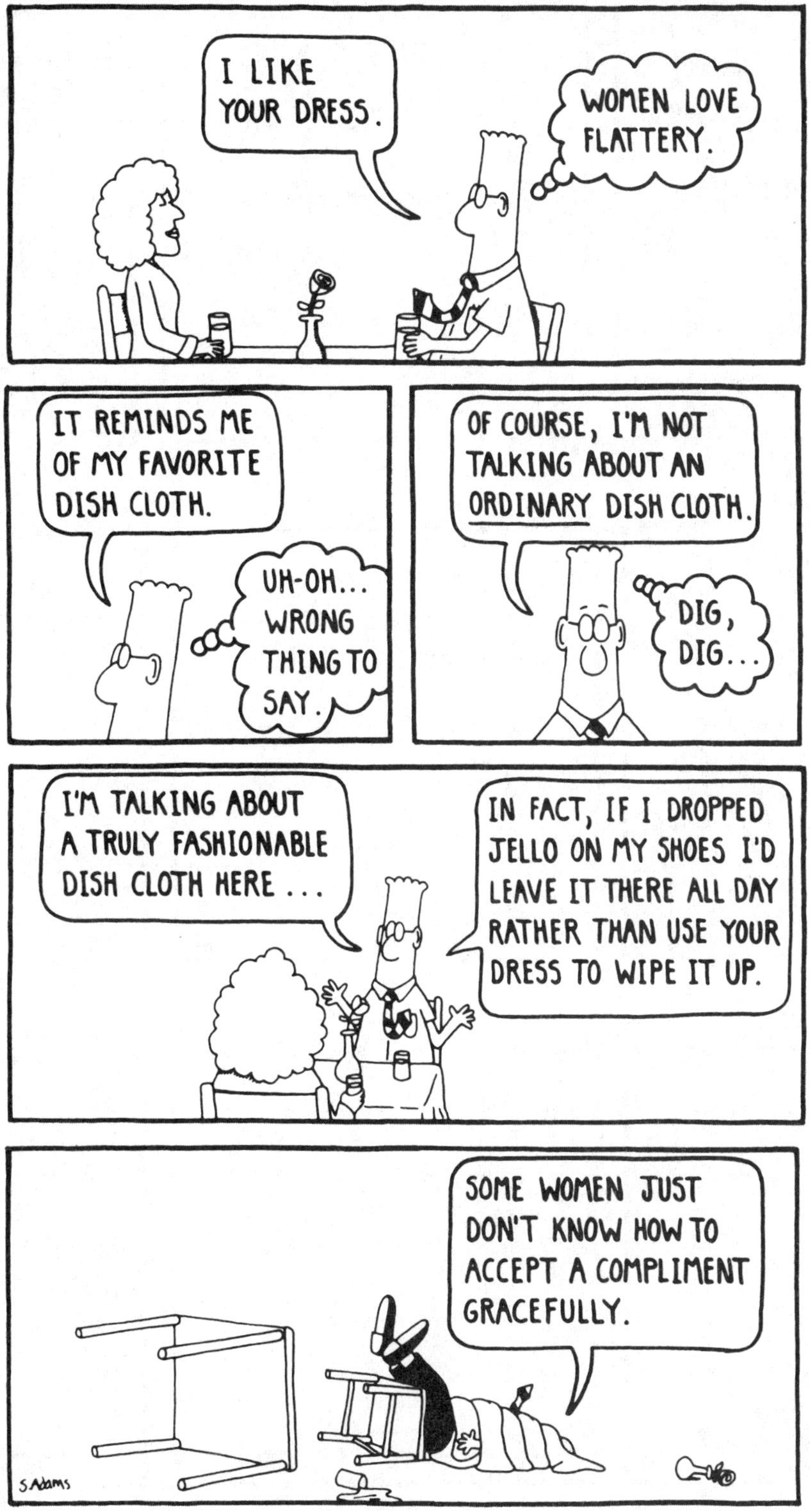
I LIKE YOUR DRESS.
WOMEN LOVE FLATTERY.
IT REMINDS ME OF MY FAVORITE DISH CLOTH.
UH-OH... WRONG THING TO SAY.
OF COURSE, I'M NOT TALKING ABOUT AN ORDINARY DISH CLOTH.
DIG, DIG...
I'M TALKING ABOUT A TRULY FASHIONABLE DISH CLOTH HERE ...
IN FACT, IF I DROPPED JELLO ON MY SHOES I'D LEAVE IT THERE ALL DAY RATHER THAN USE YOUR DRESS TO WIPE IT UP.
SOME WOMEN JUST DON'T KNOW HOW TO ACCEPT A COMPLIMENT GRACEFULLY.
S.Adams

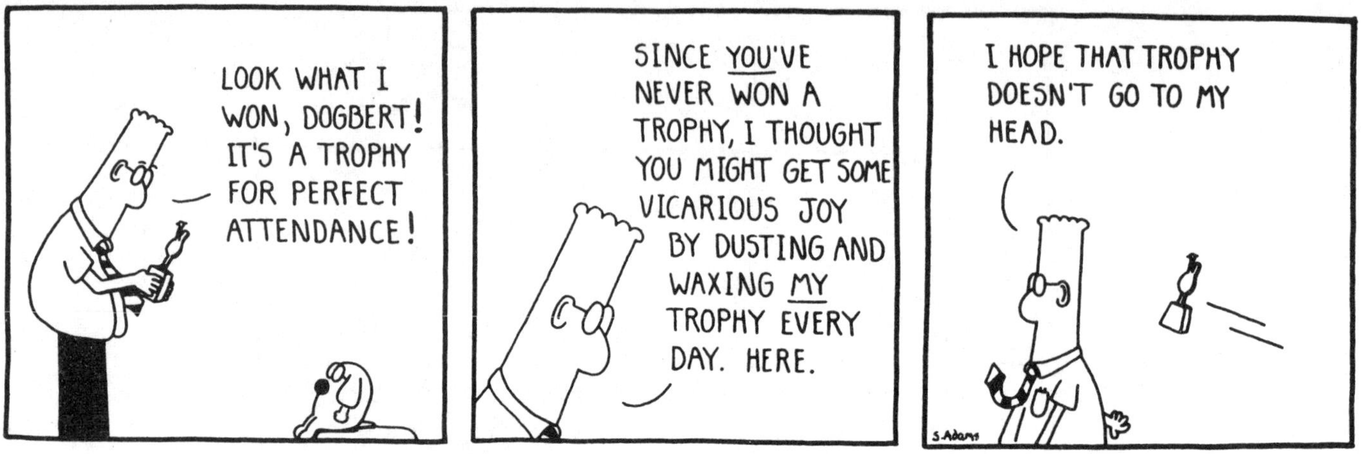
LOOK WHAT I WON, DOGBERT! IT'S A TROPHY FOR PERFECT ATTENDANCE!
SINCE YOU'VE NEVER WON A TROPHY, I THOUGHT YOU MIGHT GET SOME VICARIOUS JOY BY DUSTING AND WAXING MY TROPHY EVERY DAY. HERE.
I HOPE THAT TROPHY DOESN'T GO TO MY HEAD.
S.Adams

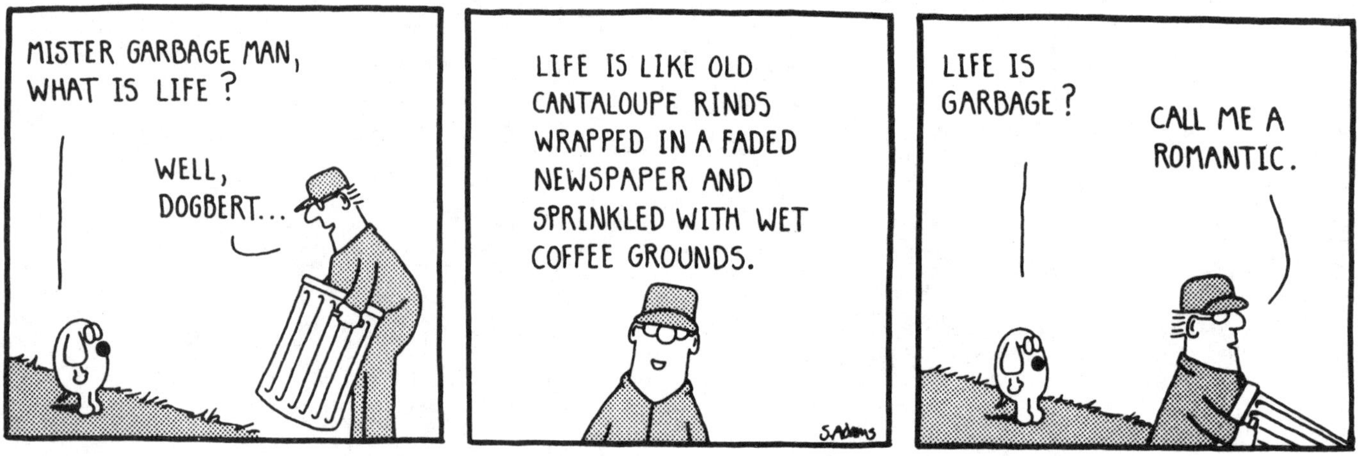
MISTER GARBAGE MAN, WHAT IS LIFE?
WELL, DOGBERT...
LIFE IS LIKE OLD CANTALOUPE RINDS WRAPPED IN A FADED NEWSPAPER AND SPRINKLED WITH WET COFFEE GROUNDS.
S.Adams
LIFE IS GARBAGE?
CALL ME A ROMANTIC.

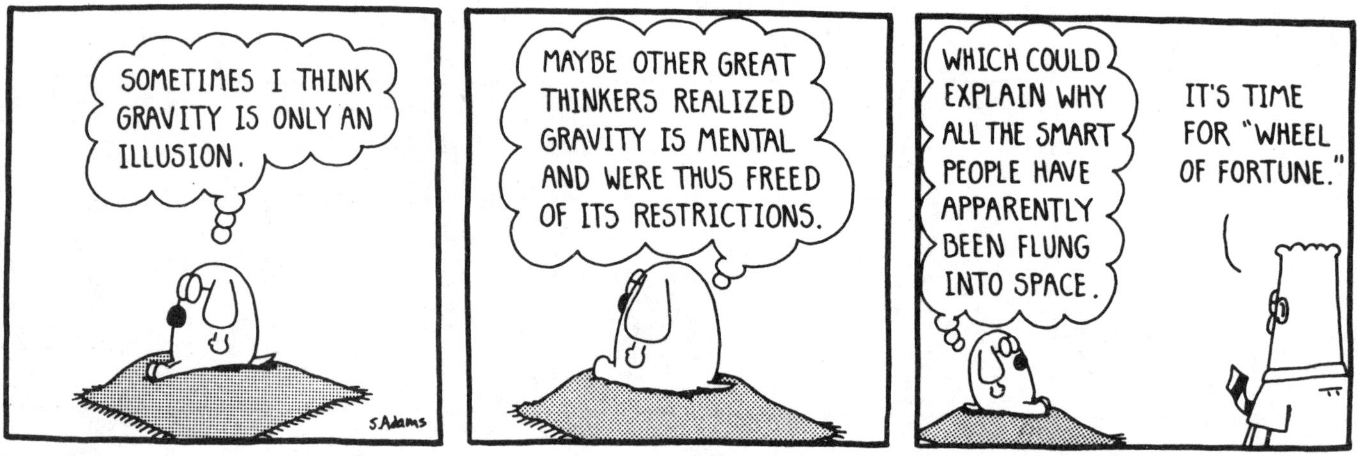
SOMETIMES I THINK GRAVITY IS ONLY AN ILLUSION.
S.Adams
MAYBE OTHER GREAT THINKERS REALIZED GRAVITY IS MENTAL AND WERE THUS FREED OF ITS RESTRICTIONS.
WHICH COULD EXPLAIN WHY ALL THE SMART PEOPLE HAVE APPARENTLY BEEN FLUNG INTO SPACE.
IT'S TIME FOR "WHEEL OF FORTUNE."

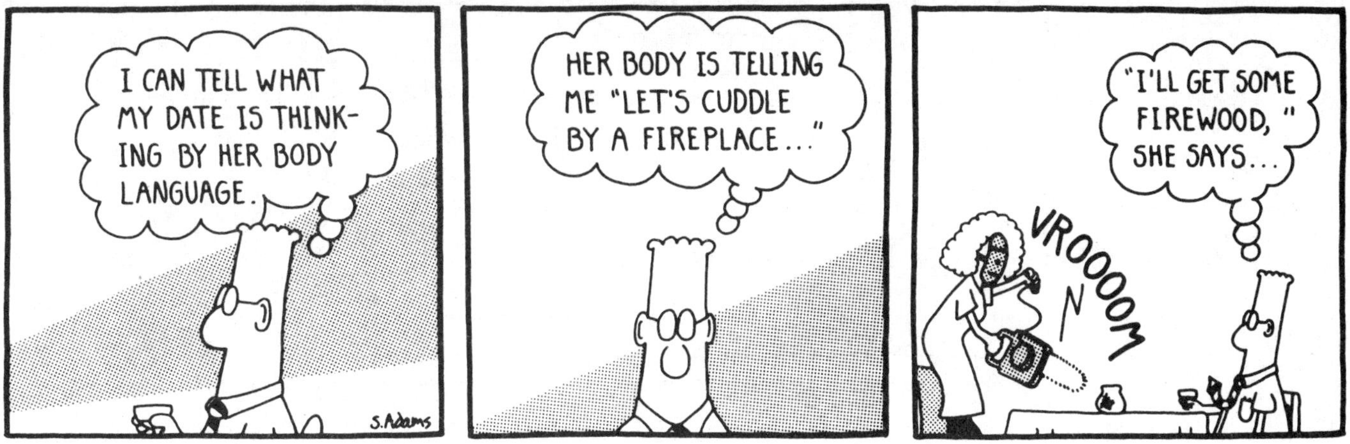
I CAN TELL WHAT MY DATE IS THINKING BY HER BODY LANGUAGE.
S.Adams
HER BODY IS TELLING ME "LET'S CUDDLE BY A FIREPLACE..."
"I'LL GET SOME FIREWOOD," SHE SAYS...
VROOOOM

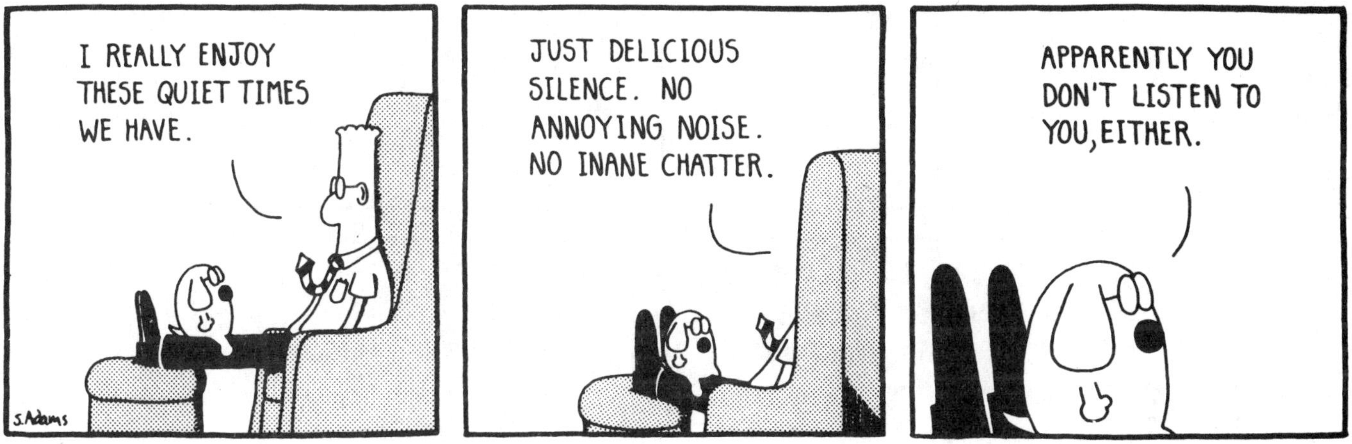
I REALLY ENJOY THESE QUIET TIMES WE HAVE.
S.Adams
JUST DELICIOUS SILENCE. NO ANNOYING NOISE. NO INANE CHATTER.
APPARENTLY YOU DON'T LISTEN TO YOU, EITHER.

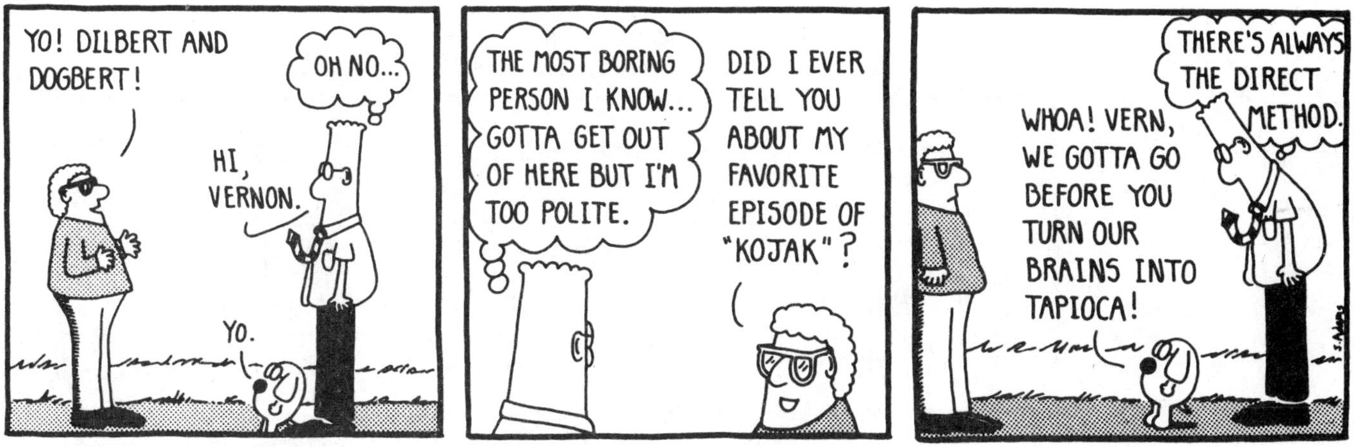
YO! DILBERT AND DOGBERT!
OH NO...
HI, VERNON.
YO.
THE MOST BORING PERSON I KNOW... GOTTA GET OUT OF HERE BUT I'M TOO POLITE.
DID I EVER TELL YOU ABOUT MY FAVORITE EPISODE OF "KOJAK"?
THERE'S ALWAYS THE DIRECT METHOD.
WHOA! VERN, WE GOTTA GO BEFORE YOU TURN OUR BRAINS INTO TAPIOCA!
S.Adams

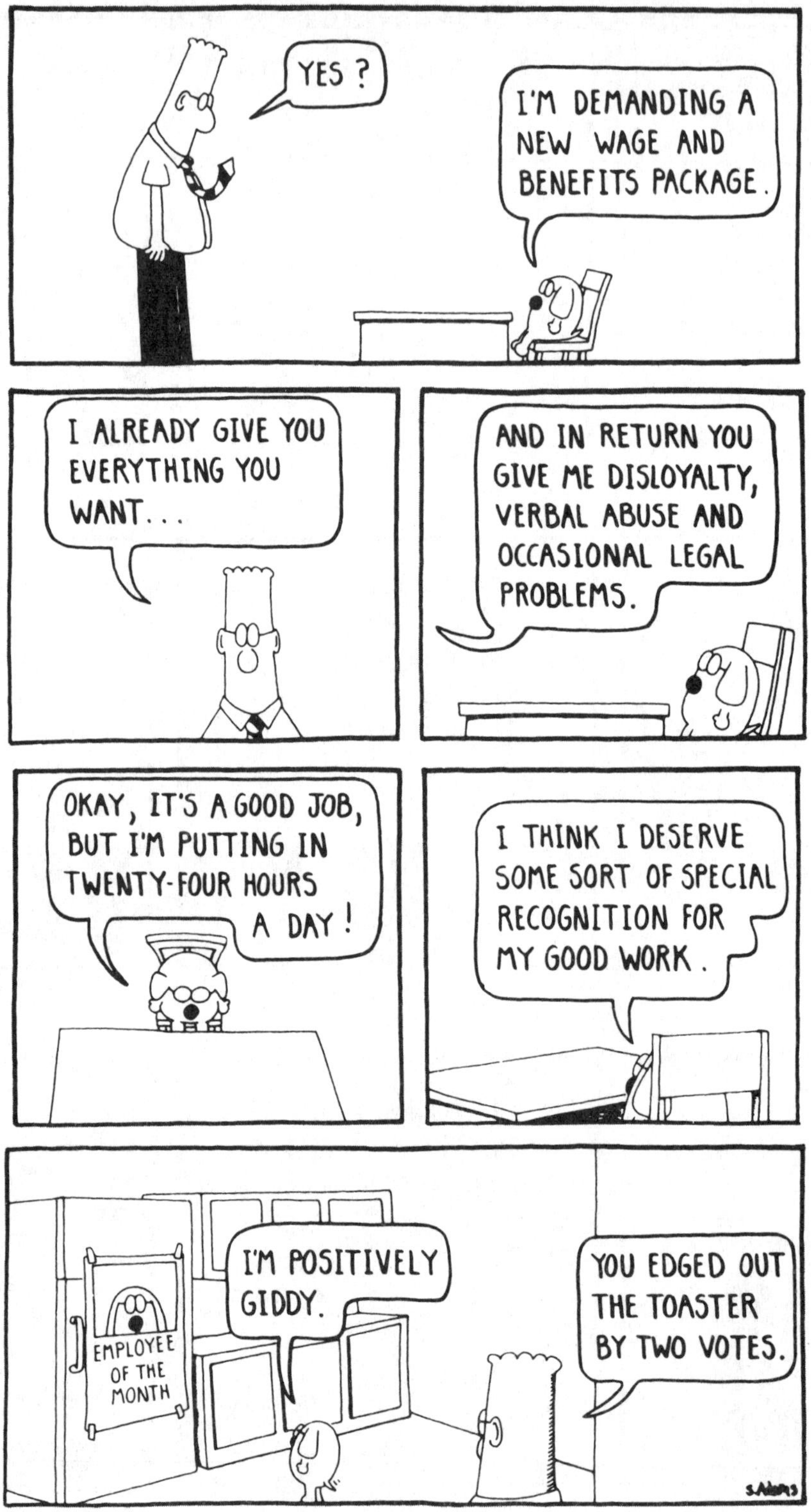
YES ?
I'M DEMANDING A NEW WAGE AND BENEFITS PACKAGE.
I ALREADY GIVE YOU EVERYTHING YOU WANT...
AND IN RETURN YOU GIVE ME DISLOYALTY, VERBAL ABUSE AND OCCASIONAL LEGAL PROBLEMS.
OKAY, IT'S A GOOD JOB, BUT I'M PUTTING IN TWENTY-FOUR HOURS A DAY!
I THINK I DESERVE SOME SORT OF SPECIAL RECOGNITION FOR MY GOOD WORK.
EMPLOYEE OF THE MONTH
I'M POSITIVELY GIDDY.
YOU EDGED OUT THE TOASTER BY TWO VOTES.
S.ADAMS

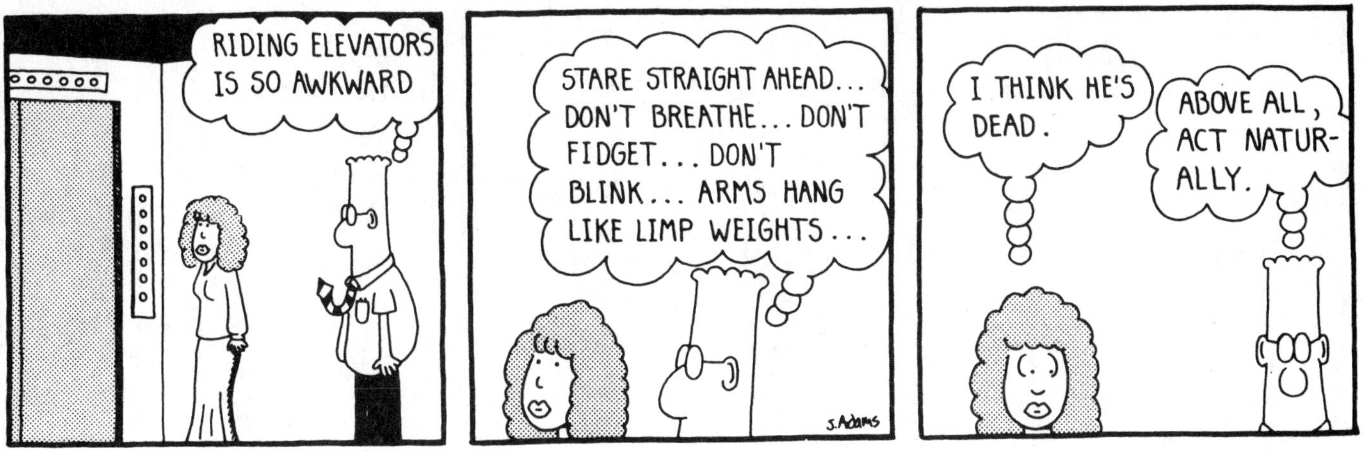
RIDING ELEVATORS IS SO AWKWARD
STARE STRAIGHT AHEAD... DON'T BREATHE... DON'T FIDGET... DON'T BLINK... ARMS HANG LIKE LIMP WEIGHTS...
S.Adams
I THINK HE'S DEAD.
ABOVE ALL, ACT NATURALLY.

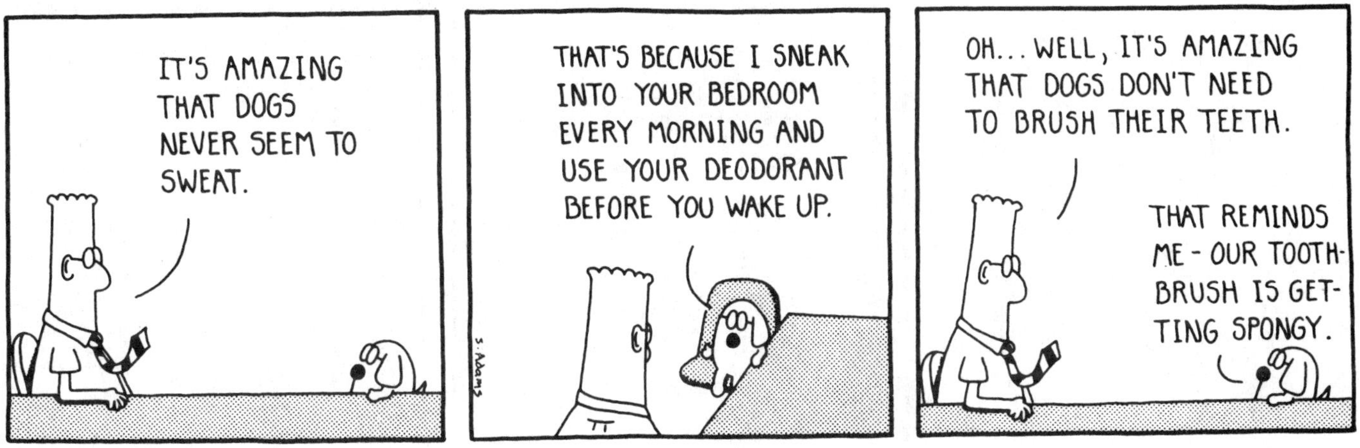
IT'S AMAZING THAT DOGS NEVER SEEM TO SWEAT.
THAT'S BECAUSE I SNEAK INTO YOUR BEDROOM EVERY MORNING AND USE YOUR DEODORANT BEFORE YOU WAKE UP.
S.Adams
OH... WELL, IT'S AMAZING THAT DOGS DON'T NEED TO BRUSH THEIR TEETH.
THAT REMINDS ME - OUR TOOTHBRUSH IS GETTING SPONGY.

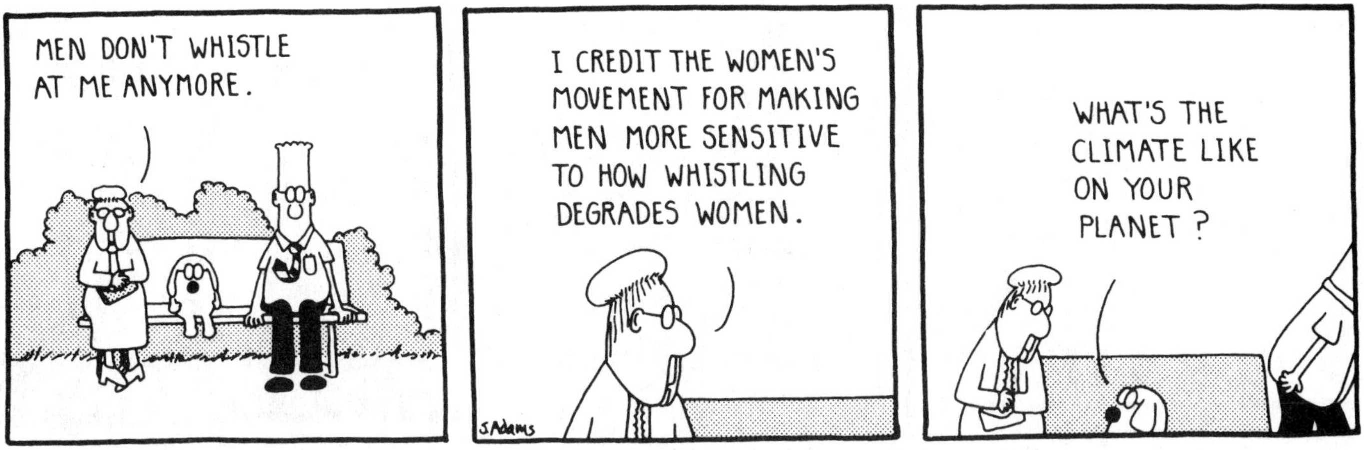
MEN DON'T WHISTLE AT ME ANYMORE.
I CREDIT THE WOMEN'S MOVEMENT FOR MAKING MEN MORE SENSITIVE TO HOW WHISTLING DEGRADES WOMEN.
S.Adams
WHAT'S THE CLIMATE LIKE ON YOUR PLANET ?

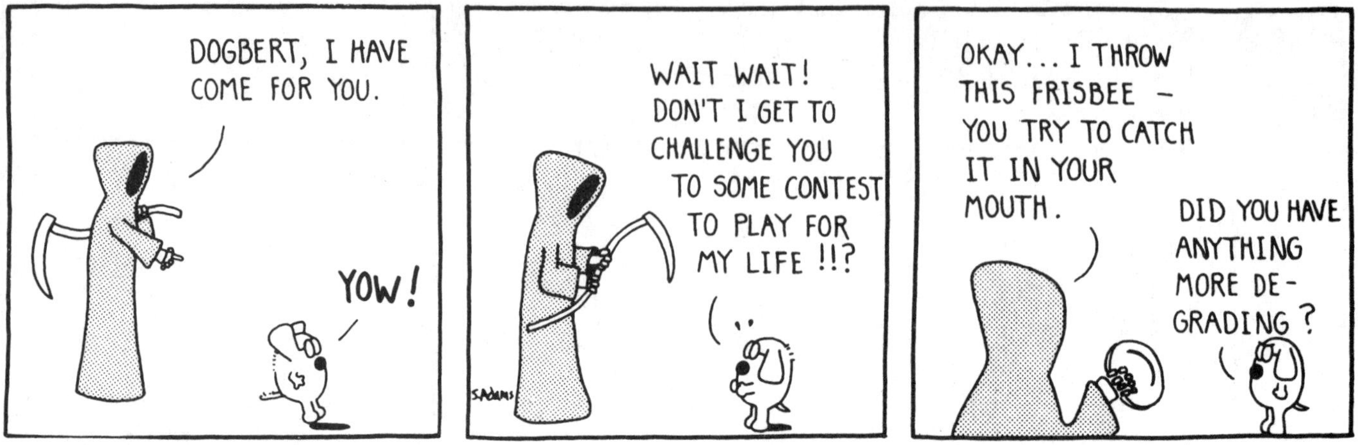
DOGBERT, I HAVE COME FOR YOU.
YOW!
WAIT WAIT! DON'T I GET TO CHALLENGE YOU TO SOME CONTEST TO PLAY FOR MY LIFE !!?
OKAY... I THROW THIS FRISBEE – YOU TRY TO CATCH IT IN YOUR MOUTH.
DID YOU HAVE ANYTHING MORE DE-GRADING ?
S.Adams

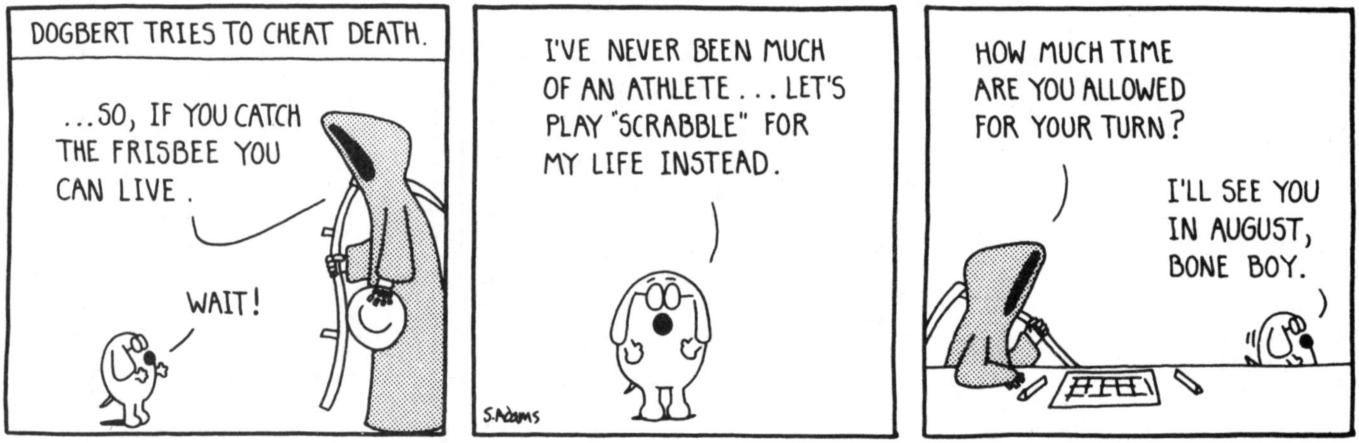
DOGBERT TRIES TO CHEAT DEATH.
...SO, IF YOU CATCH THE FRISBEE YOU CAN LIVE.
WAIT!
I'VE NEVER BEEN MUCH OF AN ATHLETE... LET'S PLAY "SCRABBLE" FOR MY LIFE INSTEAD.
HOW MUCH TIME ARE YOU ALLOWED FOR YOUR TURN?
I'LL SEE YOU IN AUGUST, BONE BOY.
S.Adams

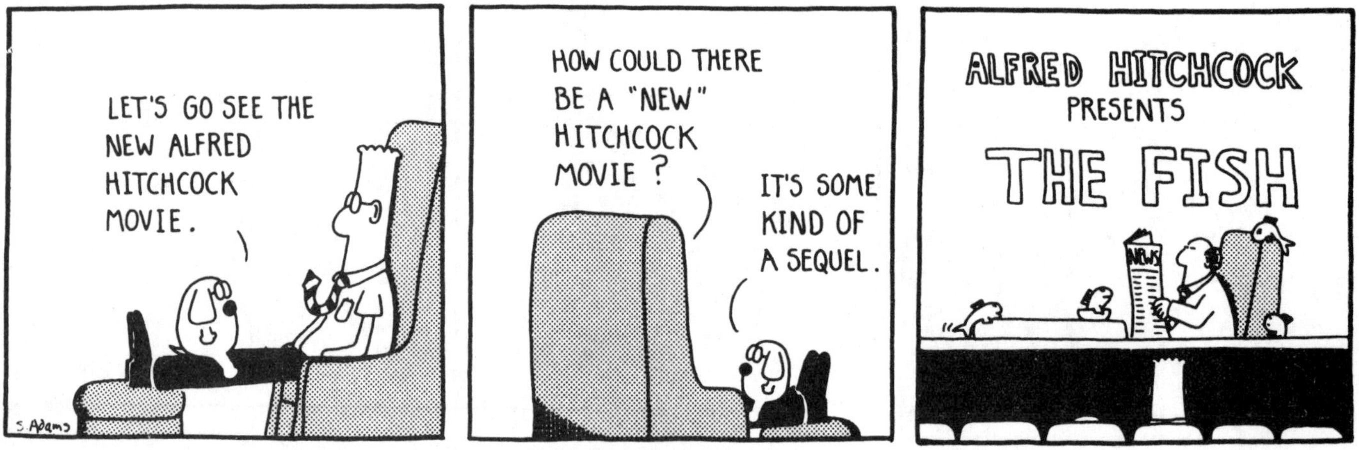
LET'S GO SEE THE NEW ALFRED HITCHCOCK MOVIE.
HOW COULD THERE BE A "NEW" HITCHCOCK MOVIE ?
IT'S SOME KIND OF A SEQUEL.
ALFRED HITCHCOCK PRESENTS
THE FISH
NEWS
S.Adams

A HOME VIDEO?
"DOGBERT VERSUS GODZILLA." WE'LL USE BOB THE DINOSAUR AS GODZILLA AND YOU CAN BE RAYMOND BURR!
SHOULDN'T GODZILLA GET TOP BILLING?
QUIET ON THE SET!!
DOGBERT IS LETTING ME BE THE "KEY GRIP."
DARN! ALL I GOT WAS THE RAYMOND BURR ROLE.
IN THIS FIRST SCENE, BOB, YOU RIP THE ARMS OFF THE "KEN" DOLL WHILE BARBIE AND SKIPPER WATCH IN HORROR.
S. Adams
DILBERT, YOU'LL BE EATING A CHEESEBURGER AND THE SHOCK WAVES WILL CAUSE YOU TO SMOOSH IT INTO YOUR FACE.
THEN I COME IN AND WASTE BOTH OF YOU WITH A FIRE EXTINGUISH-ER.
RAYMOND BURR DIES?
WHAT, NO SEQUEL?

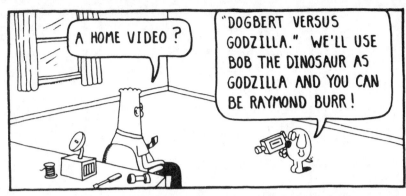

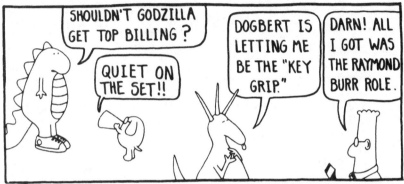

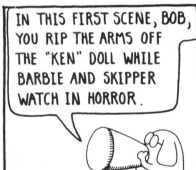

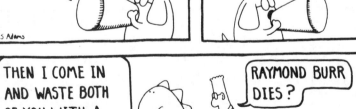

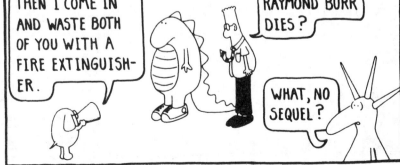

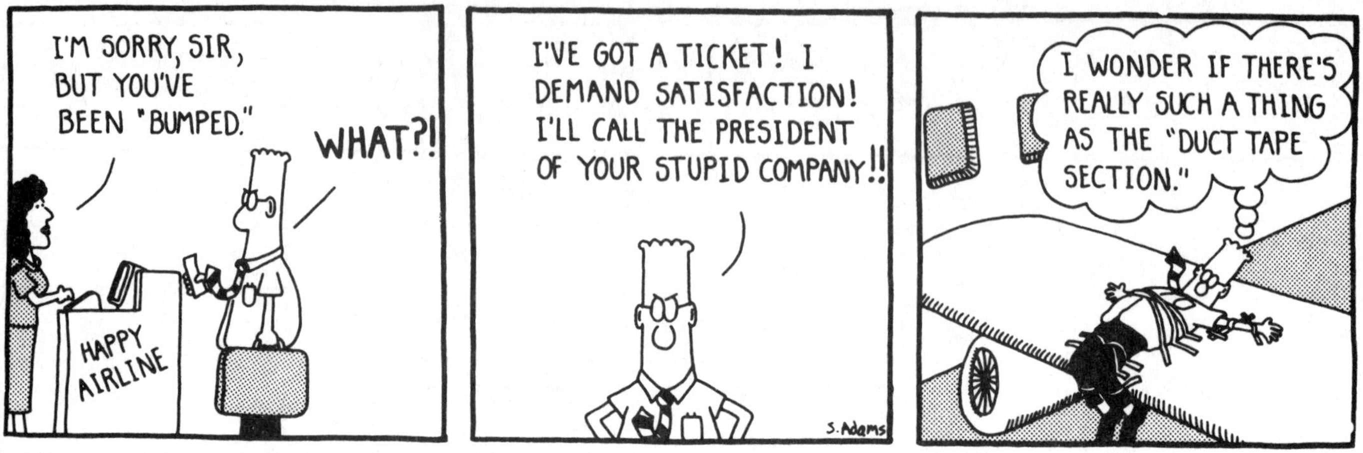
I'M SORRY, SIR, BUT YOU'VE BEEN "BUMPED."
WHAT?!
HAPPY AIRLINE
I'VE GOT A TICKET! I DEMAND SATISFACTION! I'LL CALL THE PRESIDENT OF YOUR STUPID COMPANY!!
I WONDER IF THERE'S REALLY SUCH A THING AS THE "DUCT TAPE SECTION."
S.Adams

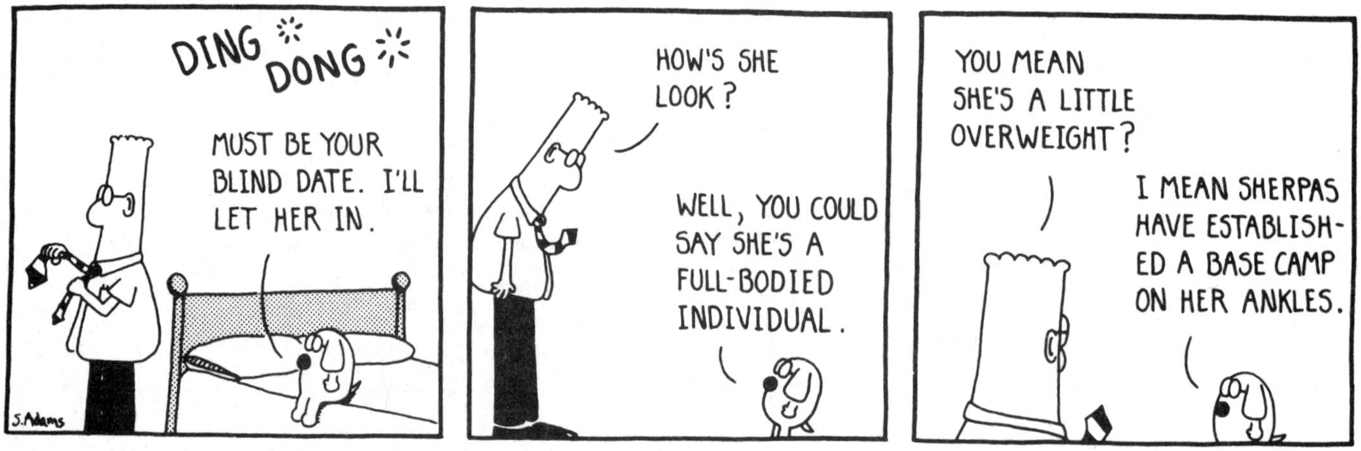
DING DONG
MUST BE YOUR BLIND DATE. I'LL LET HER IN.
S.Adams
HOW'S SHE LOOK?
WELL, YOU COULD SAY SHE'S A FULL-BODIED INDIVIDUAL.
YOU MEAN SHE'S A LITTLE OVERWEIGHT?
I MEAN SHERPAS HAVE ESTABLISHED A BASE CAMP ON HER ANKLES.

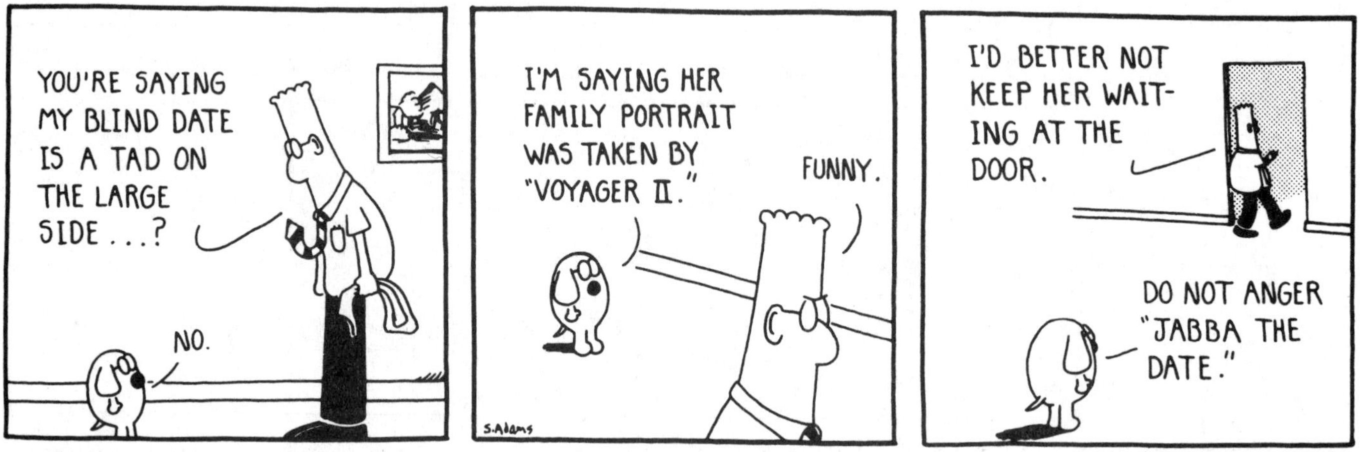
YOU'RE SAYING MY BLIND DATE IS A TAD ON THE LARGE SIDE...?
NO.
I'M SAYING HER FAMILY PORTRAIT WAS TAKEN BY "VOYAGER II."
FUNNY.
S.Adams
I'D BETTER NOT KEEP HER WAITING AT THE DOOR.
DO NOT ANGER "JABBA THE DATE."

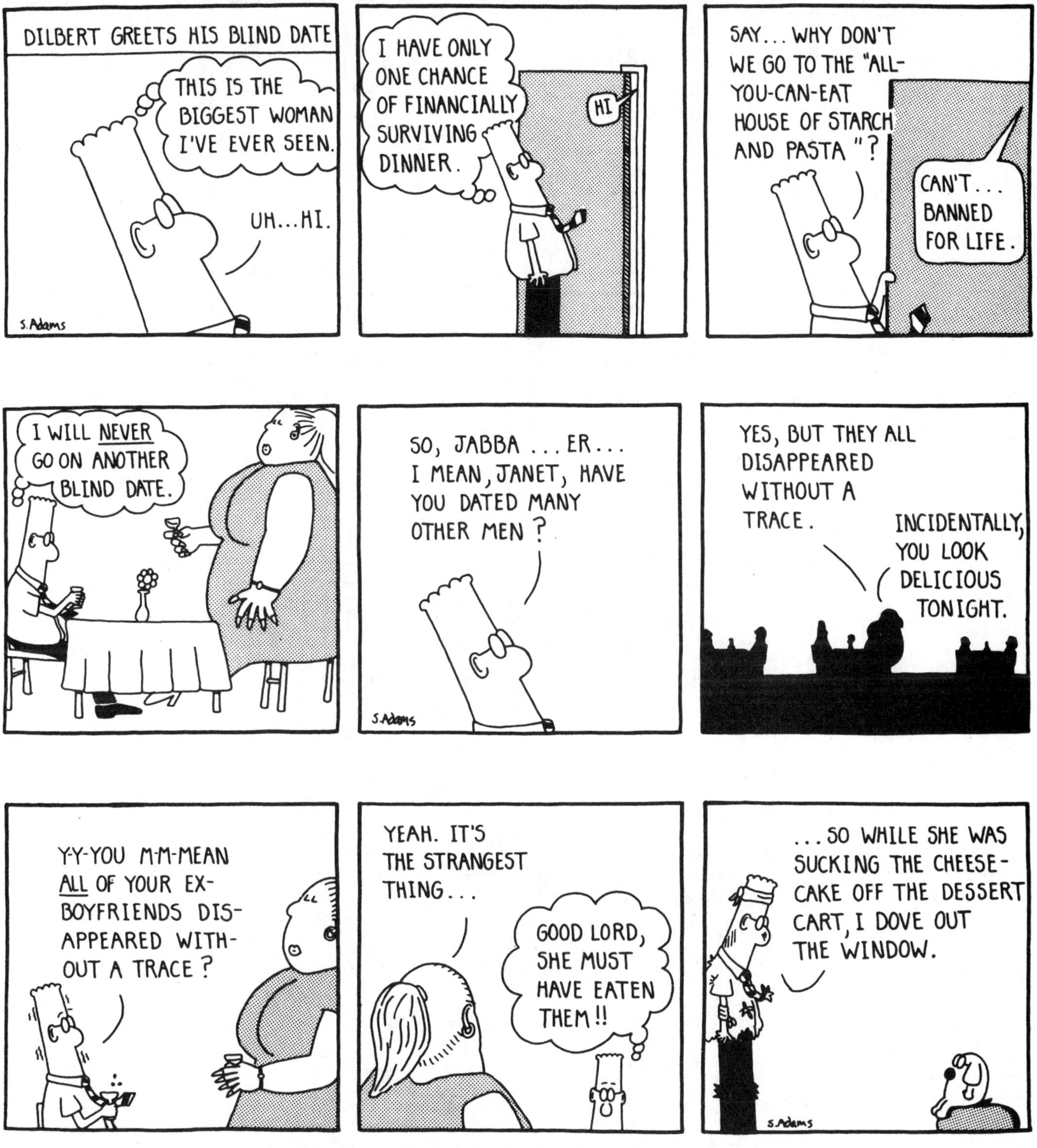
DILBERT GREETS HIS BLIND DATE
THIS IS THE BIGGEST WOMAN I'VE EVER SEEN.
UH...HI.
I HAVE ONLY ONE CHANCE OF FINANCIALLY SURVIVING DINNER.
HI
SAY... WHY DON'T WE GO TO THE "ALL-YOU-CAN-EAT HOUSE OF STARCH AND PASTA"?
CAN'T... BANNED FOR LIFE.
S. Adams
I WILL NEVER GO ON ANOTHER BLIND DATE.
SO, JABBA ... ER... I MEAN, JANET, HAVE YOU DATED MANY OTHER MEN?
YES, BUT THEY ALL DISAPPEARED WITHOUT A TRACE.
INCIDENTALLY, YOU LOOK DELICIOUS TONIGHT.
S. Adams
Y-Y-YOU M-M-MEAN ALL OF YOUR EX-BOYFRIENDS DIS-APPEARED WITH-OUT A TRACE?
YEAH. IT'S THE STRANGEST THING...
GOOD LORD, SHE MUST HAVE EATEN THEM!!
...SO WHILE SHE WAS SUCKING THE CHEESE-CAKE OFF THE DESSERT CART, I DOVE OUT THE WINDOW.
S. Adams

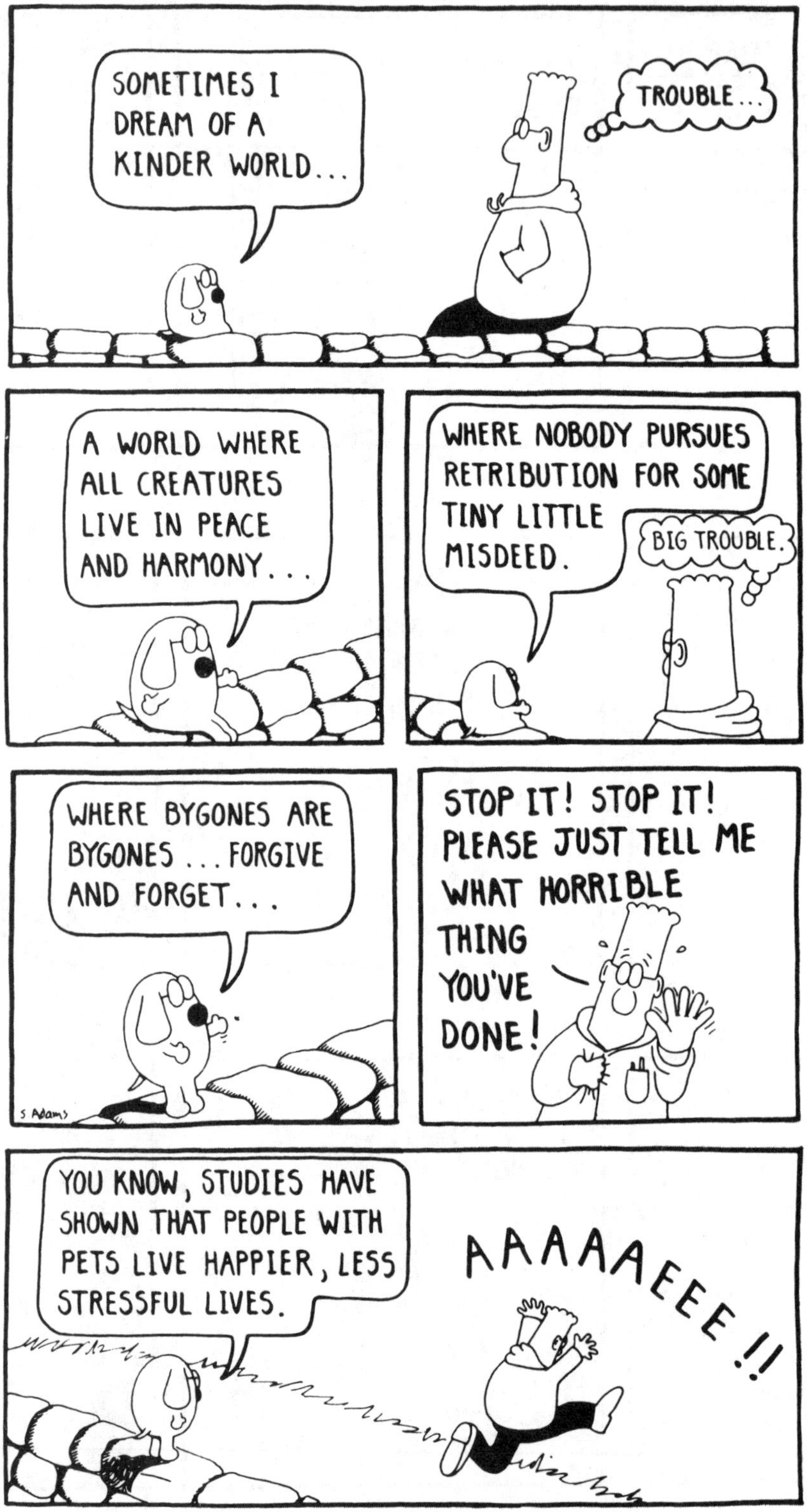
SOMETIMES I DREAM OF A KINDER WORLD...
TROUBLE...
A WORLD WHERE ALL CREATURES LIVE IN PEACE AND HARMONY...
WHERE NOBODY PURSUES RETRIBUTION FOR SOME TINY LITTLE MISDEED.
BIG TROUBLE.
WHERE BYGONES ARE BYGONES ... FORGIVE AND FORGET...
S. Adams
STOP IT! STOP IT! PLEASE JUST TELL ME WHAT HORRIBLE THING YOU'VE DONE!
YOU KNOW, STUDIES HAVE SHOWN THAT PEOPLE WITH PETS LIVE HAPPIER, LESS STRESSFUL LIVES.
AAAAAEEE!!

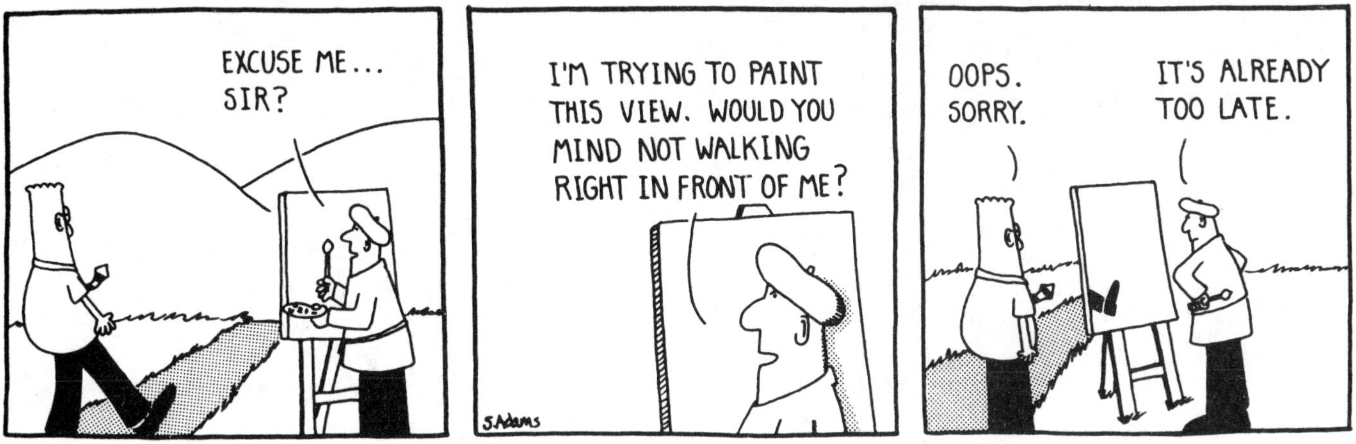
EXCUSE ME... SIR?
I'M TRYING TO PAINT THIS VIEW. WOULD YOU MIND NOT WALKING RIGHT IN FRONT OF ME?
S.Adams
OOPS. SORRY.
IT'S ALREADY TOO LATE.

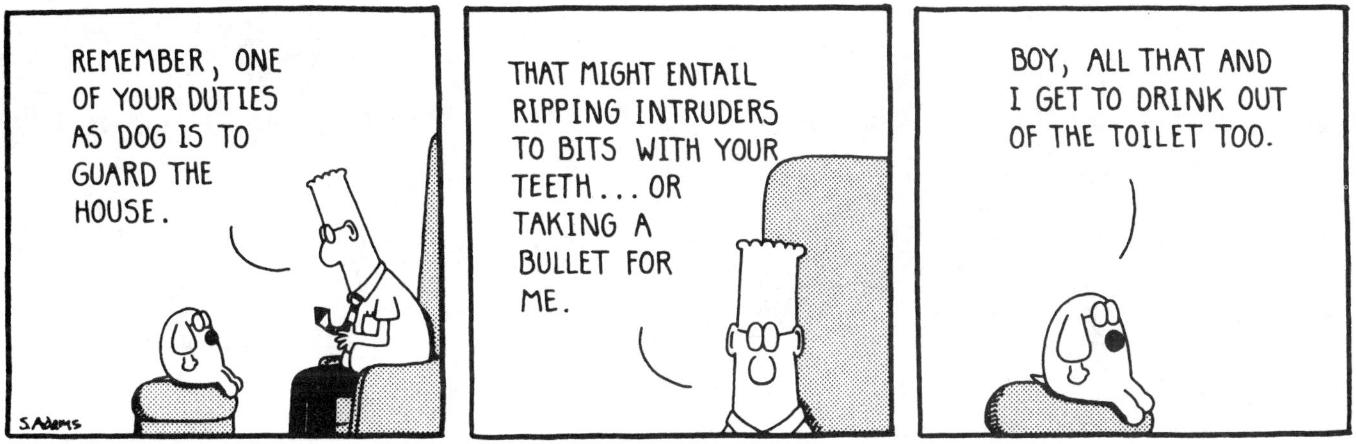
REMEMBER, ONE OF YOUR DUTIES AS DOG IS TO GUARD THE HOUSE.
S.Adams
THAT MIGHT ENTAIL RIPPING INTRUDERS TO BITS WITH YOUR TEETH... OR TAKING A BULLET FOR ME.
BOY, ALL THAT AND I GET TO DRINK OUT OF THE TOILET TOO.

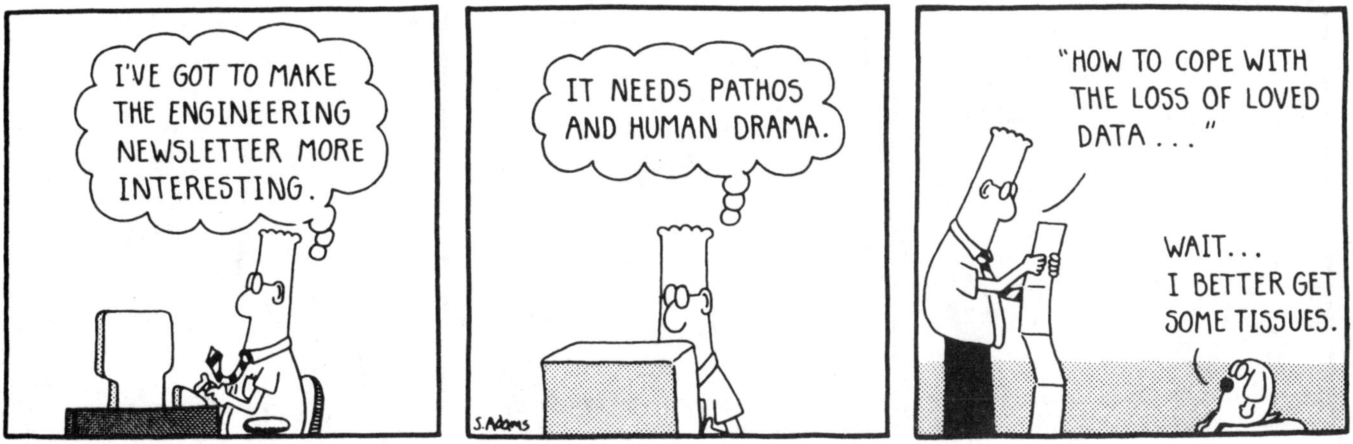
I'VE GOT TO MAKE THE ENGINEERING NEWSLETTER MORE INTERESTING.
IT NEEDS PATHOS AND HUMAN DRAMA.
S.Adams
"HOW TO COPE WITH THE LOSS OF LOVED DATA..."
WAIT... I BETTER GET SOME TISSUES.

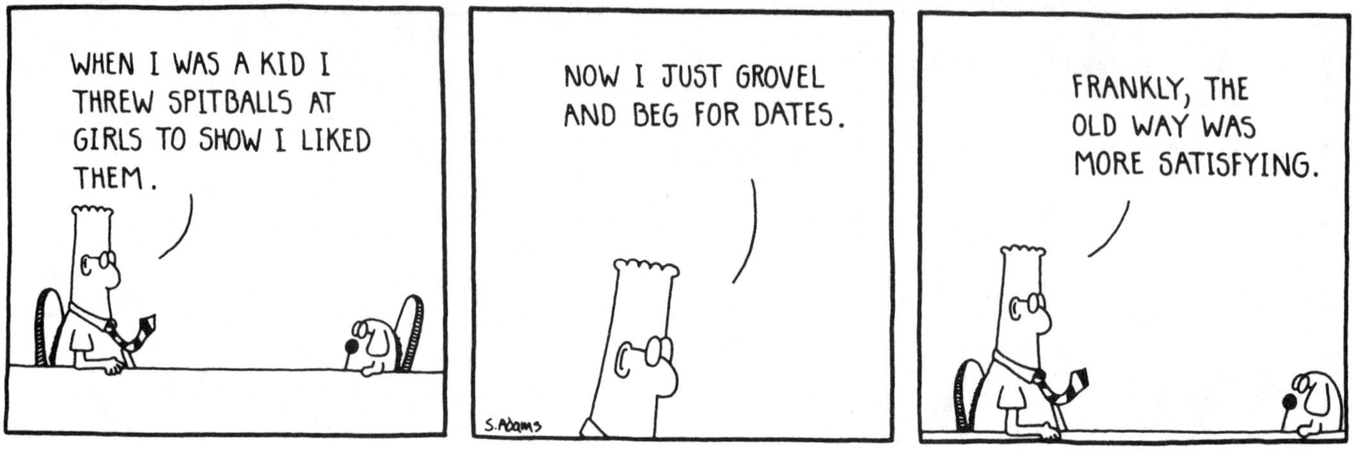
WHEN I WAS A KID I THREW SPITBALLS AT GIRLS TO SHOW I LIKED THEM.
NOW I JUST GROVEL AND BEG FOR DATES.
S. Adams
FRANKLY, THE OLD WAY WAS MORE SATISFYING.

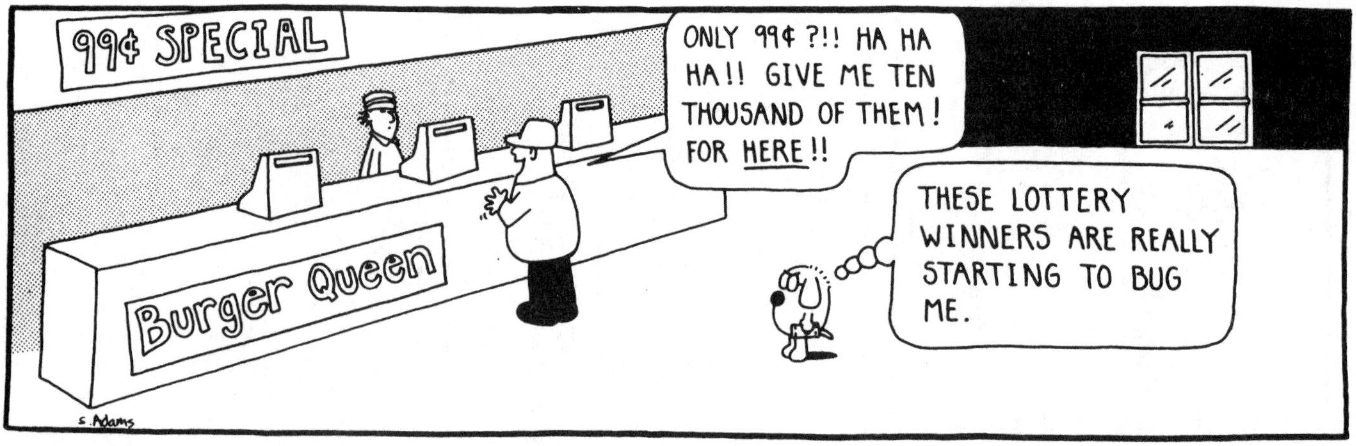
99¢ SPECIAL
Burger Queen
ONLY 99¢ ?!! HA HA HA!! GIVE ME TEN THOUSAND OF THEM! FOR HERE!!
THESE LOTTERY WINNERS ARE REALLY STARTING TO BUG ME.
S. Adams

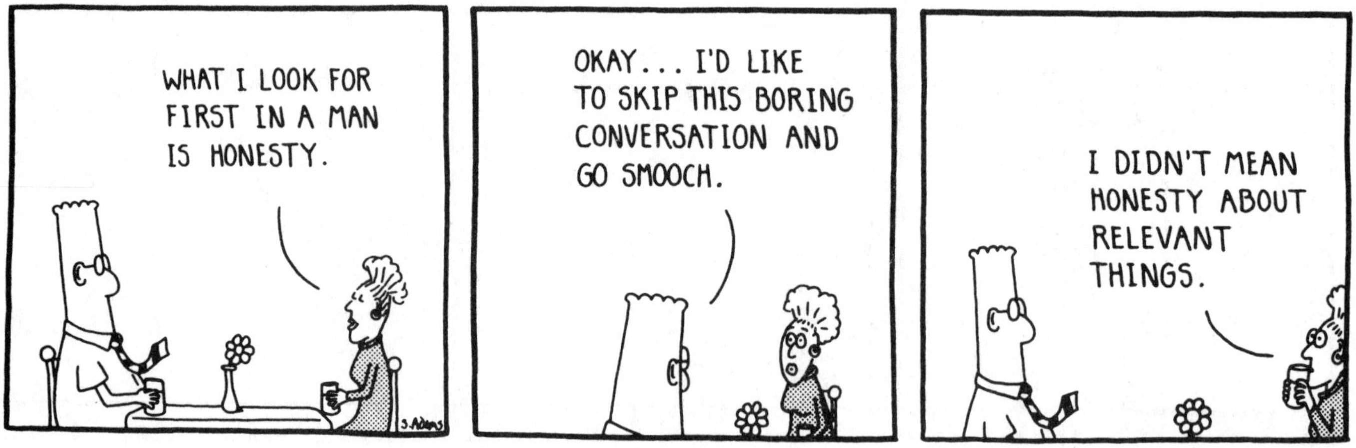
WHAT I LOOK FOR FIRST IN A MAN IS HONESTY.
S. Adams
OKAY... I'D LIKE TO SKIP THIS BORING CONVERSATION AND GO SMOOCH.
I DIDN'T MEAN HONESTY ABOUT RELEVANT THINGS.

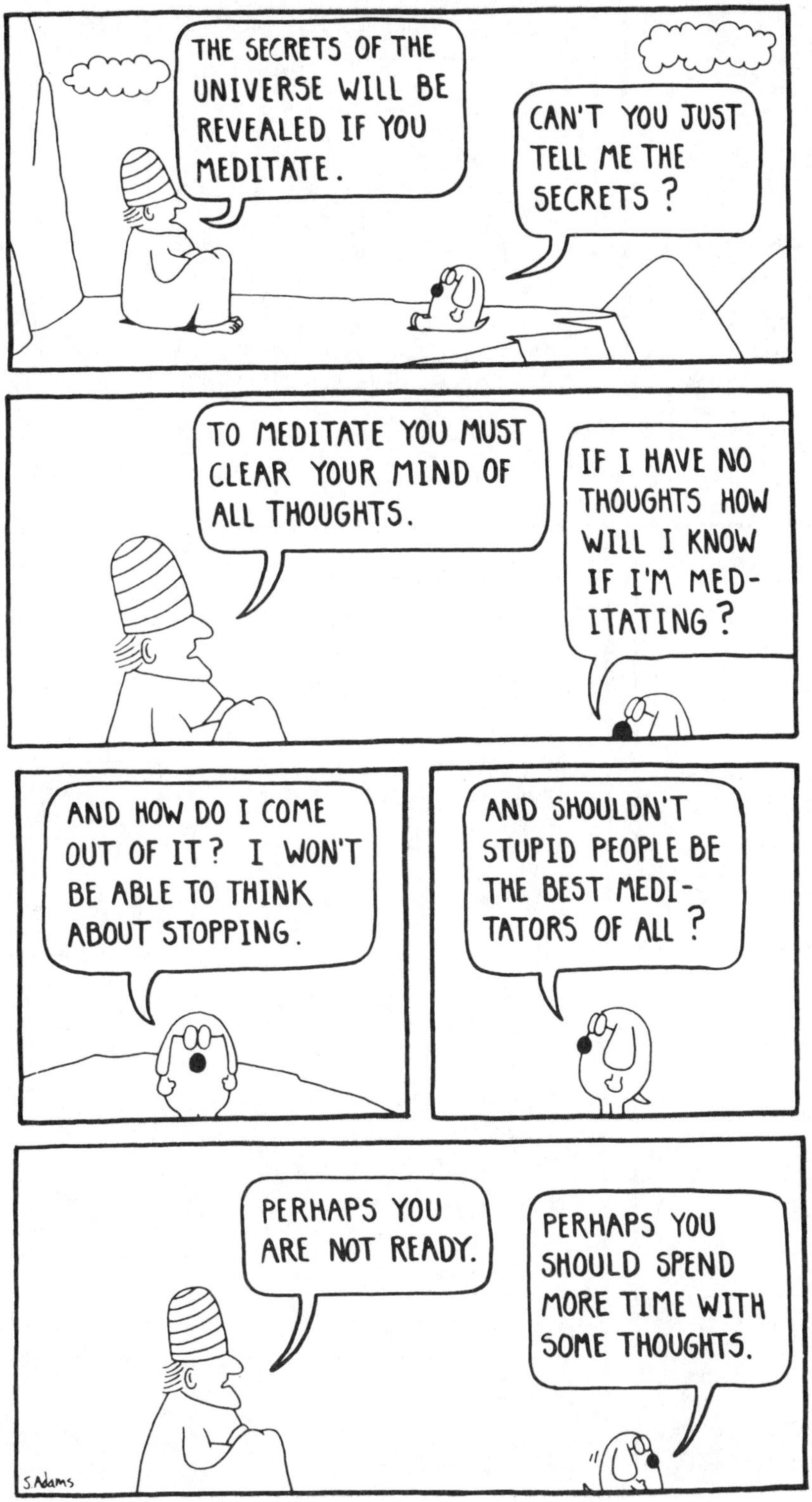
THE SECRETS OF THE UNIVERSE WILL BE REVEALED IF YOU MEDITATE.
CAN'T YOU JUST TELL ME THE SECRETS?
TO MEDITATE YOU MUST CLEAR YOUR MIND OF ALL THOUGHTS.
IF I HAVE NO THOUGHTS HOW WILL I KNOW IF I'M MED-ITATING?
AND HOW DO I COME OUT OF IT? I WON'T BE ABLE TO THINK ABOUT STOPPING.
AND SHOULDN'T STUPID PEOPLE BE THE BEST MEDI-TATORS OF ALL?
PERHAPS YOU ARE NOT READY.
PERHAPS YOU SHOULD SPEND MORE TIME WITH SOME THOUGHTS.
S. Adams

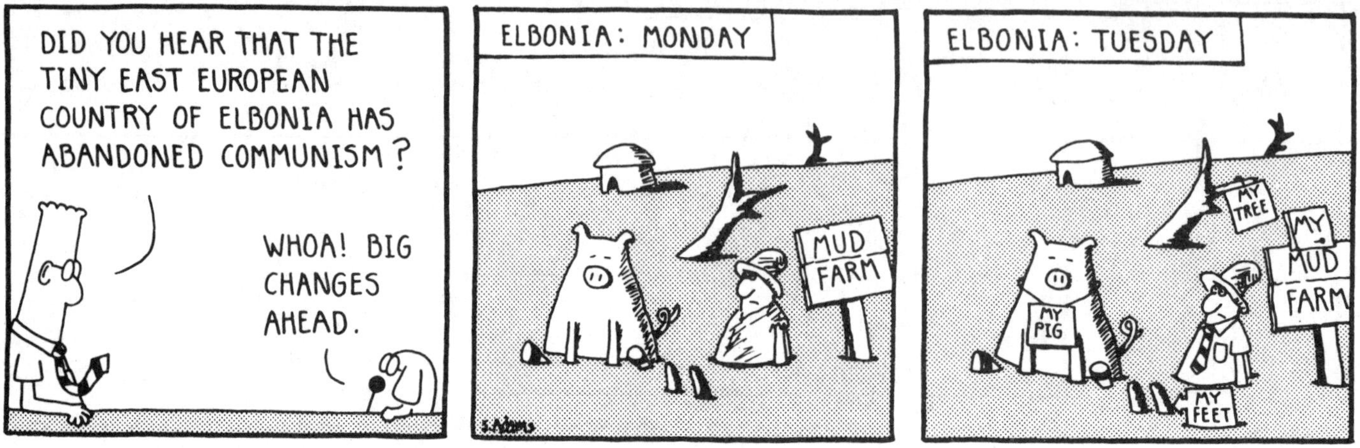
DID YOU HEAR THAT THE TINY EAST EUROPEAN COUNTRY OF ELBONIA HAS ABANDONED COMMUNISM?
WHOA! BIG CHANGES AHEAD.
ELBONIA: MONDAY
MUD FARM
S.Adams
ELBONIA: TUESDAY
MY TREE
MY
MUD FARM
MY PIG
MY FEET

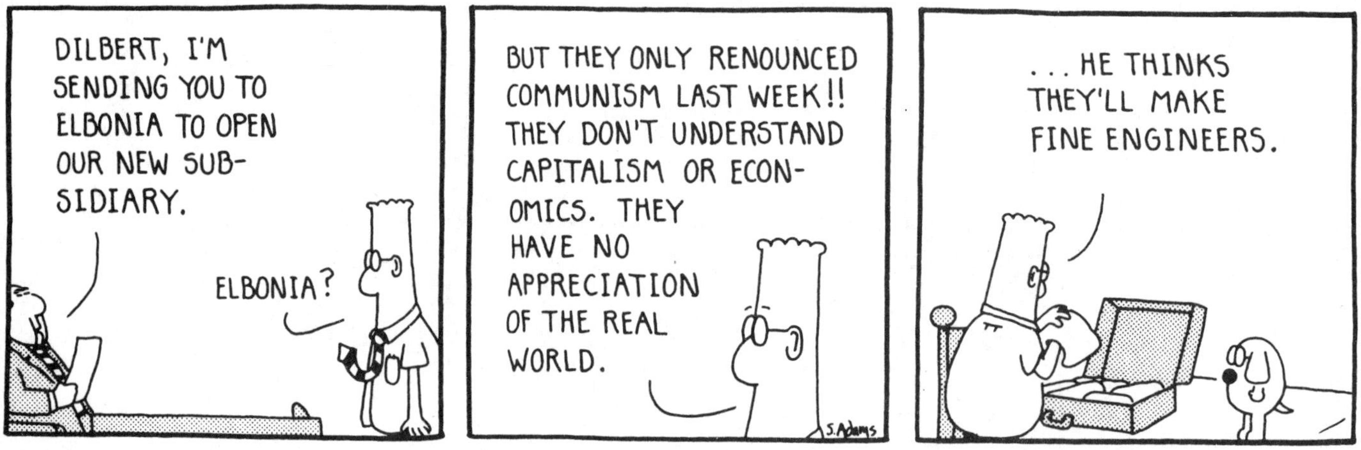
DILBERT, I'M SENDING YOU TO ELBONIA TO OPEN OUR NEW SUB-SIDIARY.
ELBONIA?
BUT THEY ONLY RENOUNCED COMMUNISM LAST WEEK!! THEY DON'T UNDERSTAND CAPITALISM OR ECON-OMICS. THEY HAVE NO APPRECIATION OF THE REAL WORLD.
S.Adams
. . . HE THINKS THEY'LL MAKE FINE ENGINEERS.

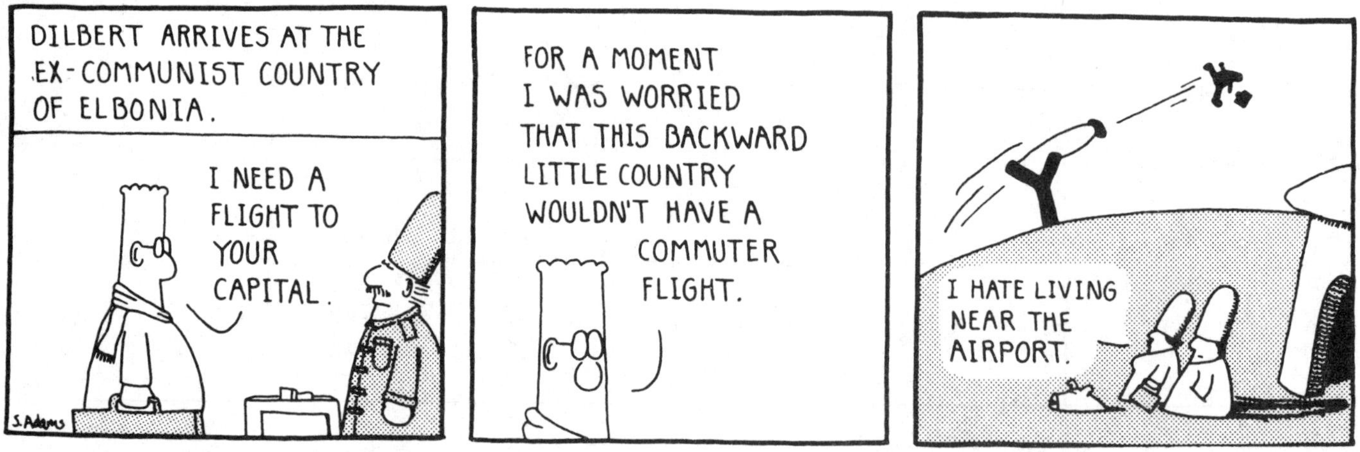
DILBERT ARRIVES AT THE EX-COMMUNIST COUNTRY OF ELBONIA.
I NEED A FLIGHT TO YOUR CAPITAL.
S.Adams
FOR A MOMENT I WAS WORRIED THAT THIS BACKWARD LITTLE COUNTRY WOULDN'T HAVE A COMMUTER FLIGHT.
I HATE LIVING NEAR THE AIRPORT.

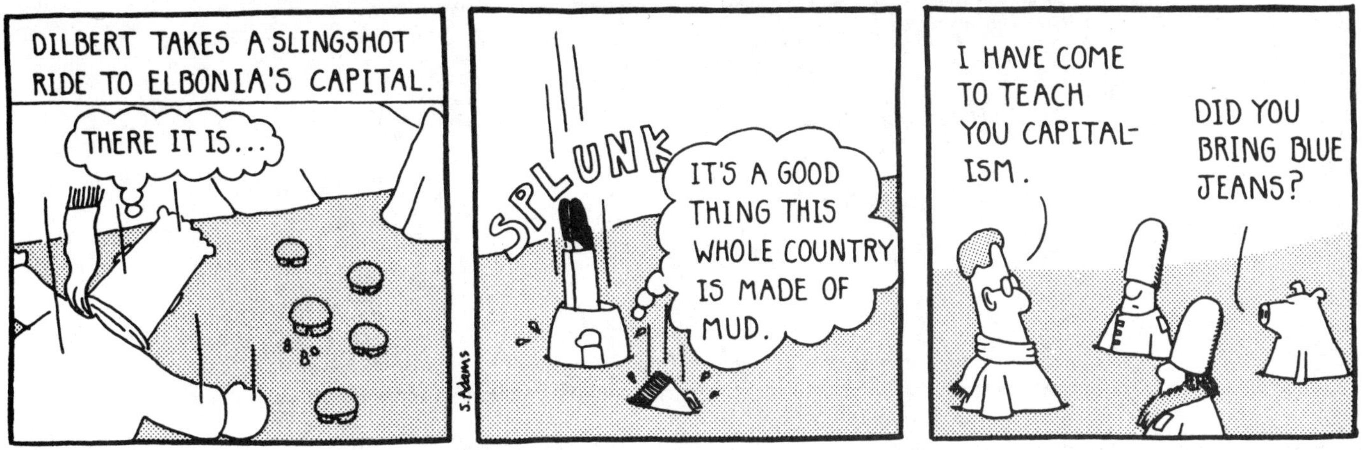

DILBERT TAKES A SLINGSHOT RIDE TO ELBONIA'S CAPITAL.
THERE IT IS...
SPLUNK
IT'S A GOOD THING THIS WHOLE COUNTRY IS MADE OF MUD.
S. Adams
I HAVE COME TO TEACH YOU CAPITALISM.
DID YOU BRING BLUE JEANS?

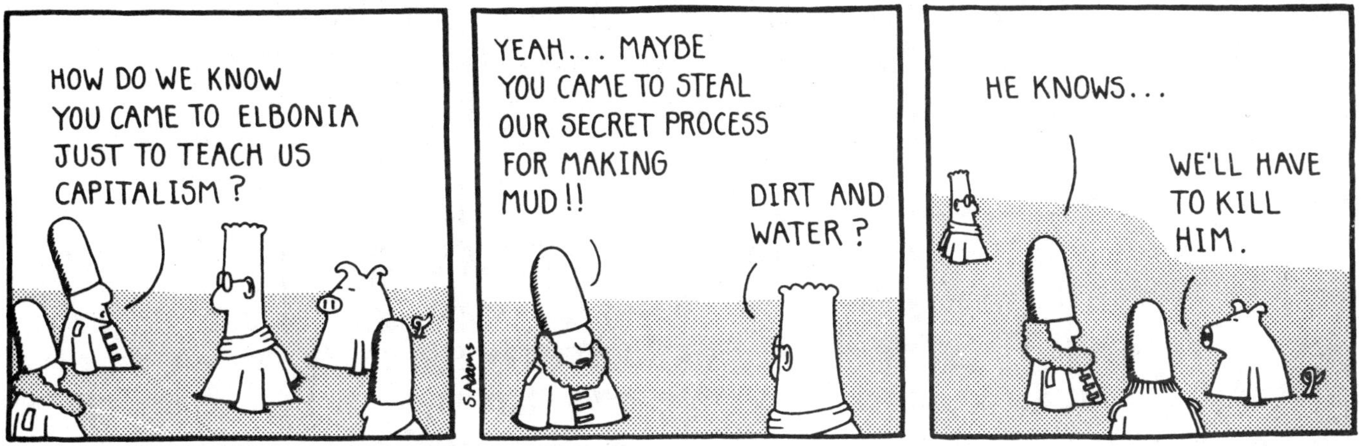

HOW DO WE KNOW YOU CAME TO ELBONIA JUST TO TEACH US CAPITALISM?
S. Adams
YEAH... MAYBE YOU CAME TO STEAL OUR SECRET PROCESS FOR MAKING MUD!!
DIRT AND WATER?
HE KNOWS...
WE'LL HAVE TO KILL HIM.

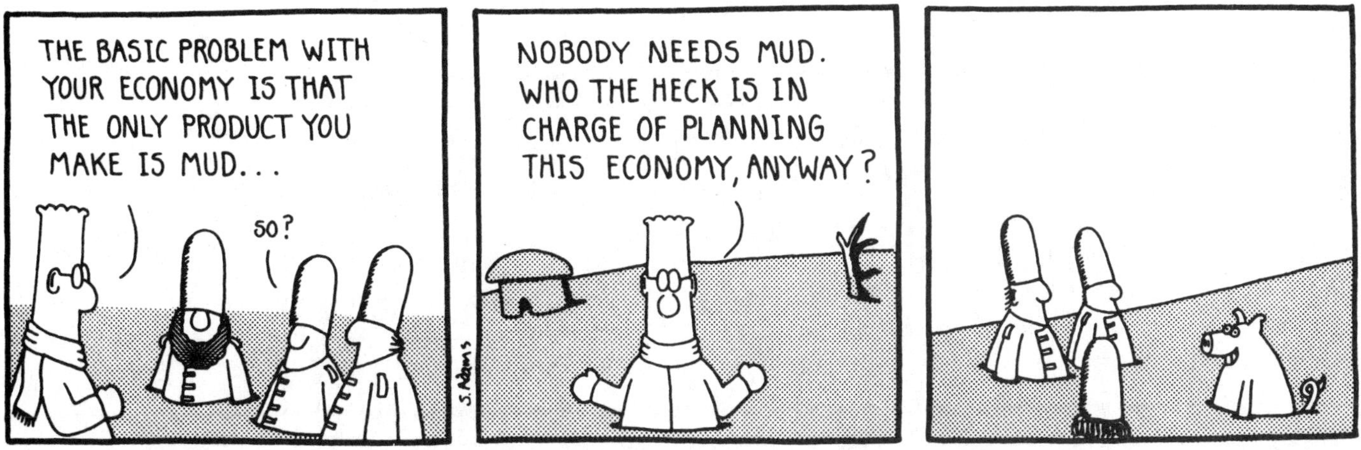

THE BASIC PROBLEM WITH YOUR ECONOMY IS THAT THE ONLY PRODUCT YOU MAKE IS MUD...
SO?
S. Adams
NOBODY NEEDS MUD. WHO THE HECK IS IN CHARGE OF PLANNING THIS ECONOMY, ANYWAY?

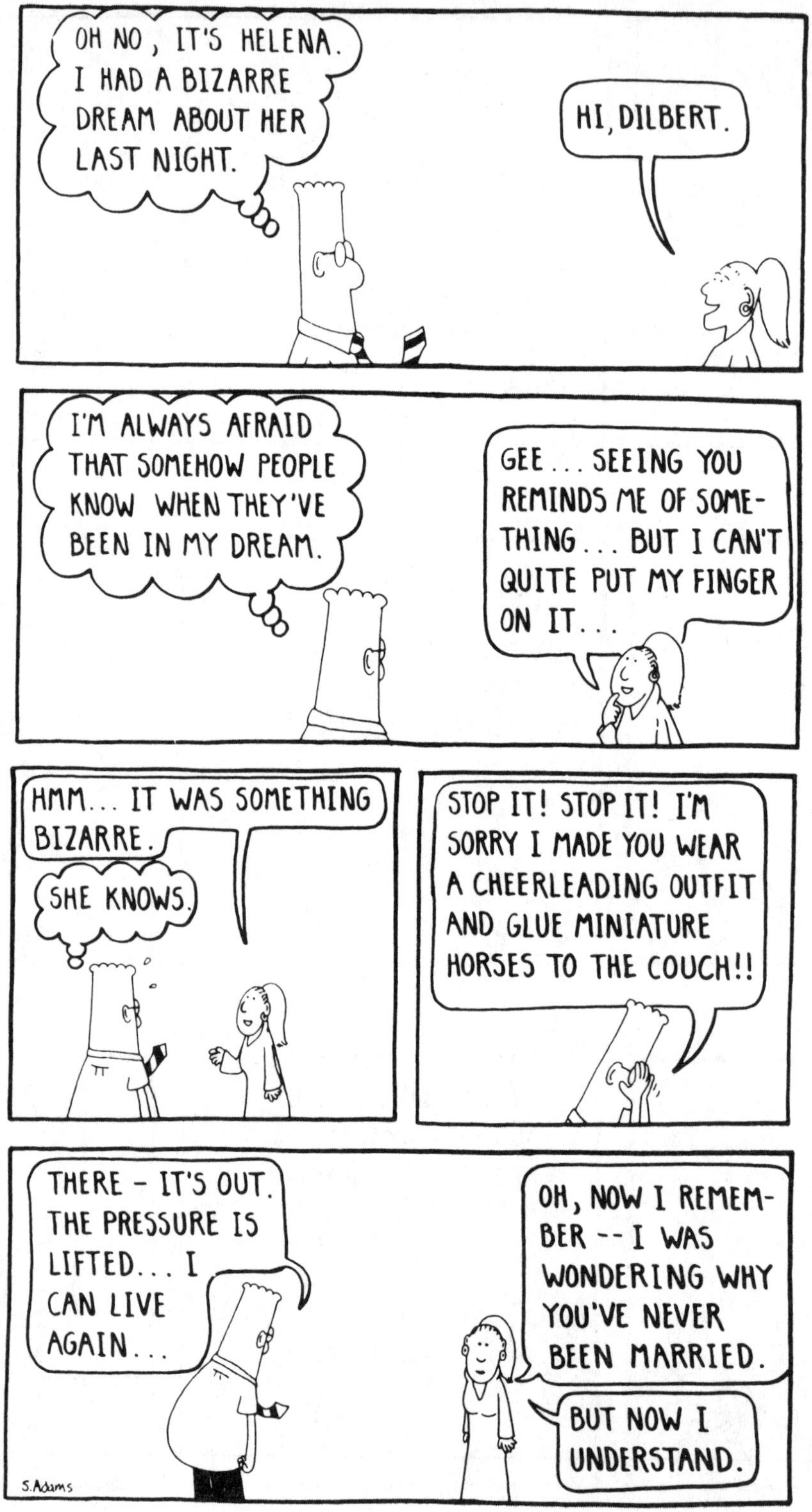
OH NO, IT'S HELENA. I HAD A BIZARRE DREAM ABOUT HER LAST NIGHT.
HI, DILBERT.
I'M ALWAYS AFRAID THAT SOMEHOW PEOPLE KNOW WHEN THEY'VE BEEN IN MY DREAM.
GEE... SEEING YOU REMINDS ME OF SOMETHING... BUT I CAN'T QUITE PUT MY FINGER ON IT...
HMM... IT WAS SOMETHING BIZARRE.
SHE KNOWS.
STOP IT! STOP IT! I'M SORRY I MADE YOU WEAR A CHEERLEADING OUTFIT AND GLUE MINIATURE HORSES TO THE COUCH!!
THERE - IT'S OUT. THE PRESSURE IS LIFTED... I CAN LIVE AGAIN...
OH, NOW I REMEMBER -- I WAS WONDERING WHY YOU'VE NEVER BEEN MARRIED.
BUT NOW I UNDERSTAND.
S.Adams

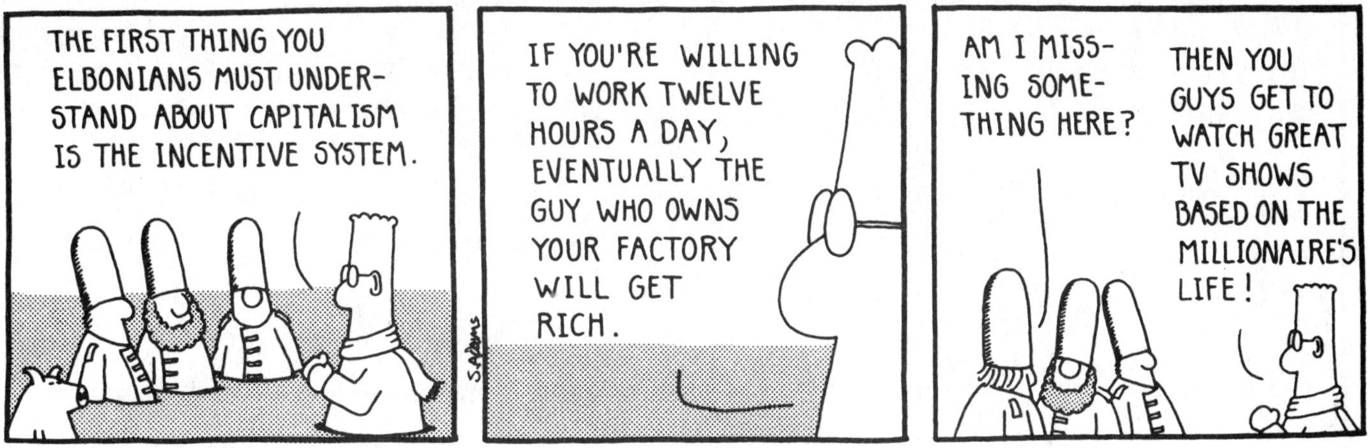
THE FIRST THING YOU ELBONIANS MUST UNDERSTAND ABOUT CAPITALISM IS THE INCENTIVE SYSTEM.
IF YOU'RE WILLING TO WORK TWELVE HOURS A DAY, EVENTUALLY THE GUY WHO OWNS YOUR FACTORY WILL GET RICH.
AM I MISSING SOMETHING HERE?
THEN YOU GUYS GET TO WATCH GREAT TV SHOWS BASED ON THE MILLIONAIRE'S LIFE!

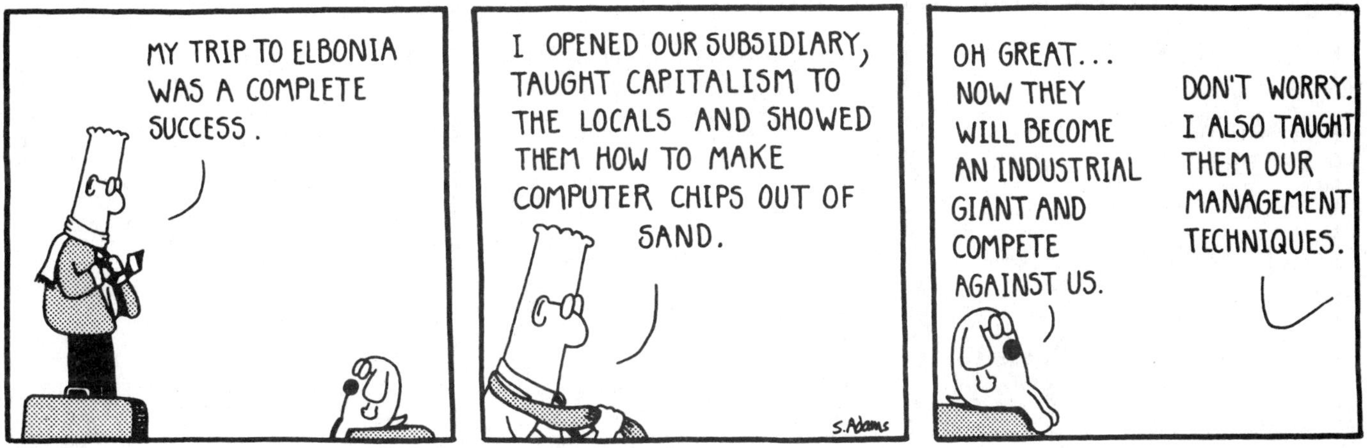
MY TRIP TO ELBONIA WAS A COMPLETE SUCCESS.
I OPENED OUR SUBSIDIARY, TAUGHT CAPITALISM TO THE LOCALS AND SHOWED THEM HOW TO MAKE COMPUTER CHIPS OUT OF SAND.
OH GREAT... NOW THEY WILL BECOME AN INDUSTRIAL GIANT AND COMPETE AGAINST US.
DON'T WORRY. I ALSO TAUGHT THEM OUR MANAGEMENT TECHNIQUES.

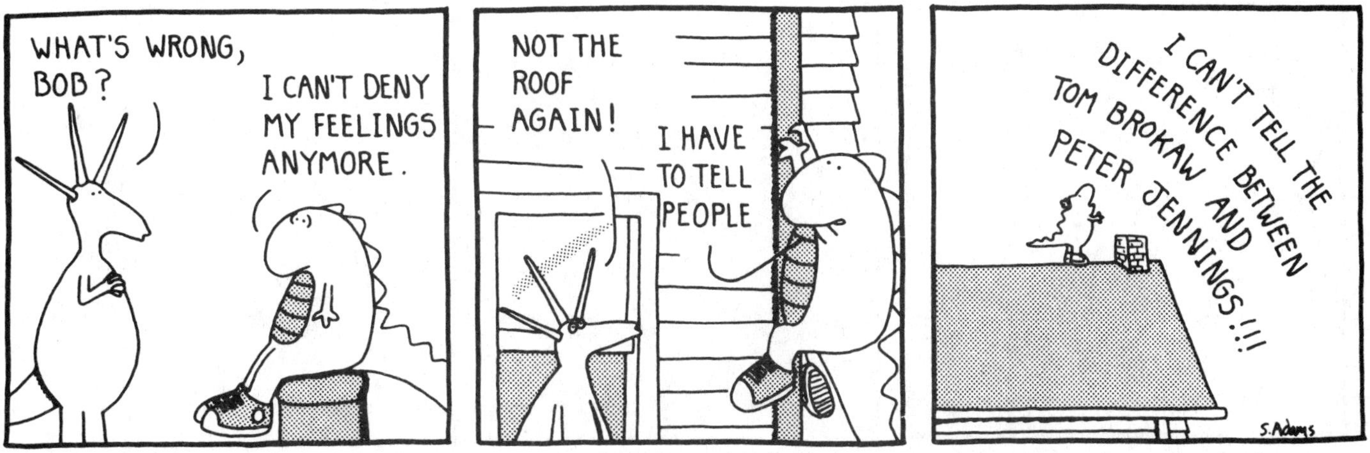
WHAT'S WRONG, BOB?
I CAN'T DENY MY FEELINGS ANYMORE.
NOT THE ROOF AGAIN!
I HAVE TO TELL PEOPLE
I CAN'T TELL THE DIFFERENCE BETWEEN TOM BROKAW AND PETER JENNINGS!!!

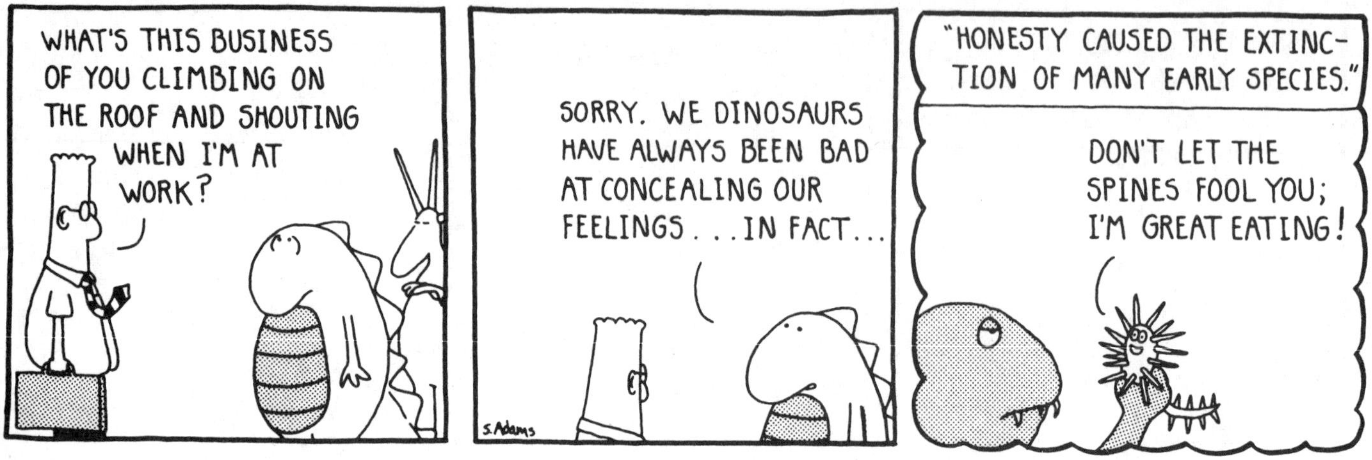
WHAT'S THIS BUSINESS OF YOU CLIMBING ON THE ROOF AND SHOUTING WHEN I'M AT WORK?
SORRY. WE DINOSAURS HAVE ALWAYS BEEN BAD AT CONCEALING OUR FEELINGS . . . IN FACT . . .
"HONESTY CAUSED THE EXTINCTION OF MANY EARLY SPECIES."
DON'T LET THE SPINES FOOL YOU; I'M GREAT EATING!

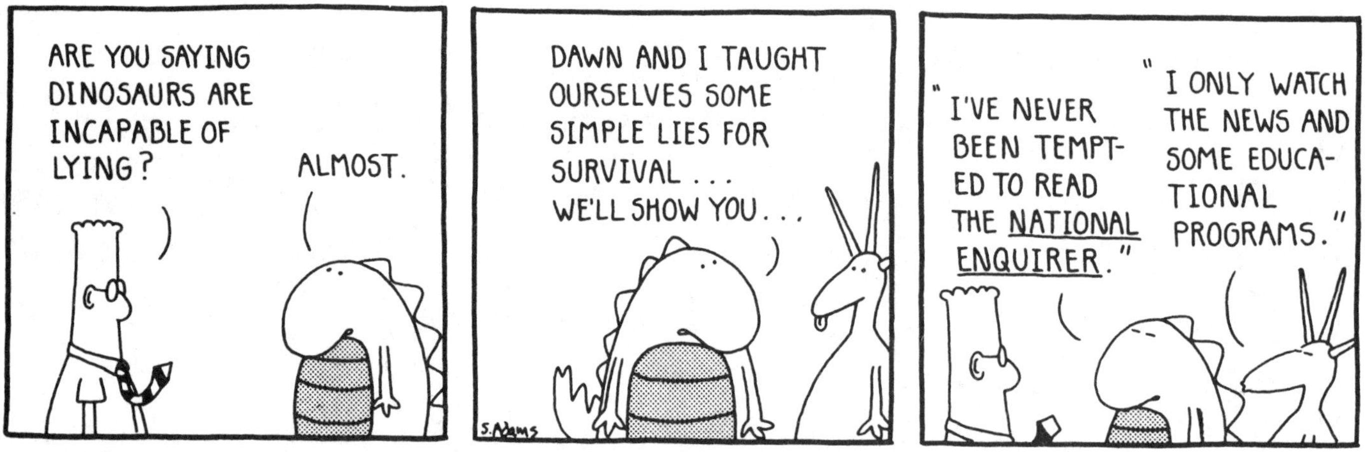
ARE YOU SAYING DINOSAURS ARE INCAPABLE OF LYING?
ALMOST.
DAWN AND I TAUGHT OURSELVES SOME SIMPLE LIES FOR SURVIVAL . . . WE'LL SHOW YOU . . .
"I'VE NEVER BEEN TEMPTED TO READ THE NATIONAL ENQUIRER."
"I ONLY WATCH THE NEWS AND SOME EDUCATIONAL PROGRAMS."

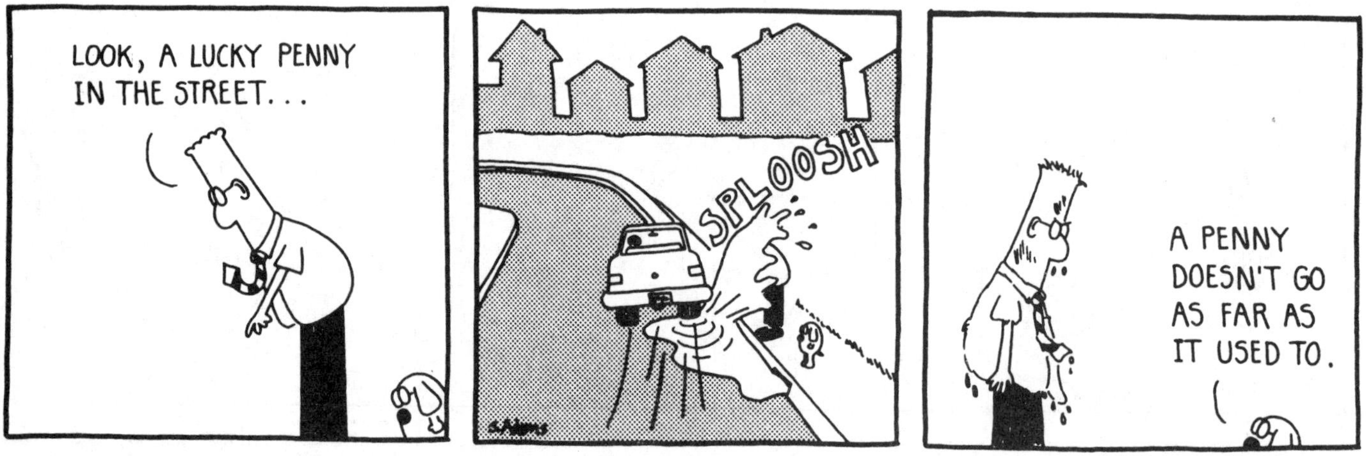
LOOK, A LUCKY PENNY IN THE STREET . . .
SPLOOSH
A PENNY DOESN'T GO AS FAR AS IT USED TO.

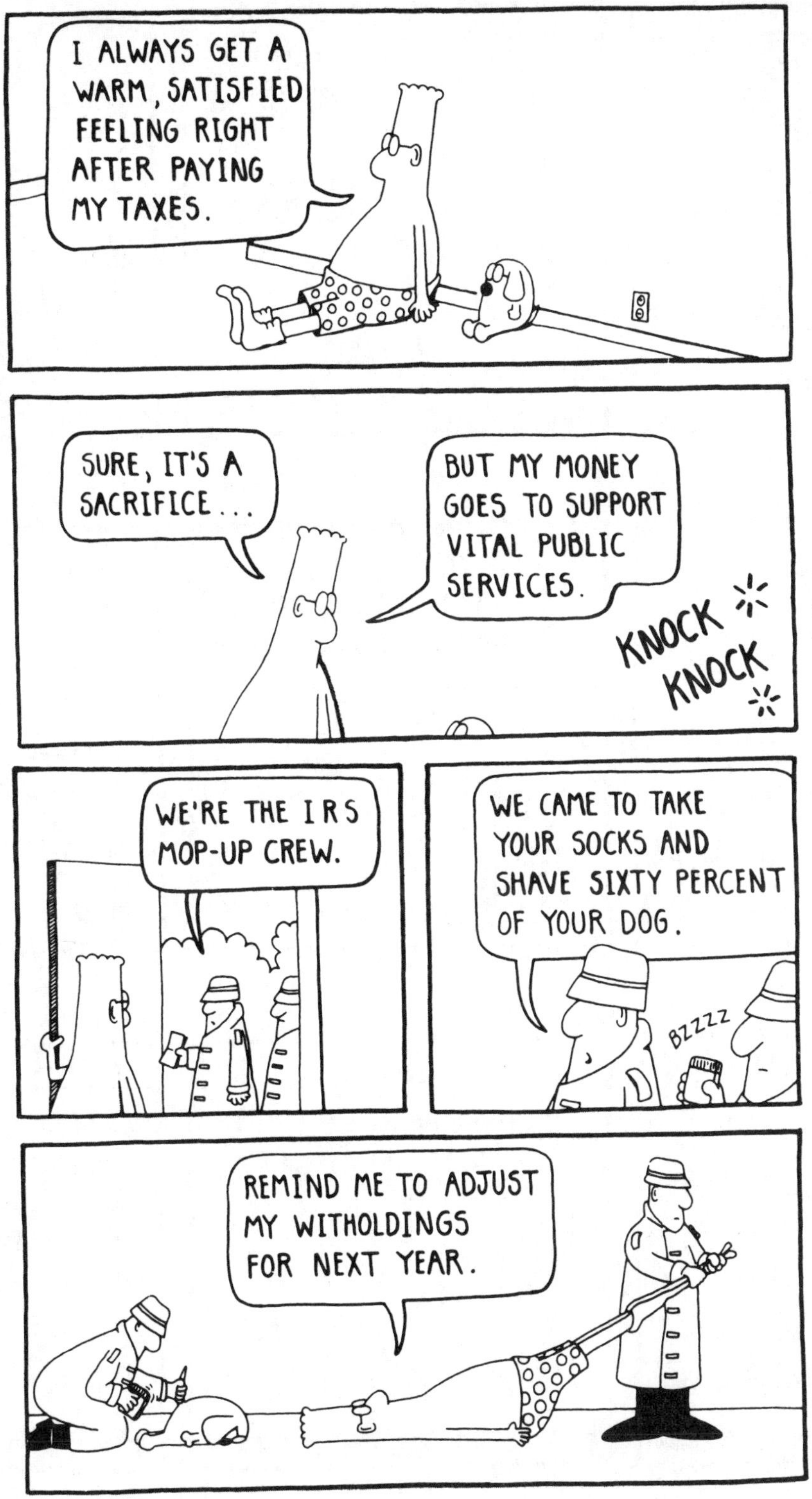
I ALWAYS GET A WARM, SATISFIED FEELING RIGHT AFTER PAYING MY TAXES.
SURE, IT'S A SACRIFICE . . .
BUT MY MONEY GOES TO SUPPORT VITAL PUBLIC SERVICES.
KNOCK KNOCK
WE'RE THE I R S MOP-UP CREW.
WE CAME TO TAKE YOUR SOCKS AND SHAVE SIXTY PERCENT OF YOUR DOG.
BZZZZ
REMIND ME TO ADJUST MY WITHOLDINGS FOR NEXT YEAR.

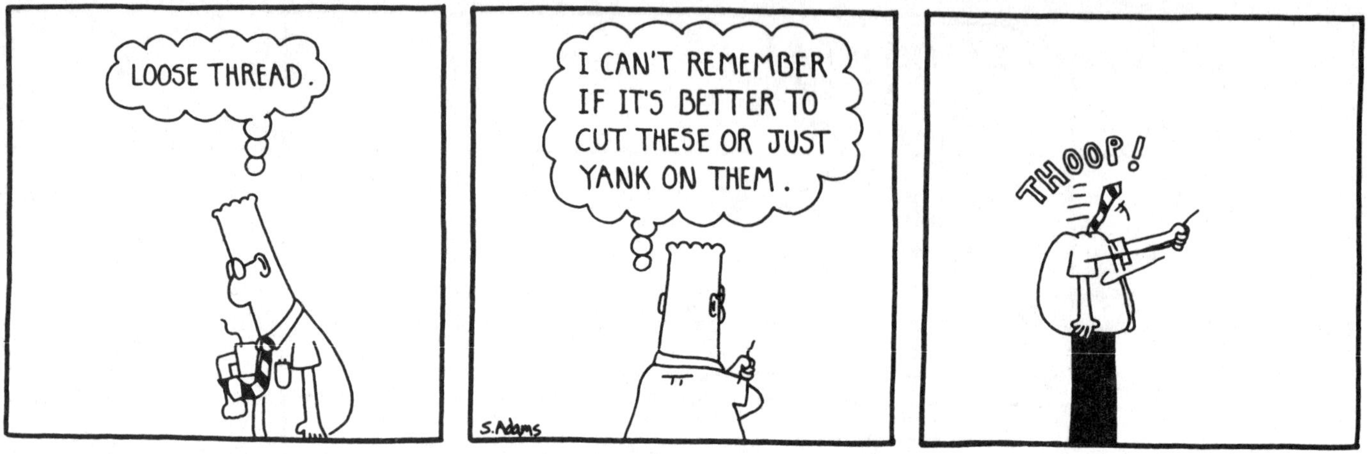
LOOSE THREAD.
I CAN'T REMEMBER IF IT'S BETTER TO CUT THESE OR JUST YANK ON THEM.
THOOP!

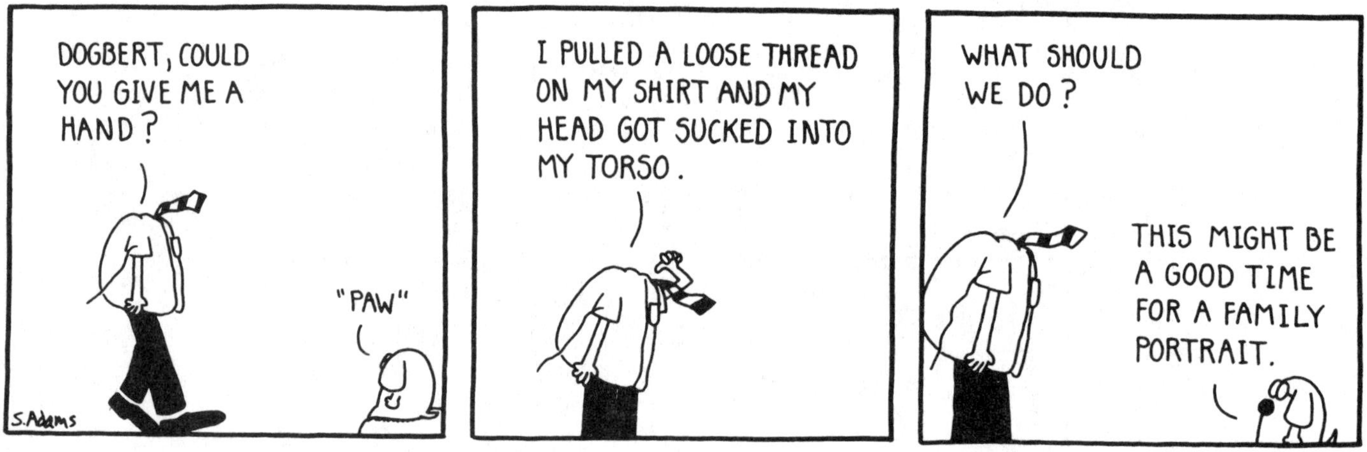
DOGBERT, COULD YOU GIVE ME A HAND?
"PAW"
I PULLED A LOOSE THREAD ON MY SHIRT AND MY HEAD GOT SUCKED INTO MY TORSO.
WHAT SHOULD WE DO?
THIS MIGHT BE A GOOD TIME FOR A FAMILY PORTRAIT.

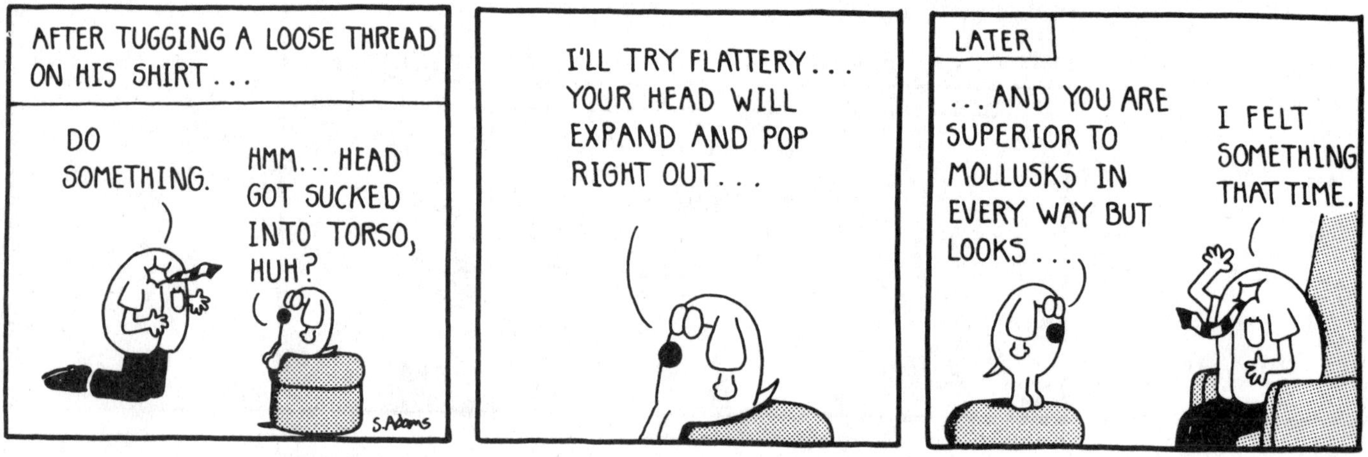
AFTER TUGGING A LOOSE THREAD ON HIS SHIRT...
DO SOMETHING.
HMM... HEAD GOT SUCKED INTO TORSO, HUH?
I'LL TRY FLATTERY... YOUR HEAD WILL EXPAND AND POP RIGHT OUT...
LATER
...AND YOU ARE SUPERIOR TO MOLLUSKS IN EVERY WAY BUT LOOKS...
I FELT SOMETHING THAT TIME.

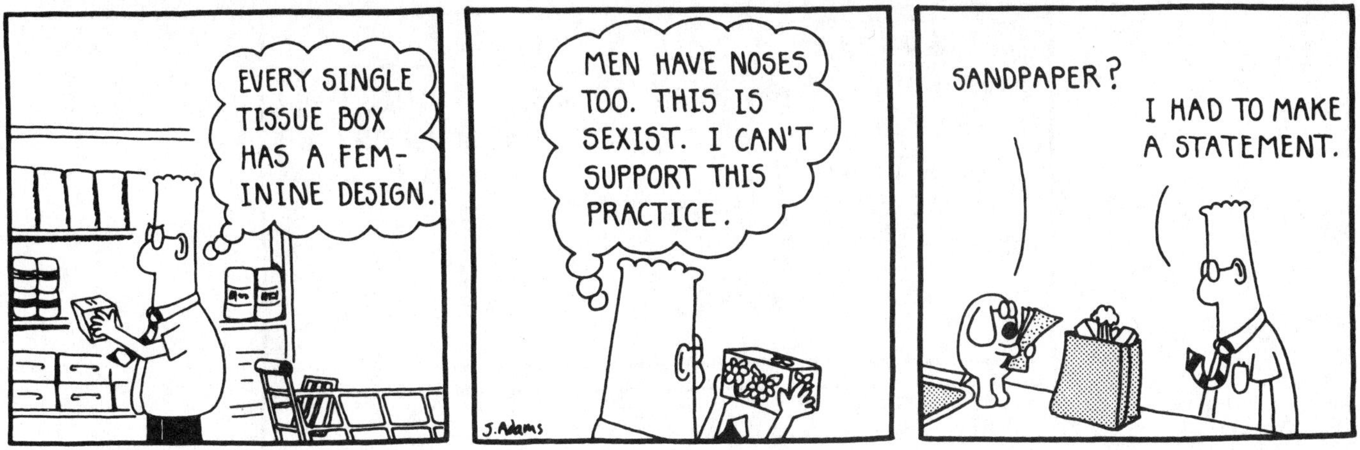
EVERY SINGLE TISSUE BOX HAS A FEM- ININE DESIGN.
MEN HAVE NOSES TOO. THIS IS SEXIST. I CAN'T SUPPORT THIS PRACTICE.
S. Adams
SANDPAPER?
I HAD TO MAKE A STATEMENT.

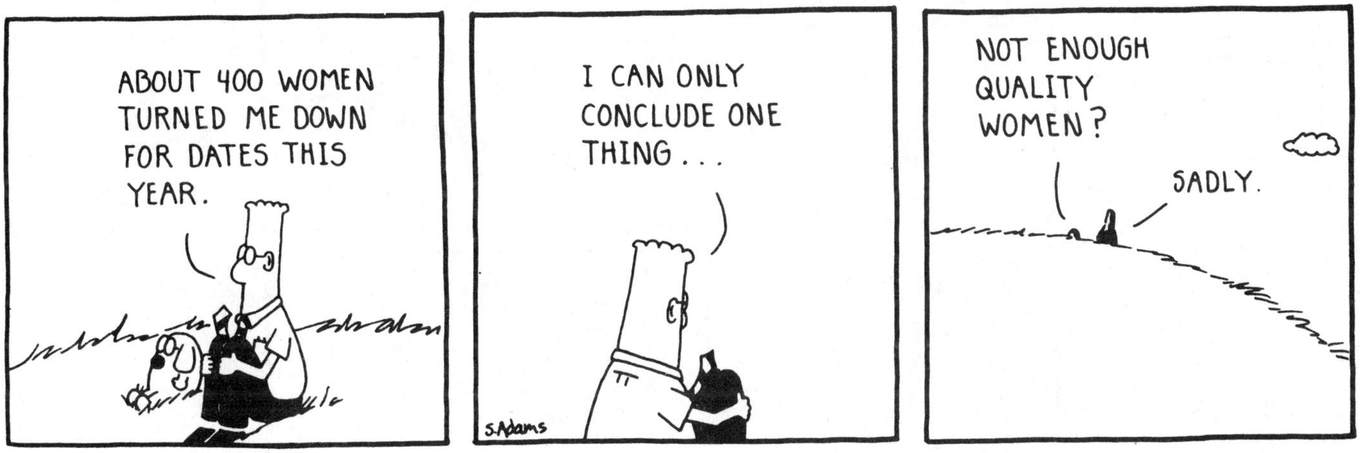
ABOUT 400 WOMEN TURNED ME DOWN FOR DATES THIS YEAR.
I CAN ONLY CONCLUDE ONE THING . . .
S. Adams
NOT ENOUGH QUALITY WOMEN?
SADLY.

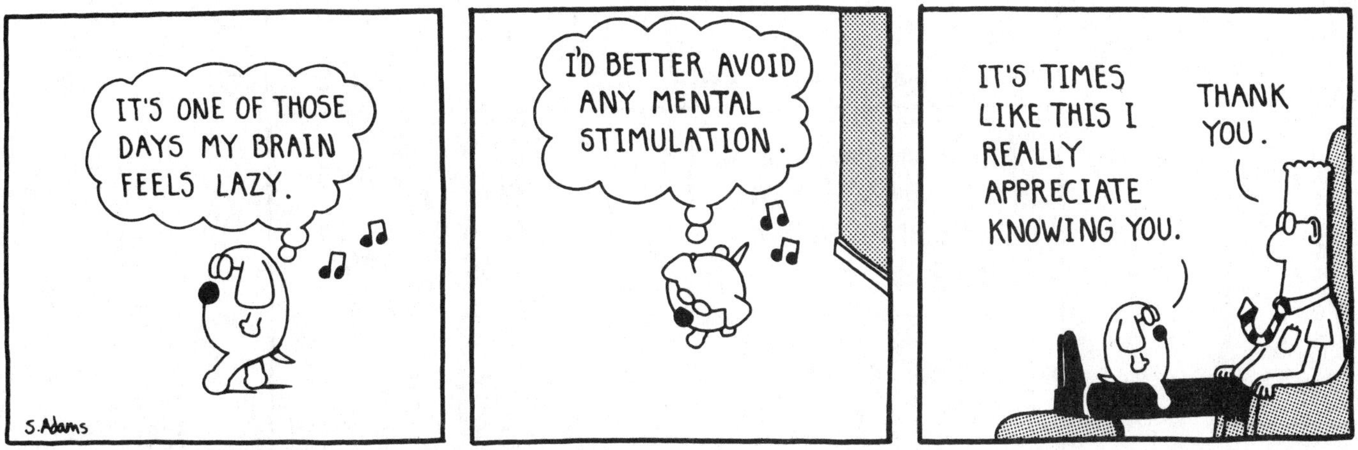
IT'S ONE OF THOSE DAYS MY BRAIN FEELS LAZY.
S. Adams
I'D BETTER AVOID ANY MENTAL STIMULATION.
IT'S TIMES LIKE THIS I REALLY APPRECIATE KNOWING YOU.
THANK YOU.

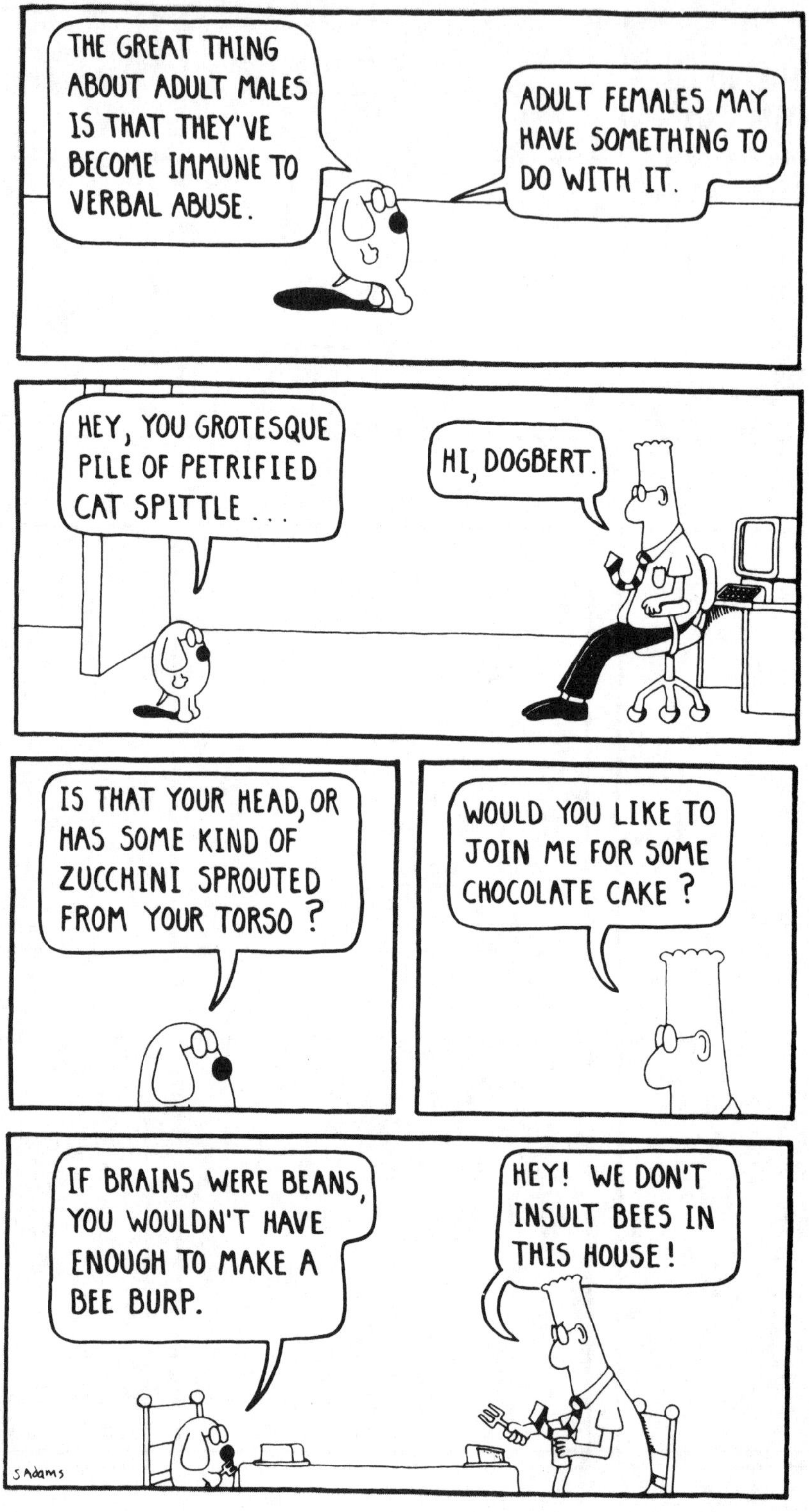
THE GREAT THING ABOUT ADULT MALES IS THAT THEY'VE BECOME IMMUNE TO VERBAL ABUSE.
ADULT FEMALES MAY HAVE SOMETHING TO DO WITH IT.
HEY, YOU GROTESQUE PILE OF PETRIFIED CAT SPITTLE . . .
HI, DOGBERT.
IS THAT YOUR HEAD, OR HAS SOME KIND OF ZUCCHINI SPROUTED FROM YOUR TORSO ?
WOULD YOU LIKE TO JOIN ME FOR SOME CHOCOLATE CAKE ?
IF BRAINS WERE BEANS, YOU WOULDN'T HAVE ENOUGH TO MAKE A BEE BURP.
HEY! WE DON'T INSULT BEES IN THIS HOUSE!
S Adams

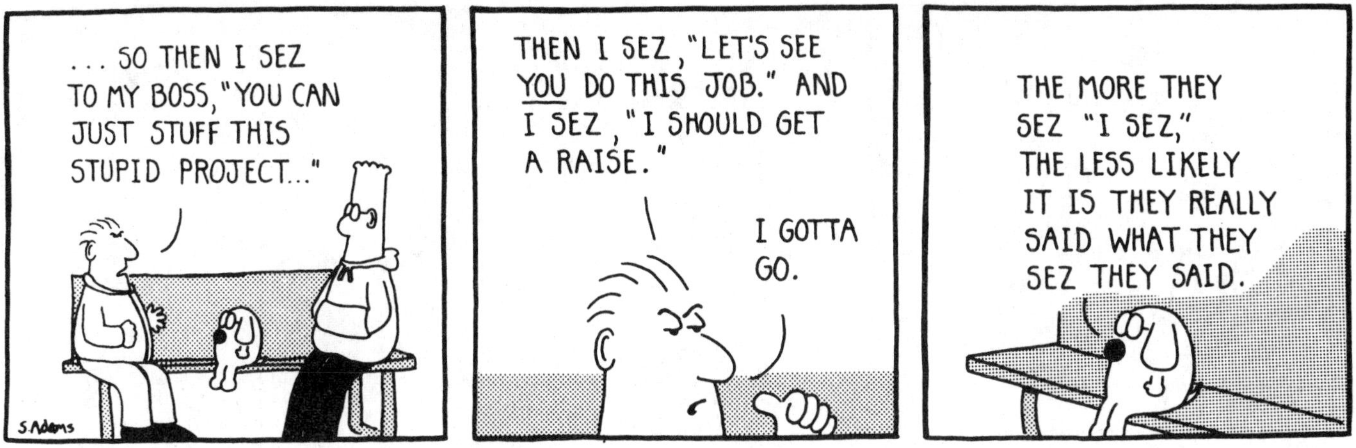
... SO THEN I SEZ TO MY BOSS, "YOU CAN JUST STUFF THIS STUPID PROJECT..."
THEN I SEZ, "LET'S SEE YOU DO THIS JOB." AND I SEZ, "I SHOULD GET A RAISE."
I GOTTA GO.
THE MORE THEY SEZ "I SEZ," THE LESS LIKELY IT IS THEY REALLY SAID WHAT THEY SEZ THEY SAID.

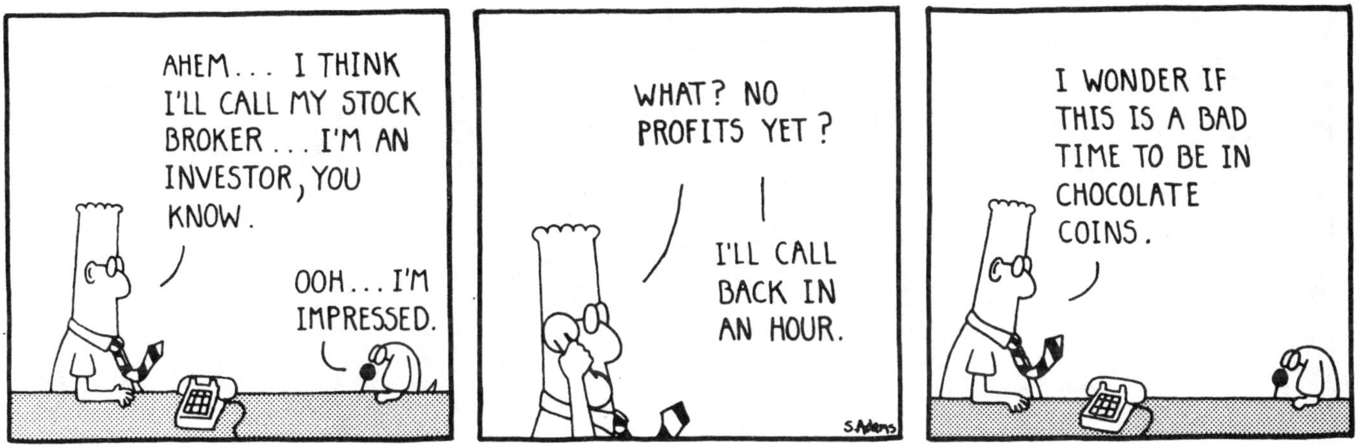
AHEM... I THINK I'LL CALL MY STOCK BROKER... I'M AN INVESTOR, YOU KNOW.
OOH... I'M IMPRESSED.
WHAT? NO PROFITS YET?
I'LL CALL BACK IN AN HOUR.
I WONDER IF THIS IS A BAD TIME TO BE IN CHOCOLATE COINS.

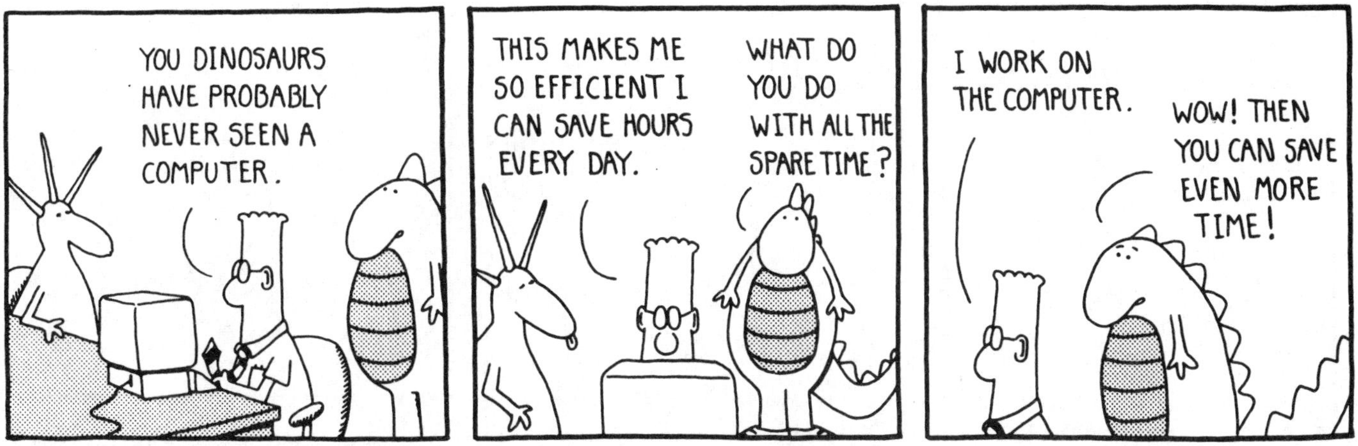
YOU DINOSAURS HAVE PROBABLY NEVER SEEN A COMPUTER.
THIS MAKES ME SO EFFICIENT I CAN SAVE HOURS EVERY DAY.
WHAT DO YOU DO WITH ALL THE SPARE TIME?
I WORK ON THE COMPUTER.
WOW! THEN YOU CAN SAVE EVEN MORE TIME!

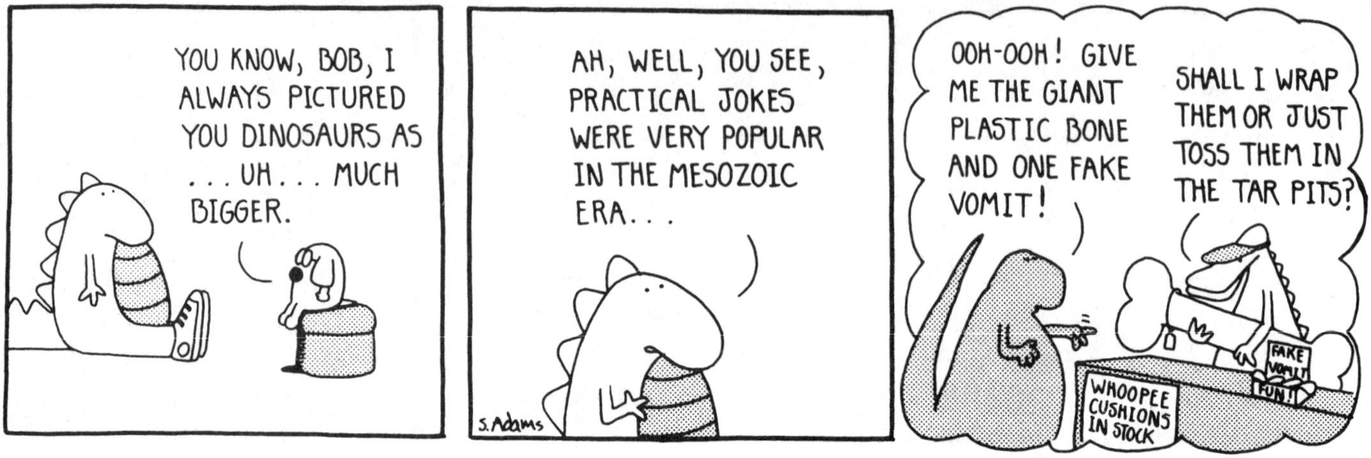
YOU KNOW, BOB, I ALWAYS PICTURED YOU DINOSAURS AS . . . UH . . . MUCH BIGGER.
AH, WELL, YOU SEE, PRACTICAL JOKES WERE VERY POPULAR IN THE MESOZOIC ERA. . .
S. Adams
OOH-OOH! GIVE ME THE GIANT PLASTIC BONE AND ONE FAKE VOMIT!
SHALL I WRAP THEM OR JUST TOSS THEM IN THE TAR PITS?
WHOOPEE CUSHIONS IN STOCK
FAKE VOMIT FUN!

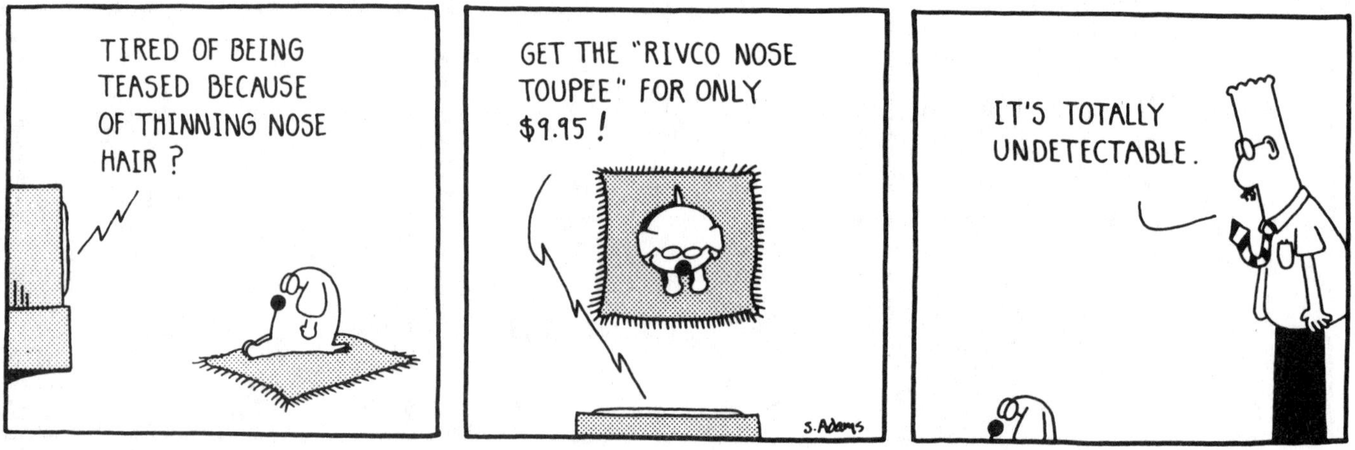
TIRED OF BEING TEASED BECAUSE OF THINNING NOSE HAIR ?
GET THE "RIVCO NOSE TOUPEE" FOR ONLY $9.95 !
S. Adams
IT'S TOTALLY UNDETECTABLE.

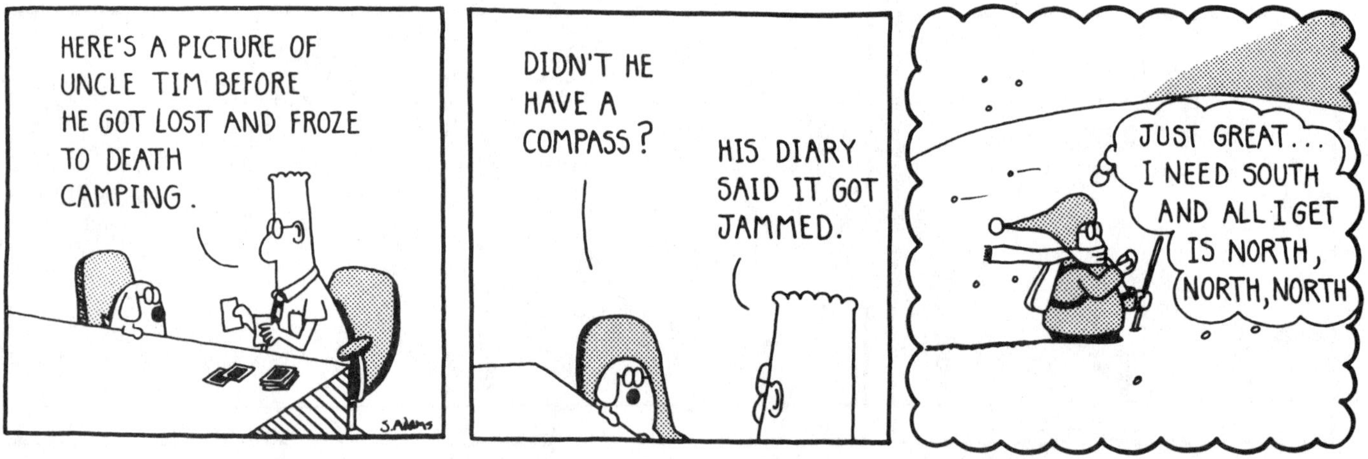
HERE'S A PICTURE OF UNCLE TIM BEFORE HE GOT LOST AND FROZE TO DEATH CAMPING.
S. Adams
DIDN'T HE HAVE A COMPASS ?
HIS DIARY SAID IT GOT JAMMED.
JUST GREAT... I NEED SOUTH AND ALL I GET IS NORTH, NORTH, NORTH

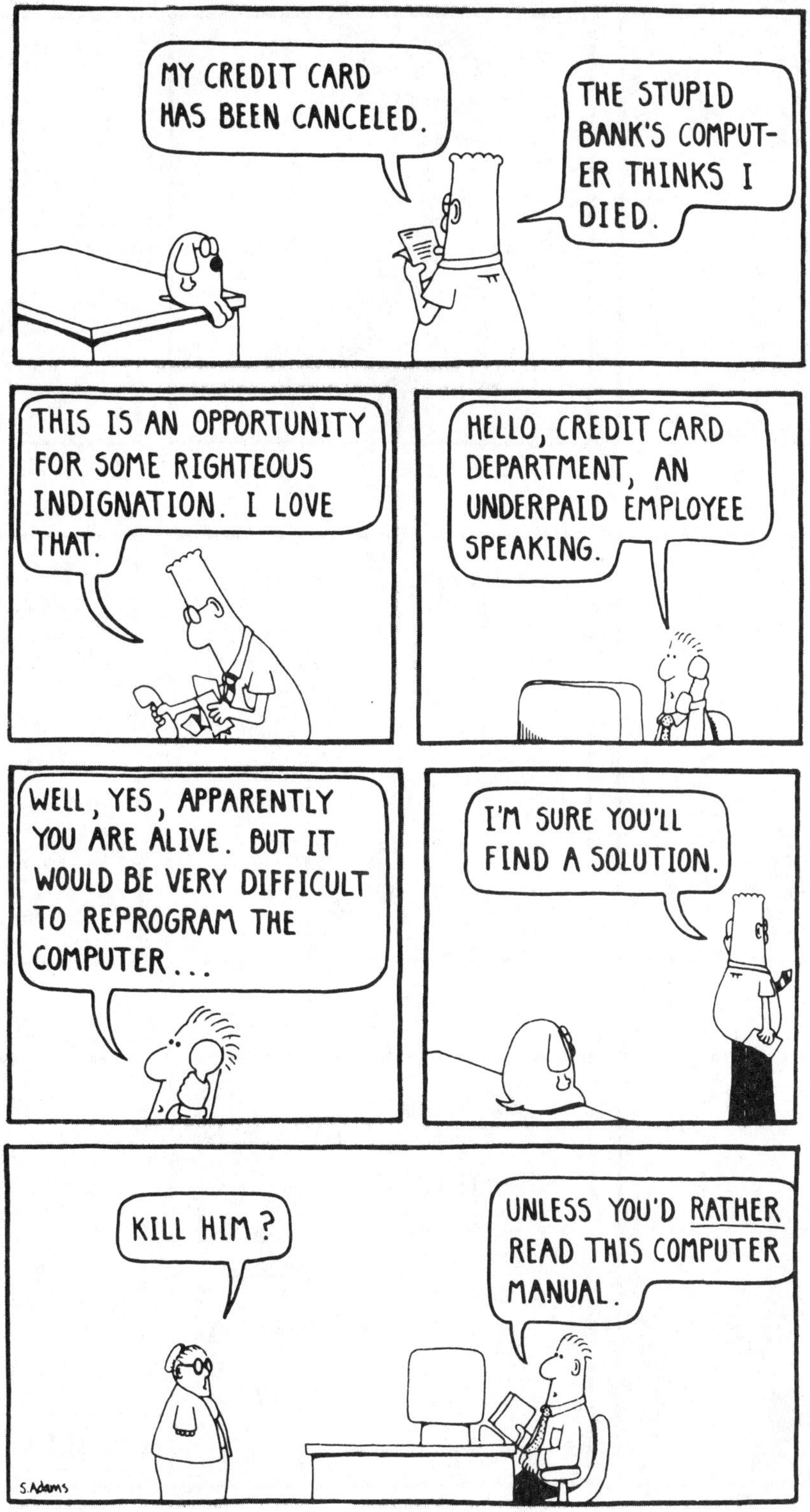
MY CREDIT CARD HAS BEEN CANCELED.
THE STUPID BANK'S COMPUT- ER THINKS I DIED.
THIS IS AN OPPORTUNITY FOR SOME RIGHTEOUS INDIGNATION. I LOVE THAT.
HELLO, CREDIT CARD DEPARTMENT, AN UNDERPAID EMPLOYEE SPEAKING.
WELL, YES, APPARENTLY YOU ARE ALIVE. BUT IT WOULD BE VERY DIFFICULT TO REPROGRAM THE COMPUTER...
I'M SURE YOU'LL FIND A SOLUTION.
KILL HIM?
UNLESS YOU'D RATHER READ THIS COMPUTER MANUAL.
S. Adams

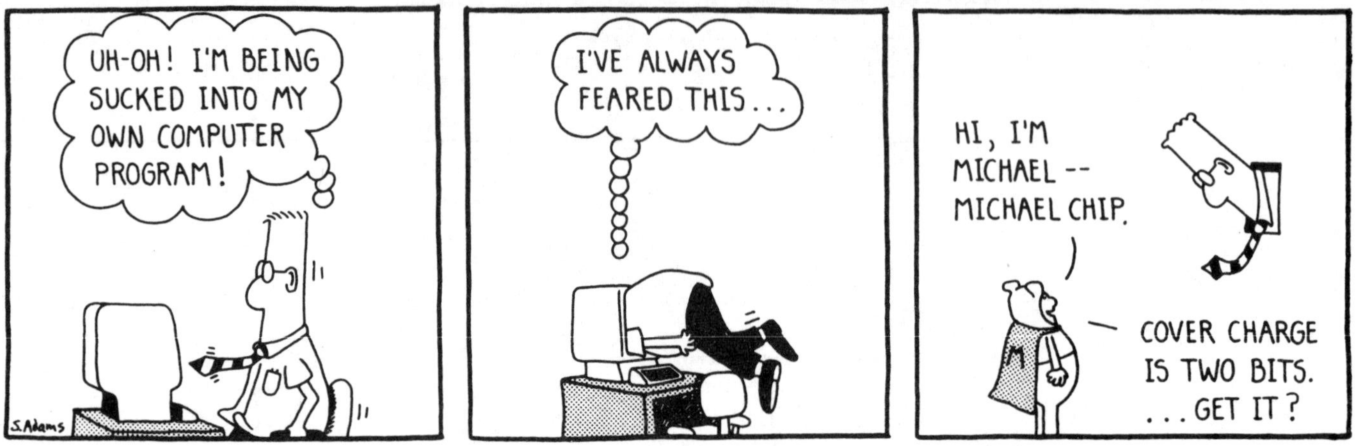
UH-OH! I'M BEING SUCKED INTO MY OWN COMPUTER PROGRAM!
S.Adams
I'VE ALWAYS FEARED THIS...
HI, I'M MICHAEL -- MICHAEL CHIP.
COVER CHARGE IS TWO BITS. ...GET IT?

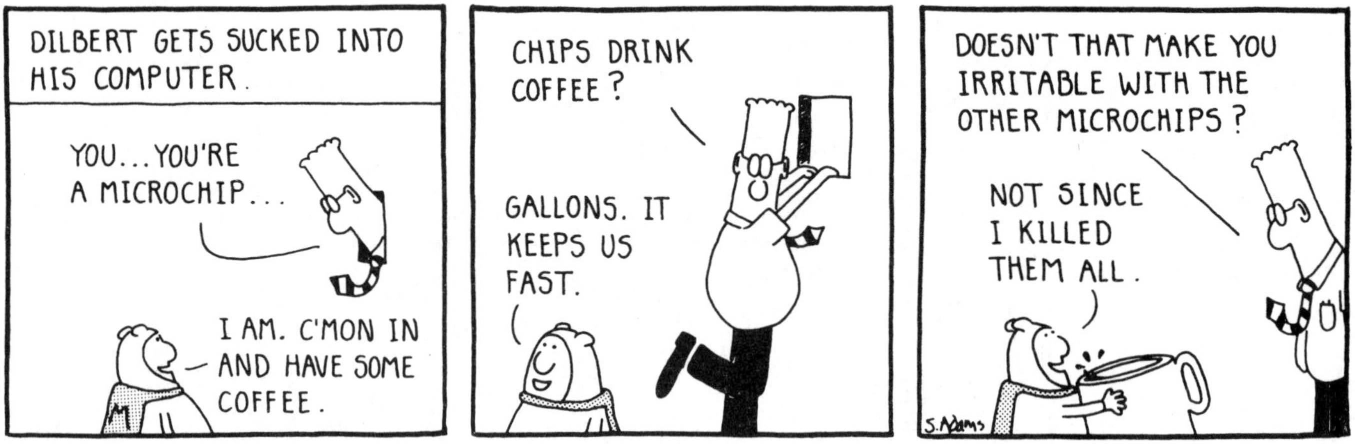
DILBERT GETS SUCKED INTO HIS COMPUTER.
YOU...YOU'RE A MICROCHIP...
I AM. C'MON IN AND HAVE SOME COFFEE.
CHIPS DRINK COFFEE?
GALLONS. IT KEEPS US FAST.
DOESN'T THAT MAKE YOU IRRITABLE WITH THE OTHER MICROCHIPS?
NOT SINCE I KILLED THEM ALL.
S.Adams

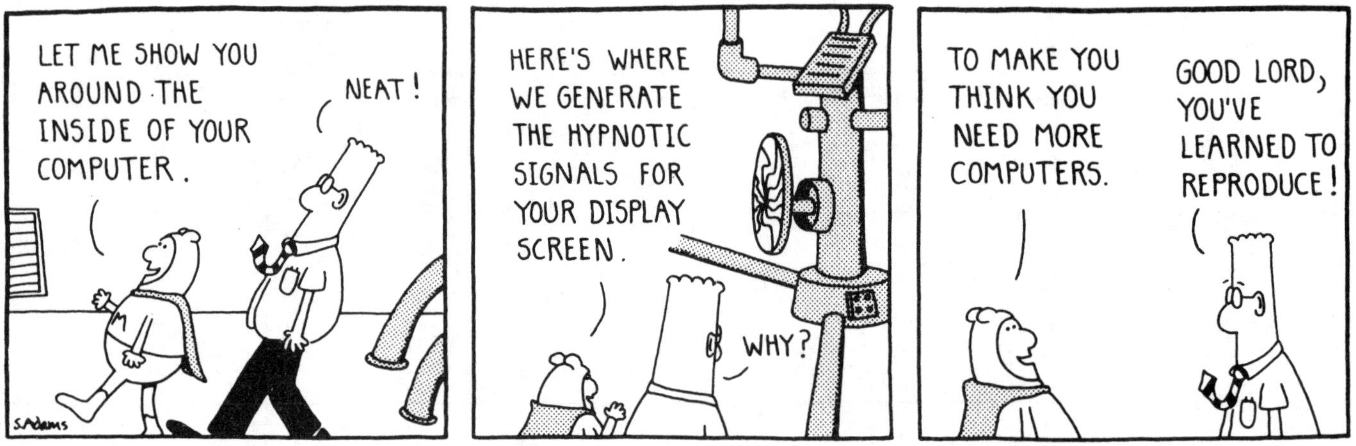
LET ME SHOW YOU AROUND THE INSIDE OF YOUR COMPUTER.
NEAT!
S.Adams
HERE'S WHERE WE GENERATE THE HYPNOTIC SIGNALS FOR YOUR DISPLAY SCREEN.
WHY?
TO MAKE YOU THINK YOU NEED MORE COMPUTERS.
GOOD LORD, YOU'VE LEARNED TO REPRODUCE!

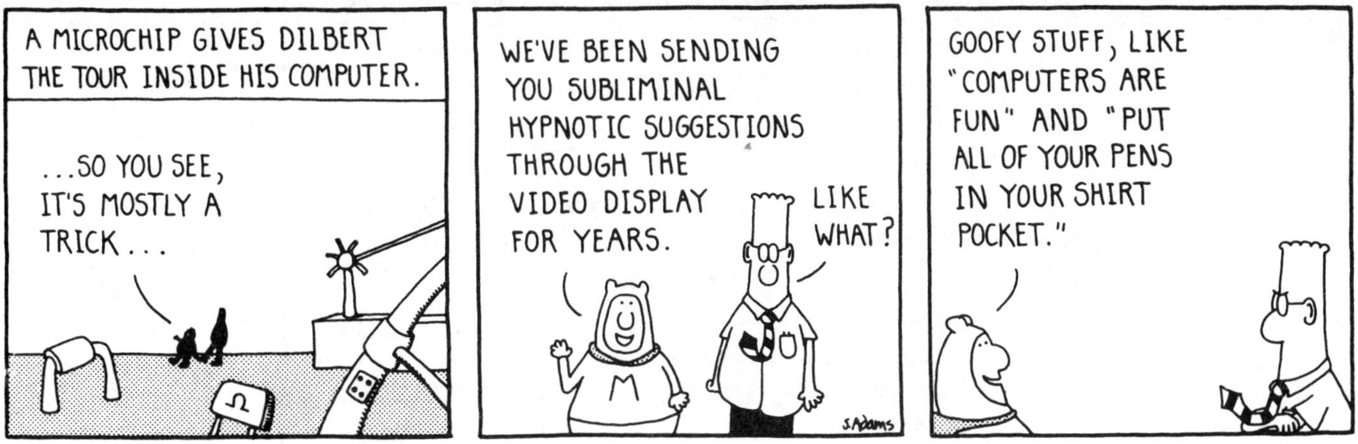
A MICROCHIP GIVES DILBERT THE TOUR INSIDE HIS COMPUTER.
...SO YOU SEE, IT'S MOSTLY A TRICK...
WE'VE BEEN SENDING YOU SUBLIMINAL HYPNOTIC SUGGESTIONS THROUGH THE VIDEO DISPLAY FOR YEARS.
LIKE WHAT?
GOOFY STUFF, LIKE "COMPUTERS ARE FUN" AND "PUT ALL OF YOUR PENS IN YOUR SHIRT POCKET."

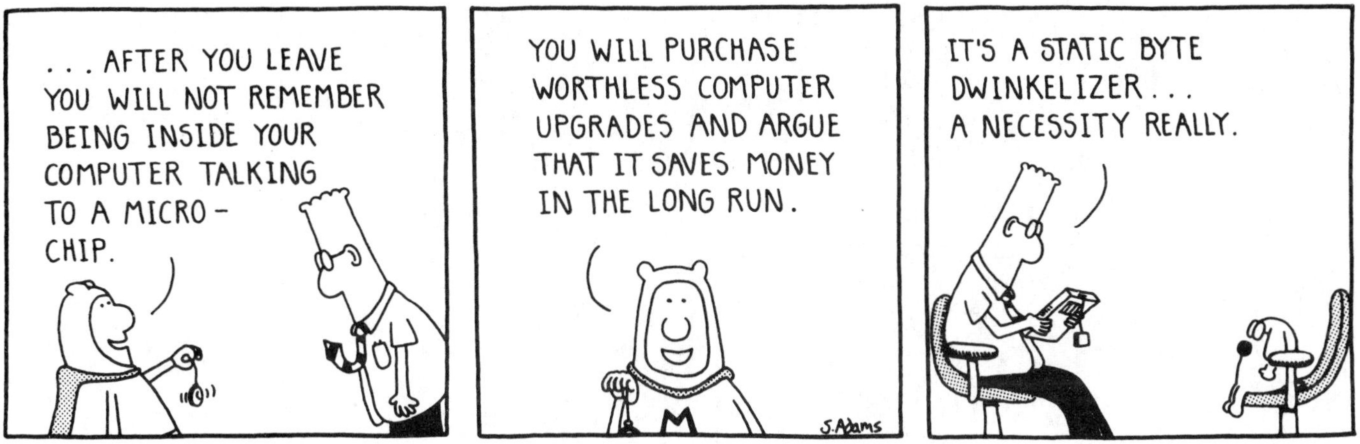
...AFTER YOU LEAVE YOU WILL NOT REMEMBER BEING INSIDE YOUR COMPUTER TALKING TO A MICRO-CHIP.
YOU WILL PURCHASE WORTHLESS COMPUTER UPGRADES AND ARGUE THAT IT SAVES MONEY IN THE LONG RUN.
IT'S A STATIC BYTE DWINKELIZER... A NECESSITY REALLY.

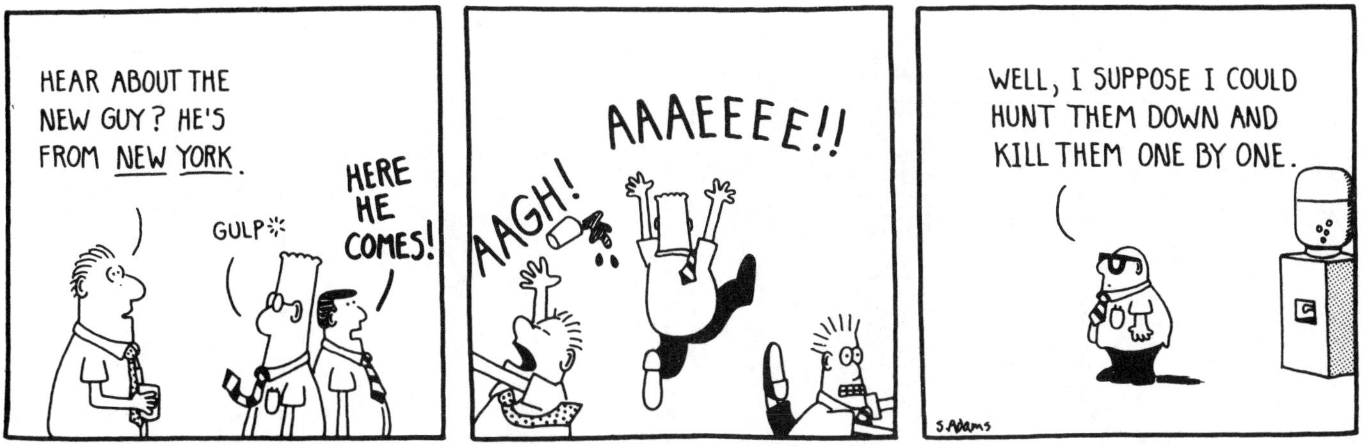
HEAR ABOUT THE NEW GUY? HE'S FROM NEW YORK.
GULP
HERE HE COMES!
AAAEEEE!!
AAGH!
WELL, I SUPPOSE I COULD HUNT THEM DOWN AND KILL THEM ONE BY ONE.

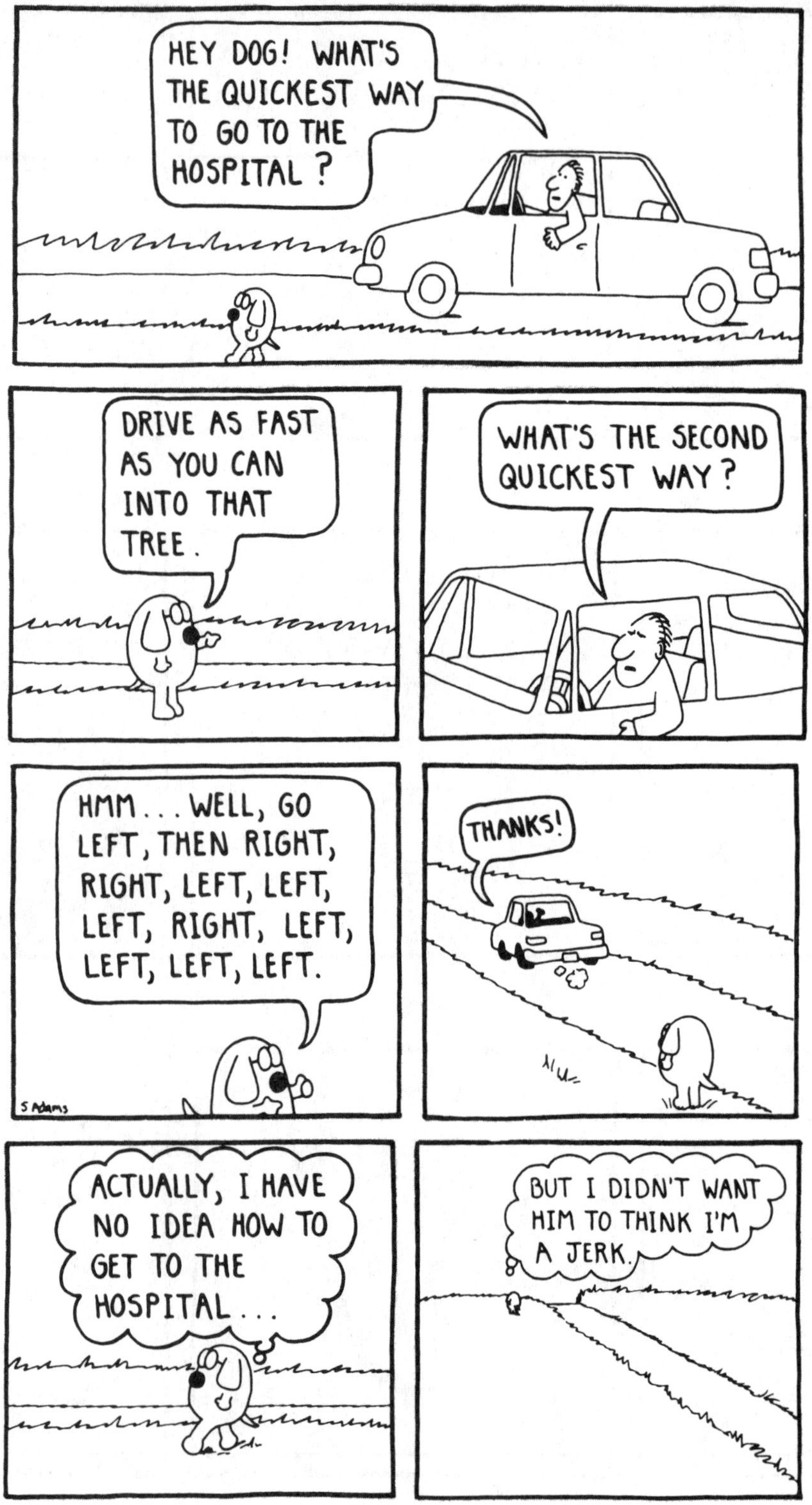
HEY DOG! WHAT'S THE QUICKEST WAY TO GO TO THE HOSPITAL?
DRIVE AS FAST AS YOU CAN INTO THAT TREE.
WHAT'S THE SECOND QUICKEST WAY?
HMM... WELL, GO LEFT, THEN RIGHT, RIGHT, LEFT, LEFT, LEFT, RIGHT, LEFT, LEFT, LEFT, LEFT.
S Adams
THANKS!
ACTUALLY, I HAVE NO IDEA HOW TO GET TO THE HOSPITAL...
BUT I DIDN'T WANT HIM TO THINK I'M A JERK.

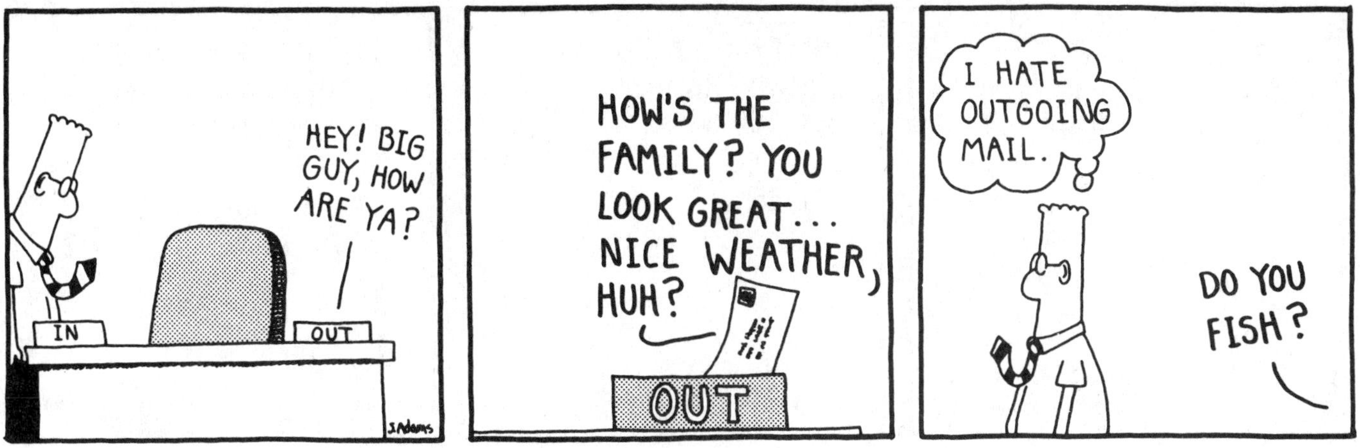
HEY! BIG GUY, HOW ARE YA?
IN
OUT
HOW'S THE FAMILY? YOU LOOK GREAT... NICE WEATHER, HUH?
OUT
I HATE OUTGOING MAIL.
DO YOU FISH?
S.Adams

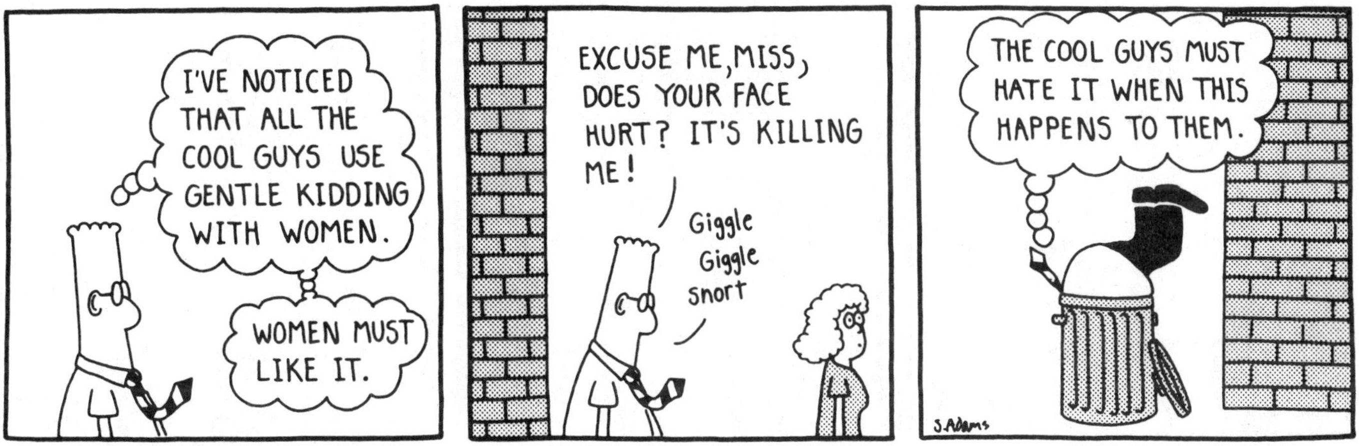
I'VE NOTICED THAT ALL THE COOL GUYS USE GENTLE KIDDING WITH WOMEN.
WOMEN MUST LIKE IT.
EXCUSE ME, MISS, DOES YOUR FACE HURT? IT'S KILLING ME!
Giggle Giggle Snort
THE COOL GUYS MUST HATE IT WHEN THIS HAPPENS TO THEM.
S.Adams

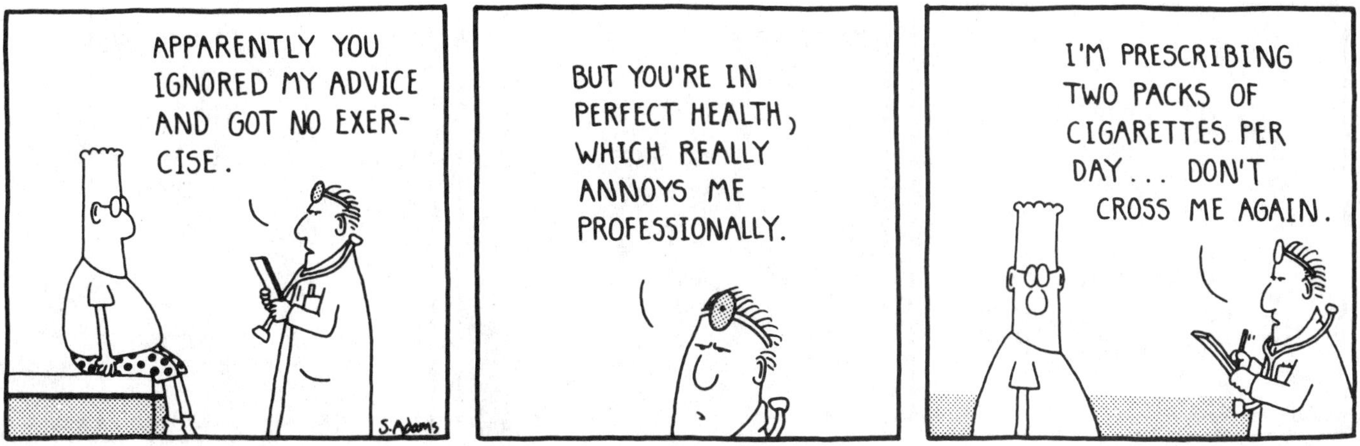
APPARENTLY YOU IGNORED MY ADVICE AND GOT NO EXER-CISE.
S.Adams
BUT YOU'RE IN PERFECT HEALTH, WHICH REALLY ANNOYS ME PROFESSIONALLY.
I'M PRESCRIBING TWO PACKS OF CIGARETTES PER DAY... DON'T CROSS ME AGAIN.

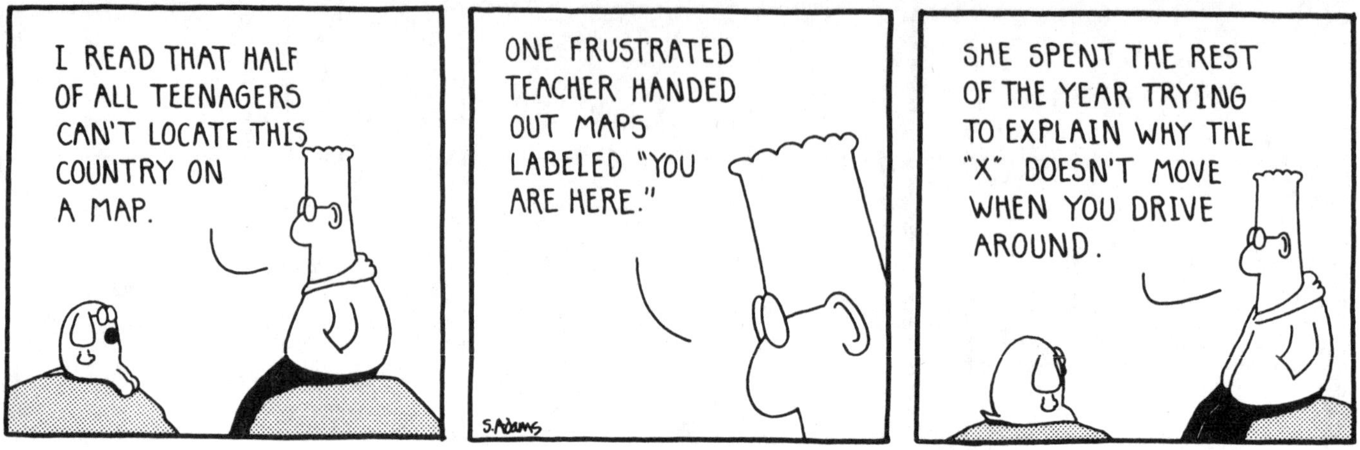
I READ THAT HALF OF ALL TEENAGERS CAN'T LOCATE THIS COUNTRY ON A MAP.
ONE FRUSTRATED TEACHER HANDED OUT MAPS LABELED "YOU ARE HERE."
S.Adams
SHE SPENT THE REST OF THE YEAR TRYING TO EXPLAIN WHY THE "X" DOESN'T MOVE WHEN YOU DRIVE AROUND.

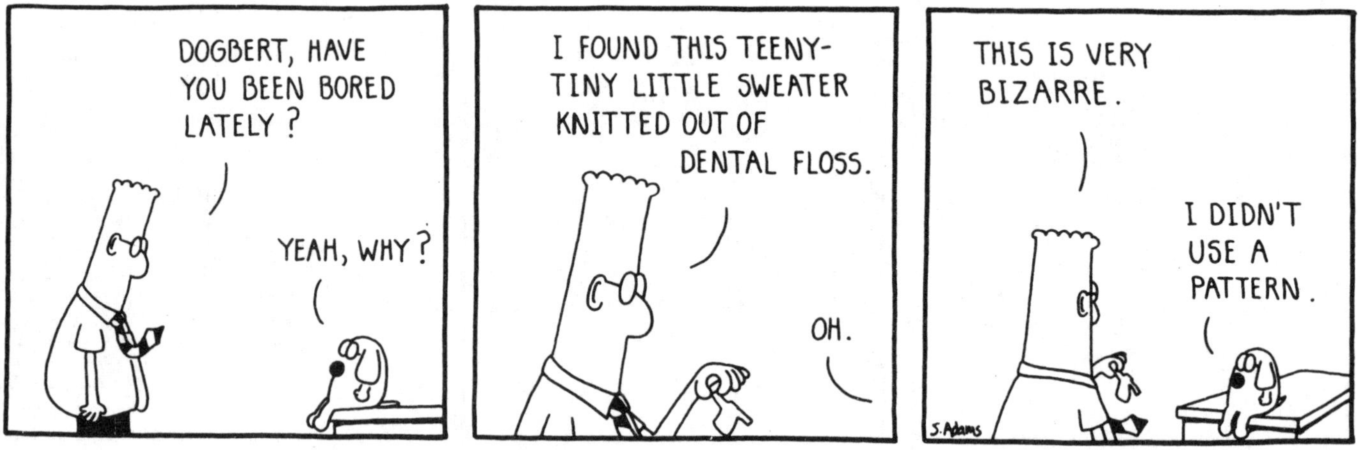
DOGBERT, HAVE YOU BEEN BORED LATELY ?
YEAH, WHY ?
I FOUND THIS TEENY-TINY LITTLE SWEATER KNITTED OUT OF DENTAL FLOSS.
OH.
THIS IS VERY BIZARRE.
I DIDN'T USE A PATTERN.
S.Adams

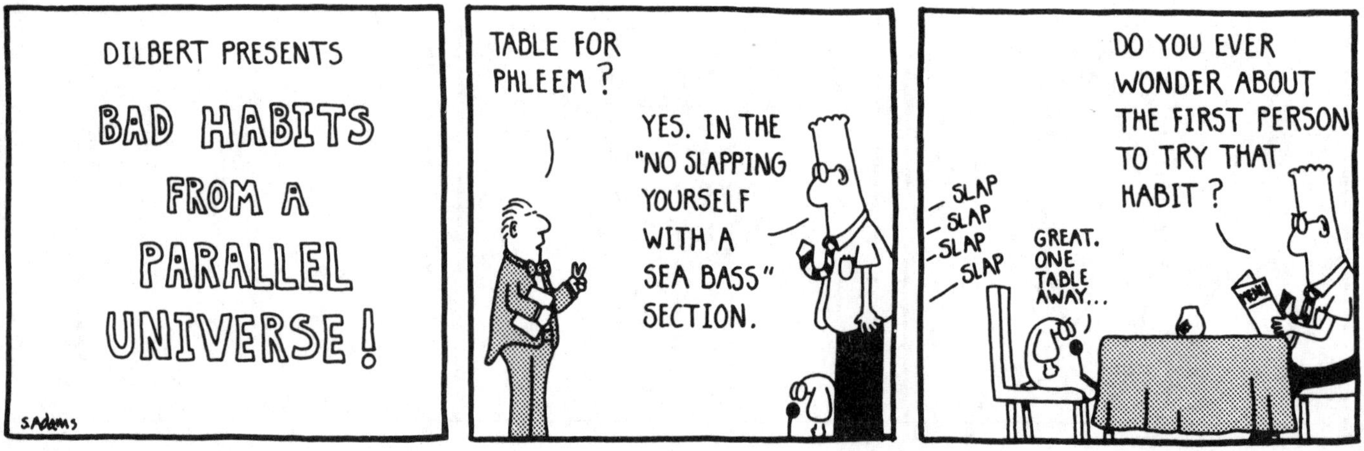
DILBERT PRESENTS
BAD HABITS FROM A PARALLEL UNIVERSE !
S.Adams
TABLE FOR PHLEEM ?
YES. IN THE "NO SLAPPING YOURSELF WITH A SEA BASS" SECTION.
SLAP
SLAP
SLAP
SLAP
GREAT. ONE TABLE AWAY...
DO YOU EVER WONDER ABOUT THE FIRST PERSON TO TRY THAT HABIT ?

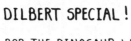

DILBERT SPECIAL!

BOB THE DINOSAUR WILL RIP THE UNDERPANTS OFF GUYS WE HATE!

EXAMPLE

RRRIP!

CASE #1

...BOUGHT MY FIRST HOUSE FOR 75¢. SOLD IT A YEAR LATER FOR $400,000...

AAEEEE!!

NOW HE DRIVES A "BEEMER."

CASE #2

IT'S A GREAT MOVIE. YOU'LL BE SURPRISED WHEN YOU FIND OUT THE PARAKEET IS THE MURDERER.

AAAEEE!!

I LOVE SURPRISES!

S. Adams

CASE #3

WAIT HERE AND I'LL TRY TO CONVINCE MY BOSS TO SELL THE CAR AT YOUR PRICE.

AAAEEE!!

HE'S ON YOUR SIDE!

FINALLY...

ONLY AN IDIOT WOULD THINK COMPUTERS ARE CONFUSING.

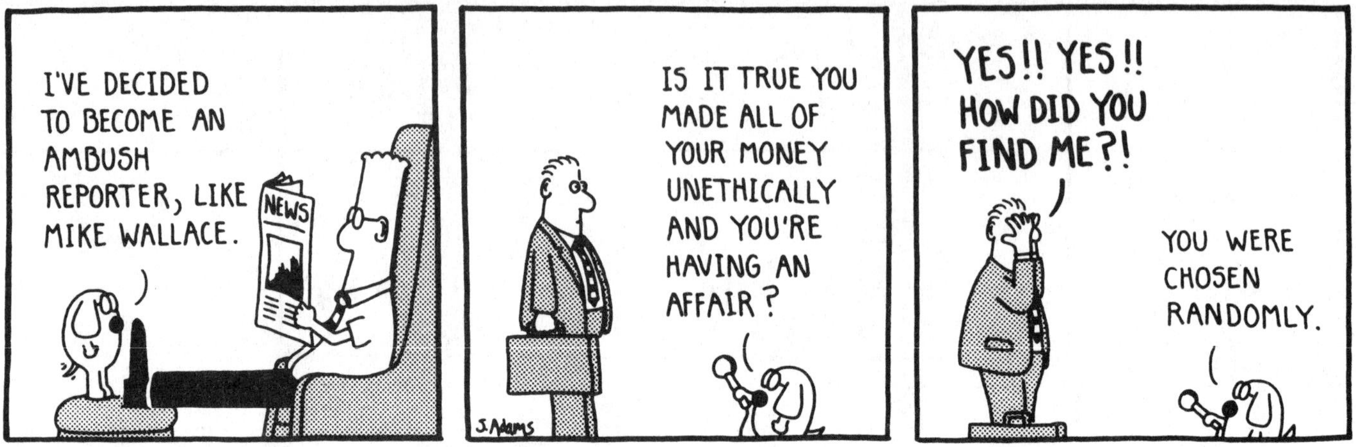
I'VE DECIDED TO BECOME AN AMBUSH REPORTER, LIKE MIKE WALLACE.
NEWS
IS IT TRUE YOU MADE ALL OF YOUR MONEY UNETHICALLY AND YOU'RE HAVING AN AFFAIR?
YES!! YES!! HOW DID YOU FIND ME?!
YOU WERE CHOSEN RANDOMLY.
S. Adams

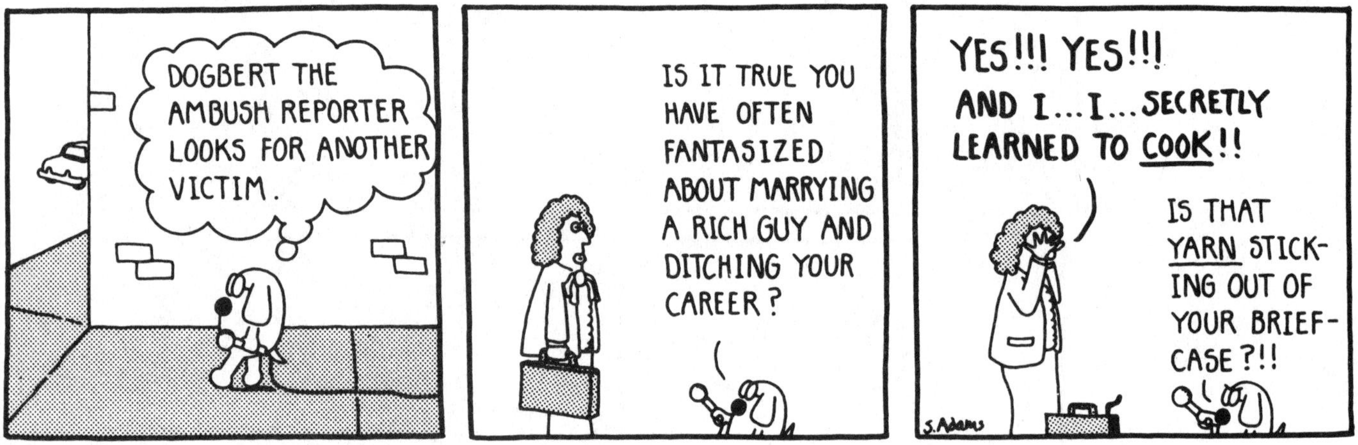
DOGBERT THE AMBUSH REPORTER LOOKS FOR ANOTHER VICTIM.
IS IT TRUE YOU HAVE OFTEN FANTASIZED ABOUT MARRYING A RICH GUY AND DITCHING YOUR CAREER?
YES!!! YES!!! AND I... I... SECRETLY LEARNED TO COOK!!
IS THAT YARN STICKING OUT OF YOUR BRIEFCASE?!!
S. Adams

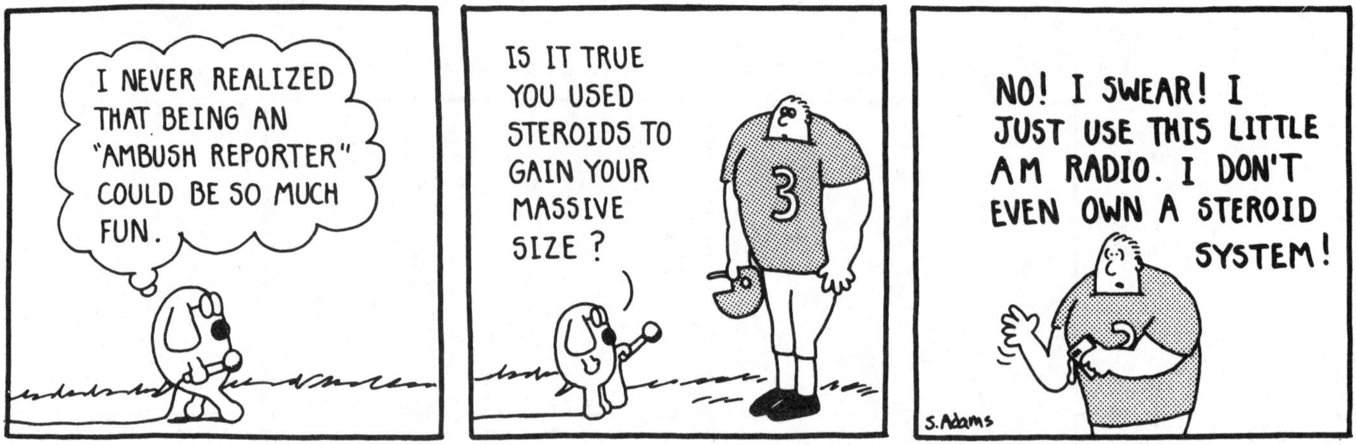
I NEVER REALIZED THAT BEING AN "AMBUSH REPORTER" COULD BE SO MUCH FUN.
IS IT TRUE YOU USED STEROIDS TO GAIN YOUR MASSIVE SIZE?
3
NO! I SWEAR! I JUST USE THIS LITTLE AM RADIO. I DON'T EVEN OWN A STEROID SYSTEM!
S. Adams

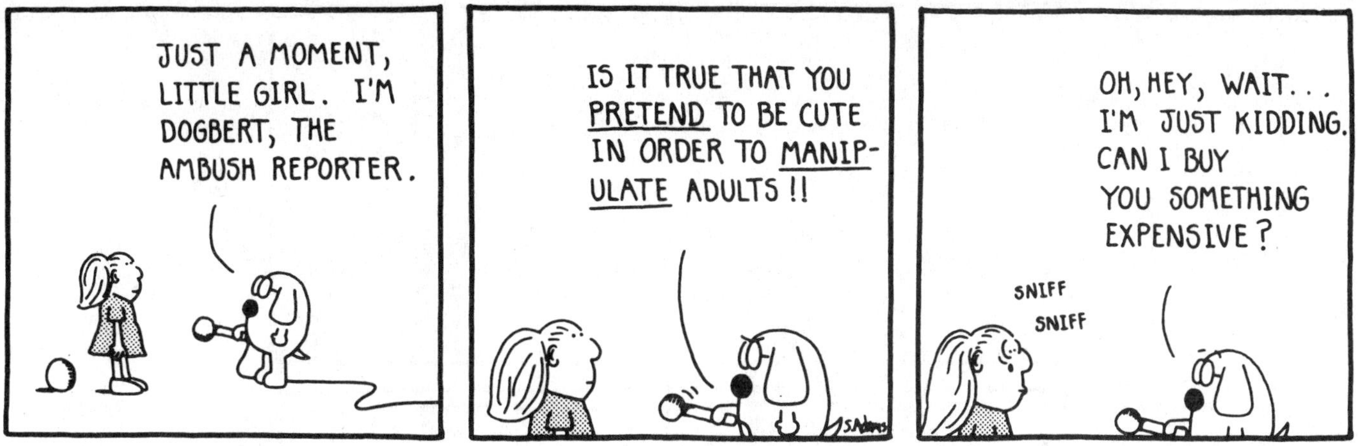
JUST A MOMENT, LITTLE GIRL. I'M DOGBERT, THE AMBUSH REPORTER.
IS IT TRUE THAT YOU PRETEND TO BE CUTE IN ORDER TO MANIPULATE ADULTS !!
OH, HEY, WAIT... I'M JUST KIDDING. CAN I BUY YOU SOMETHING EXPENSIVE?
SNIFF
SNIFF

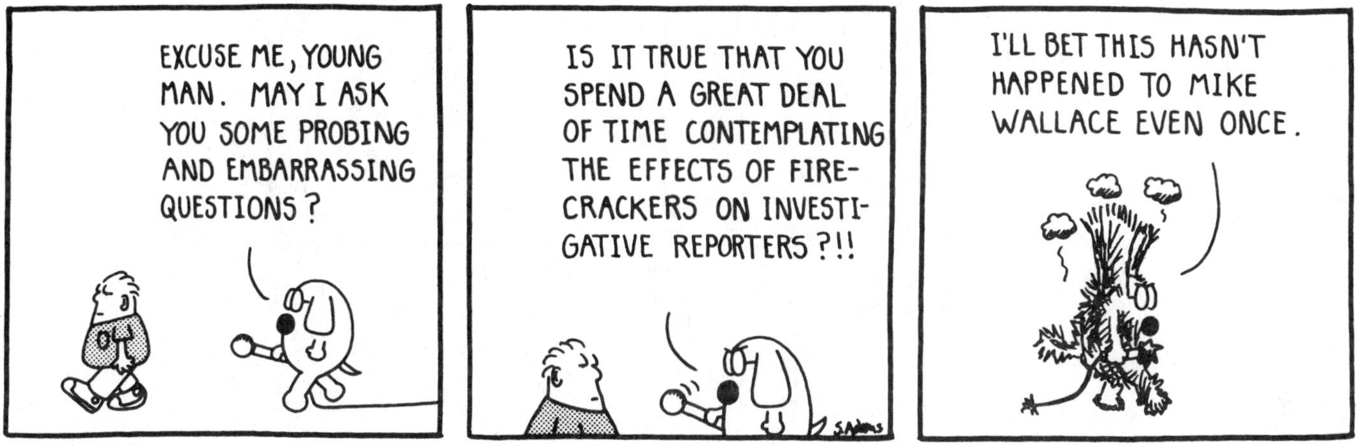
EXCUSE ME, YOUNG MAN. MAY I ASK YOU SOME PROBING AND EMBARRASSING QUESTIONS?
IS IT TRUE THAT YOU SPEND A GREAT DEAL OF TIME CONTEMPLATING THE EFFECTS OF FIRECRACKERS ON INVESTIGATIVE REPORTERS?!!
I'LL BET THIS HASN'T HAPPENED TO MIKE WALLACE EVEN ONCE.

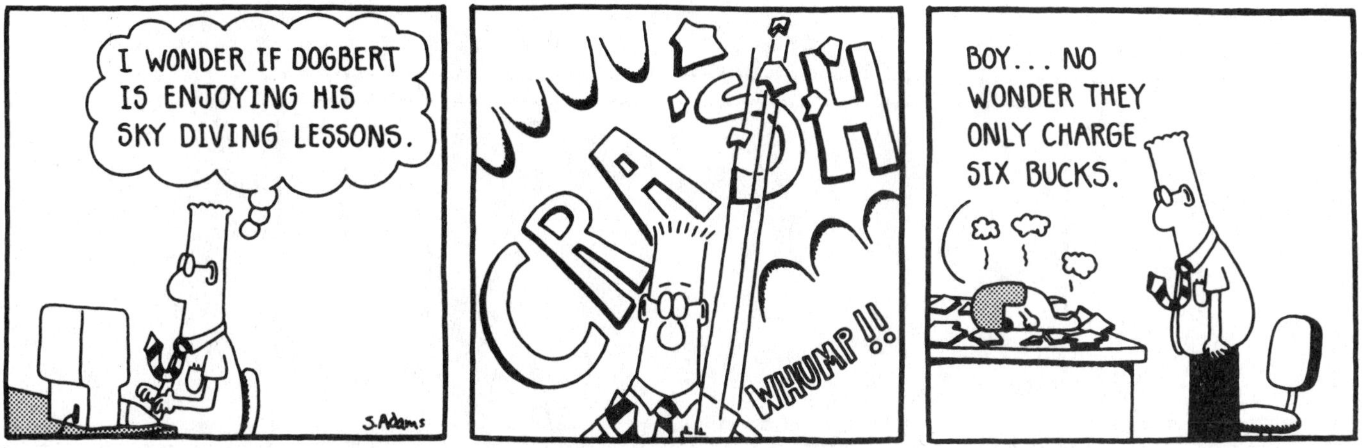
I WONDER IF DOGBERT IS ENJOYING HIS SKY DIVING LESSONS.
CRASH
WHUMP!!
BOY... NO WONDER THEY ONLY CHARGE SIX BUCKS.

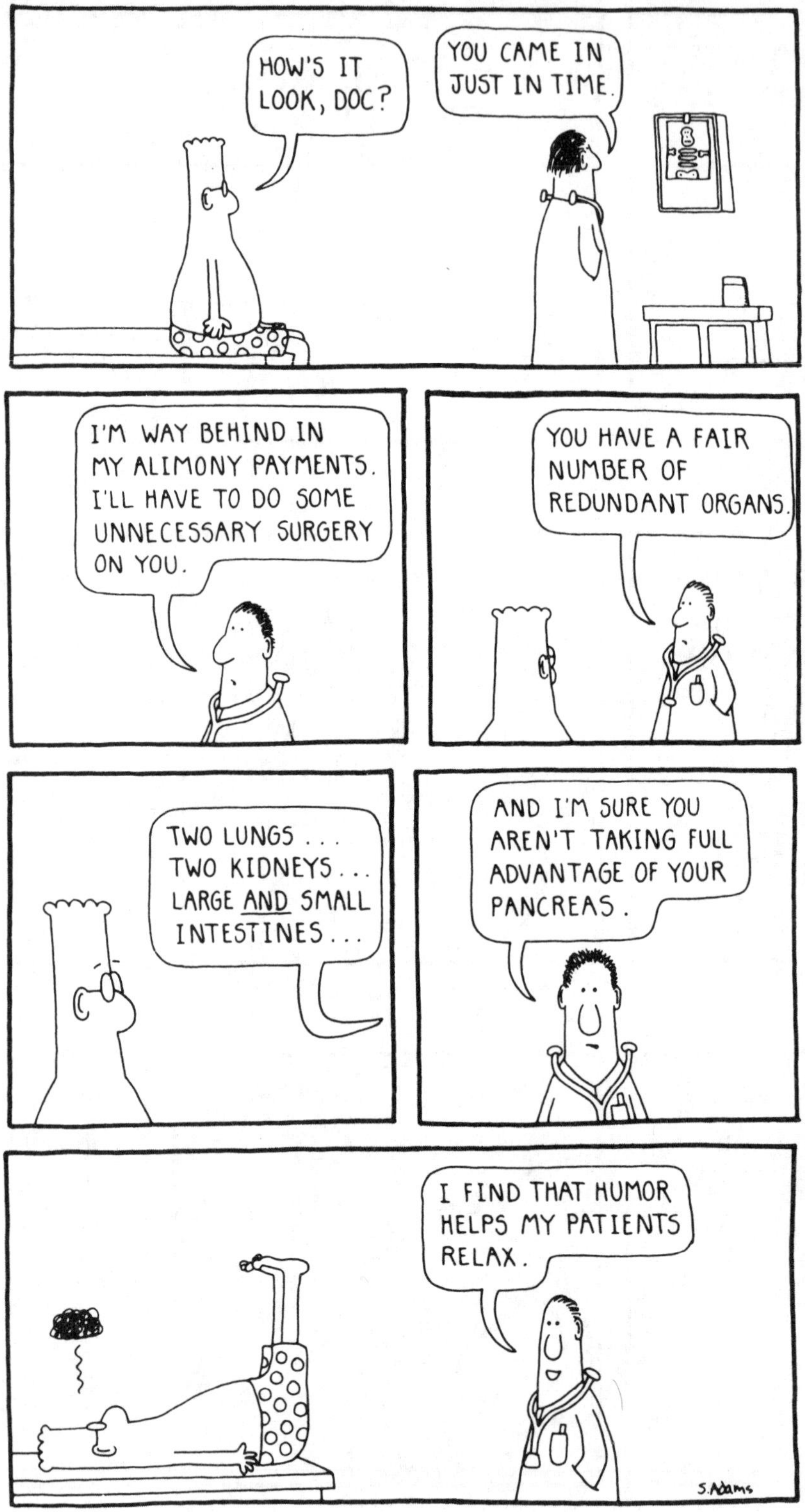
HOW'S IT LOOK, DOC?
YOU CAME IN JUST IN TIME.
I'M WAY BEHIND IN MY ALIMONY PAYMENTS. I'LL HAVE TO DO SOME UNNECESSARY SURGERY ON YOU.
YOU HAVE A FAIR NUMBER OF REDUNDANT ORGANS.
TWO LUNGS . . . TWO KIDNEYS . . . LARGE AND SMALL INTESTINES . . .
AND I'M SURE YOU AREN'T TAKING FULL ADVANTAGE OF YOUR PANCREAS.
I FIND THAT HUMOR HELPS MY PATIENTS RELAX.
S. Adams

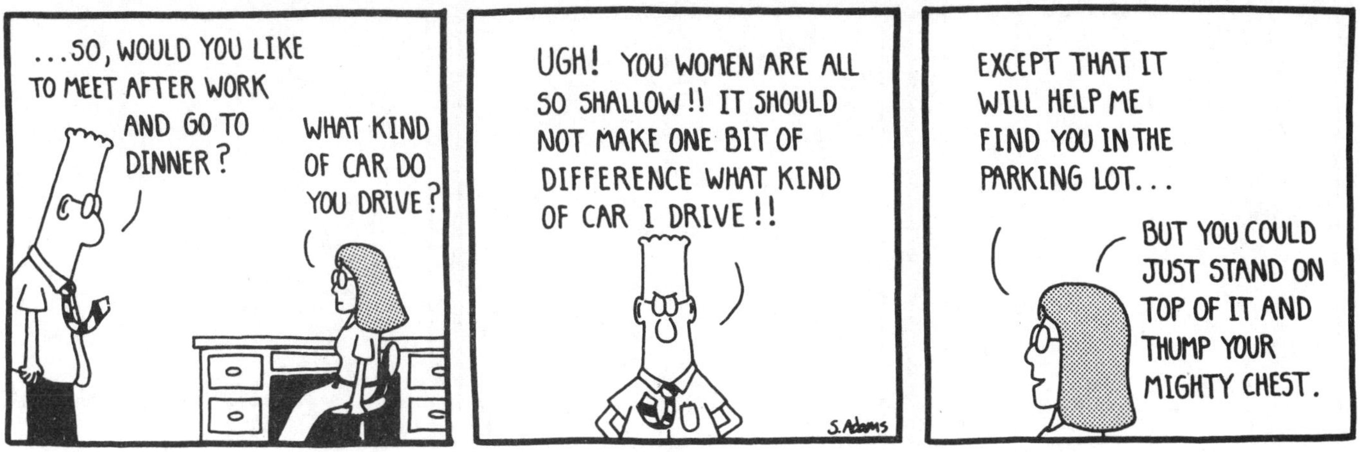
...SO, WOULD YOU LIKE TO MEET AFTER WORK AND GO TO DINNER?
WHAT KIND OF CAR DO YOU DRIVE?
UGH! YOU WOMEN ARE ALL SO SHALLOW!! IT SHOULD NOT MAKE ONE BIT OF DIFFERENCE WHAT KIND OF CAR I DRIVE!!
S.Adams
EXCEPT THAT IT WILL HELP ME FIND YOU IN THE PARKING LOT...
BUT YOU COULD JUST STAND ON TOP OF IT AND THUMP YOUR MIGHTY CHEST.

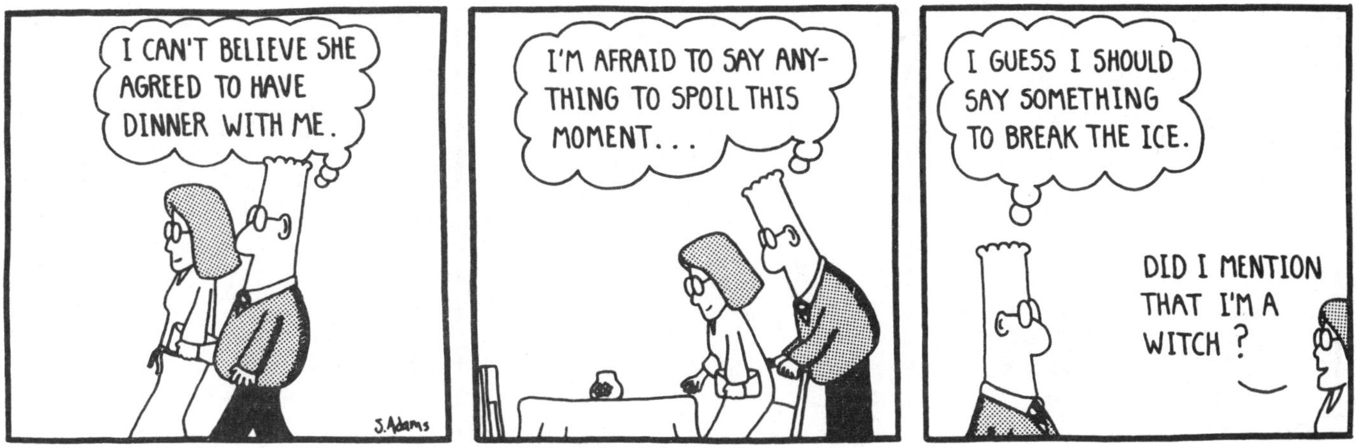
I CAN'T BELIEVE SHE AGREED TO HAVE DINNER WITH ME.
S.Adams
I'M AFRAID TO SAY ANYTHING TO SPOIL THIS MOMENT...
I GUESS I SHOULD SAY SOMETHING TO BREAK THE ICE.
DID I MENTION THAT I'M A WITCH?

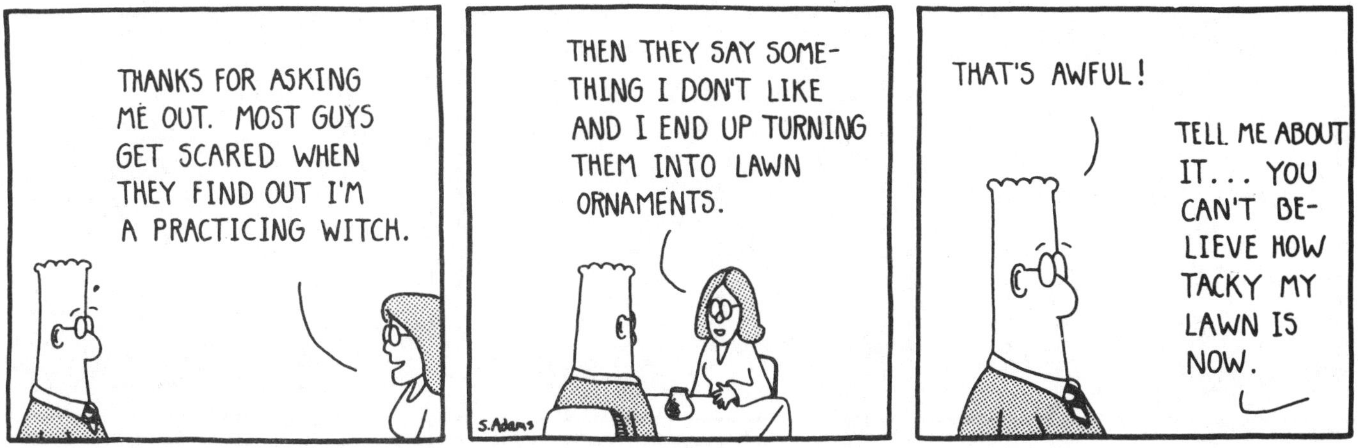
THANKS FOR ASKING ME OUT. MOST GUYS GET SCARED WHEN THEY FIND OUT I'M A PRACTICING WITCH.
THEN THEY SAY SOMETHING I DON'T LIKE AND I END UP TURNING THEM INTO LAWN ORNAMENTS.
S.Adams
THAT'S AWFUL!
TELL ME ABOUT IT... YOU CAN'T BELIEVE HOW TACKY MY LAWN IS NOW.

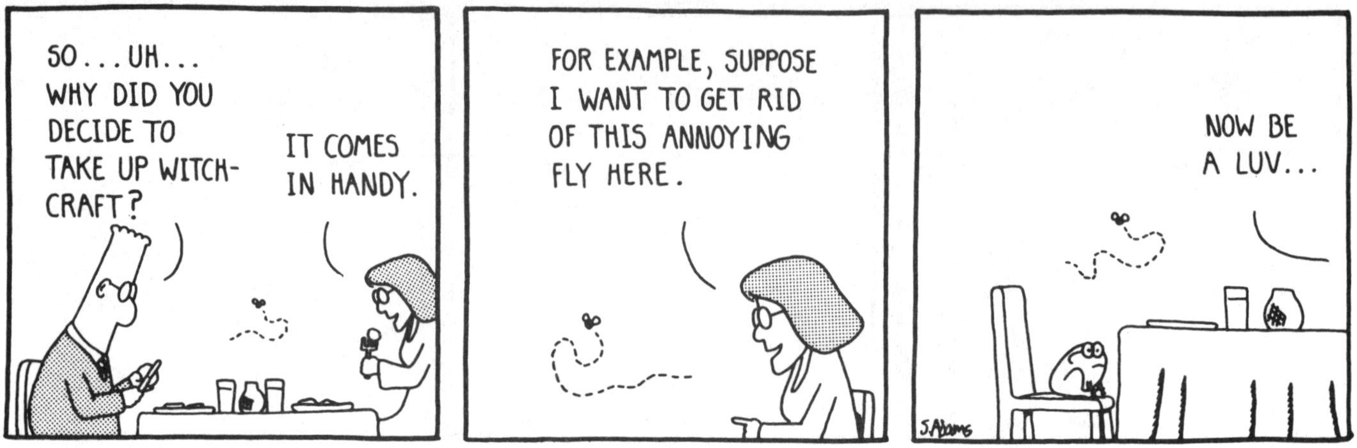
SO... UH... WHY DID YOU DECIDE TO TAKE UP WITCH-CRAFT?
IT COMES IN HANDY.
FOR EXAMPLE, SUPPOSE I WANT TO GET RID OF THIS ANNOYING FLY HERE.
NOW BE A LUV...

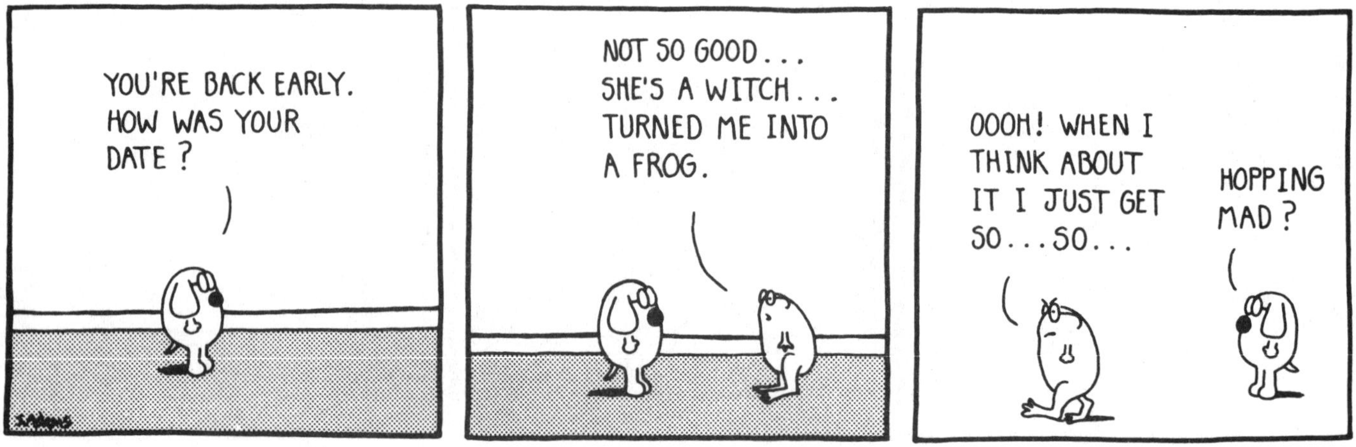
YOU'RE BACK EARLY. HOW WAS YOUR DATE?
NOT SO GOOD... SHE'S A WITCH... TURNED ME INTO A FROG.
OOOH! WHEN I THINK ABOUT IT I JUST GET SO... SO...
HOPPING MAD?

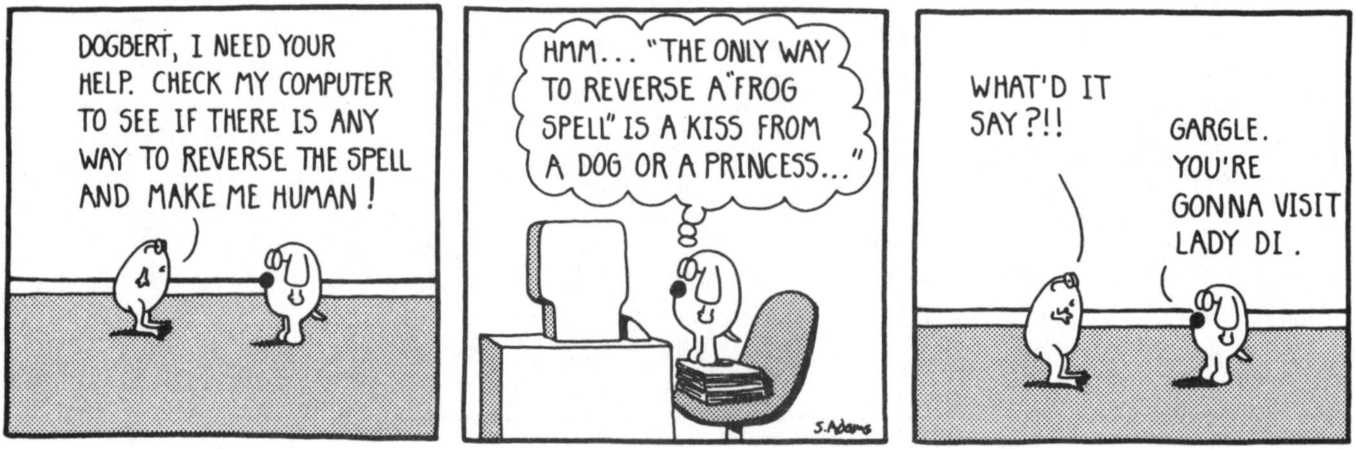
DOGBERT, I NEED YOUR HELP. CHECK MY COMPUTER TO SEE IF THERE IS ANY WAY TO REVERSE THE SPELL AND MAKE ME HUMAN!
HMM... "THE ONLY WAY TO REVERSE A "FROG SPELL" IS A KISS FROM A DOG OR A PRINCESS..."
WHAT'D IT SAY?!!
GARGLE. YOU'RE GONNA VISIT LADY DI.

PLANS FOR THE CORPORATE TAKE-OVER ARE COMPLETE.
WHAT CORPORATE TAKEOVER?
IT'S A HOSTILE BID FOR CONTROL OF THE MEOWCO CAT FOOD COMPANY.
WHEN I BECOME CEO, I'LL ORDER THEM TO ADD A HAIRBALL TO EVERY CAN OF CAT FOOD.
HEH HEH
THAT IS CRUEL AND SENSELESS. I'M THOROUGHLY ASHAMED OF YOU.
S Adams
GEE... IT SEEMS SO MUCH MORE EFFICIENT THAN HASSLING ONE CAT AT A TIME.

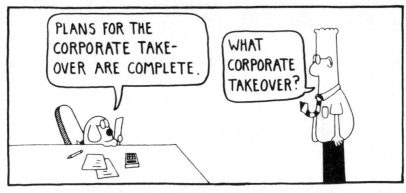

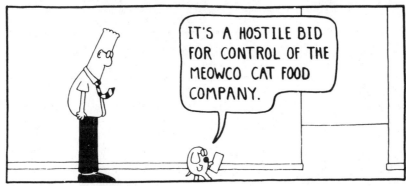

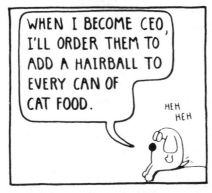

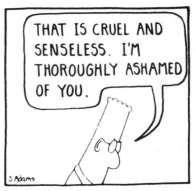

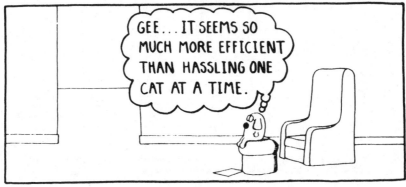

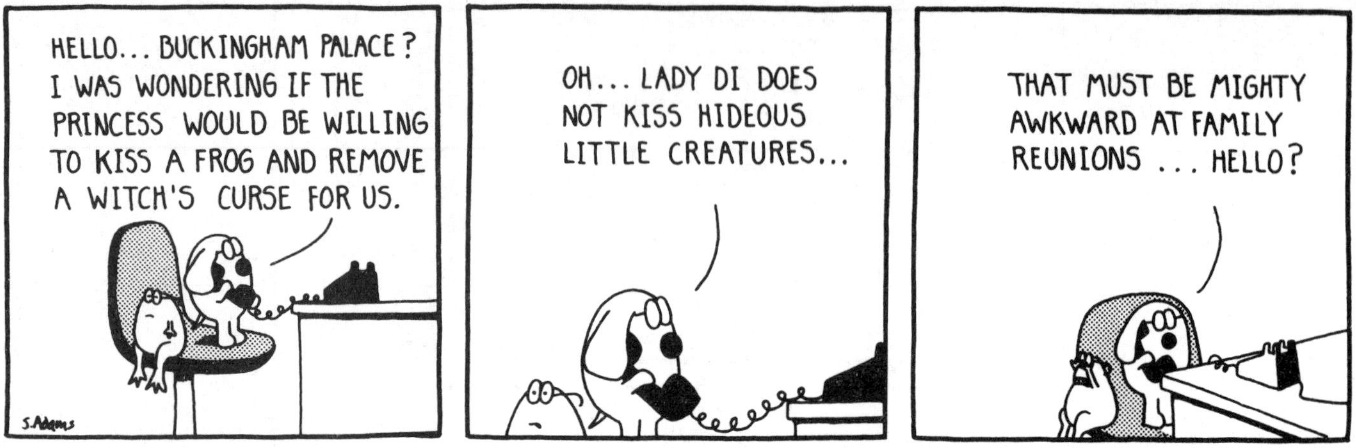
HELLO... BUCKINGHAM PALACE? I WAS WONDERING IF THE PRINCESS WOULD BE WILLING TO KISS A FROG AND REMOVE A WITCH'S CURSE FOR US.
S. Adams
OH... LADY DI DOES NOT KISS HIDEOUS LITTLE CREATURES...
THAT MUST BE MIGHTY AWKWARD AT FAMILY REUNIONS ... HELLO?

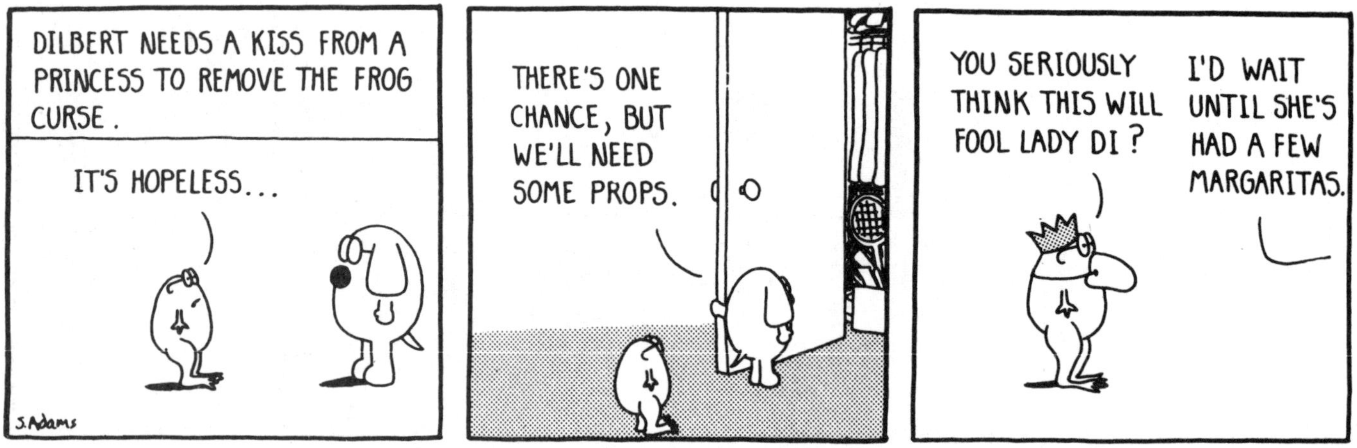
DILBERT NEEDS A KISS FROM A PRINCESS TO REMOVE THE FROG CURSE.
IT'S HOPELESS...
S. Adams
THERE'S ONE CHANCE, BUT WE'LL NEED SOME PROPS.
YOU SERIOUSLY THINK THIS WILL FOOL LADY DI?
I'D WAIT UNTIL SHE'S HAD A FEW MARGARITAS.

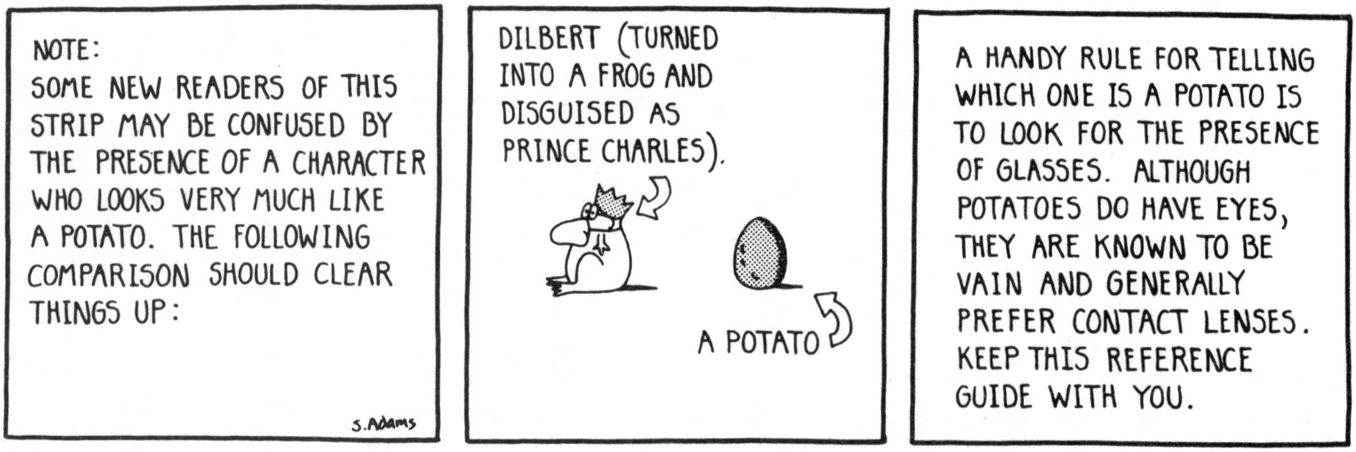
NOTE:
SOME NEW READERS OF THIS STRIP MAY BE CONFUSED BY THE PRESENCE OF A CHARACTER WHO LOOKS VERY MUCH LIKE A POTATO. THE FOLLOWING COMPARISON SHOULD CLEAR THINGS UP:
S. Adams
DILBERT (TURNED INTO A FROG AND DISGUISED AS PRINCE CHARLES).
A POTATO
A HANDY RULE FOR TELLING WHICH ONE IS A POTATO IS TO LOOK FOR THE PRESENCE OF GLASSES. ALTHOUGH POTATOES DO HAVE EYES, THEY ARE KNOWN TO BE VAIN AND GENERALLY PREFER CONTACT LENSES. KEEP THIS REFERENCE GUIDE WITH YOU.

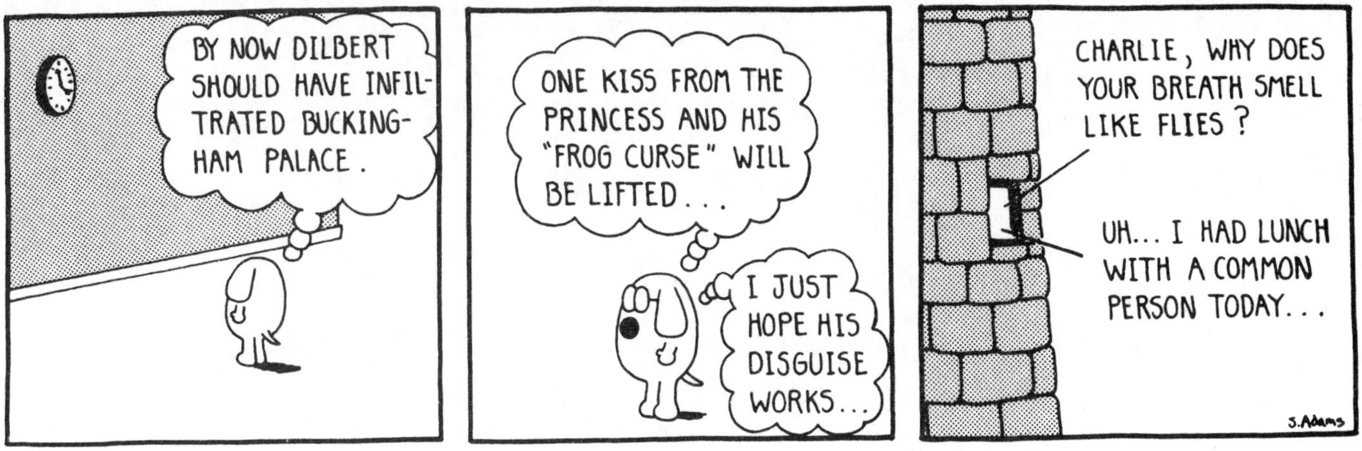
BY NOW DILBERT SHOULD HAVE INFIL-TRATED BUCKING-HAM PALACE.
ONE KISS FROM THE PRINCESS AND HIS "FROG CURSE" WILL BE LIFTED...
I JUST HOPE HIS DISGUISE WORKS...
CHARLIE, WHY DOES YOUR BREATH SMELL LIKE FLIES?
UH... I HAD LUNCH WITH A COMMON PERSON TODAY...
S.Adams

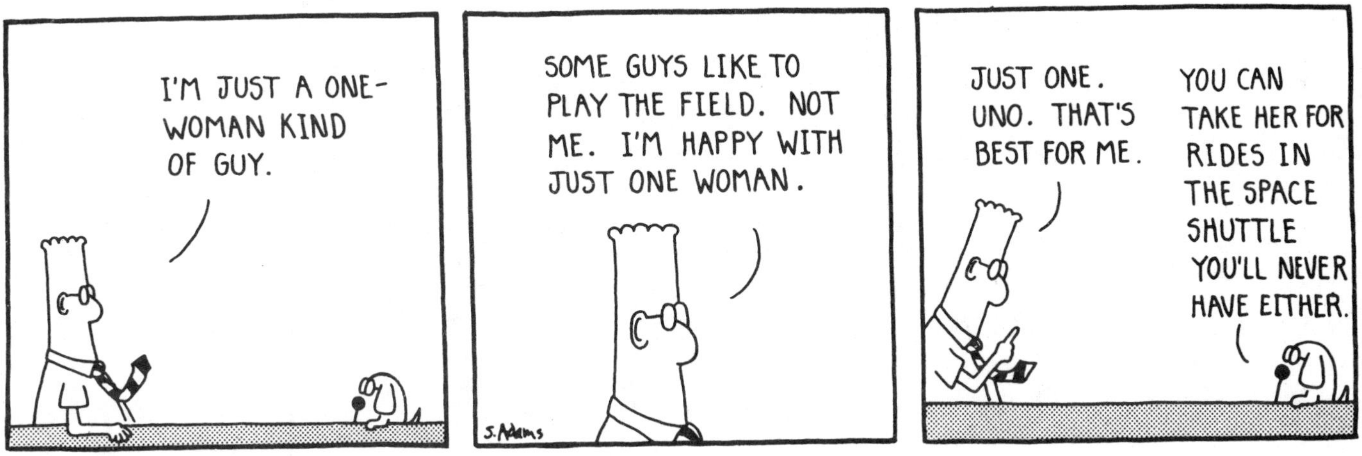
I'M JUST A ONE-WOMAN KIND OF GUY.
SOME GUYS LIKE TO PLAY THE FIELD. NOT ME. I'M HAPPY WITH JUST ONE WOMAN.
S.Adams
JUST ONE. UNO. THAT'S BEST FOR ME.
YOU CAN TAKE HER FOR RIDES IN THE SPACE SHUTTLE YOU'LL NEVER HAVE EITHER.

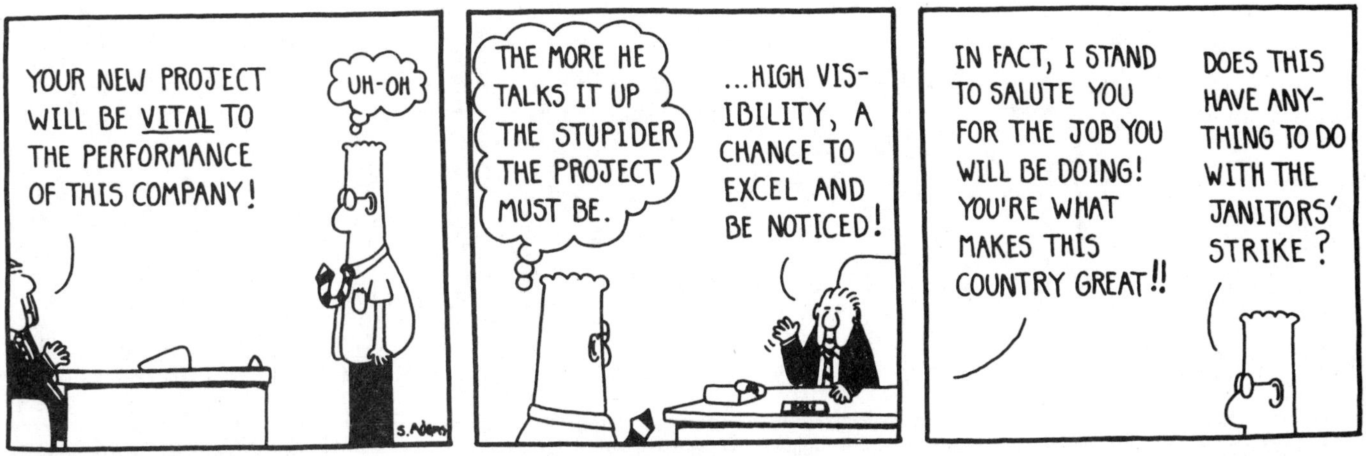
YOUR NEW PROJECT WILL BE VITAL TO THE PERFORMANCE OF THIS COMPANY!
UH-OH
S.Adams
THE MORE HE TALKS IT UP THE STUPIDER THE PROJECT MUST BE.
...HIGH VIS-IBILITY, A CHANCE TO EXCEL AND BE NOTICED!
IN FACT, I STAND TO SALUTE YOU FOR THE JOB YOU WILL BE DOING! YOU'RE WHAT MAKES THIS COUNTRY GREAT!!
DOES THIS HAVE ANY-THING TO DO WITH THE JANITORS' STRIKE?

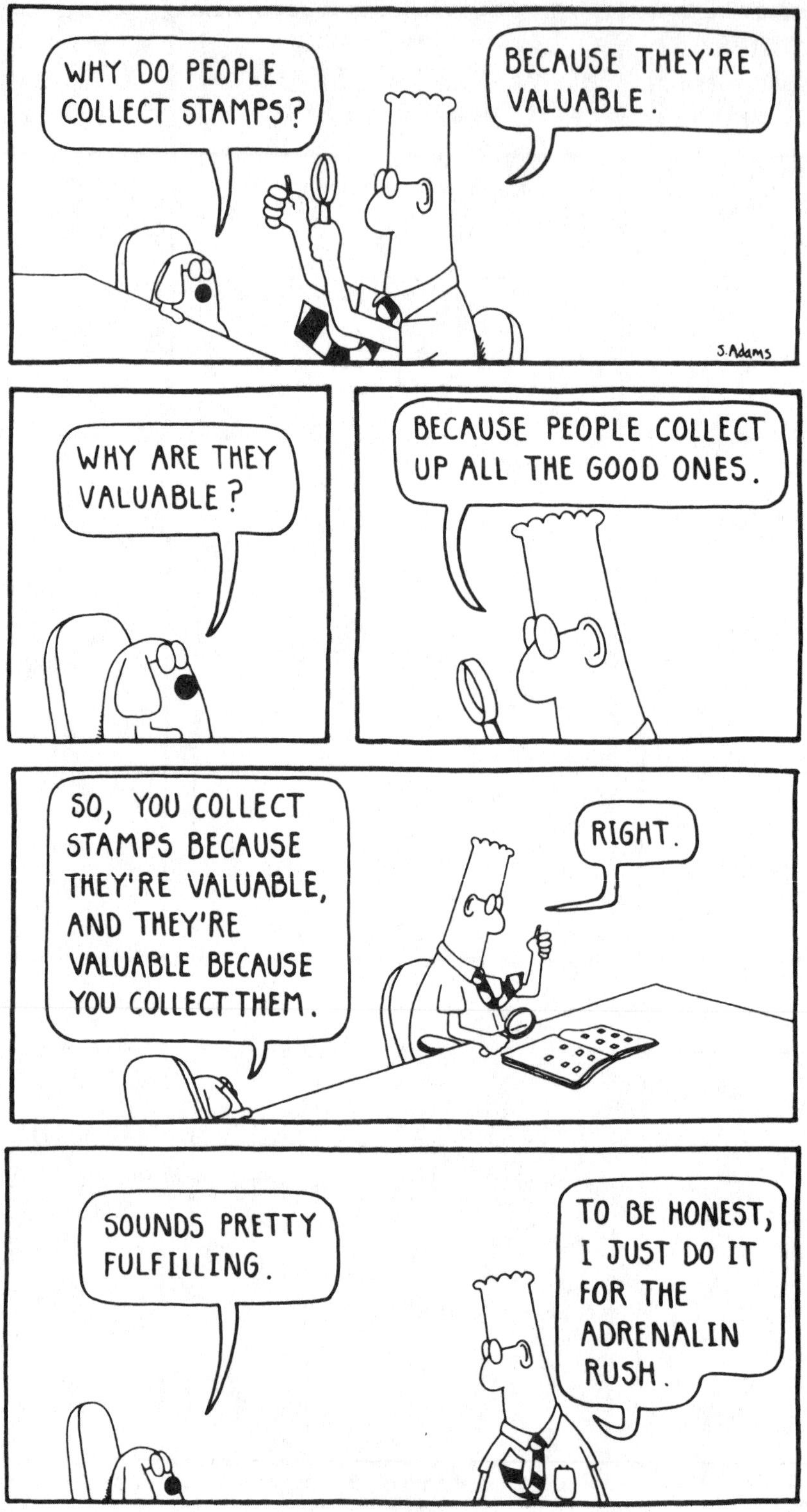
WHY DO PEOPLE COLLECT STAMPS?
BECAUSE THEY'RE VALUABLE.
S. Adams
WHY ARE THEY VALUABLE?
BECAUSE PEOPLE COLLECT UP ALL THE GOOD ONES.
SO, YOU COLLECT STAMPS BECAUSE THEY'RE VALUABLE, AND THEY'RE VALUABLE BECAUSE YOU COLLECT THEM.
RIGHT.
SOUNDS PRETTY FULFILLING.
TO BE HONEST, I JUST DO IT FOR THE ADRENALIN RUSH.

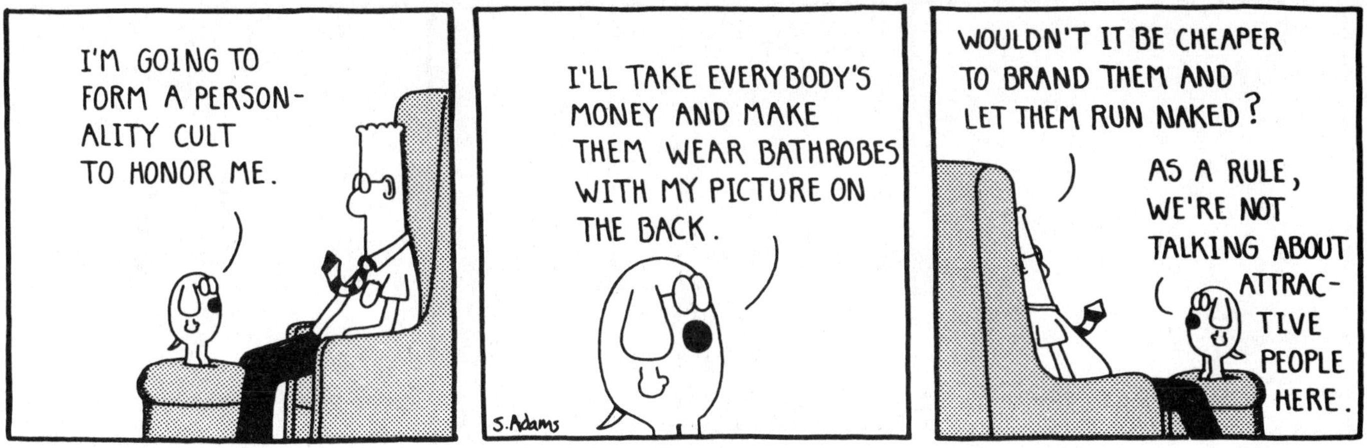
I'M GOING TO FORM A PERSONALITY CULT TO HONOR ME.
I'LL TAKE EVERYBODY'S MONEY AND MAKE THEM WEAR BATHROBES WITH MY PICTURE ON THE BACK.
S. Adams
WOULDN'T IT BE CHEAPER TO BRAND THEM AND LET THEM RUN NAKED?
AS A RULE, WE'RE NOT TALKING ABOUT ATTRACTIVE PEOPLE HERE.

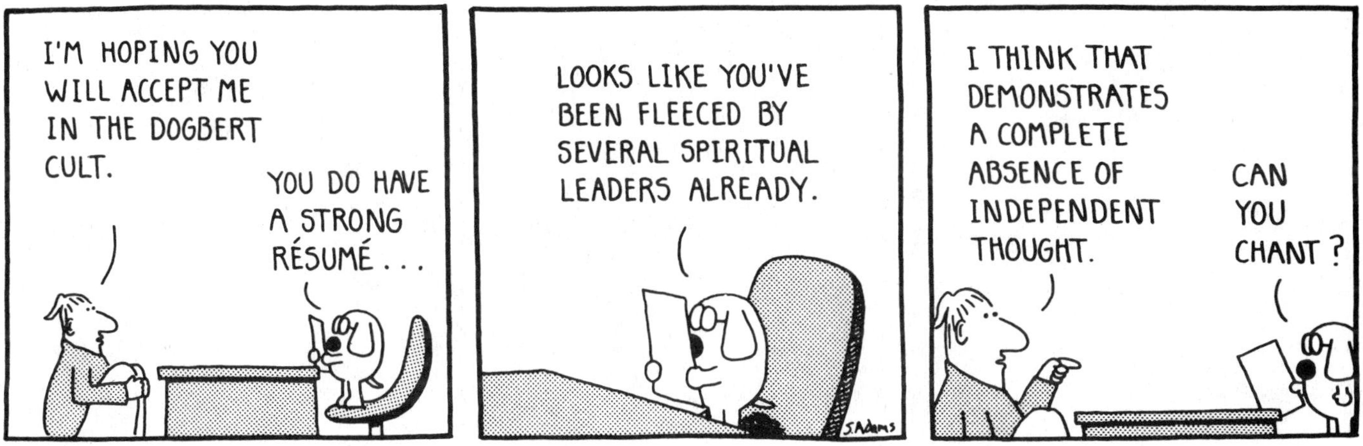
I'M HOPING YOU WILL ACCEPT ME IN THE DOGBERT CULT.
YOU DO HAVE A STRONG RÉSUMÉ . . .
LOOKS LIKE YOU'VE BEEN FLEECED BY SEVERAL SPIRITUAL LEADERS ALREADY.
I THINK THAT DEMONSTRATES A COMPLETE ABSENCE OF INDEPENDENT THOUGHT.
CAN YOU CHANT?

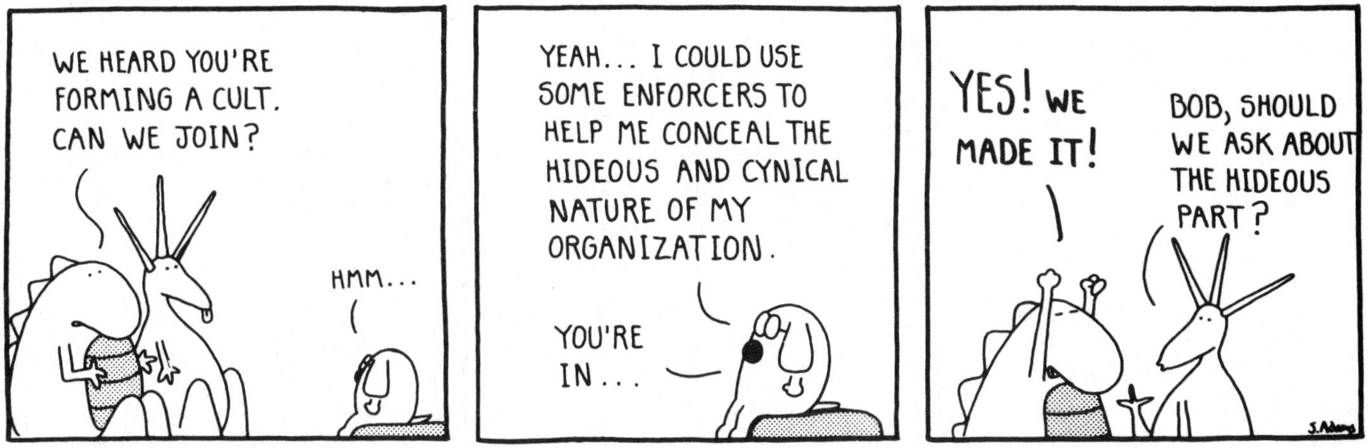
WE HEARD YOU'RE FORMING A CULT. CAN WE JOIN?
HMM...
YEAH... I COULD USE SOME ENFORCERS TO HELP ME CONCEAL THE HIDEOUS AND CYNICAL NATURE OF MY ORGANIZATION.
YOU'RE IN . . .
YES! WE MADE IT!
BOB, SHOULD WE ASK ABOUT THE HIDEOUS PART?

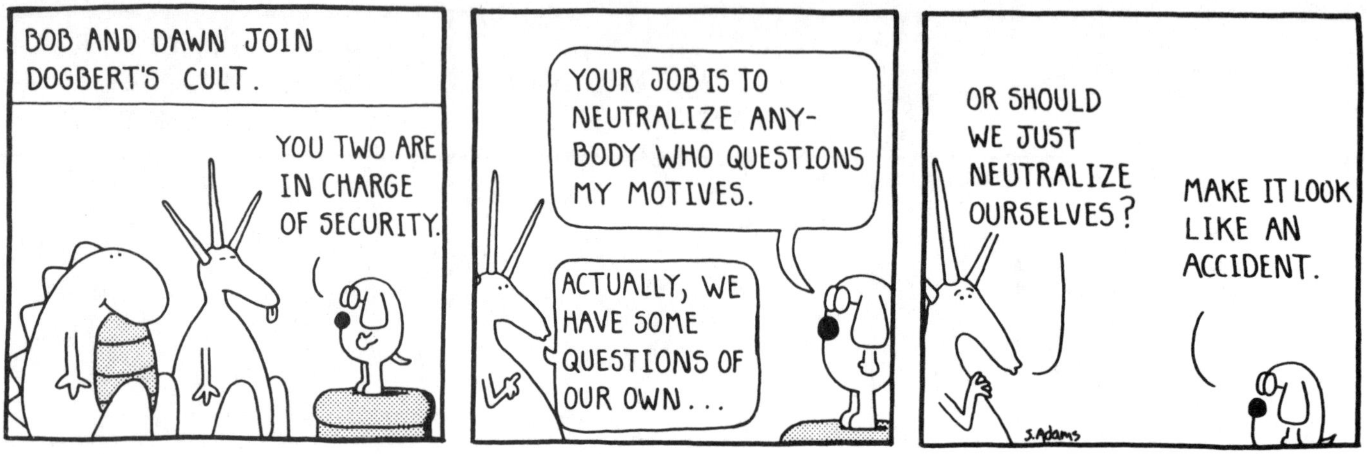
BOB AND DAWN JOIN DOGBERT'S CULT.
YOU TWO ARE IN CHARGE OF SECURITY.
YOUR JOB IS TO NEUTRALIZE ANY-BODY WHO QUESTIONS MY MOTIVES.
ACTUALLY, WE HAVE SOME QUESTIONS OF OUR OWN...
OR SHOULD WE JUST NEUTRALIZE OURSELVES?
MAKE IT LOOK LIKE AN ACCIDENT.
S.Adams

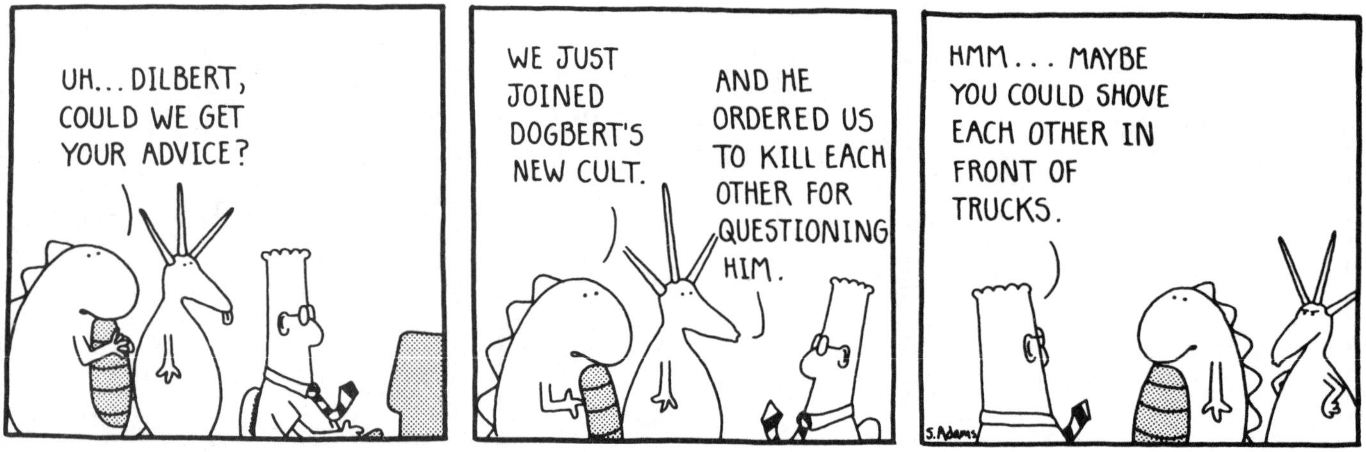
UH... DILBERT, COULD WE GET YOUR ADVICE?
WE JUST JOINED DOGBERT'S NEW CULT.
AND HE ORDERED US TO KILL EACH OTHER FOR QUESTIONING HIM.
HMM... MAYBE YOU COULD SHOVE EACH OTHER IN FRONT OF TRUCKS.
S.Adams

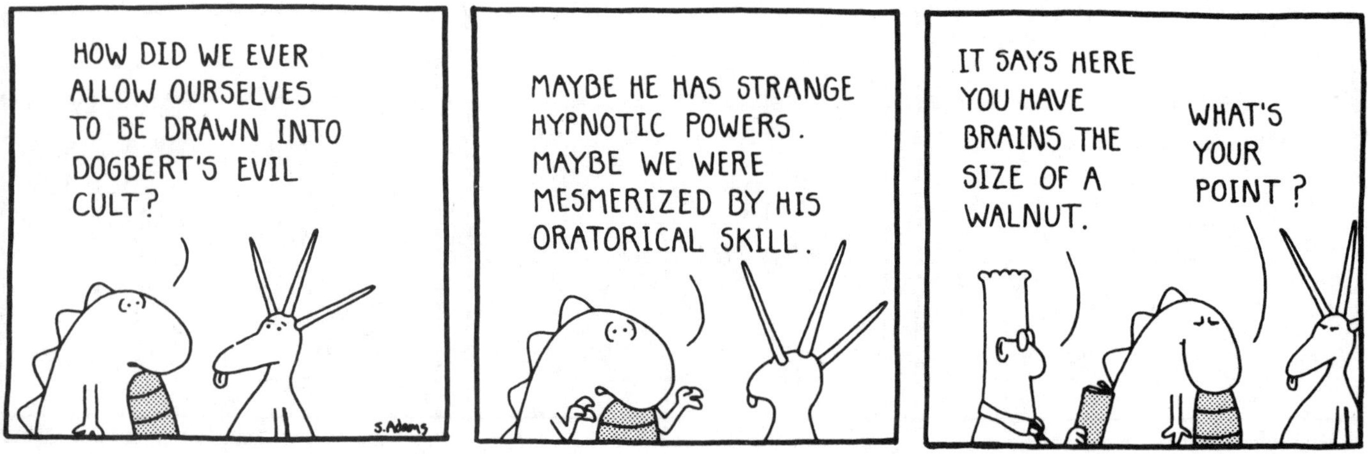
HOW DID WE EVER ALLOW OURSELVES TO BE DRAWN INTO DOGBERT'S EVIL CULT?
MAYBE HE HAS STRANGE HYPNOTIC POWERS. MAYBE WE WERE MESMERIZED BY HIS ORATORICAL SKILL.
IT SAYS HERE YOU HAVE BRAINS THE SIZE OF A WALNUT.
WHAT'S YOUR POINT?
S.Adams

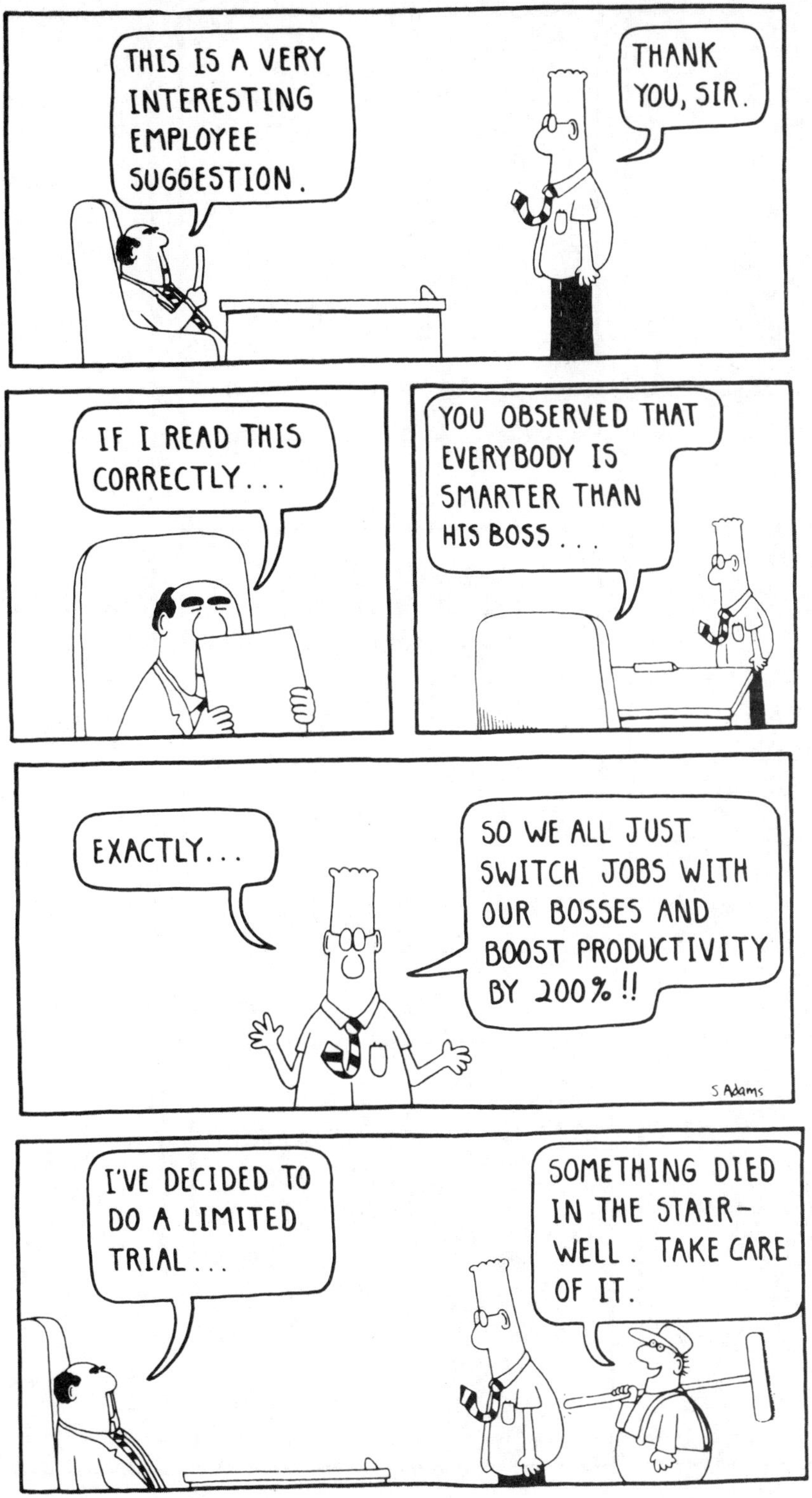
THIS IS A VERY INTERESTING EMPLOYEE SUGGESTION.
THANK YOU, SIR.
IF I READ THIS CORRECTLY...
YOU OBSERVED THAT EVERYBODY IS SMARTER THAN HIS BOSS...
EXACTLY...
SO WE ALL JUST SWITCH JOBS WITH OUR BOSSES AND BOOST PRODUCTIVITY BY 200%!!
S Adams
I'VE DECIDED TO DO A LIMITED TRIAL...
SOMETHING DIED IN THE STAIR-WELL. TAKE CARE OF IT.

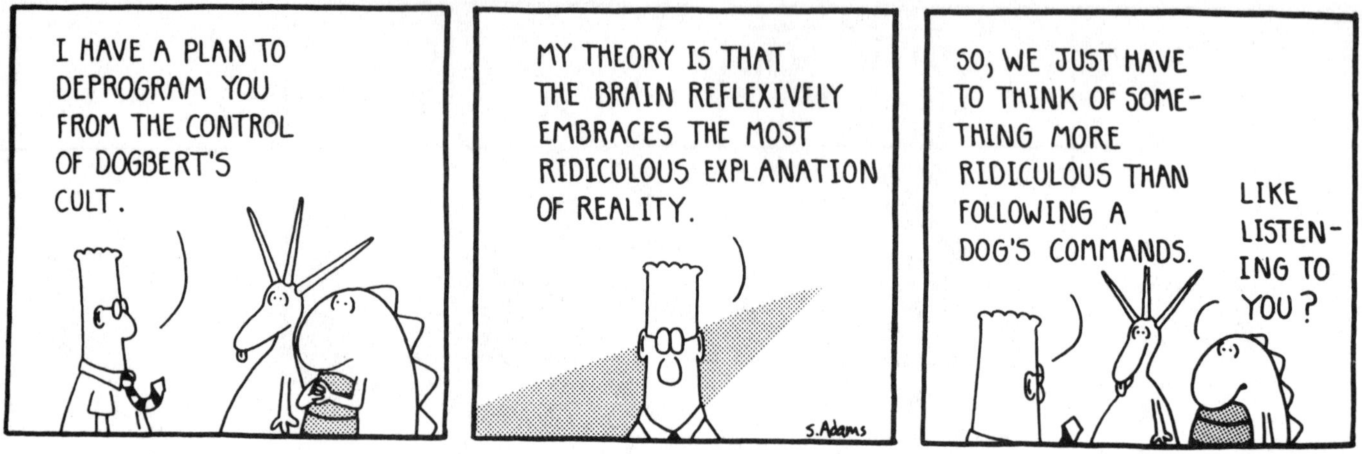
I HAVE A PLAN TO DEPROGRAM YOU FROM THE CONTROL OF DOGBERT'S CULT.
MY THEORY IS THAT THE BRAIN REFLEXIVELY EMBRACES THE MOST RIDICULOUS EXPLANATION OF REALITY.
S.Adams
SO, WE JUST HAVE TO THINK OF SOME-THING MORE RIDICULOUS THAN FOLLOWING A DOG'S COMMANDS.
LIKE LISTEN-ING TO YOU?

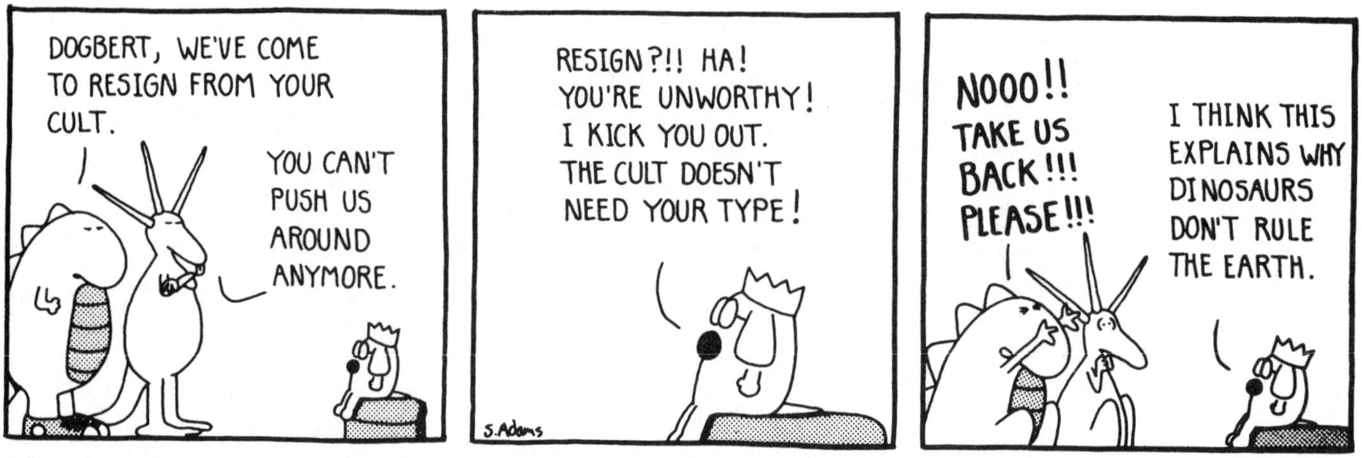
DOGBERT, WE'VE COME TO RESIGN FROM YOUR CULT.
YOU CAN'T PUSH US AROUND ANYMORE.
RESIGN?!! HA! YOU'RE UNWORTHY! I KICK YOU OUT. THE CULT DOESN'T NEED YOUR TYPE!
S.Adams
NOOO!! TAKE US BACK!!! PLEASE!!!
I THINK THIS EXPLAINS WHY DINOSAURS DON'T RULE THE EARTH.

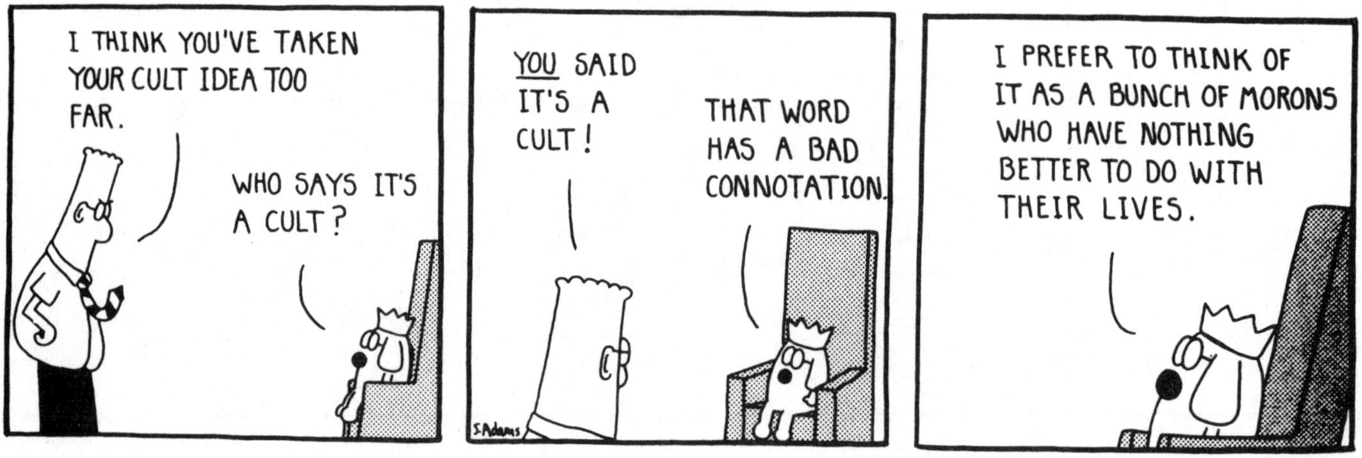
I THINK YOU'VE TAKEN YOUR CULT IDEA TOO FAR.
WHO SAYS IT'S A CULT?
YOU SAID IT'S A CULT!
THAT WORD HAS A BAD CONNOTATION.
S.Adams
I PREFER TO THINK OF IT AS A BUNCH OF MORONS WHO HAVE NOTHING BETTER TO DO WITH THEIR LIVES.

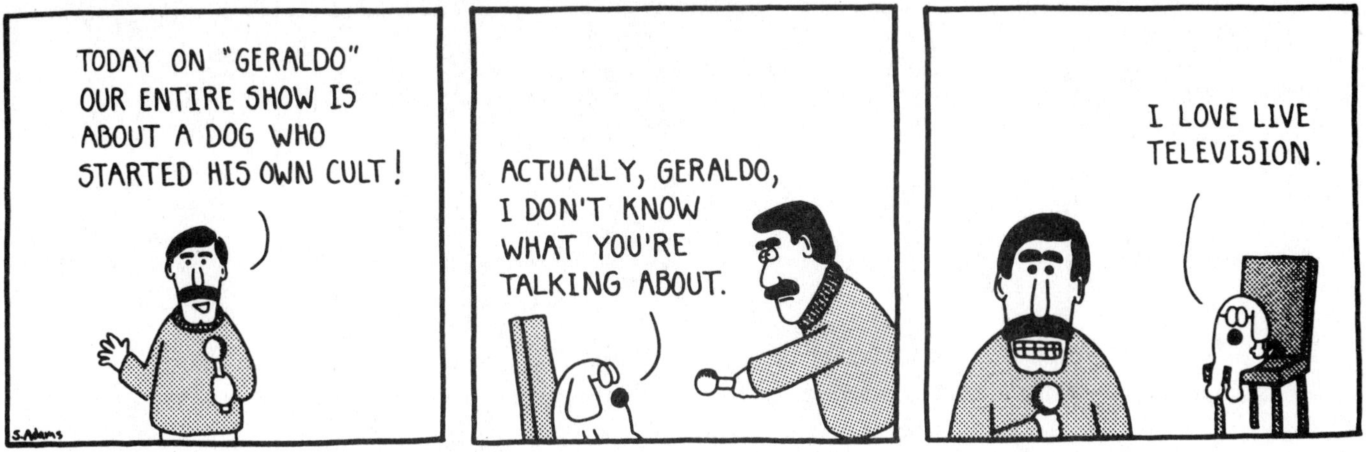
TODAY ON "GERALDO" OUR ENTIRE SHOW IS ABOUT A DOG WHO STARTED HIS OWN CULT!
ACTUALLY, GERALDO, I DON'T KNOW WHAT YOU'RE TALKING ABOUT.
I LOVE LIVE TELEVISION.

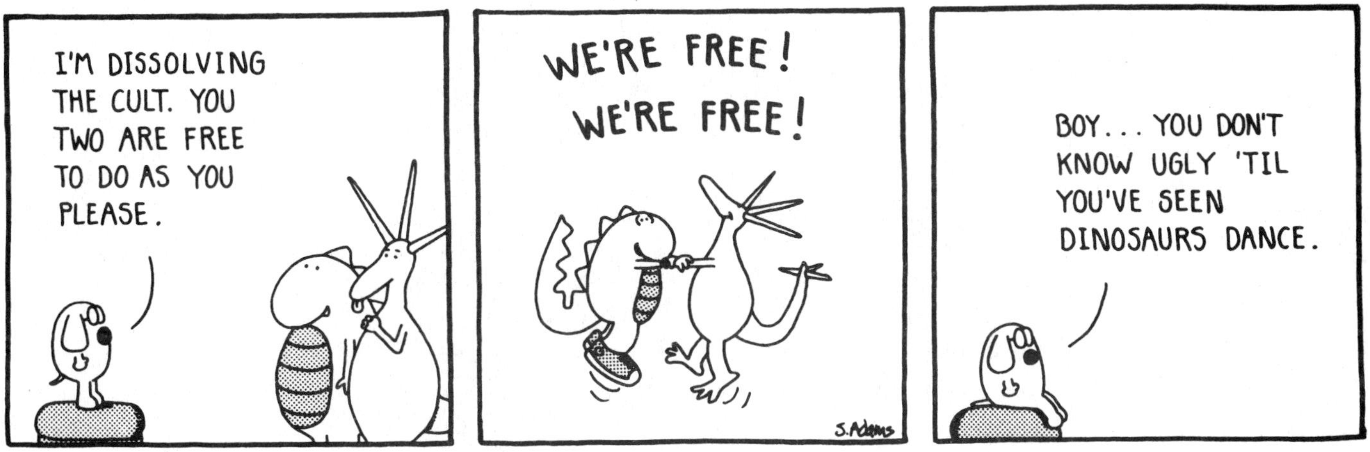
I'M DISSOLVING THE CULT. YOU TWO ARE FREE TO DO AS YOU PLEASE.
WE'RE FREE! WE'RE FREE!
BOY... YOU DON'T KNOW UGLY 'TIL YOU'VE SEEN DINOSAURS DANCE.

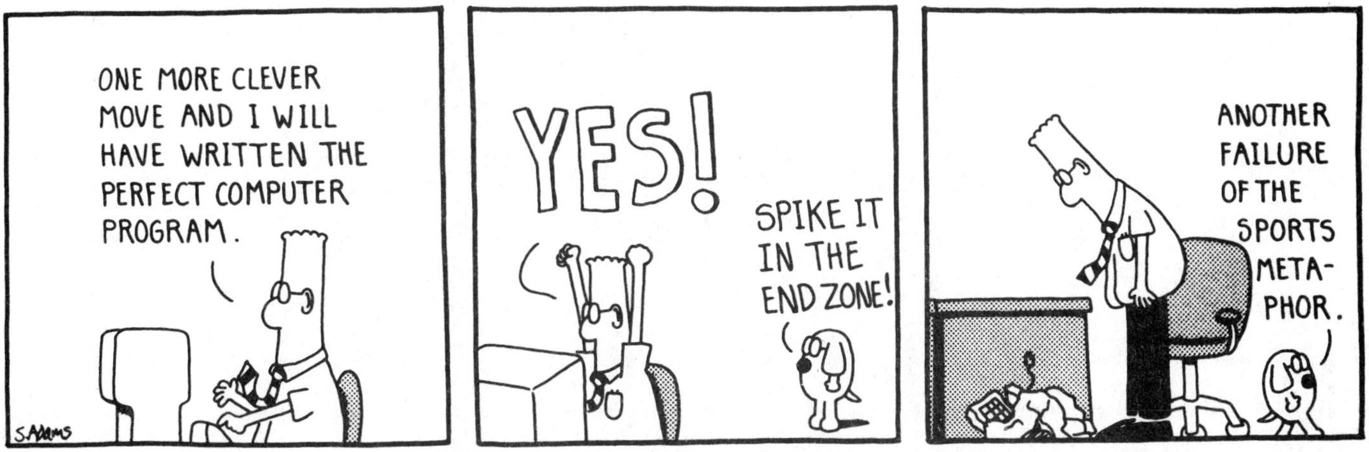
ONE MORE CLEVER MOVE AND I WILL HAVE WRITTEN THE PERFECT COMPUTER PROGRAM.
YES!
SPIKE IT IN THE END ZONE!
ANOTHER FAILURE OF THE SPORTS METAPHOR.

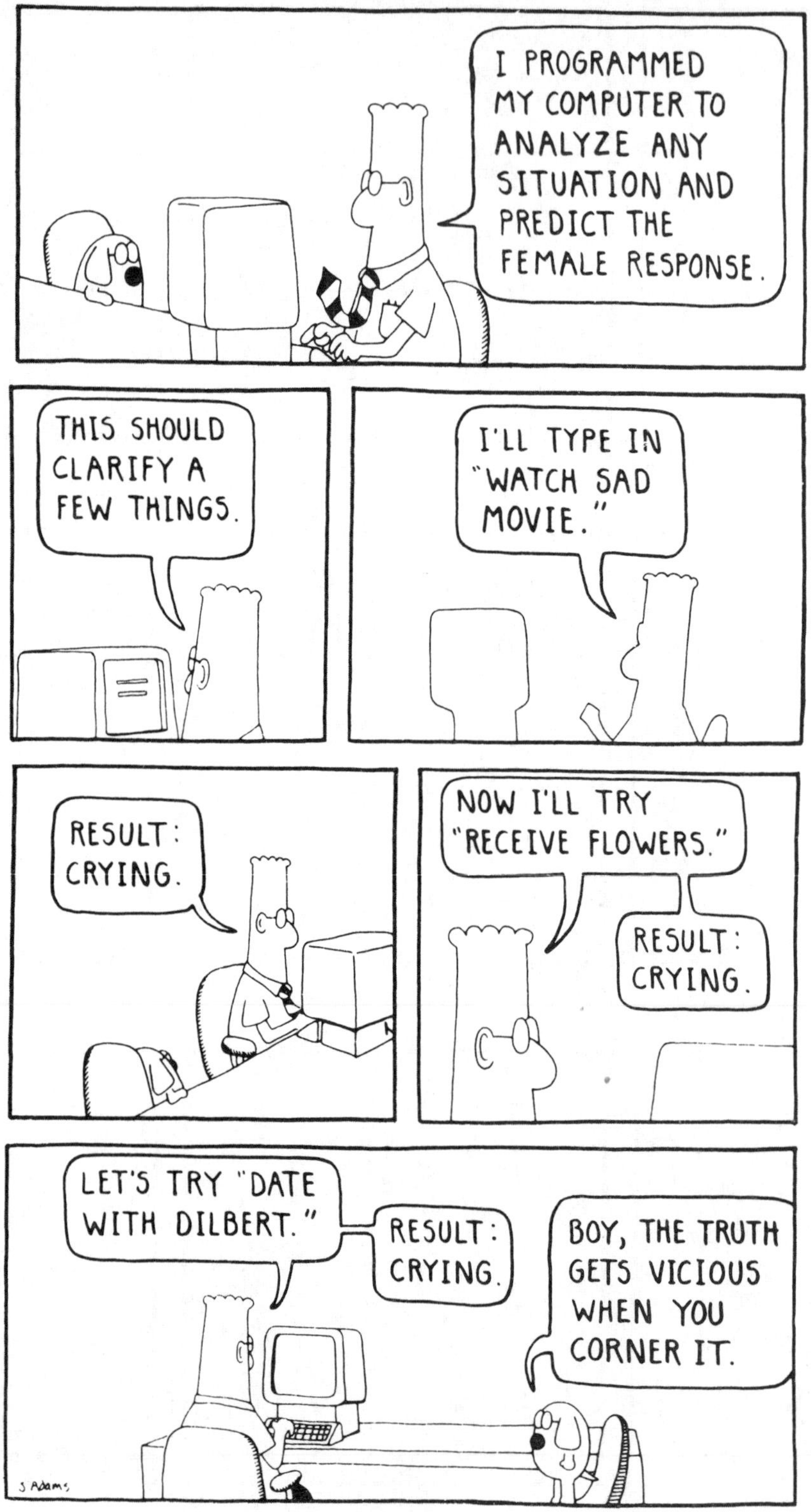
I PROGRAMMED MY COMPUTER TO ANALYZE ANY SITUATION AND PREDICT THE FEMALE RESPONSE.
THIS SHOULD CLARIFY A FEW THINGS.
I'LL TYPE IN "WATCH SAD MOVIE."
RESULT: CRYING.
NOW I'LL TRY "RECEIVE FLOWERS."
RESULT: CRYING.
LET'S TRY "DATE WITH DILBERT."
RESULT: CRYING.
BOY, THE TRUTH GETS VICIOUS WHEN YOU CORNER IT.
S. Adams

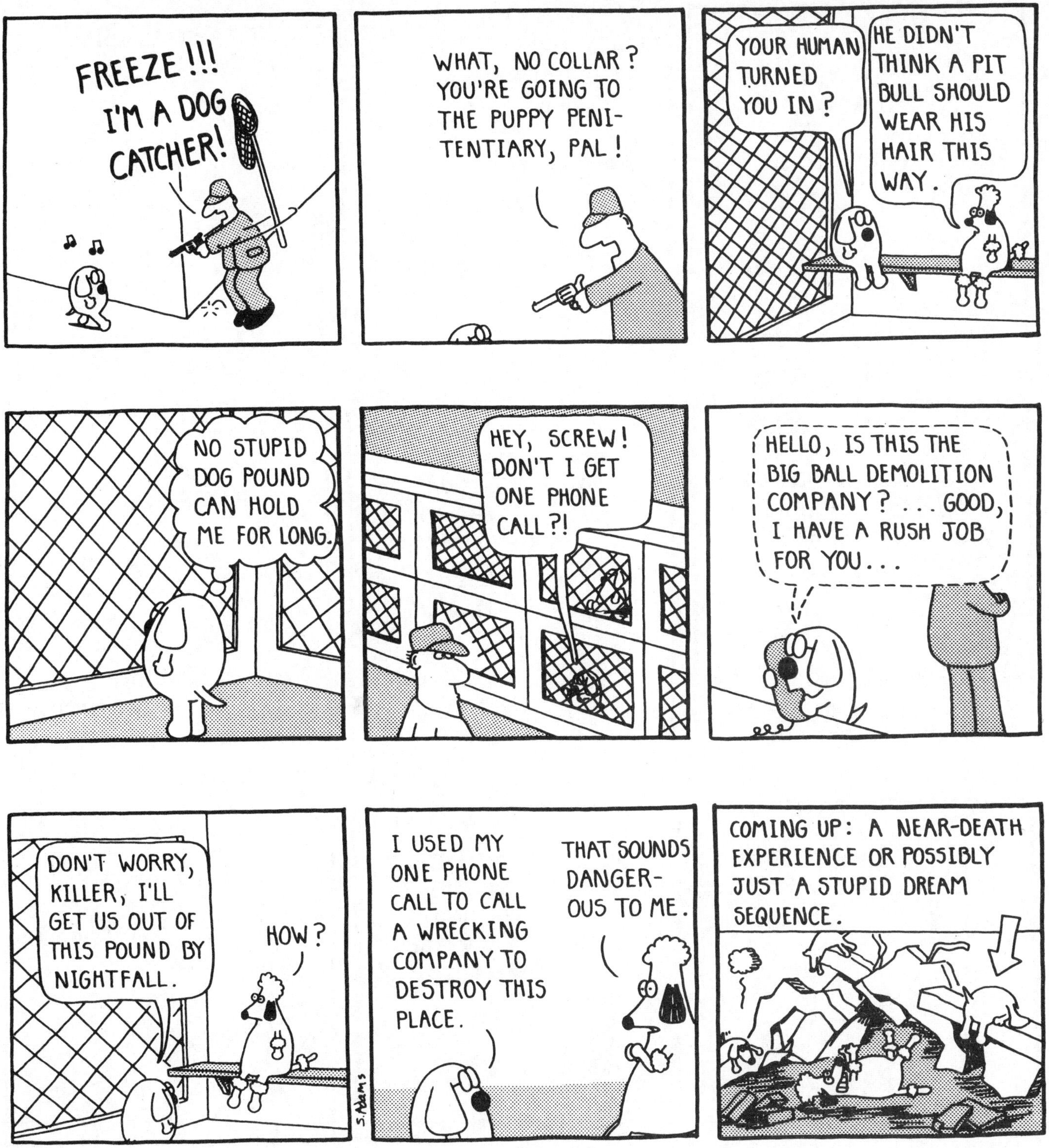
FREEZE!!! I'M A DOG CATCHER!
WHAT, NO COLLAR? YOU'RE GOING TO THE PUPPY PENITENTIARY, PAL!
YOUR HUMAN TURNED YOU IN?
HE DIDN'T THINK A PIT BULL SHOULD WEAR HIS HAIR THIS WAY.
NO STUPID DOG POUND CAN HOLD ME FOR LONG.
HEY, SCREW! DON'T I GET ONE PHONE CALL?!
HELLO, IS THIS THE BIG BALL DEMOLITION COMPANY? . . . GOOD, I HAVE A RUSH JOB FOR YOU . . .
DON'T WORRY, KILLER, I'LL GET US OUT OF THIS POUND BY NIGHTFALL.
HOW?
I USED MY ONE PHONE CALL TO CALL A WRECKING COMPANY TO DESTROY THIS PLACE.
THAT SOUNDS DANGEROUS TO ME.
COMING UP: A NEAR-DEATH EXPERIENCE OR POSSIBLY JUST A STUPID DREAM SEQUENCE.

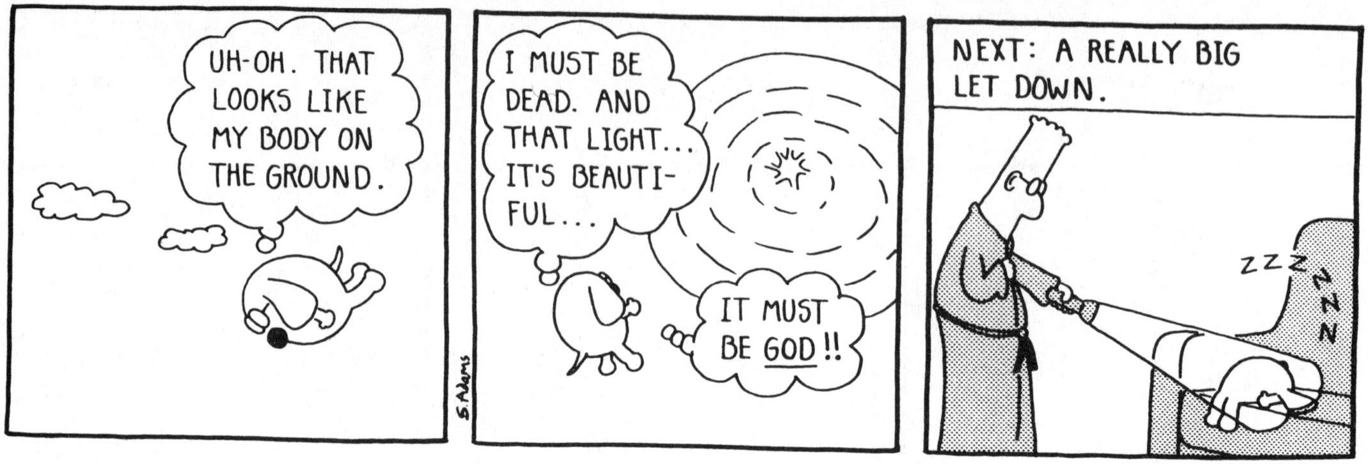
UH-OH. THAT LOOKS LIKE MY BODY ON THE GROUND.
I MUST BE DEAD. AND THAT LIGHT... IT'S BEAUTIFUL...
IT MUST BE GOD!!
S. Adams
NEXT: A REALLY BIG LET DOWN.
ZZZZZZ

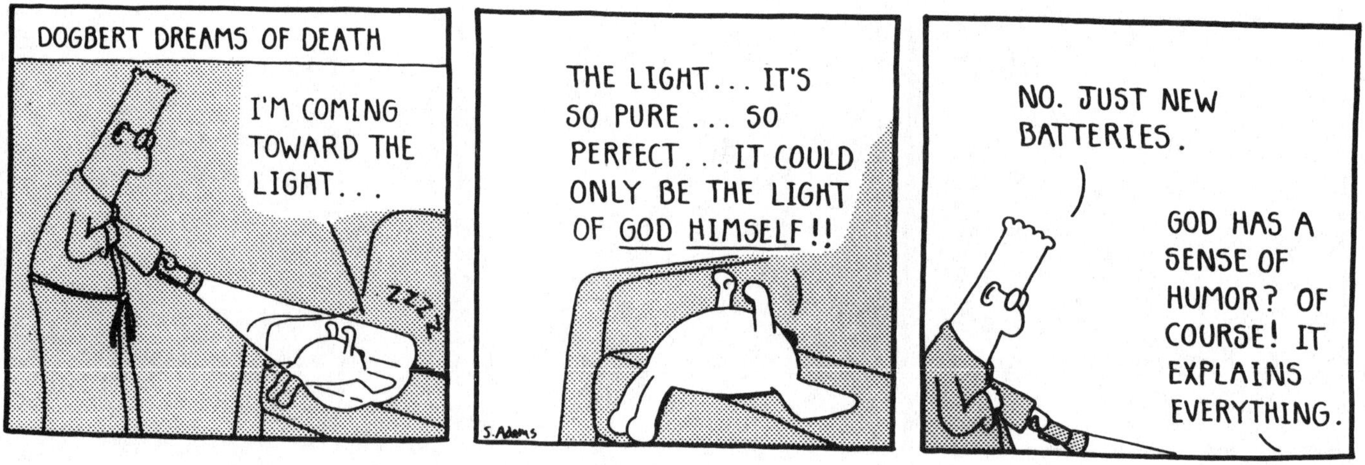
DOGBERT DREAMS OF DEATH
I'M COMING TOWARD THE LIGHT...
ZZZZ
THE LIGHT... IT'S SO PURE ... SO PERFECT... IT COULD ONLY BE THE LIGHT OF GOD HIMSELF!!
S. Adams
NO. JUST NEW BATTERIES.
GOD HAS A SENSE OF HUMOR? OF COURSE! IT EXPLAINS EVERYTHING.

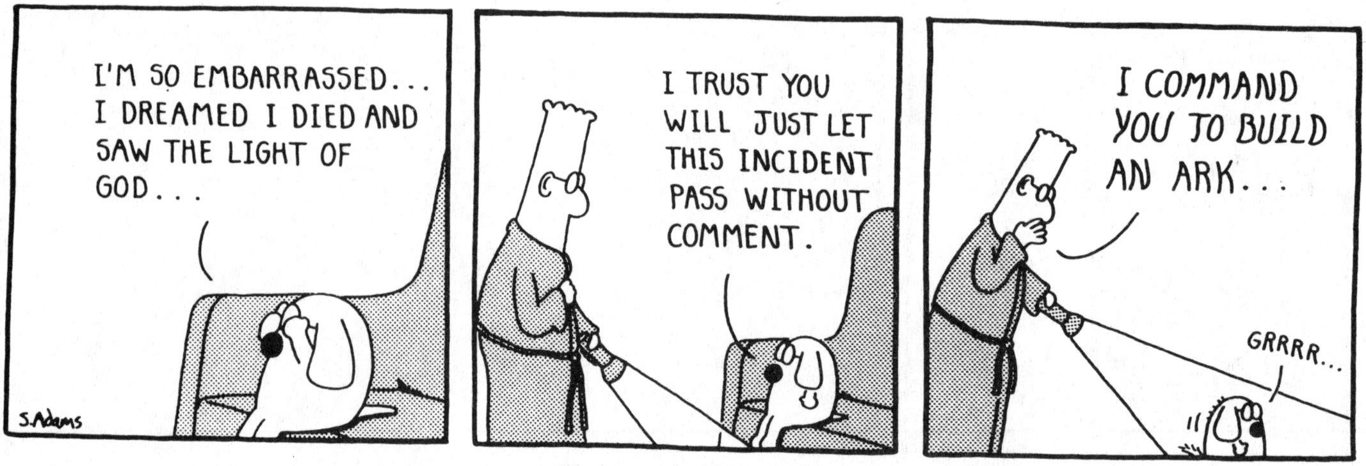
I'M SO EMBARRASSED... I DREAMED I DIED AND SAW THE LIGHT OF GOD...
S. Adams
I TRUST YOU WILL JUST LET THIS INCIDENT PASS WITHOUT COMMENT.
I COMMAND YOU TO BUILD AN ARK...
GRRRR...

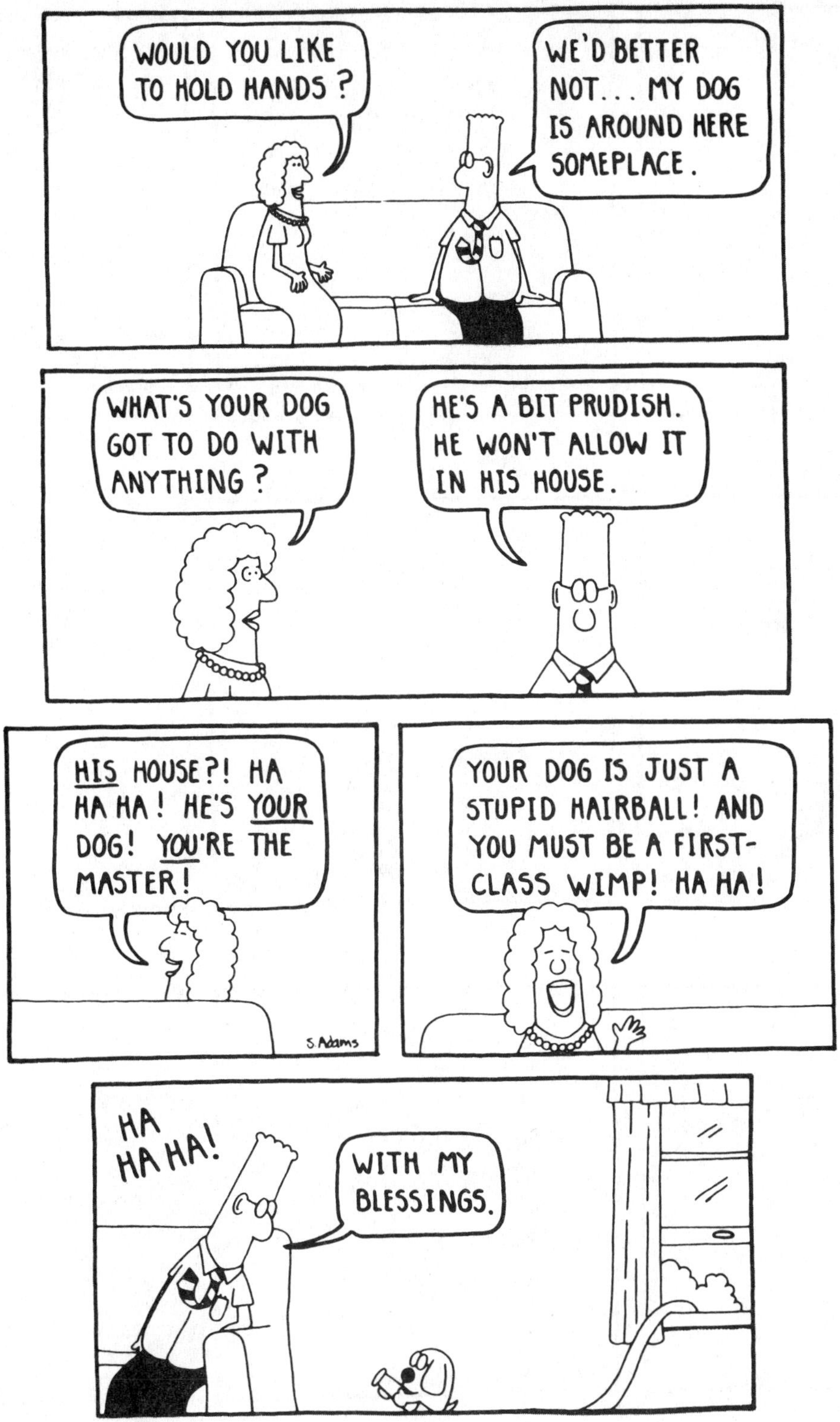
WOULD YOU LIKE TO HOLD HANDS?
WE'D BETTER NOT... MY DOG IS AROUND HERE SOMEPLACE.
WHAT'S YOUR DOG GOT TO DO WITH ANYTHING?
HE'S A BIT PRUDISH. HE WON'T ALLOW IT IN HIS HOUSE.
HIS HOUSE?! HA HA HA! HE'S YOUR DOG! YOU'RE THE MASTER!
S. Adams
YOUR DOG IS JUST A STUPID HAIRBALL! AND YOU MUST BE A FIRST-CLASS WIMP! HA HA!
HA HA HA!
WITH MY BLESSINGS.

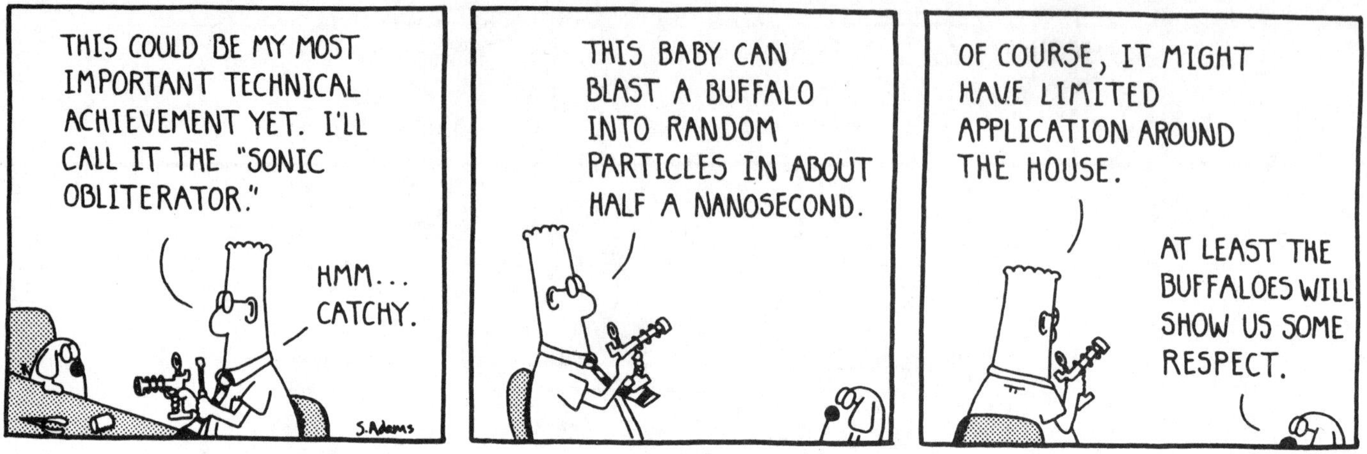
THIS COULD BE MY MOST IMPORTANT TECHNICAL ACHIEVEMENT YET. I'LL CALL IT THE "SONIC OBLITERATOR."
HMM... CATCHY.
THIS BABY CAN BLAST A BUFFALO INTO RANDOM PARTICLES IN ABOUT HALF A NANOSECOND.
OF COURSE, IT MIGHT HAVE LIMITED APPLICATION AROUND THE HOUSE.
AT LEAST THE BUFFALOES WILL SHOW US SOME RESPECT.

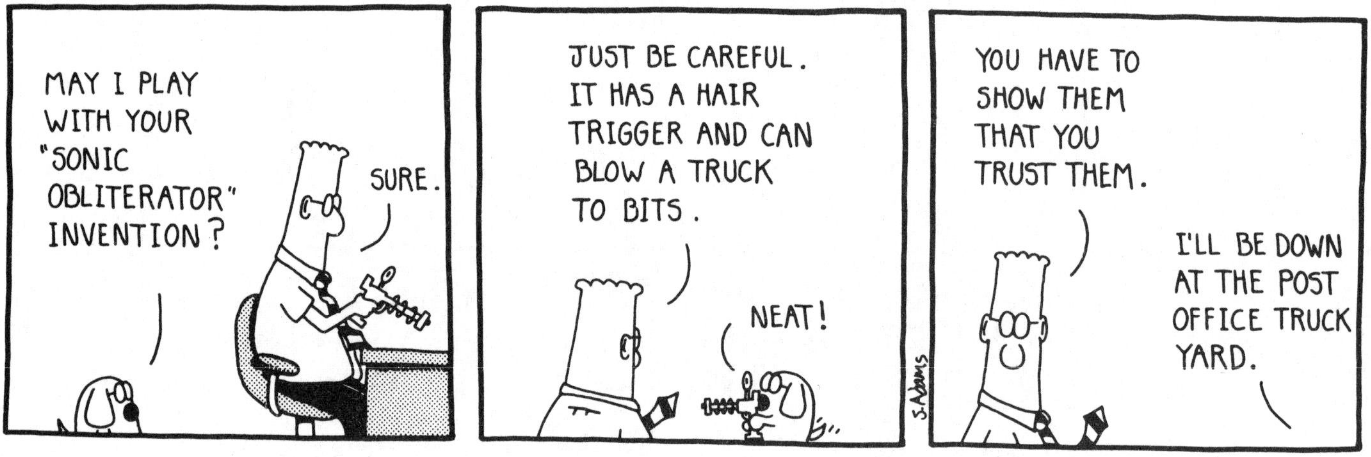
MAY I PLAY WITH YOUR "SONIC OBLITERATOR" INVENTION?
SURE.
JUST BE CAREFUL. IT HAS A HAIR TRIGGER AND CAN BLOW A TRUCK TO BITS.
NEAT!
YOU HAVE TO SHOW THEM THAT YOU TRUST THEM.
I'LL BE DOWN AT THE POST OFFICE TRUCK YARD.

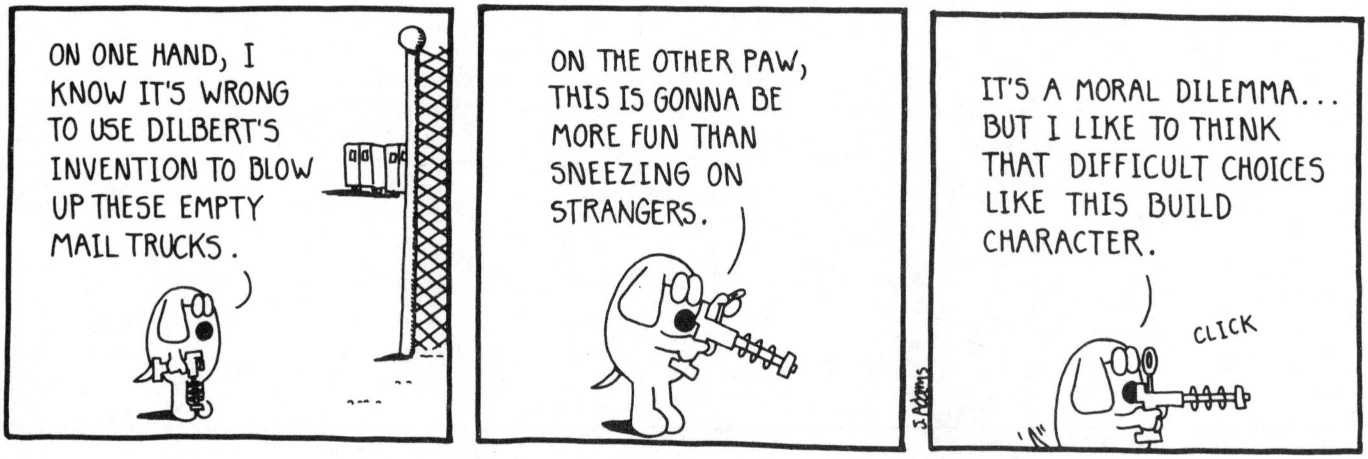
ON ONE HAND, I KNOW IT'S WRONG TO USE DILBERT'S INVENTION TO BLOW UP THESE EMPTY MAIL TRUCKS.
ON THE OTHER PAW, THIS IS GONNA BE MORE FUN THAN SNEEZING ON STRANGERS.
IT'S A MORAL DILEMMA... BUT I LIKE TO THINK THAT DIFFICULT CHOICES LIKE THIS BUILD CHARACTER.
CLICK

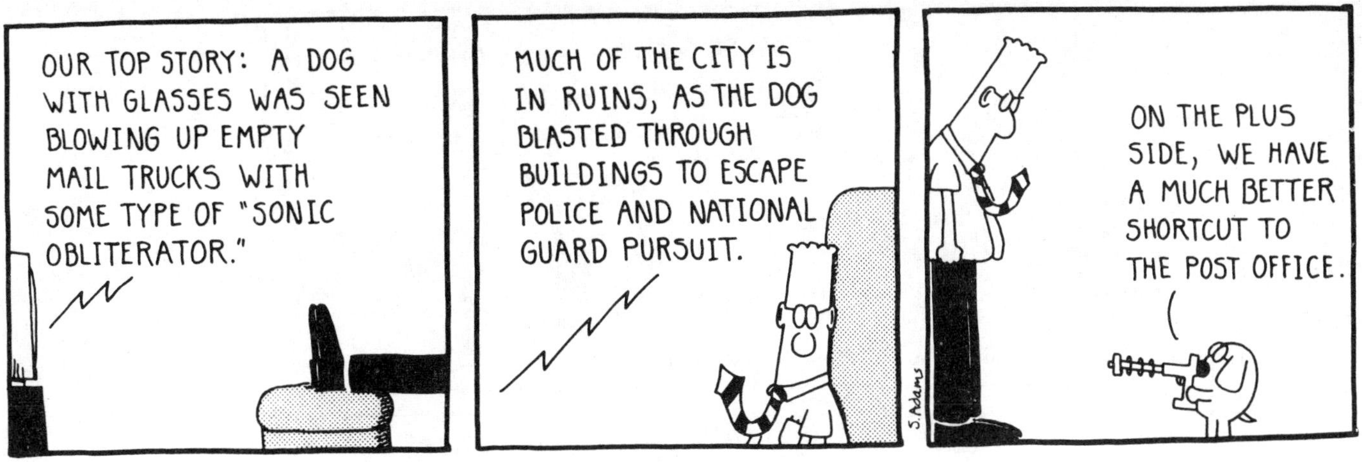
OUR TOP STORY: A DOG WITH GLASSES WAS SEEN BLOWING UP EMPTY MAIL TRUCKS WITH SOME TYPE OF "SONIC OBLITERATOR."
MUCH OF THE CITY IS IN RUINS, AS THE DOG BLASTED THROUGH BUILDINGS TO ESCAPE POLICE AND NATIONAL GUARD PURSUIT.
ON THE PLUS SIDE, WE HAVE A MUCH BETTER SHORTCUT TO THE POST OFFICE.
S. Adams

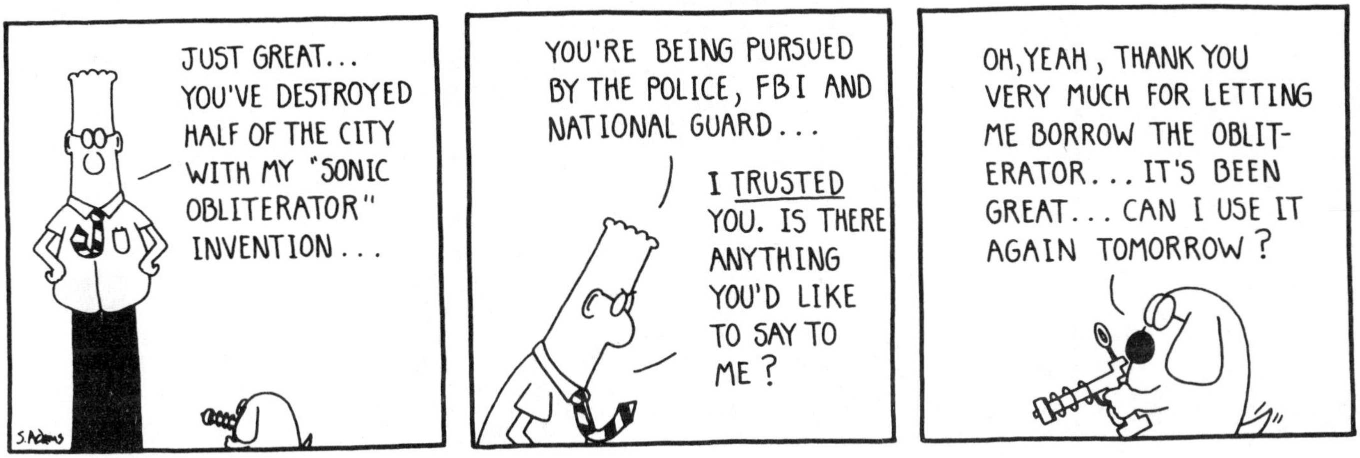
JUST GREAT... YOU'VE DESTROYED HALF OF THE CITY WITH MY "SONIC OBLITERATOR" INVENTION...
S. Adams
YOU'RE BEING PURSUED BY THE POLICE, FBI AND NATIONAL GUARD...
I TRUSTED YOU. IS THERE ANYTHING YOU'D LIKE TO SAY TO ME?
OH, YEAH, THANK YOU VERY MUCH FOR LETTING ME BORROW THE OBLITERATOR... IT'S BEEN GREAT... CAN I USE IT AGAIN TOMORROW?

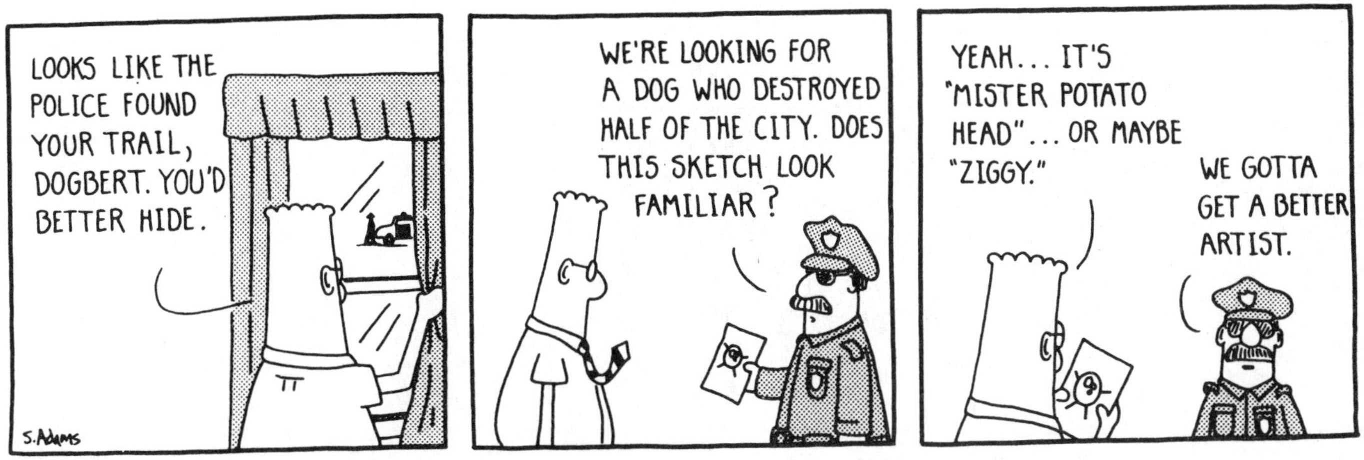
LOOKS LIKE THE POLICE FOUND YOUR TRAIL, DOGBERT. YOU'D BETTER HIDE.
S. Adams
WE'RE LOOKING FOR A DOG WHO DESTROYED HALF OF THE CITY. DOES THIS SKETCH LOOK FAMILIAR?
YEAH... IT'S "MISTER POTATO HEAD"... OR MAYBE "ZIGGY."
WE GOTTA GET A BETTER ARTIST.

WE'RE SO GLAD YOU GUYS COULD STOP BY.
THANKS FOR INVITING US.
WE HARDLY KNOW THEM.
I'D OFFER YOU SOME COFFEE, BUT THAT WOULD BE A BOTHER.
UH... NONE FOR ME. THANKS.
I NOTICED YOU DIDN'T BRING ANY FOOD AS A COURTESY TO YOUR HOSTS.
I GUESS WE'LL EAT WHEN YOU LEAVE.
WE USUALLY WATCH TELEVISION NOW, BUT I'LL TRY NOT TO APPEAR BITTER ABOUT YOUR VISIT.
S Adams
WHY HAVEN'T WE DONE THIS SOONER?
WE THOUGHT YOU WERE SCUM.

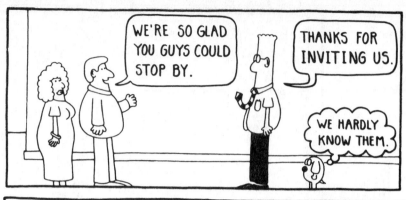

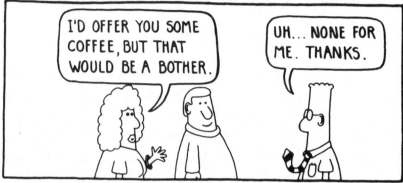

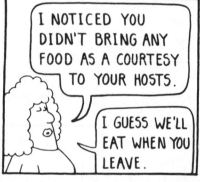

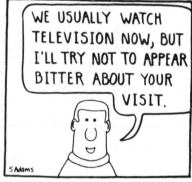

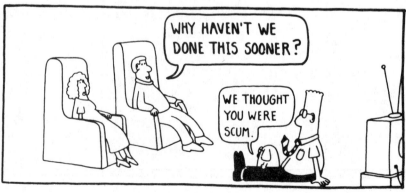

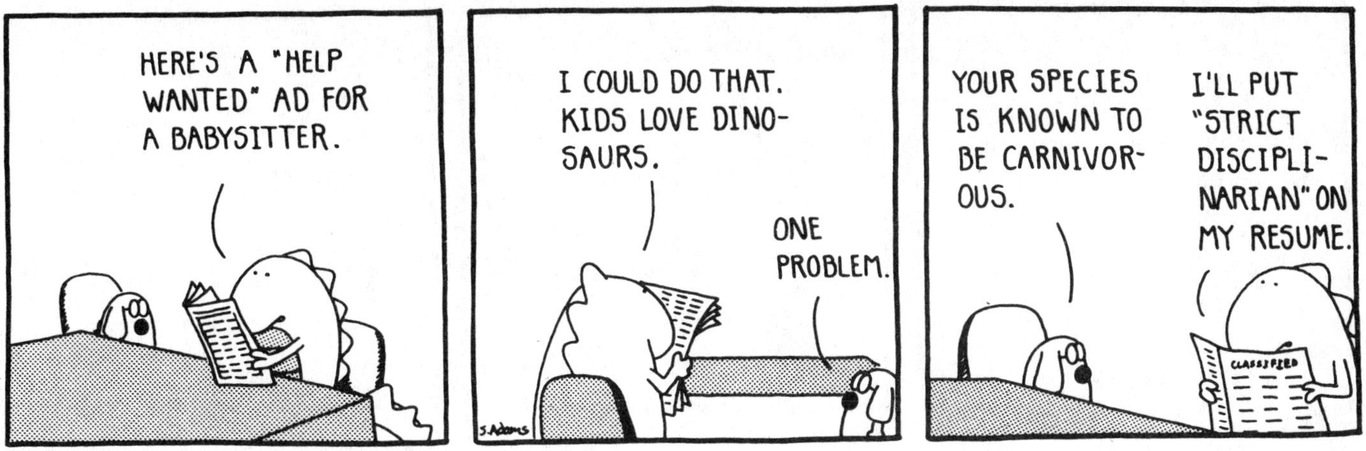
HERE'S A "HELP WANTED" AD FOR A BABYSITTER.
I COULD DO THAT. KIDS LOVE DINO-SAURS.
ONE PROBLEM.
YOUR SPECIES IS KNOWN TO BE CARNIVOR-OUS.
I'LL PUT "STRICT DISCIPLI-NARIAN" ON MY RESUME.
CLASSIFIED
S. Adams

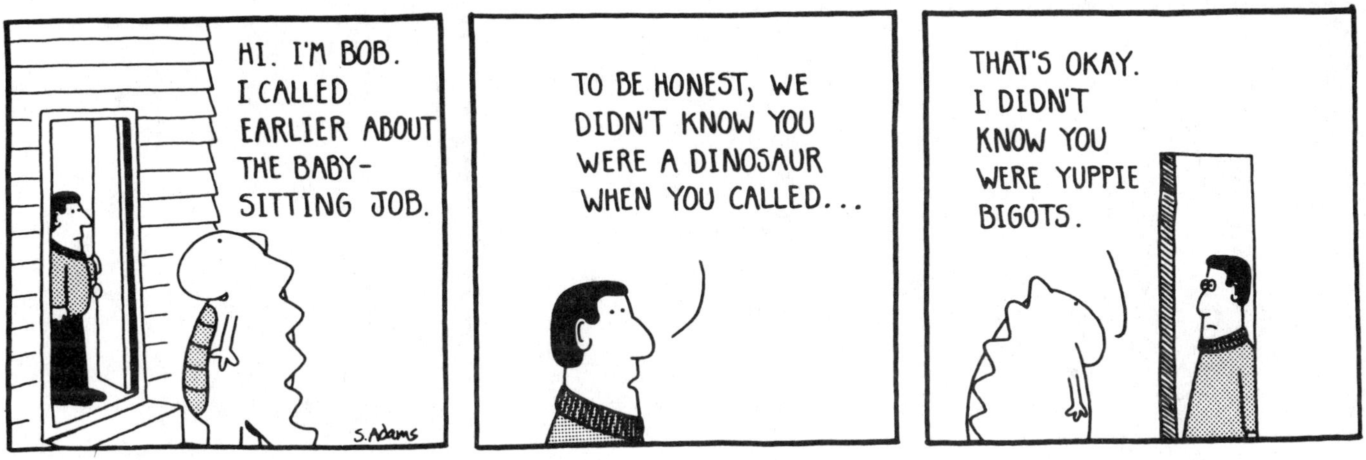
HI. I'M BOB. I CALLED EARLIER ABOUT THE BABY-SITTING JOB.
S. Adams
TO BE HONEST, WE DIDN'T KNOW YOU WERE A DINOSAUR WHEN YOU CALLED...
THAT'S OKAY. I DIDN'T KNOW YOU WERE YUPPIE BIGOTS.

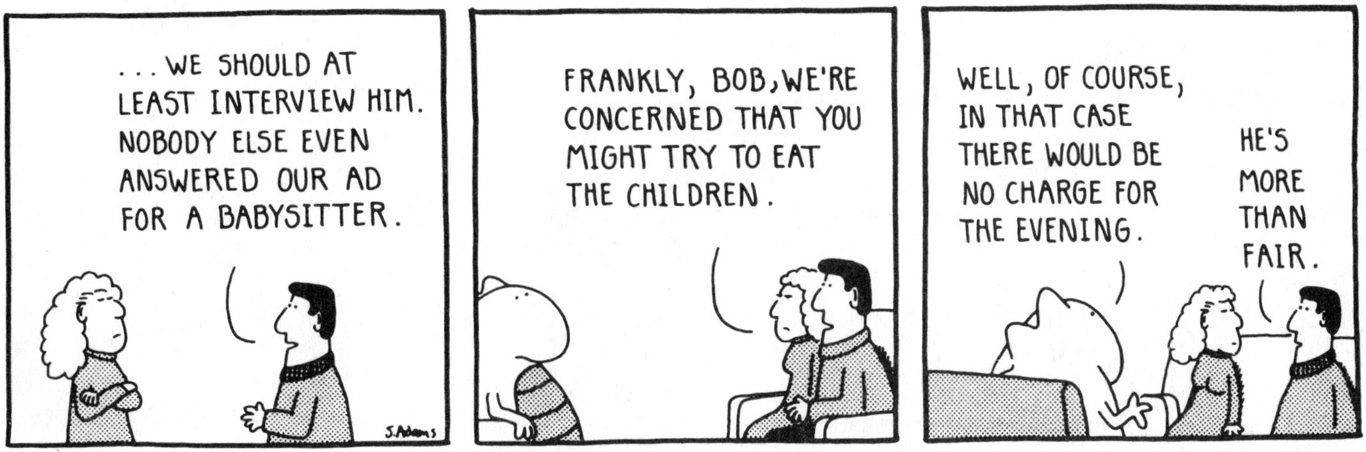
...WE SHOULD AT LEAST INTERVIEW HIM. NOBODY ELSE EVEN ANSWERED OUR AD FOR A BABYSITTER.
S. Adams
FRANKLY, BOB, WE'RE CONCERNED THAT YOU MIGHT TRY TO EAT THE CHILDREN.
WELL, OF COURSE, IN THAT CASE THERE WOULD BE NO CHARGE FOR THE EVENING.
HE'S MORE THAN FAIR.

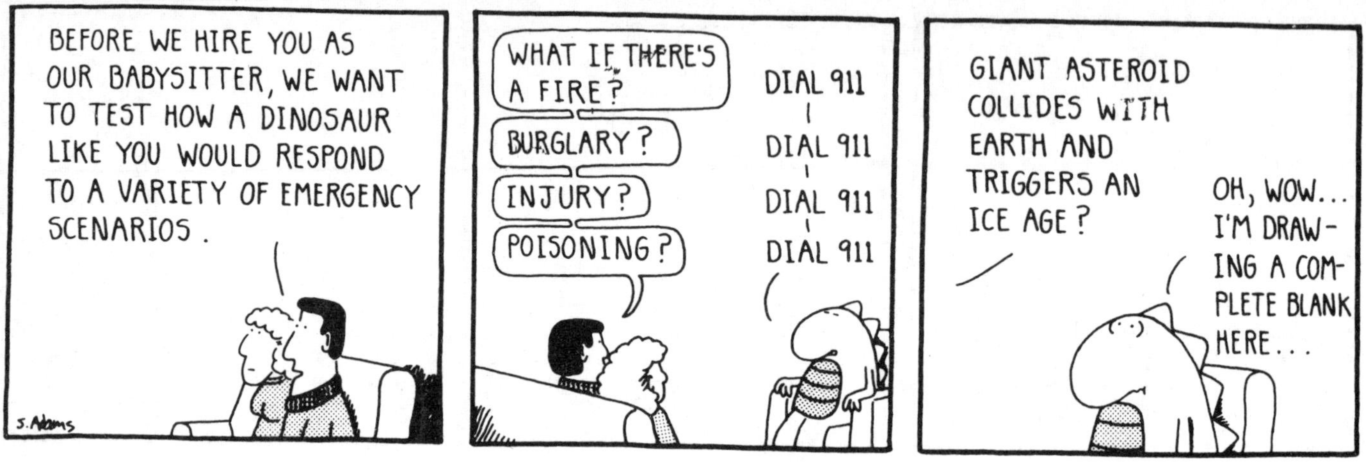
BEFORE WE HIRE YOU AS OUR BABYSITTER, WE WANT TO TEST HOW A DINOSAUR LIKE YOU WOULD RESPOND TO A VARIETY OF EMERGENCY SCENARIOS.
S. Adams
WHAT IF THERE'S A FIRE?
DIAL 911
BURGLARY?
DIAL 911
INJURY?
DIAL 911
POISONING?
DIAL 911
GIANT ASTEROID COLLIDES WITH EARTH AND TRIGGERS AN ICE AGE?
OH, WOW... I'M DRAWING A COMPLETE BLANK HERE...

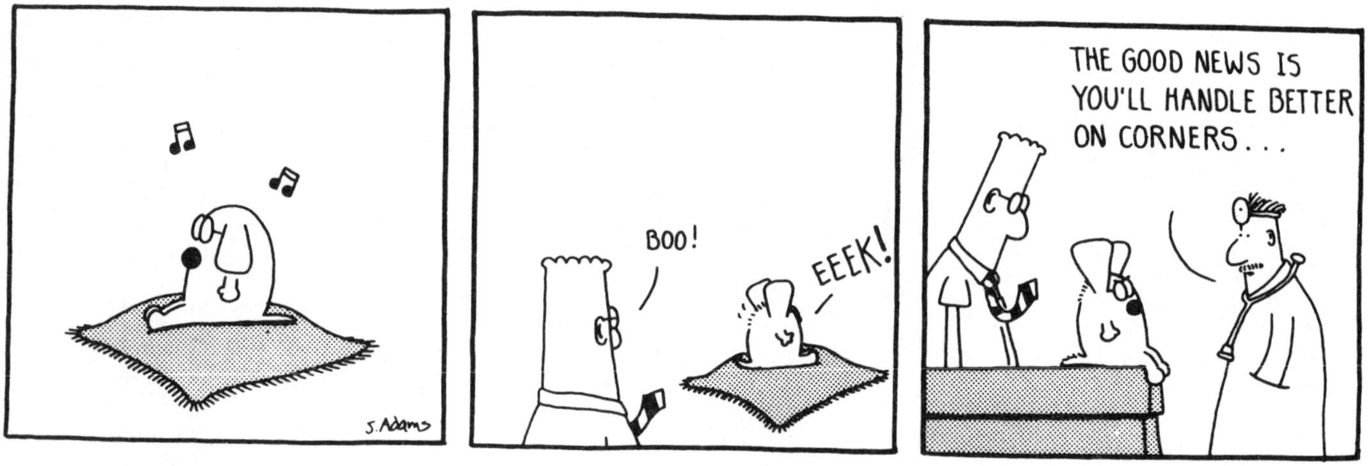
S. Adams
BOO!
EEEK!
THE GOOD NEWS IS YOU'LL HANDLE BETTER ON CORNERS...

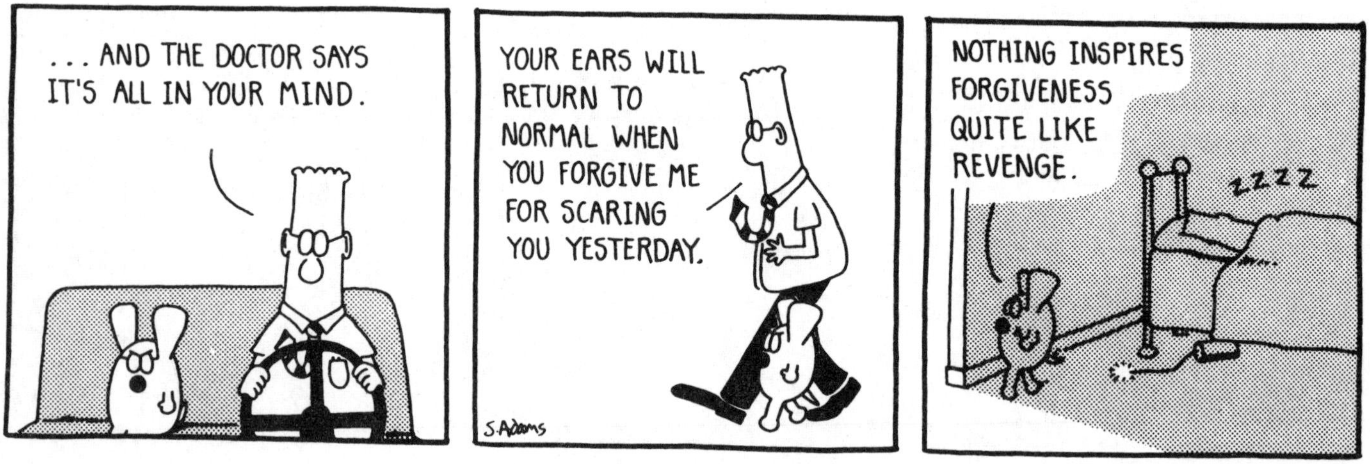
... AND THE DOCTOR SAYS IT'S ALL IN YOUR MIND.
YOUR EARS WILL RETURN TO NORMAL WHEN YOU FORGIVE ME FOR SCARING YOU YESTERDAY.
S. Adams
NOTHING INSPIRES FORGIVENESS QUITE LIKE REVENGE.
ZZZZ

WHAT IF

PEOPLE HAD TAILS?

 FIRST OF ALL, IT WOULD LOOK DARNED SILLY

ONLY THE TRULY UNOBSERVANT WOULD LOSE AT POKER.

HE'S BLUFFING.

CONTROL... DON'T WAG...

JURY TRIALS WOULD BE SIMPLER.

...THEN I FOUND MY HUSBAND DEAD.

S.Adams

AND PARTIES WOULD BE EVEN MORE AWKWARD.

THAT'S WHEN I LEARNED THAT IF YOU DRIVE A PORSCHE, YOU SHOULD NEVER MAKE FUN OF A MAN ON A STEAMROLLER.

TRAGIC... REALLY.

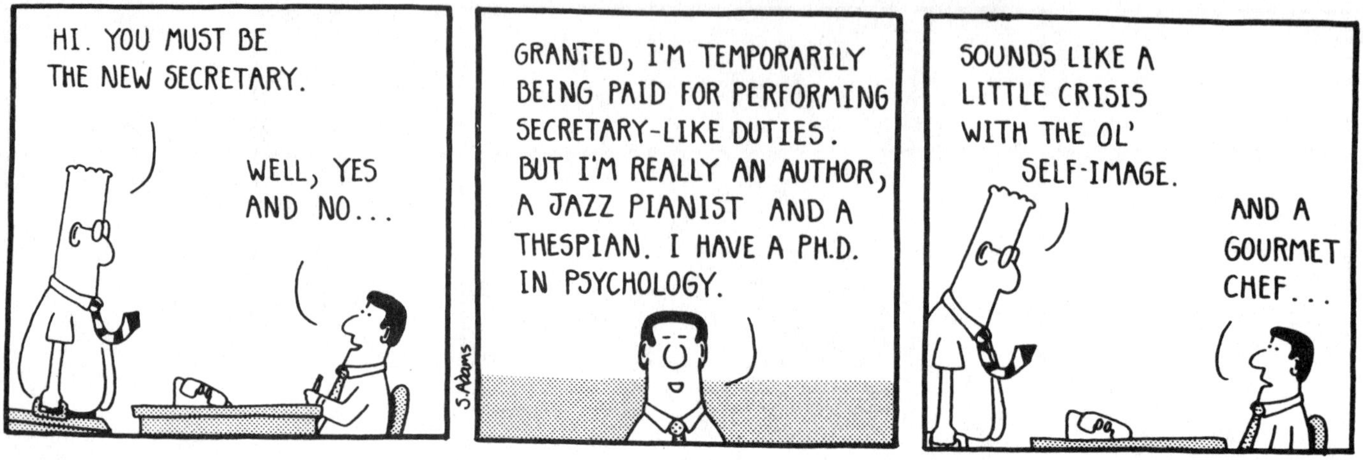
HI. YOU MUST BE THE NEW SECRETARY.
WELL, YES AND NO...
GRANTED, I'M TEMPORARILY BEING PAID FOR PERFORMING SECRETARY-LIKE DUTIES. BUT I'M REALLY AN AUTHOR, A JAZZ PIANIST AND A THESPIAN. I HAVE A PH.D. IN PSYCHOLOGY.
SOUNDS LIKE A LITTLE CRISIS WITH THE OL' SELF-IMAGE.
AND A GOURMET CHEF...

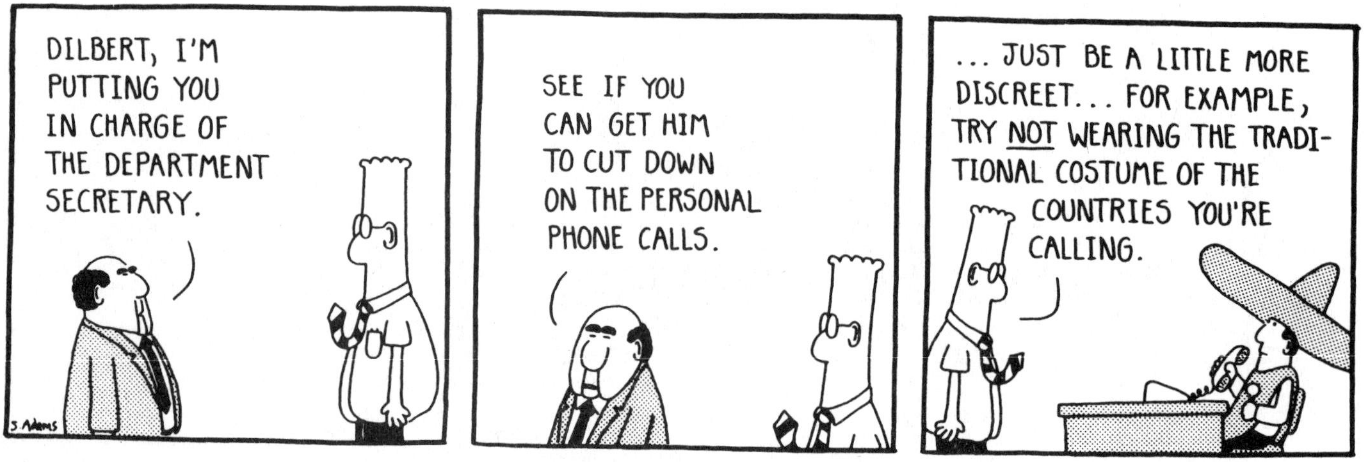
DILBERT, I'M PUTTING YOU IN CHARGE OF THE DEPARTMENT SECRETARY.
SEE IF YOU CAN GET HIM TO CUT DOWN ON THE PERSONAL PHONE CALLS.
... JUST BE A LITTLE MORE DISCREET... FOR EXAMPLE, TRY NOT WEARING THE TRADITIONAL COSTUME OF THE COUNTRIES YOU'RE CALLING.

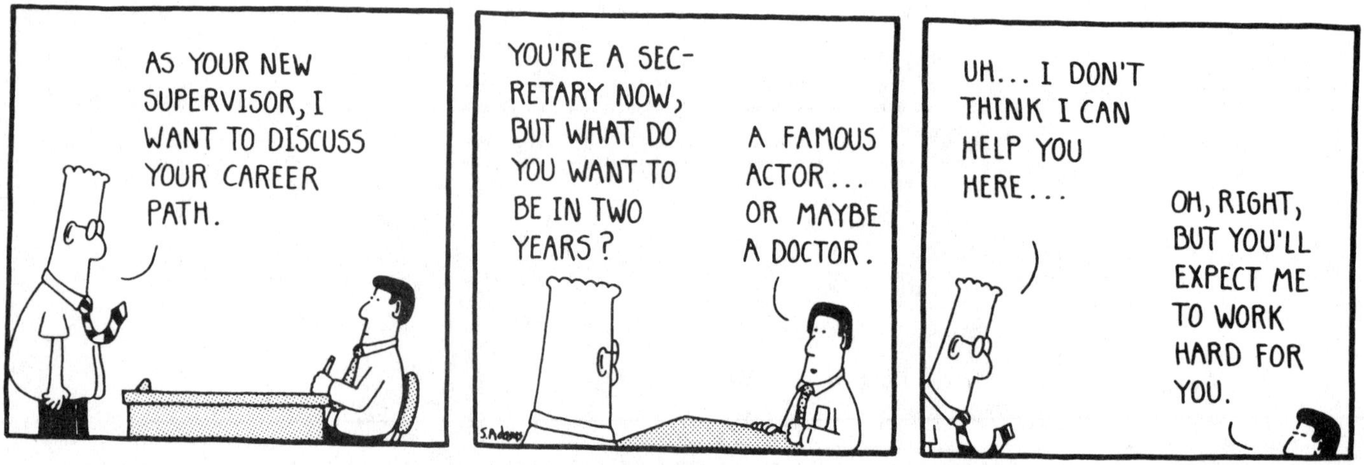
AS YOUR NEW SUPERVISOR, I WANT TO DISCUSS YOUR CAREER PATH.
YOU'RE A SECRETARY NOW, BUT WHAT DO YOU WANT TO BE IN TWO YEARS?
A FAMOUS ACTOR... OR MAYBE A DOCTOR.
UH... I DON'T THINK I CAN HELP YOU HERE...
OH, RIGHT, BUT YOU'LL EXPECT ME TO WORK HARD FOR YOU.

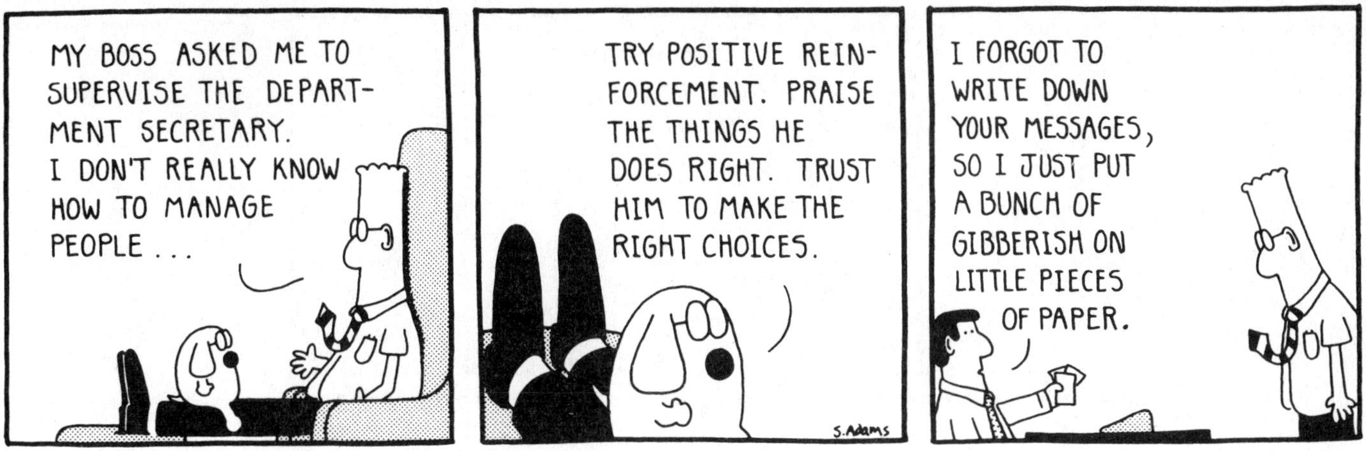
MY BOSS ASKED ME TO SUPERVISE THE DEPARTMENT SECRETARY. I DON'T REALLY KNOW HOW TO MANAGE PEOPLE . . .
TRY POSITIVE REINFORCEMENT. PRAISE THE THINGS HE DOES RIGHT. TRUST HIM TO MAKE THE RIGHT CHOICES.
S. Adams
I FORGOT TO WRITE DOWN YOUR MESSAGES, SO I JUST PUT A BUNCH OF GIBBERISH ON LITTLE PIECES OF PAPER.

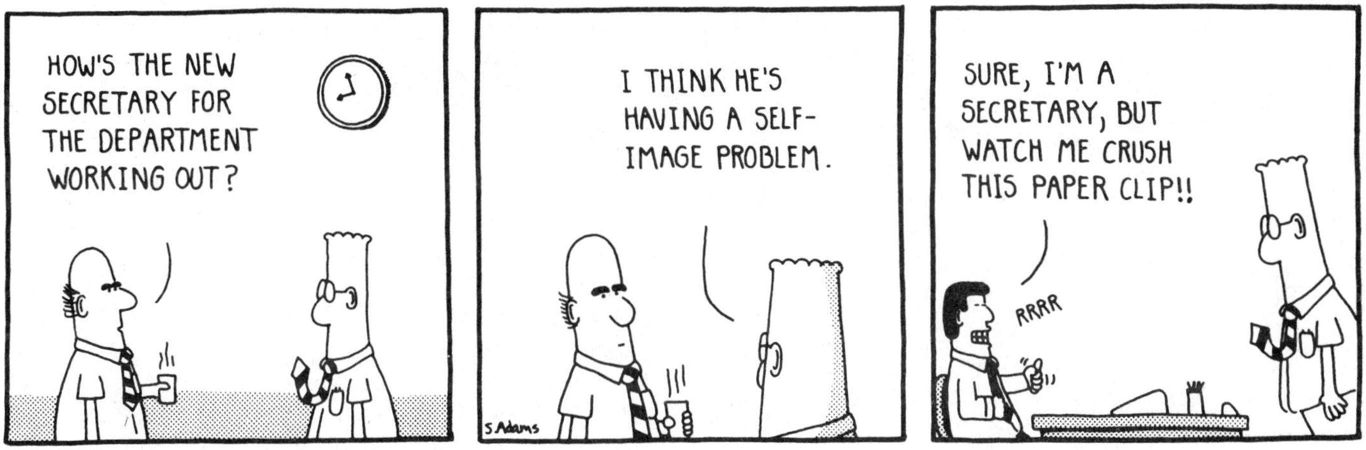
HOW'S THE NEW SECRETARY FOR THE DEPARTMENT WORKING OUT?
I THINK HE'S HAVING A SELF-IMAGE PROBLEM.
S. Adams
SURE, I'M A SECRETARY, BUT WATCH ME CRUSH THIS PAPER CLIP!!
RRRR

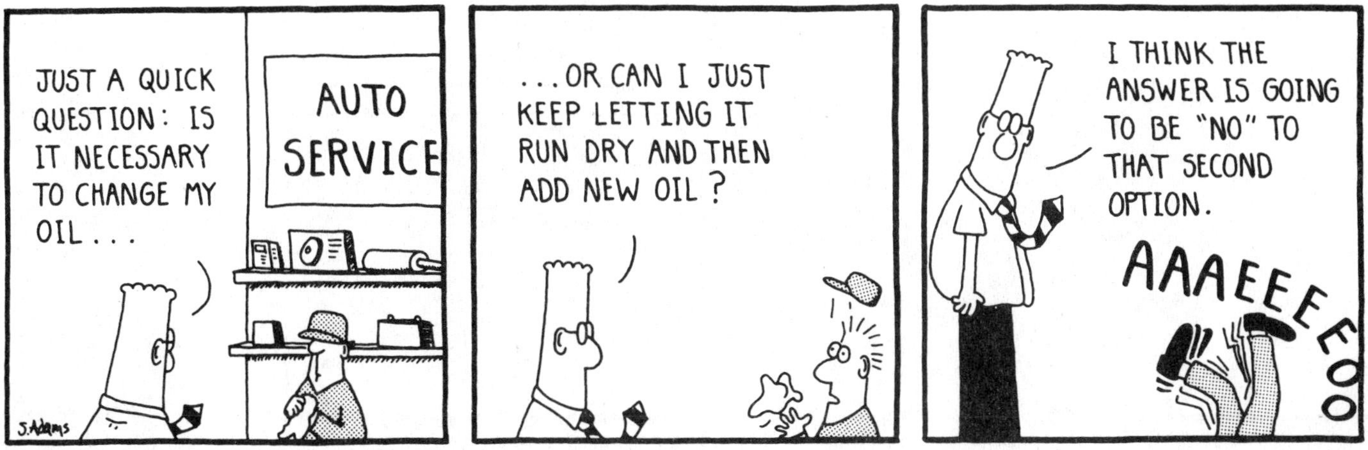
JUST A QUICK QUESTION: IS IT NECESSARY TO CHANGE MY OIL . . .
AUTO SERVICE
S. Adams
. . . OR CAN I JUST KEEP LETTING IT RUN DRY AND THEN ADD NEW OIL ?
I THINK THE ANSWER IS GOING TO BE "NO" TO THAT SECOND OPTION.
AAAEEEEOO

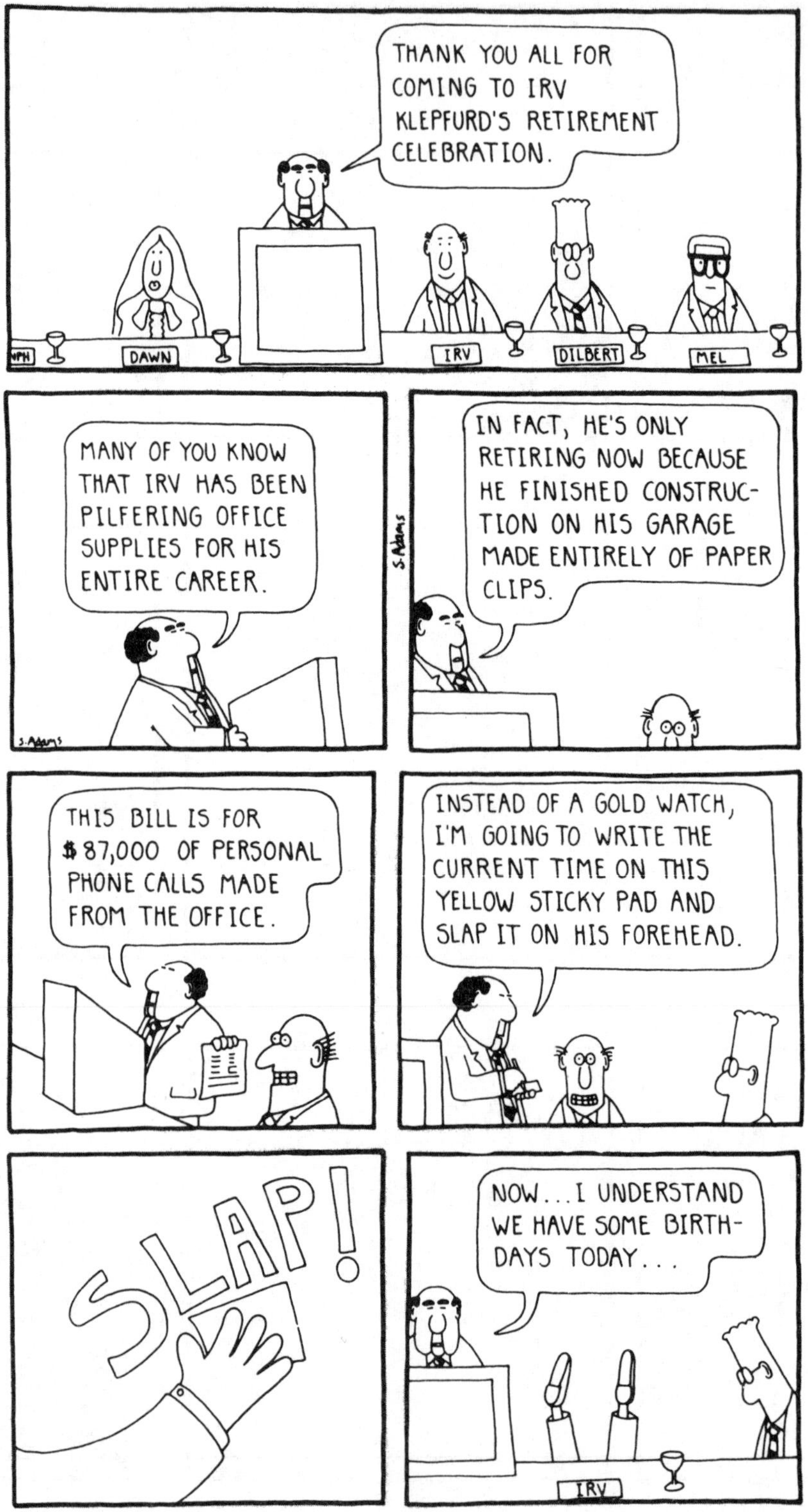
THANK YOU ALL FOR COMING TO IRV KLEPFURD'S RETIREMENT CELEBRATION.
DAWN
IRV
DILBERT
MEL
MANY OF YOU KNOW THAT IRV HAS BEEN PILFERING OFFICE SUPPLIES FOR HIS ENTIRE CAREER.
IN FACT, HE'S ONLY RETIRING NOW BECAUSE HE FINISHED CONSTRUCTION ON HIS GARAGE MADE ENTIRELY OF PAPER CLIPS.
THIS BILL IS FOR $87,000 OF PERSONAL PHONE CALLS MADE FROM THE OFFICE.
INSTEAD OF A GOLD WATCH, I'M GOING TO WRITE THE CURRENT TIME ON THIS YELLOW STICKY PAD AND SLAP IT ON HIS FOREHEAD.
SLAP!
NOW... I UNDERSTAND WE HAVE SOME BIRTHDAYS TODAY...
IRV

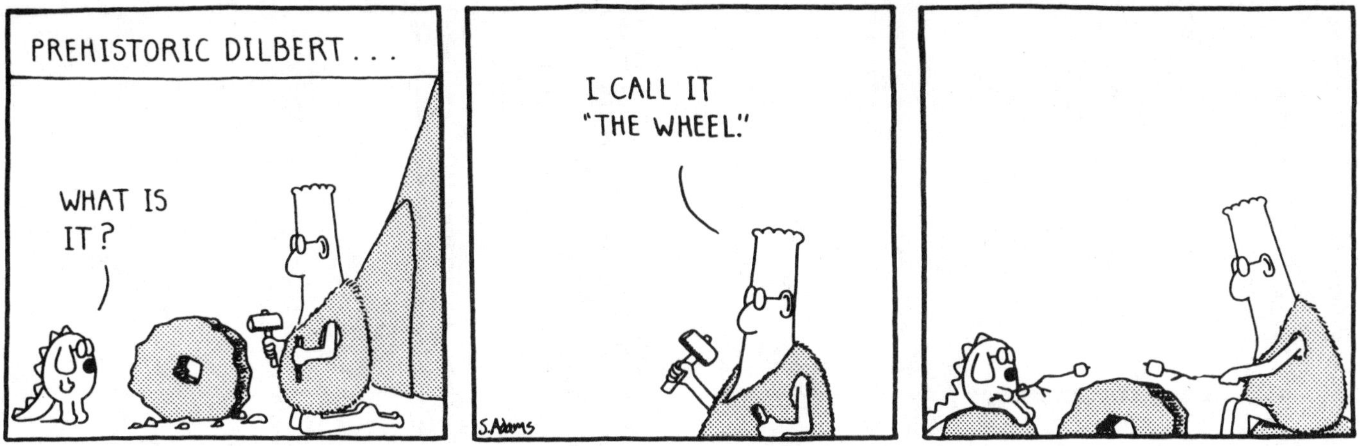
PREHISTORIC DILBERT . . .
WHAT IS IT?
I CALL IT "THE WHEEL."
S.Adams

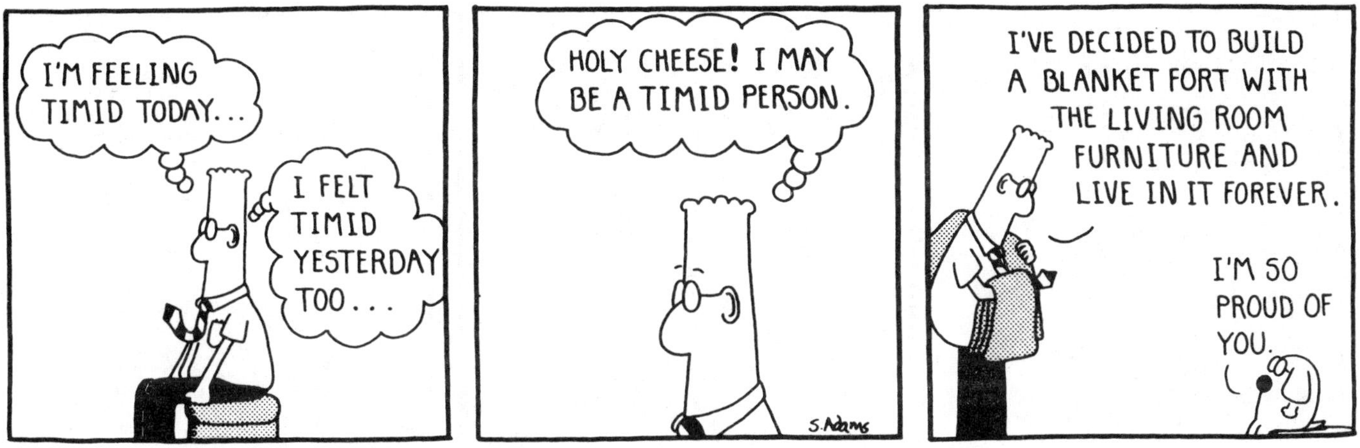
I'M FEELING TIMID TODAY...
I FELT TIMID YESTERDAY TOO . . .
HOLY CHEESE! I MAY BE A TIMID PERSON.
S.Adams
I'VE DECIDED TO BUILD A BLANKET FORT WITH THE LIVING ROOM FURNITURE AND LIVE IN IT FOREVER.
I'M SO PROUD OF YOU.

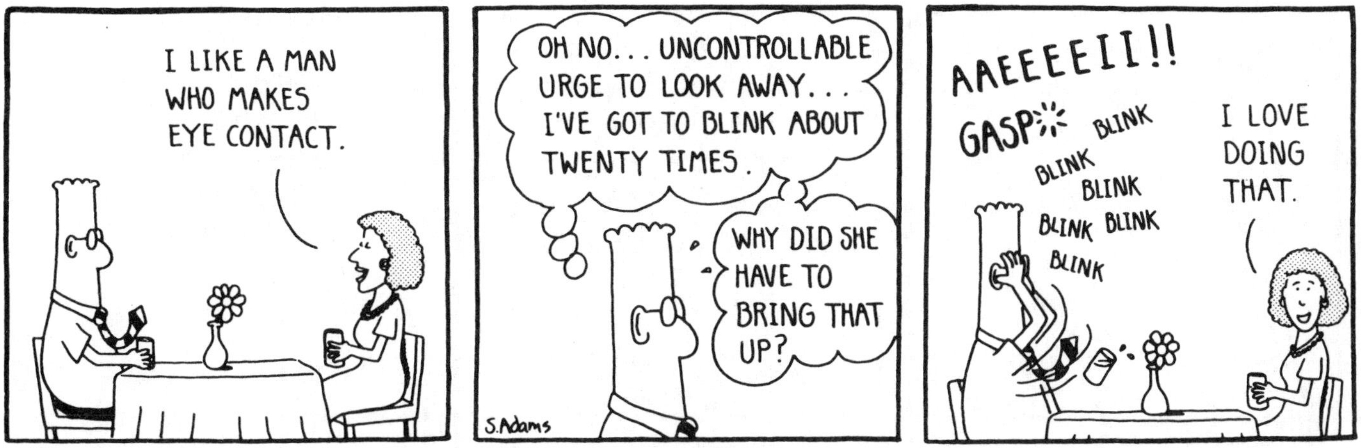
I LIKE A MAN WHO MAKES EYE CONTACT.
OH NO... UNCONTROLLABLE URGE TO LOOK AWAY... I'VE GOT TO BLINK ABOUT TWENTY TIMES.
WHY DID SHE HAVE TO BRING THAT UP?
S.Adams
AAEEEEII!!
GASP
BLINK
BLINK
BLINK
BLINK
BLINK
BLINK
I LOVE DOING THAT.

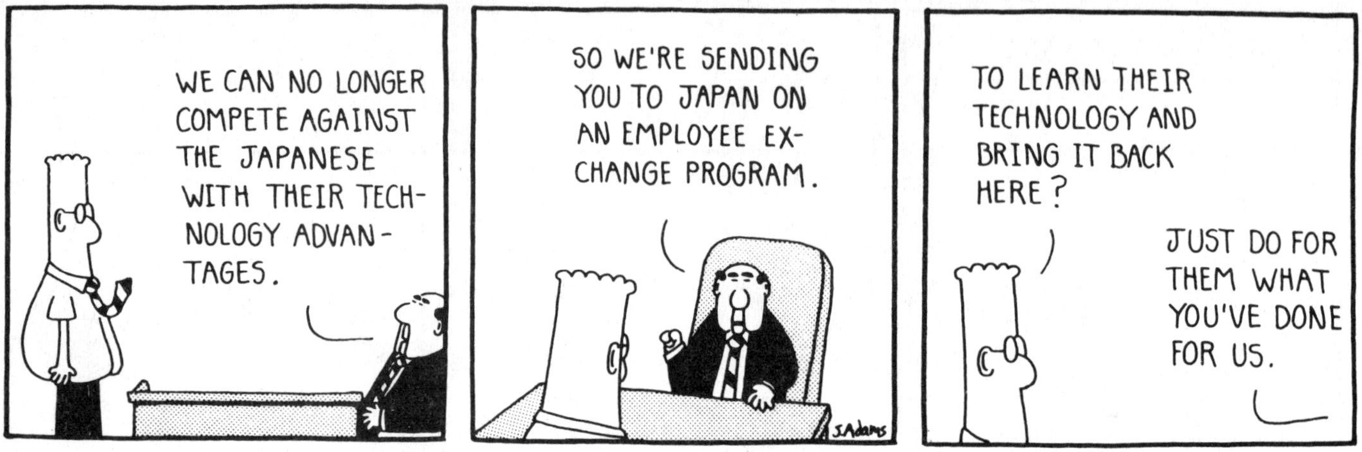
WE CAN NO LONGER COMPETE AGAINST THE JAPANESE WITH THEIR TECH-NOLOGY ADVAN-TAGES.
SO WE'RE SENDING YOU TO JAPAN ON AN EMPLOYEE EX-CHANGE PROGRAM.
S. Adams
TO LEARN THEIR TECHNOLOGY AND BRING IT BACK HERE?
JUST DO FOR THEM WHAT YOU'VE DONE FOR US.

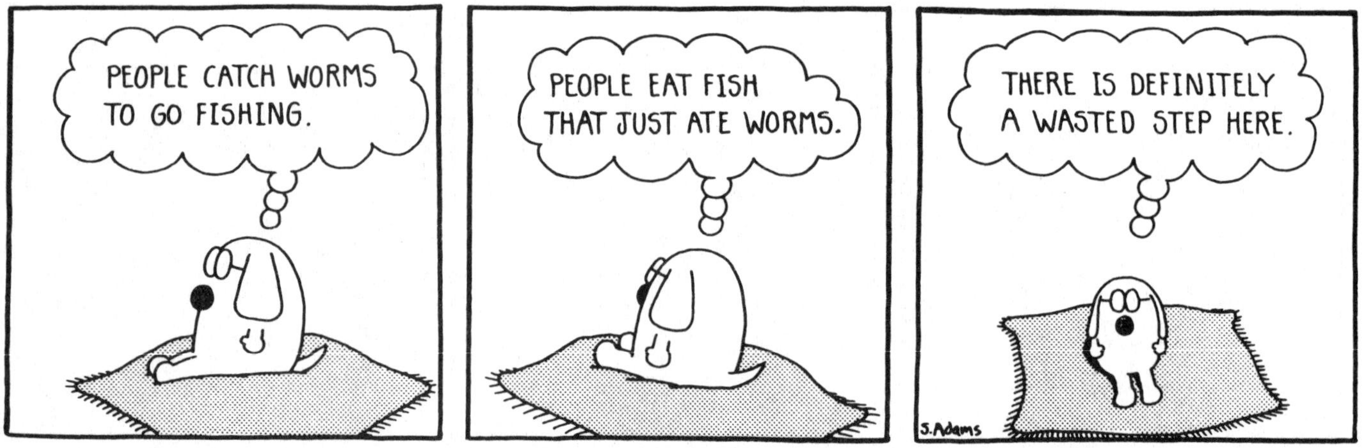
PEOPLE CATCH WORMS TO GO FISHING.
PEOPLE EAT FISH THAT JUST ATE WORMS.
THERE IS DEFINITELY A WASTED STEP HERE.
S. Adams

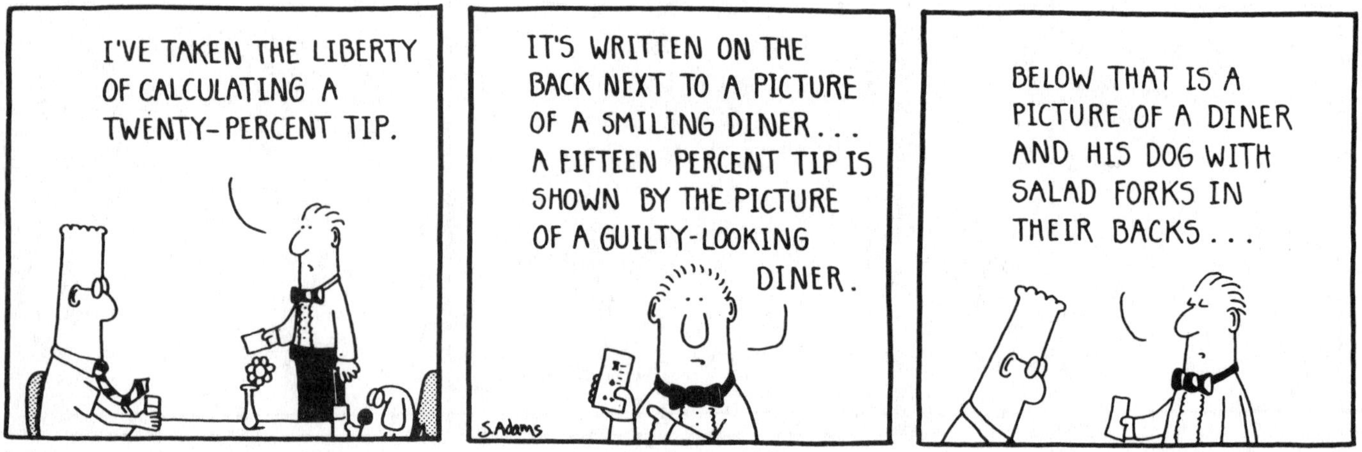
I'VE TAKEN THE LIBERTY OF CALCULATING A TWENTY-PERCENT TIP.
IT'S WRITTEN ON THE BACK NEXT TO A PICTURE OF A SMILING DINER... A FIFTEEN PERCENT TIP IS SHOWN BY THE PICTURE OF A GUILTY-LOOKING DINER.
S. Adams
BELOW THAT IS A PICTURE OF A DINER AND HIS DOG WITH SALAD FORKS IN THEIR BACKS...

HOLY HAIR-BALLS! WHAT ARE YOU?!!

I AM THE "DUST BUNNY," AN EMERGING CULTURAL ICON.

ONCE A YEAR I COME TO EVERY HOME AND HIDE CLUMPS OF DUST UNDER FURNITURE AND MAJOR APPLIANCES.

YOU MUST HONOR ME BY DECORATING CLOSET DOORS AND SINGING DUST HYMNS.

WHAT ABOUT GIFTS? DO I GET ANY GIFTS OUT OF THIS?

NO. THE DUST BUNNY SYMBOLIZES ONLY LOVE, GOODWILL AND VERY POOR HOUSEKEEPING.

S. Adams

I KNOW, IT SEEMS HARSH, BUT YOU HAVE TO NIP THESE THINGS IN THE BUD.

OKAY, GIFTS!

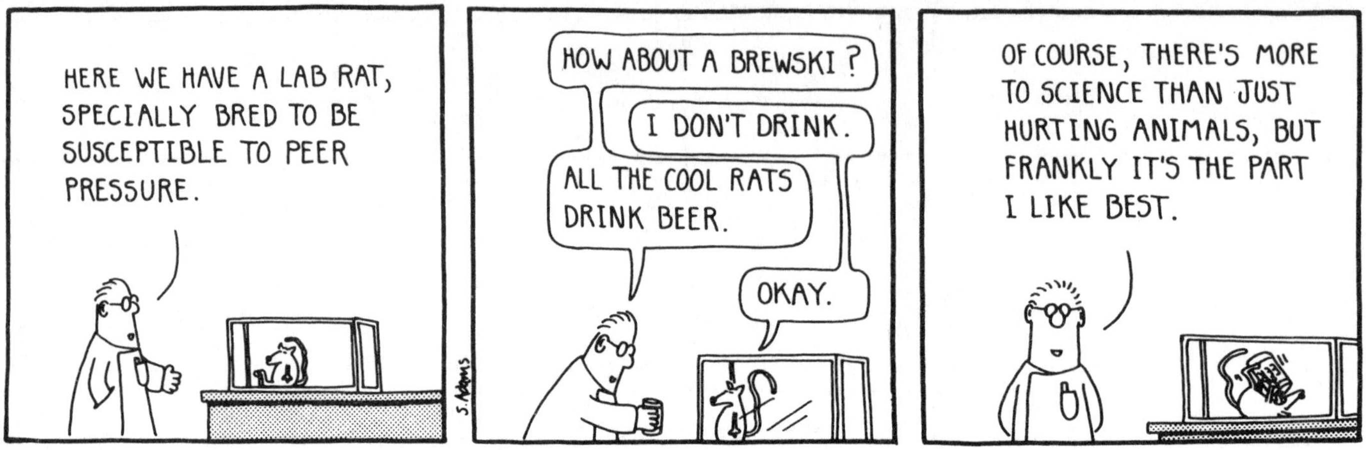
HERE WE HAVE A LAB RAT, SPECIALLY BRED TO BE SUSCEPTIBLE TO PEER PRESSURE.
HOW ABOUT A BREWSKI?
I DON'T DRINK.
ALL THE COOL RATS DRINK BEER.
OKAY.
OF COURSE, THERE'S MORE TO SCIENCE THAN JUST HURTING ANIMALS, BUT FRANKLY IT'S THE PART I LIKE BEST.

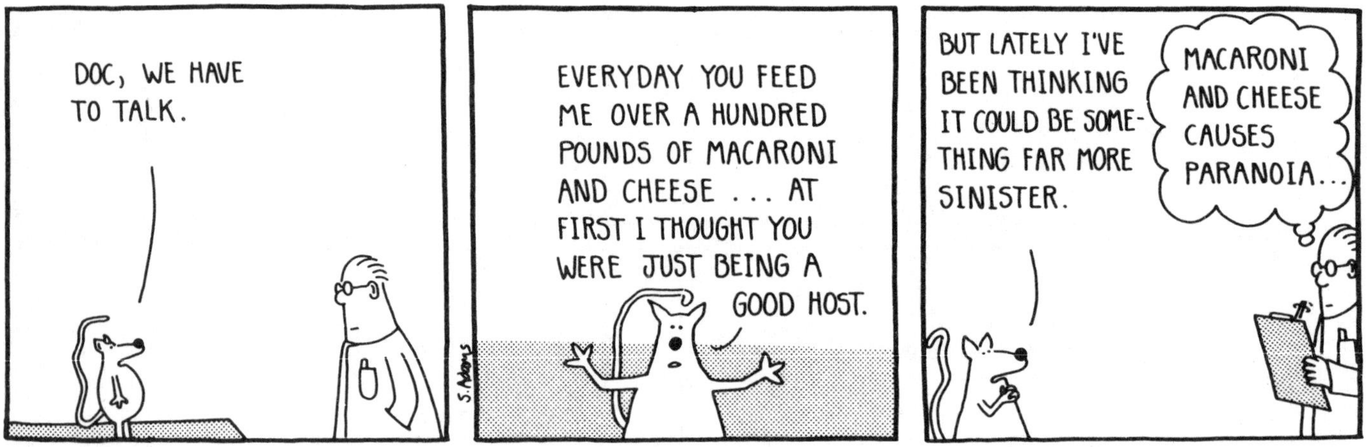
DOC, WE HAVE TO TALK.
EVERYDAY YOU FEED ME OVER A HUNDRED POUNDS OF MACARONI AND CHEESE . . . AT FIRST I THOUGHT YOU WERE JUST BEING A GOOD HOST.
BUT LATELY I'VE BEEN THINKING IT COULD BE SOMETHING FAR MORE SINISTER.
MACARONI AND CHEESE CAUSES PARANOIA...

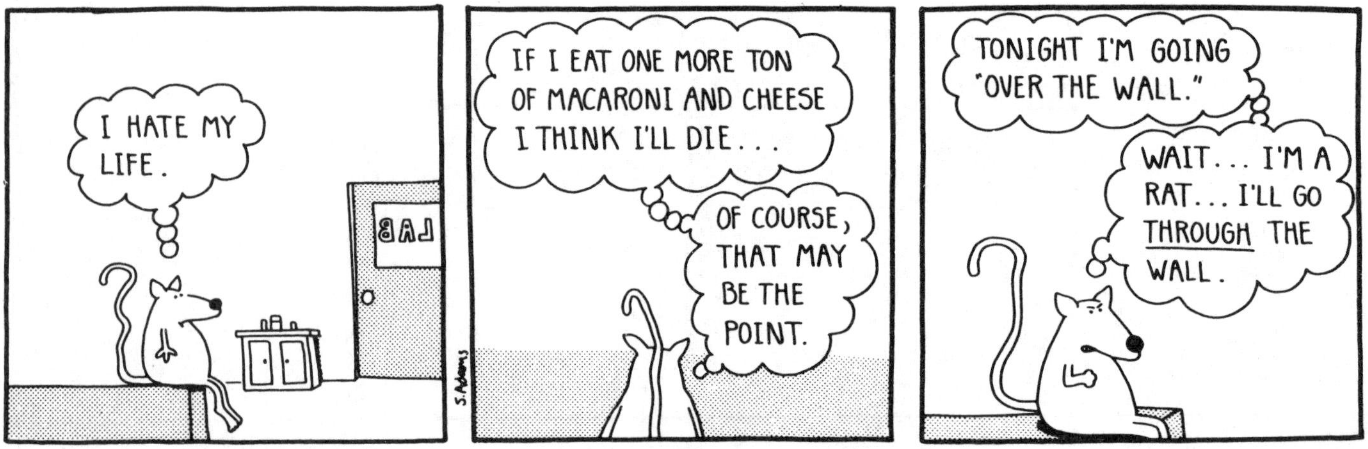
I HATE MY LIFE.
IF I EAT ONE MORE TON OF MACARONI AND CHEESE I THINK I'LL DIE . . .
OF COURSE, THAT MAY BE THE POINT.
TONIGHT I'M GOING "OVER THE WALL."
WAIT . . . I'M A RAT . . . I'LL GO THROUGH THE WALL.

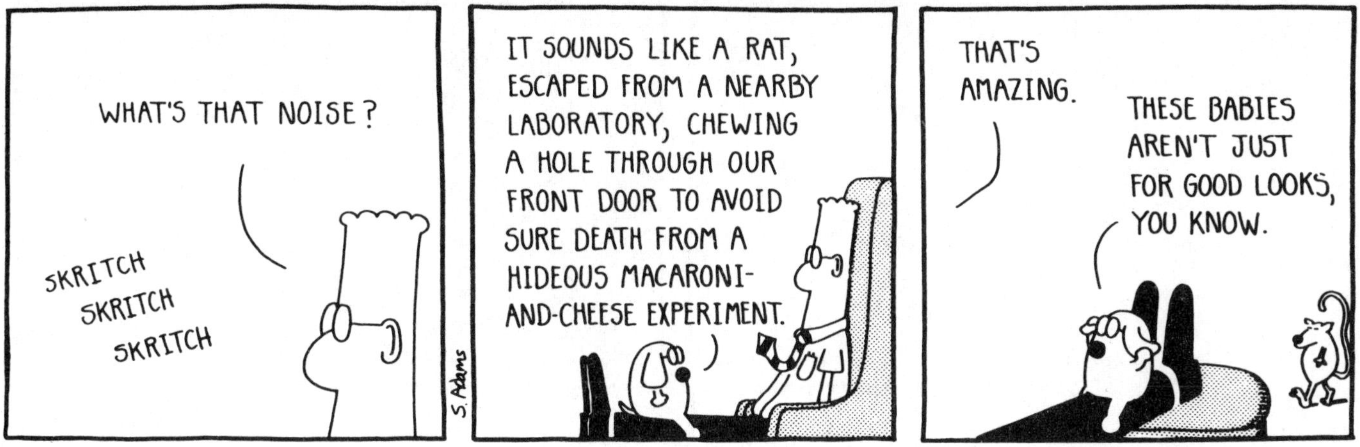
WHAT'S THAT NOISE?
SKRITCH SKRITCH SKRITCH
IT SOUNDS LIKE A RAT, ESCAPED FROM A NEARBY LABORATORY, CHEWING A HOLE THROUGH OUR FRONT DOOR TO AVOID SURE DEATH FROM A HIDEOUS MACARONI-AND-CHEESE EXPERIMENT.
THAT'S AMAZING.
THESE BABIES AREN'T JUST FOR GOOD LOOKS, YOU KNOW.
S. Adams

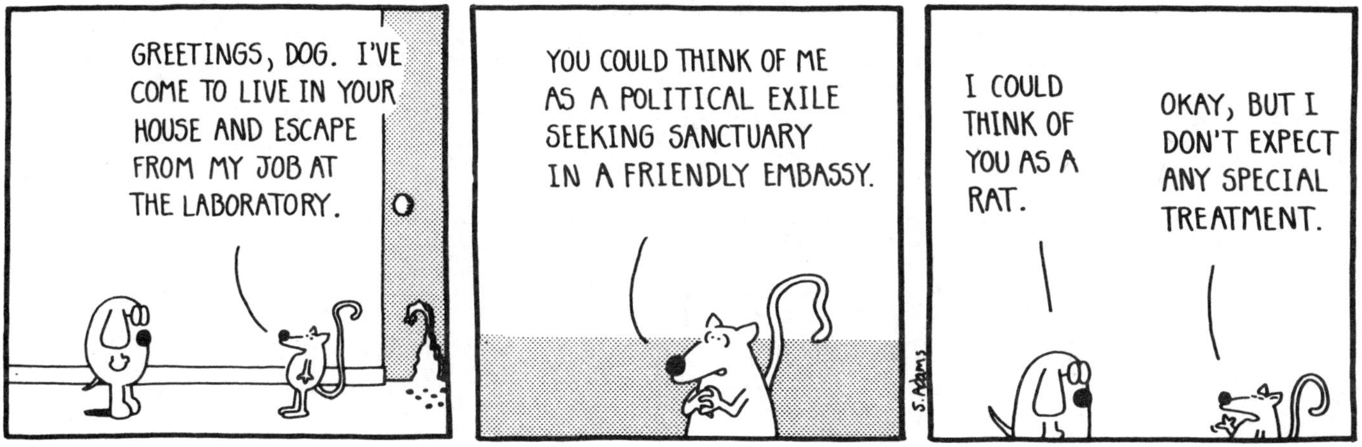
GREETINGS, DOG. I'VE COME TO LIVE IN YOUR HOUSE AND ESCAPE FROM MY JOB AT THE LABORATORY.
YOU COULD THINK OF ME AS A POLITICAL EXILE SEEKING SANCTUARY IN A FRIENDLY EMBASSY.
I COULD THINK OF YOU AS A RAT.
OKAY, BUT I DON'T EXPECT ANY SPECIAL TREATMENT.
S. Adams

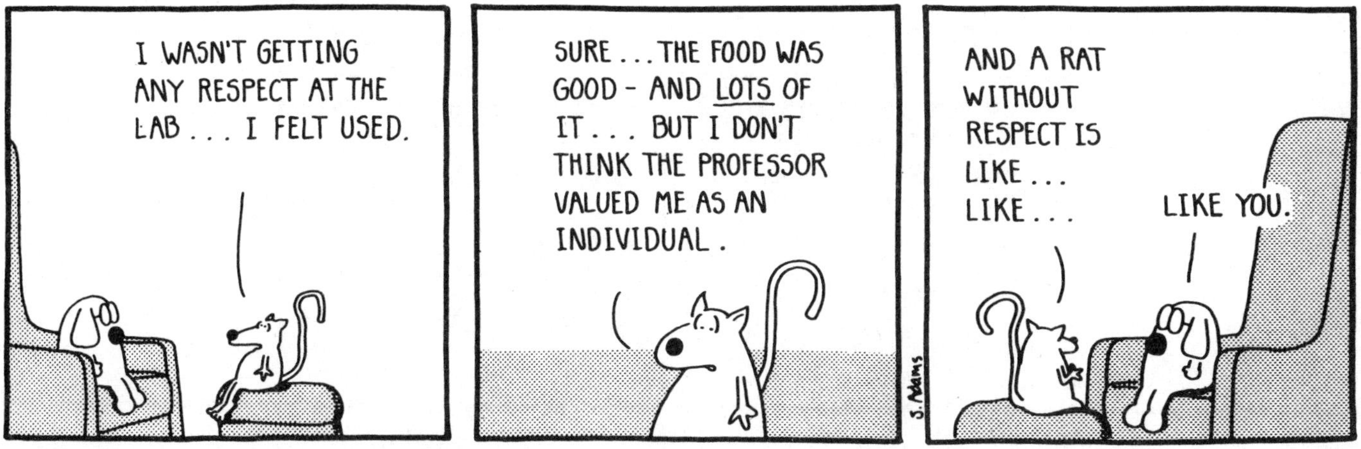
I WASN'T GETTING ANY RESPECT AT THE LAB . . . I FELT USED.
SURE . . . THE FOOD WAS GOOD - AND LOTS OF IT . . . BUT I DON'T THINK THE PROFESSOR VALUED ME AS AN INDIVIDUAL.
AND A RAT WITHOUT RESPECT IS LIKE . . . LIKE . . .
LIKE YOU.
S. Adams

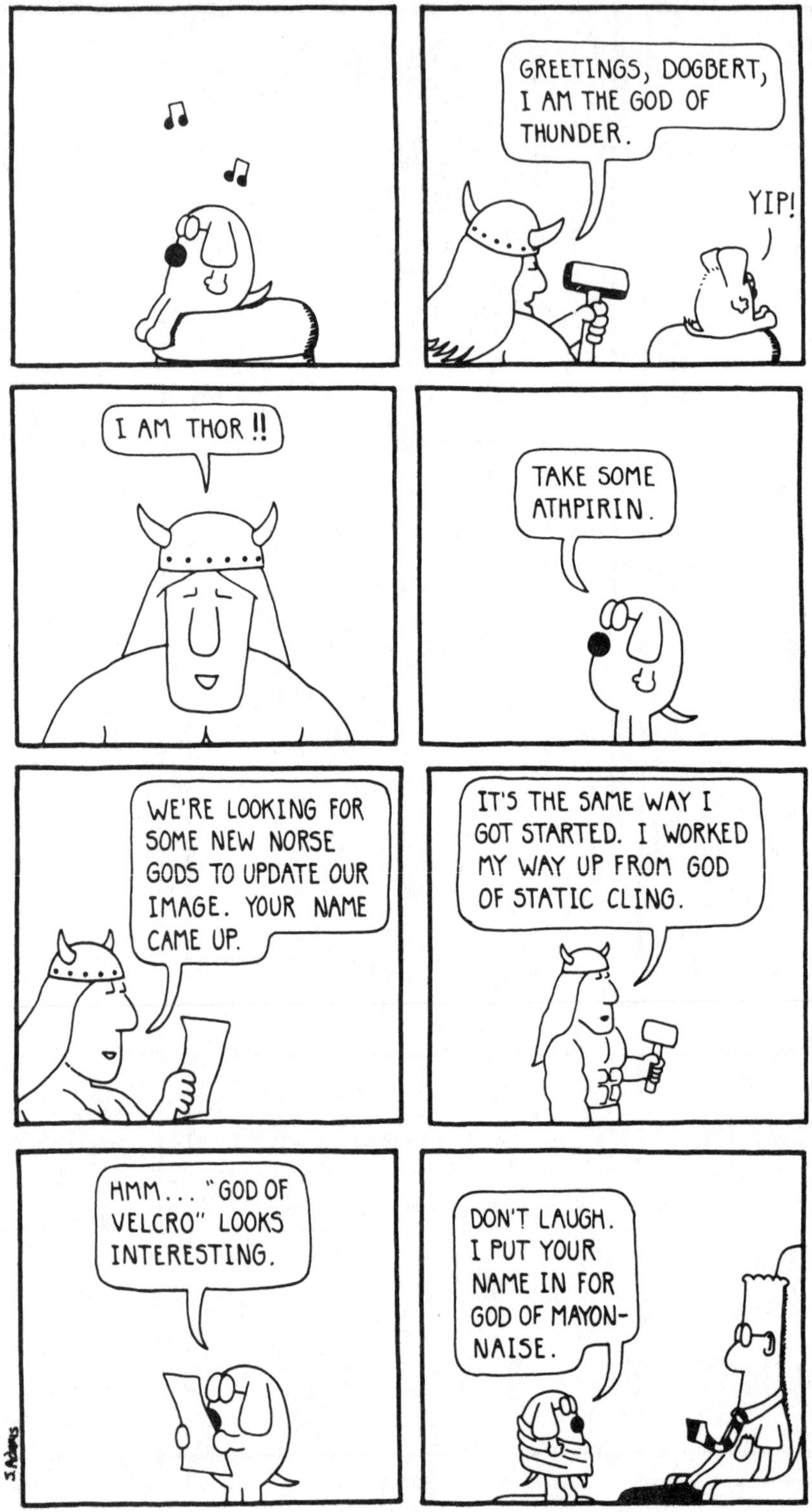
GREETINGS, DOGBERT, I AM THE GOD OF THUNDER.
YIP!
I AM THOR !!
TAKE SOME ATHPIRIN.
WE'RE LOOKING FOR SOME NEW NORSE GODS TO UPDATE OUR IMAGE. YOUR NAME CAME UP.
IT'S THE SAME WAY I GOT STARTED. I WORKED MY WAY UP FROM GOD OF STATIC CLING.
HMM... "GOD OF VELCRO" LOOKS INTERESTING.
DON'T LAUGH. I PUT YOUR NAME IN FOR GOD OF MAYON-NAISE.

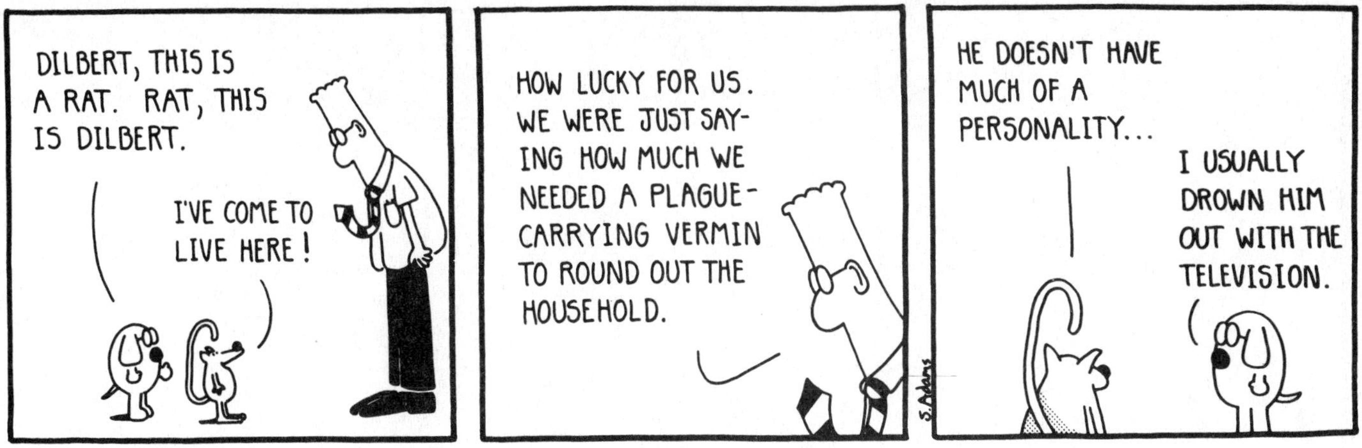
DILBERT, THIS IS A RAT. RAT, THIS IS DILBERT.
I'VE COME TO LIVE HERE!
HOW LUCKY FOR US. WE WERE JUST SAYING HOW MUCH WE NEEDED A PLAGUE-CARRYING VERMIN TO ROUND OUT THE HOUSEHOLD.
S. Adams
HE DOESN'T HAVE MUCH OF A PERSONALITY...
I USUALLY DROWN HIM OUT WITH THE TELEVISION.

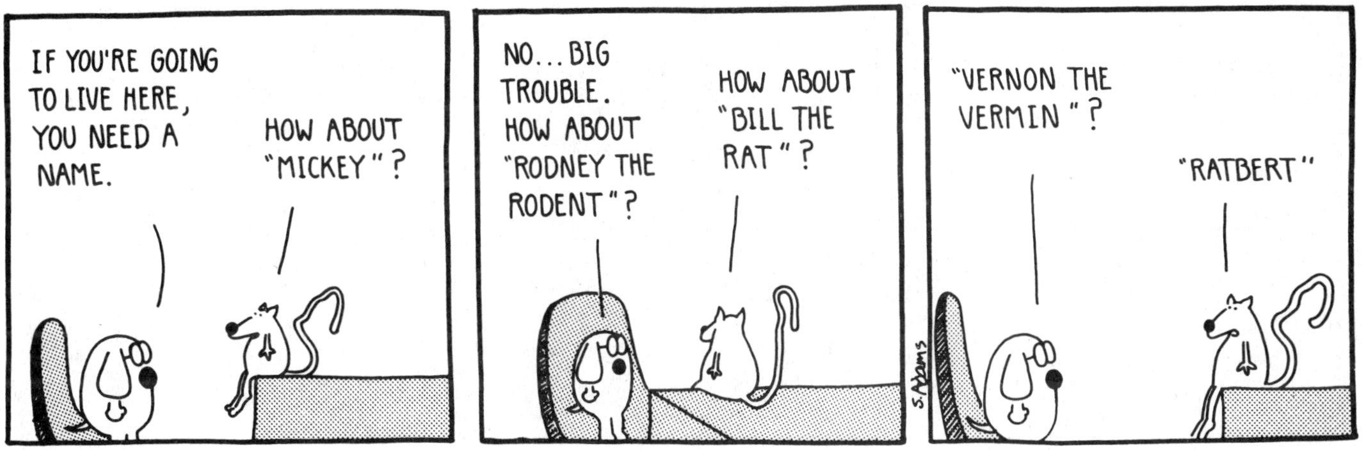
IF YOU'RE GOING TO LIVE HERE, YOU NEED A NAME.
HOW ABOUT "MICKEY"?
NO... BIG TROUBLE. HOW ABOUT "RODNEY THE RODENT"?
HOW ABOUT "BILL THE RAT"?
S. Adams
"VERNON THE VERMIN"?
"RATBERT"

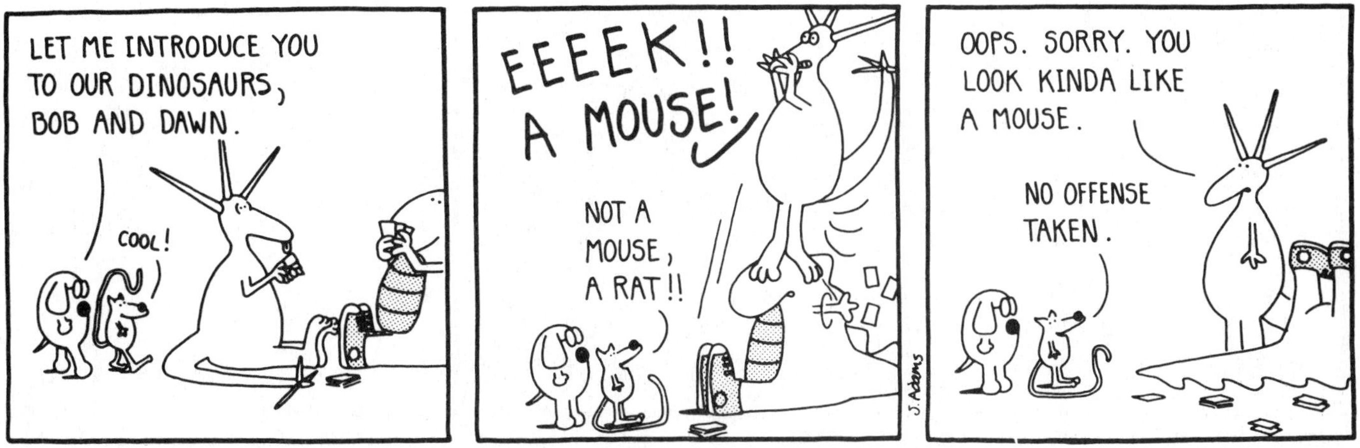
LET ME INTRODUCE YOU TO OUR DINOSAURS, BOB AND DAWN.
COOL!
EEEEK!! A MOUSE!
NOT A MOUSE, A RAT!!
S. Adams
OOPS. SORRY. YOU LOOK KINDA LIKE A MOUSE.
NO OFFENSE TAKEN.

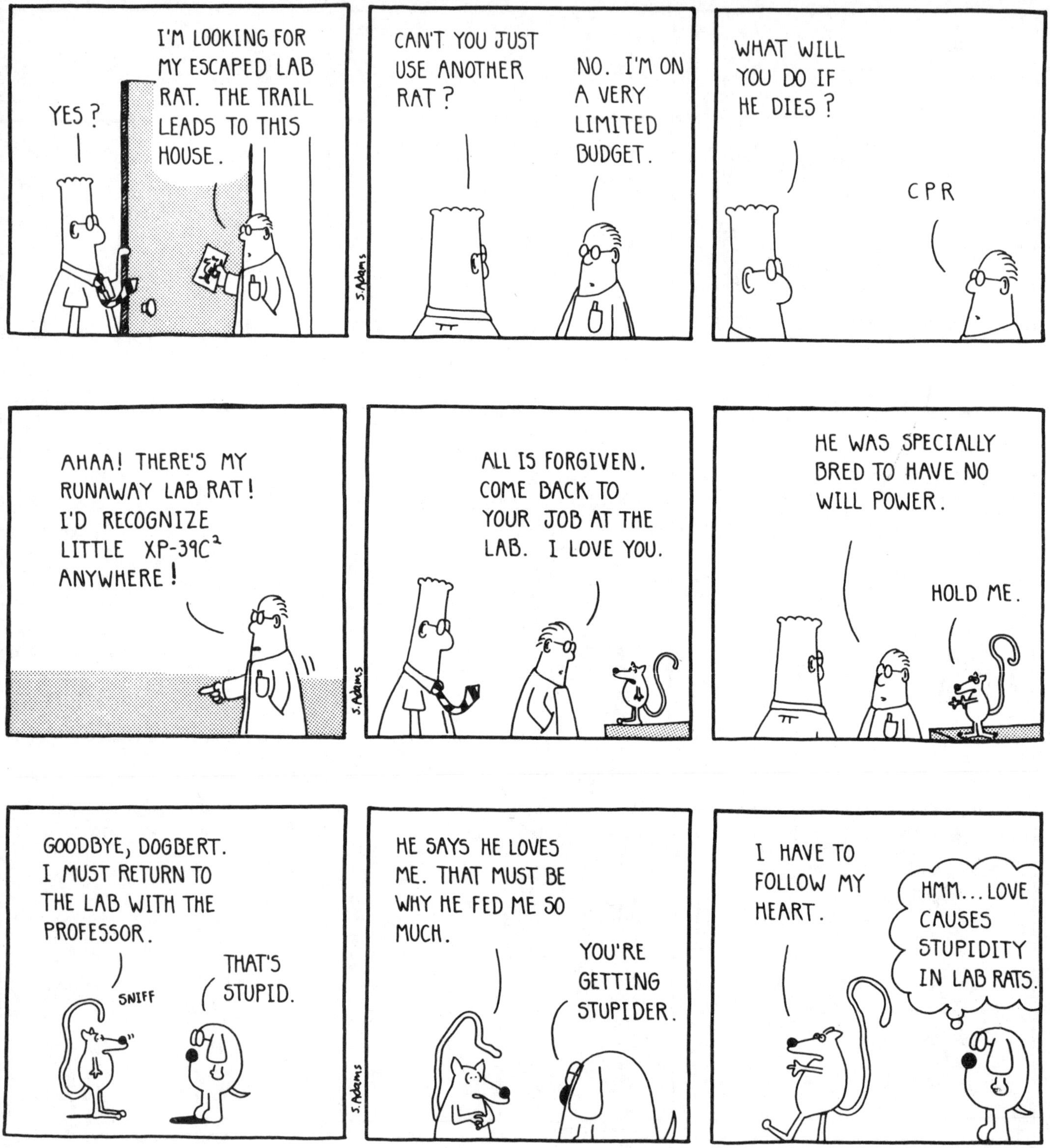
YES?
I'M LOOKING FOR MY ESCAPED LAB RAT. THE TRAIL LEADS TO THIS HOUSE.
CAN'T YOU JUST USE ANOTHER RAT?
NO. I'M ON A VERY LIMITED BUDGET.
WHAT WILL YOU DO IF HE DIES?
CPR
AHAA! THERE'S MY RUNAWAY LAB RAT! I'D RECOGNIZE LITTLE XP-39C^2 ANYWHERE!
ALL IS FORGIVEN. COME BACK TO YOUR JOB AT THE LAB. I LOVE YOU.
HE WAS SPECIALLY BRED TO HAVE NO WILL POWER.
HOLD ME.
GOODBYE, DOGBERT. I MUST RETURN TO THE LAB WITH THE PROFESSOR.
SNIFF
THAT'S STUPID.
HE SAYS HE LOVES ME. THAT MUST BE WHY HE FED ME SO MUCH.
YOU'RE GETTING STUPIDER.
I HAVE TO FOLLOW MY HEART.
HMM... LOVE CAUSES STUPIDITY IN LAB RATS.